In praise of *Dynamic Supply Chains*

'*Dynamic Supply Chains* represents leading edge thinking in designing end-to-end supply chains. Recognizing that people, and people alone, make the difference in enterprise supply chains, John provides an excellent, albeit pragmatic, "how-to" approach to build the supply chain as a "living organism", able to adapt and proactively respond to rapidly changing conditions. Certainly the best reference work available and particularly relevant in today's turbulent and complex business environment.'

Deon van As, VP, Brewery Operations, Miller Coors, USA

'In these unprecedented times of opportunity *Dynamic Supply Chains* is a must read for business leaders seeking to gain competitive advantage by truly aligning their supply chain strategy with customers' ever evolving needs. In highlighting the importance of leadership, organizational design and culture in dynamic alignment, John Gattorna outlines the opportunity backed up by a tangible, practical framework which will allow organizations to unlock their true potential.'

Andy Johnson, UK Logistics Director, Computer 2000, UK

'*Dynamic Supply Chains* is a must read, not only for supply chain managers but for every senior executive from the C-suite down. The articulated dynamic supply chains are a critical component of every business and corporate strategy. The book is terrific. Congratulations.'

Yoram (Jerry) Wind, The Lauder Professor of Marketing, The Wharton School, University of Pennsylvania, USA

'I really liked the structure of the book – organizing specific chapters around each supply chain type – Lean, Continuous Replenishment, Fully Flexible, and Agile is incredibly helpful, and provides easy and instant access to information on key topics. General themes of organizational structure, job description(s), people, and prevalent culture as keys to successful performance of supply chains are incredibly relevant. Companies such as Dell that go through major change must reassess at some point and conduct massive "job analysis" activities to determine the scope of new roles and best organization structure pre- and post- change. Finally, I love the concept of "Hybrid" supply chains – Lean on Lean, Continuous replenishment on Lean, Flexible on Lean, etc.'

Annette Clayton, VP Global Supply Chain, Dell Global B.V., USA

'John Gattorna's thought leadership is both pragmatic and profound. His leading-edge work is helping companies transform traditionally "siloed" supply chain functions into dynamically balanced and "living" value-networks. John recognizes that the business goal is to meaningfully reduce end-to-end complexity by first understanding and then translating "outside-in" buying behaviors into sustainable "inside-out" supply chains – rather than just trying to make all the disconnected pieces more efficient, faster, and leaner! This book is a must read for CEOs, and global supply chain executives.'

Roddy Martin, SVP & Research Fellow, AMR Research-Gartner, USA

'*Dynamic Supply Chains* presents a brilliant framework that will enable enterprises to achieve alignment of their business/supply chain strategies, organizational structure, and culture with their customers. Gattorna's research is sound, his conclusions are spot-on and the resulting model for achieving dynamic alignment is very powerful. The world and global business environment in which we operate is constantly changing customer needs and what they value is in constant flux. Our supply chains must be dynamically aligned through these changing conditions – enabling this, along with its comprehensive scope, is what separates Gattorna's approach from the rest. It helps address the brutal fact that "one-size-does-not-fit-all", while keeping the complexity of the supply chains and sub-cultures in the global enterprise to a very manageable level.'

Ron Woodward, Manufacturing, Engineering and Global Operations Director, Strategic Change and Risk Mgmt, Dow Corning Corporation, USA

'An exceptional book that I enjoyed reading immensely. *Dynamic Supply Chains* has achieved something rather unusual: a comprehensive and innovative look at end-to-end customer-centric supply chains that reads like a pragmatic narrative – taking the business contribution of supply chains to a whole new level. I have on my shelves a number of "must read" books. Such books must be engaging and absorbing, offer me something new or challenging to think about and above all must be the kind of book I just cannot put down until I've finished reading it. John Gattorna's book sits in this category on my shelf.'

Regina Lemgruber, Director, Supply Planning & Replenishment, *Magazine Luiza*, Brazil

'John Gattorna highlights the need and urgency for changing the way we have approached supply chains in the past. He makes a very compelling case to change to a new business model for contemporary supply chains called "dynamic alignment", and suggests that the real driver of today's supply chains are people. John takes a holistic supply chain perspective, and, in a very comprehensive and structured way, this book is practical and immediately applicable in all industries. It will help companies move quickly from crisis mode to growth mode.'

Roger Crook, CEO, DHL Express Americas, USA

'Gattorna manages to tackle the sticky, but essential, "soft" issues around culture while still providing a highly structured and usable approach to developing supply chain strategy based on extensive real-world examples. This is a well-researched and compelling book.'

Kevin O'Marah, Group Vice President, Supply Chain Research, Gartner, USA

'John Gattorna tangibly validates why he is considered one of the global thought leaders in supply chain management. He not only introduces and refines four key supply chain types, which can creatively be adapted by most companies, but more importantly, focuses on the hidden ingredient essential to all successful transformations – the human element. Of equal importance, John takes the definition of supply/demand chain management to a new multi-dimensional structure as he explains the transition to "value networks". That's where his is leading us, and those companies who creatively adapt their business models to this new frontier will gain significant competitive advantage. Those who don't will be at significant risk. I strongly endorse this book as an essential framework for international business leaders.'

Paul W.l. Bradley, Chairman and CEO, Caprica International, Singapore

'Yet another great piece from Dr John Gattorna where he is able to wonderfully explain fresh concepts that help us understand the "art" of supply chain rather than just thinking about the "science" associated with it.'

Ajay Mittal, Chairman and Managing Director, Arshiya International, India

'It is akin to extra virgin oil produced from freshly-harvested olives that are pressed to squeeze the juice from the fruit. When reading John's book it feels just like your mind is in there, in the olive oil press, squeezed to produce novel ideas, fresh insights and new ways of thinking.'
Alexander Katsiotis, Managing Director, Elgeka S.A., Greece

'A very well organized book laying out the future of supply chains. John has a knack of taking a very abstract concept and rendering a picture that is both intuitive and common sense. It is a very in-depth, comprehensive, practical book for every supply chain professional at all levels and would rate as my best ever read on the topic.'
Shekar Natarajan, Director of Supply Chain, Pepsi Bottling Group, USA

'I'm convinced that your segmentation model is a must for every manager to understand and build solid business models for each venture in the market. Congratulations.'
Vicente Moliterno, Managing Director, Staroup S.A., Brazil

'John's latest book is, for me, one of the best and most relevant books I have read on the supply chain topic. I have already started to promote it among my MBA students as well as with executives, not only in Spain but also in Mexico and the Middle East.'
Dr Luis E. Solis, Associate Dean and Professor of Operations and Technology Management, Instituto de Empresa Business School, Spain

'*Dynamic Supply Chains* is a practitioner's handbook written by an academic who clearly knows the challenges of operating supply chains. Dr Gattorna describes what is required to build successful and sustainable competitive advantage, premised on understanding the dynamics of different types of supply chains shaped by different types of customer behavior, and emphasizing in the process the important role of the human element. Filled with real-life examples, *Dynamic Supply Chains* provides a vital roadmap for companies that wish to survive and excel in the rapidly and ever-changing world of global trade.'
Bassam Fawaz, CIO, Agility Global Integrated Logistics, Switzerland

'Few understand in today's competitive market that ignoring the organizational and cultural elements when designing and executing a Demand Driven Supply Network (DDSN), spells certain failure – John does, and in his book he presents insights that are unique and deserve to be heard.'
C.J (Jake) Barr, Global Operations Leader, Supply Network Operations and Director Product Supply, Procter & Gamble, USA

'Human behavior and leadership are still the most forgotten elements of successful supply chain management. In *Dynamic Supply Chains*, John Gattorna again explains why humans are the key factor in supply chain performance. The interaction between the various parties in supply chains determines its success, and the supply chain manager is the leader in the chain to make everyone work jointly together. Excellent reading for all C-level executives, and a must-read for supply chain managers with CEO ambitions.'
Edwin Tuyn, Director, Inspired-Search, The Netherlands

'In *Dynamic Supply Chains*, John has once again put together a thought-provoking visionary perspective on the future of supply chain management. Specifically, his perspective on need-based supply chain segmentation is refreshing. This cross-disciplinary perspective on supply chains is an essential read for anyone in the field.'

**Dr Zachary Williams, A/ Professor of Logistics and Marketing,
Central Michigan University, USA**

'John Gattorna has introduced an insightful concept in his book – Dynamic Alignment. Indeed, "alignment" is not just the work of a great consumer-focused company or great leader, it is their opportunity and their art.'

John Pollaers, CEO, Fosters Brewing, Australia

'The various approaches introduced by John Gattorna in *Dynamic Supply Chains* provide a unique recipe for developing the exact capabilities required in most, if not all, contemporary organizations. Indeed, responding effectively to customers' expectations is the only unassailable strategy to follow if we wish to maintain a leadership position in our market or industry.'

Evangelos Angeletopoulos, Managing Director, Business Logistics Services Ltd, Greece

'John Gattorna does an exceptional job providing not only the thinking, but also the tools to turn supply chains (which are inherently internally focused) into market-focused living supply chains delivering value to the customer.'

Dr Chris Roberts, CEO/President, Cochlear Limited, Australia

'In *Dynamic Supply Chains*, John Gattorna's concepts of Dynamic Alignment clearly demonstrates how modern supply chain thinking will not only improve operational effectiveness in organizations, but also make a significant improvement in business and revenue growth. In today's highly competitive world of Private Equity it will be those firms who can materially improve the inherent value of their portfolio companies, which will be successful. *Dynamic Supply Chains* is an extremely powerful tool to help realize this value.'

Jamie Bolton, Director, KKR Capstone Asia Limited, Hong Kong

'This book provides a full menu for business-driven supply chain implementation, describing how different philosophies (e.g. lean, VMI), processes and leadership styles fit with four basic types of supply chains. Supply chains are finally seen from a total business perspective and, at the same time, with a very practical approach.'

Hille Korhonen, VP Operations, Fiskars Corp., Finland

'John has produced a simple, yet effective and practical, roadmap for business executives to align their enterprise to their target market. The emphasis on people across the enterprise value chain, as well as the focus on integration, is refreshing. Companies who can implement and execute the concepts in this book will create competitive advantage and will grow profits well ahead of their competitors.'

Burger Van der Merwe, Supply Chain Director, Woolworths S.A., South Africa

'Finally, a genuinely innovative approach on how supply chains should be designed and managed. With this book, John brings the supply chain management discipline to a new and much more comprehensive level, addressing vital elements which are mostly ignored by organizations. His messages will drive business improvements in the decades ahead, all around the world.'

Dr Rodrigo Cambiaghi, COO, Axia Value Chain, USA

Dynamic Supply Chains

DELIVERING VALUE THROUGH PEOPLE

2nd Edition

John Gattorna

Financial Times
Prentice Hall
is an imprint of

Harlow, England • London • New York • Boston • San Francisco • Toronto • Sydney • Singapore • Hong Kong
Tokyo • Seoul • Taipei • New Delhi • Cape Town • Madrid • Mexico City • Amsterdam • Munich • Paris • Milan

PEARSON EDUCATION LIMITED

Edinburgh Gate
Harlow CM20 2JE
Tel: +44 (0)1279 623623
Fax: +44 (0)1279 431059
Website: www.pearsoned.co.uk

First published in Great Britain in 2006
Second edition published 2010

© Pearson Education Limited 2006, 2010

Pearson Education is not responsible for the content of third party Internet sites.

ISBN: 978-0-273-73040-8

British Library Cataloguing-in-Publication Data
A catalogue record for this book is available from the British Library

Library of Congress Cataloging-in-Publication Data
Dynamic supply chains : delivering value through people / [edited by] John Gattorna. -- 2nd ed.
    p. cm.
  Includes bibliographical references and index.
  Previously published under title: Dynamic supply chain alignment.
  ISBN 978-0-273-73040-8 (pbk.)
  1. Business logistics. 2. Delivery of goods--Management. I. Gattorna, John.
  HD38.5.D96 2010
  658.7--dc22
                            2010026325

10 9 8 7 6 5 4 3 2 1
14 13 12 11 10

Typeset in 10/14 Plantin by 30
Printed and bound in Great Britain by Henry Ling Ltd, Dorchester, Dorset

To Charlie, whose smile lights up everyone's day, love Paps

Contents

CONTENTS

A word about the title

T he title of the forerunner to this book was *Living Supply Chains* (FT Prentice Hall, Harlow, 2006). Unfortunately, experience shows that too few readers understood the subtlety implicit in the word 'living'. So as I started to write this new edition I was determined to find a title that was accurate yet resonated with senior executives around the world – my readers. The chosen title, *Dynamic Supply Chains*, is better, but still not perfect, although the accompanying sub-title is helpful, because it makes the point that in supply chains we are dealing with people everywhere in the form of customers, consumers and end-users, suppliers and third parties.

For a long time I have been of the school that resisted changing terminology as things progressed, because I thought we should avoid additional jargon, and simply redefine what goes inside the term 'supply chain' as understanding of its scope grew. However, I have to admit failure, and never was this more evident than at a recent 'thought leadership' forum in Sydney where we had a room full of CEOs and Managing Directors – mention of the term 'supply chain' immediately brought forth narrow understandings, mostly focused on cost reduction. There was little recognition of the revenue potential and all the other value-enhancing opportunities implicit in the term. So despite years of trying to get executives to understand that there is a big difference between 'logistics' and 'supply chain', few have changed their mental scope. And as for including human behavior and relationships, the business world is still largely in denial. Something has to change and maybe it is me this time!

The term '*supply chain management*' was originally coined by the consulting house Booz Allen & Hamilton circa 1982. It never was a good term because it immediately conjured up in one's mind the 'supply' side of the enterprise. The 'chain' descriptor doesn't help either, as it implies we are dealing with linear chains or strings of enterprises, when in fact the real world involves three-dimensional arrays of enterprises. Indeed, our future world, whether we like it or not, is moving inexorably towards a *'network of networks'*, and we had better get on board with that reality.

Over the past decade, various commentators have broken ranks in search of more meaningful terminology. For example, *value chain; demand-chain; demand-networks*. When the Sydney forum discussed this issue, the term which ultimately emerged was *'value networks'*. However, although it is probably a little early to move straight to this term, I forecast that it will become widely adopted within ten years. Why? Because the term 'value networks' beautifully encompasses everything we want included; supply-side supply chains; demand-side supply chains; and the idea that enterprises have many supply chains (or pathways) flowing through them. It also allows us to explain the concept of 'alignment' and describe the *dynamism* involved as combinations of different supply chain configurations mix and match to form aligned 'value networks'.

By ultimately embracing 'value networks' as the accepted vernacular in the future we automatically include all parties on the supply-side, all parties on the demand-side, and all parties in between, e.g. service-providers. When that happens we will have finally cracked the definitional problem that has bedevilled us for decades and been one of the primary inhibitors to the development of this relatively new sub-field of management science. We still have to overcome other impediments to end-to-end integration such as organization design, but we are well on the way, and technology is more of an enabler than an inhibiter these days.

In this book I will talk a lot about components such as supply chains (plural); supply chain configurations; and 'hybrid' supply chains, but the over-arching, albeit subliminal, concept will be 'value networks' – because this is the end-game. That's where I am heading in the future, what about you?

Foreword

E nlightened. This is how I felt the first time I read *Living Supply Chains*, the forerunner to *Dynamic Supply Chains*. Since then the concepts described in both of these books have helped me and my company to migrate to a new level of performance.

The first time I heard about the 'dynamic alignment' model developed by John Gattorna was in February 2007. We were implementing a global S&OP model for a leading global manufacturing company, based on what we thought at the time was best practice.

Our problem was that we were having difficulty implementing a process that was aligned to the company's marketing and sales departments, let alone the real needs of its customers. We kept trying to achieve this alignment by using traditional techniques-customer segmentation and demand forecasting.

Then, quite fortuitously, one of our consultants stumbled on the book *Living Supply Chains*, which contained details of the dynamic alignment model. I was so absorbed by the content of the book that I was unable to put it down for two days, and since then I have been revising many of my concepts and beliefs about enterprise supply chains, and the approach we at Axia Value Chain take with our clients. In effect, we went from a static, one-size-fits-all model to a dynamic model of multiple supply chains.

We started to segment our clients' customers based on buying behavior, and then we aligned them to the value proposition, culture and leadership of the firm, thereby enabling a deep understanding in a short period of time of just how to design, build and implement supply chains that add value.

The outcome of our relationship with John Gattorna since that first experience is that we have been applying the dynamic alignment concept to our customers and to each new project with significant results, leading to our consultancy firm tripling in size in two years and entering new markets, all this despite the negative effects of the GFC crisis in 2008/09.

In addition to expanding our range of solutions in designing and implementing new supply chains for our clients, the content of these two books has forced us to ask the right questions. So, like us, you need to read this book with an open mind, open to a whole new, but very coherent, set of ideas on how to design and implement enterprise supply chains.

You should start questioning yourself about your beliefs in Chapter 1, where John deconstructs our existing static, operations-oriented, and one-size-fits-all model. In Chapter 2, he reconstructs a new model of thought based on customers and their buying behaviors, and aligns the value propositions (Chapter 3), culture, and value delivery (Chapter 4), and leadership capability (Chapter 5), to present a whole new way of viewing the business; 'outside-in' rather than the conventional 'inside-out'.

In Chapter 6, John discusses the major obstacle we face today when implementing the dynamic alignment model: our existing organizational structures, which need to be revised and radically reformulated.

From Chapter 7 to 10, he describes each of the four generic supply chain types, providing a deep understanding of what they mean and how we should design and implement each in turn.

From Chapter 10 onwards, you will be able to read complementary analyses designed to help understand the dynamic alignment proposal, from its refinement of Lee's Triple-A model, through to how we relate to our suppliers and the reality of 'hybrid' chains.

In Chapters 14 and 15, the book provides us with a view of likely future trends, which forces us to reflect even more, and stimulates us to face the challenges that are fast approaching.

Finally, the great merit of this book is the way it succeeds in turning such a complex issue into something simple and understandable, with an obvious repetitive pattern: the elements that align our chains, the humans who are involved at every stage along the way. Their behaviors are cleverly encoded in the PADI structure, and this provides a rich albeit simple-to-use method for converting everything into the same metric thereby facilitating easy comparison.

I hope readers will feel as 'enlightened' as I did when I read it and its companion text, and now I constantly use the 'alignment' model as a frame-of-reference to make sense of current challenges – a rich source of possible solutions to these and future challenges.

Dr. Carlos Bremer, Executive Partner
Axia Value Chain
Atlanta and Sào Paulo
10 January 2010

Preface

The thrust of the ideas presented in this book are well summed up in the words of P.D. Ouspensky many years ago: 'I cannot guarantee that you will hear [find] new ideas [in this book], that is ideas you never heard before, from the start; but if you are patient you will soon begin to notice them. And then I wish you not to miss them, and to try not to interpret them in the old way.' New York 1945.[i]

Current approaches to supply chain design and operations are fundamentally flawed. Indeed, they have always been so, but we have gotten away with this less than perfect situation for a long time – so long in fact that we have convinced ourselves that we are on the right track. In the end, the convergence of the Internet, user-friendly software applications, and much more informed customers has found us out – and we must now set about developing a new business model for enterprise chains and networks of these chains. That is what this book is about, guiding you through this process towards the new world. In the words of Andrew Motion, Poet Laureate, the task ahead of me is a bit like making 'something look like water but taste like gin'.[ii]

Indeed, we need more than just a change in business model – we need a change in mindset, from one of functional specialism, to the notion that the principles and practices embodied in supply chain and value networks type thinking, should become a philosophy that permeates the enterprise, owned and contributed to by all functions.

Nick Greiner, the former Premier of New South Wales, and later board member of the large Australian retailer Coles has a poignant story to tell in this regard. Not long after being appointed to the Coles board he bumped into Roger Corbett, the then Managing Director of Woolworths, their main competitor. Roger asked Nick how often they discussed supply chain matters in Coles board meetings, and the answer was never! Roger's response was that supply chain matters were discussed in every board meeting at Woolworths. Therein lies the difference, and the rest is history.

Coles subsequently sunk to great depths, and are now slowly returning to former greatness under new ownership and new management; Woolworths in Australia continues to go from strength to strength.

Have you ever had that peculiar feeling when you have been in a room with other people and they are discussing you, without acknowledging your presence! It's weird. Yet that is how we have been treating our customers and consumers, and to a lesser extent our suppliers.

In essence, we have allowed the company (tail) to wag the head of the dog, which means in plain language we have been working from the 'inside-out', largely ignoring particular customers' special needs and wants, and feeding them a diet that suits our own selfish purposes. In turn, this has led to much guessing and second-guessing inside the enterprise, and ultimately service failures and loss of customers.

The new business model being proposed in this book, *dynamic alignment*, has been under test and development for two decades, and we have learned a lot in that time, about ourselves and our customers and suppliers. This is a genuine whole-of-business B2B/B2C model, that starts with interpreting the way customers and consumers prefer to buy products and services. Customers are the ultimate reference point for all subsequent action inside the enterprise, and you better believe that if you want to survive and thrive in the new world ahead. I am describing the enlightened 'outside-in' orientation of the Third Millennium.

Once you establish the customer *frame-of-reference* through behavioral segmentation it is possible to reverse engineer the corresponding '*value propositions*,' operational strategies, and internal *capabilities* that will shape the sub-cultures necessary to propel these into the marketplace. All this activity has to be driven by a leadership team that is especially empathetic with the target marketplace . . . or else nothing worthwhile can or will happen.

So, internal capabilities and operational strategies (and actions) must be developed coincidentally, because they are closely inter-related. This is part of the 'genetic' engineering task of contemporary supply chain/value networks designers and operators; and Human Resource personnel must be brought into help in these early developmental stages, or else it is too late.

Finally, 'collaboration' is an activity which should only be attempted between consenting adults! You only collaborate with those who possess genuine collaborative values – and do something else with the rest. 'Requisite' collaboration is a better way to describe this part of the overall supply chain activity.

And make sure you re-connect the Sourcing/Procurement function to the integrated supply chains that constitute your value networks. They are being wasted while they stand apart, another consequence of flawed organization design and years of posturing and neglect.

As you can see, there's a lot of lost ground to make up quickly. Those that follow this path will quickly go to the top of the league table as the best-of-the-best enterprise supply chains and value networks in the world. But then, this is a fact of life – the best enterprises will only get better, and the rest will fall further behind. It is the way the world works. Make the choice now to be one of the winners.

Dr John Gattorna
Sydney, 1 January 2010

i P.D. Ouspensky, *The Psychology of Man's Possible Evolution*, Vintage Books Edition, New York, January, 1974, p. xiii.
ii Motion, Andrew, Poet Laureate, 1999–2009, a comment made during an interview with Stephen Sakur on *Hard Talk*, BBC World, 31 August 2009.

Author's acknowledgements

I t is exactly four years since I wrote my 'Acknowledgements' in *Living Supply Chains*, which was the earlier edition of this book. Now, as then, I have a number of people to thank for their unstinting support as I endeavoured to develop and update the ideas originally presented in *Living Supply Chains*.

My colleague Deborah Ellis has been a tower of strength during the writing of the new book, always ready to discuss the difficult conceptual issues encountered along the way, and to provide me with possible solutions. She is undertaking doctoral studies at MGSM in how to design and manage 'extreme' supply chains in life-critical situations, such as the reliable supply of insulin to diabetes sufferers in Third World countries. Maslada Nobhandhu, a former post-graduate student at MGSM has been my primary researcher over the last two years, and I am greatly indebted to her inspired work and dedicated support. I hope both of you get as much pleasure out of this book as I did writing it.

The other person who has been invaluable to me is Carmel McCauley at Future Perfect Communications. She has helped take a very complex subject, remove the jargon, and present a storyline that can be digested and understood by the C-suite, who after all are the real target of this book. Many thanks Carmel, and well done once again.

Of course, during the past four years I have found myself in front of many post-graduate and post-experience student groups at MGSM (Australia, Singapore and Hong Kong), Cranfield (UK), and Normandy Business School (France). These sessions have provided me with many opportunities to field-test some of my ideas, and identify and close any gaps left in the first edition.

I am also very fortunate to have Pearson Education as my publisher because they have great people. Liz Gooster provided strong editorial guidance in the early stages, before she decided to take a sabbatical to travel around South America. Martina O'Sullivan took over and has been very supportive. Special thanks goes to Sarah Wild, desk editor for this edition and Jenny Oates in her role as copy editor.

This book is also scheduled to be published by Pearson's sister company in the US, FT Press, New Jersey, so I am delighted readers in the Americas will have easier access.

My clients around the world have also been a source of constant inspiration; these are the people who provide me with in effect my own personal R&D laboratories to pursue ideas, in many cases through to implementation on the ground. Indeed, my clients are all my friends and I am deeply indebted to their support and show of confidence – these are all genuine leaders indeed. In particular I would single out Warith al Kharusi at PDO, Oman, for his pioneering work with the first 4PL® business model in the oil and gas industry, worldwide. Also, Alexander Katsiotis, Managing Director of Elgeka S.A. in Greece, who has enthusiastically embraced 'alignment' principles in his group of companies, and been an avid supporter of my work. Evangelos Angeletopoulos, Managing Director of BLS in Greece first invited me to Greece in May 2009, and I have returned several times since to collaborate with him on various ventures; thank you Evangelos for introducing me to this ancient and interesting part of the world.

There is one other person I would like to acknowledge – Ajay Mittal, Chairman and Managing Director of Arshiya International in India. Ajay, you have been an inspiration for the visionary work that you are doing in India with your new logistics business model – this will surely be world's best practice. Congratulations, and thank you for including me as part of your Global Advisory Board.

Similarly, my friends at the burgeoning Brazilian consultancy, Axia Value Chain, have demonstrated their faith in the *dynamic* alignment model by universally adopting it as their standard framework on all consulting assignments in Brazil and the US. In particular, I would like to mention Dr Carlos Bremer, Executive Partner, and Dr Rodrigo Cambiaghi, COO in the US, both very big supporters of my work and respected colleagues as we set out together to 'align' the world! It has been a real pleasure working with both of you, and meeting your wonderful team of smart young people at Axia.

It is always exciting to meet someone who is especially passionate about their work, and in this case it means being passionate about supply chain/value networks 'thought leadership'. One such person is Roddy Martin, Vice President Research and Research Fellow at AMR Research-Gartner, based in Boston. He has been a most enthusiastic supporter of my work, spreading the gospel of *dynamic* alignment wherever he goes; and he travels a lot! Thank you, Roddy, for all your help in spreading the new gospel.

I have been particularly fortunate to have great executive assistants during the course of the writing of the book; Graciela Parker-Day in the early stages, and Jacqui Turner in the latter stages. Thank you both for your understanding and support as I struggled to complete on schedule despite a demanding work/travel schedule.

Finally, loving thanks to my wife Lea for putting up with me while I ploughed through the chapters; maybe it's time to take some holidays free of any thinking about supply chains and value networks, and smell the roses.

John Gattorna
Sydney, 26 January 2010, *Australia* Day

Publisher's acknowledgments

We are grateful to the following for permission to reproduce copyright material:

Figures

Figure 1.9 developed in discussion with Deborah Ellis, Carpenter Ellis, 2009; Figure 12.1 adapted from Bueler, Diane (2006) 'Supplier Segmentation – The Tool for Differentiation and Results'; Figure 12.6 from information supplied by Axia Consulting, Axia Value Chain, Brazil (2008); Figure 14.2 from Credit Suisse HOLT ValueSearch®, © 2010 Credit Suisse Group AG and its subsidiaries and affiliates. All rights reserved. Used by permission. HOLT, ValueSearch and CFROI are registered trademarks of Credit Suisse Group AG or its affiliates in the United States and other countries. HOLT is a corporate performance and valuation advisory service of Credit Suisse; Figure 14.11 from Deborah Ellis, Carpenter Ellis; Figure 14.12 from unpublished PWCS presentations 01/03/2008, Gattorna Alignment Pty Ltd, reproduced with permission; Figure 4.5 prepared for John Gattorna by The Ryder Self Group, Sydney, 2004; Figures 4.6, 4.7, 4.8 adapted from *Cultural Dimensions*, (1980), Geert Hofstede™, and prepared for John Gattorna by The Ryder Self Group, 2009; Figure 6.3 from Nobhandhu, M. (2008) unpublished MBA research paper, MGSM.

Photos

Photo 1.1 from Getty Images/Mike Hewitt; Photo 9.1 © Schlegelmilch Photography.

In some instances we have been unable to trace the owners of copyright material, and we would appreciate any information that would enable us to do so.

CHAPTER 1

A new business model for new and challenging times

Re-engaging with customers and suppliers

During 2008 the world changed in a precipitous way as the global financial crisis hit and the ensuing global recession affected people around the world. The flow of money froze, and so did the corresponding flow of goods and services. What had been obvious for some time became painfully obvious – we need to move away from the old static view of the world and embrace a new business model. We must reinvigorate moribund supply chains by capturing the dynamism that people bring to the flow of goods and services inside and outside a business. We can do this by embracing a new definition of supply chains that recognises they are living organisms made up of living, active and dynamic people. All institutions have supply chains (or pathways) running through them, connecting a diverse range of human activities and needs. In fact, supply chains in aggregate *are* the business, so, in effect, supply chains is a whole-of-business concept. This chapter breaks with convention and introduces the concept of 'dynamic alignment', which we think will re-set our enterprises and equip them to cope with the volatile times that surely lie ahead.

As I write this opening statement, the world is still experiencing the effects of the Global Financial Crisis (GFC) of 2008–09, and I can't help but feel the importance of supply chains in our society has just gone up a notch or two. Too many companies are in trouble, and it's their leadership (or lack of) that has got them where they are today. The business models of many overleveraged financial institutions are no longer sustainable in the wake of the global credit crunch. The impact has spread throughout the real economy, seriously affecting the many businesses that rely on the free flow of capital and credit. When I have previously written articles about the consequences for customers and the supply chains that serve them,[1] I have always received a heartfelt response of, 'Yes, but what can we do about it?' People throughout the business world are seeking answers, because they can see the knee-jerk way in which many companies have been responding to the crisis. Supply chain research firm AMR Research put it this way: '. . . the natural reaction in a downturn is to retreat, cancel all new initiatives, pull back to the basics, and tighten up the ship. But the smart companies across [all] industries will be much more strategic, targeting areas that will not only see them through a rough economy [in the short term], but help them thrive during and after it passes.'[2] Forget the supposed 'actions' of cancelling the daily newspapers and the flowers in reception; that is mere posturing. Such measures will not save the enterprise – we need something very much more fundamental at this pivotal time. Suffice to say that now is the time for business leaders to adopt a new model for the supply chain that will help firms get closer to their customers and establish a new growth path for their business.

Indeed, investment columnist and author Dr David James couldn't have put it better in his column for *Business Review Weekly* magazine, when he remarked that '. . . cost-cutting is not exactly the last refuge of a scoundrel, but it is probably the first refuge of managers having difficulty with direction'.[3] He was talking about the strategy of Australian retailer Coles in 2006, which at the time was slashing costs in a last-ditched effort to survive. This once iconic national firm has since been taken over, but the accusation applies equally well to the businesses that were caught unprepared in the ensuing credit crisis of 2008. We need look no further than the attitude of General Motors, which went from being the world's largest automotive maker and the symbol of industrial innovation for most of the twentieth century to financial collapse in 2008. After asset sales, staff cuts and $50 billion in government loans, the new General Motors Company of 2009 announced its rebirth 'with a vow to start listening to its customers'.[4] After two weeks in the job, the new Chief Executive

Edward Whitacre pointed out that the company could not afford 'business as usual'.[5]

But if it's not business as usual, what then? For many businesses it's time to start over and 're-set' their strategies – if not their supply chain belief system – for the volatile operating environment that surely lies ahead. No previous management experience can prepare us for this difficult and complex task. We have to **adopt** the mantra of 'learning by doing' rather than simply chant it. It's in this context that we propose a new business model for contemporary supply chains, called *dynamic alignment.*

Look at the world-leading companies such as Dell, IKEA, Nokia, Zara, Li & Fung, Apple and Cisco Systems. Many of you will know them. But do you really *know* them? Do you know what lies beneath their dynamic supply chains? Business leaders around the world admire their superior performance; they can deliver products and services to their customers in a way that makes it look easy. But not many of us can understand how they do it. Let us consider first the classic business goal of 'alignment'. Companies have been seeking to match their strategies and goals to the needs of the customer for a long time. Alignment in the supply chain is similar – but different. It means aligning your supply chain strategies to customer segments. *Dynamic alignment* is something different again, because it uses customer buying behavior as its direct reference point.

Dynamic alignment is an idea I have been developing during more than 20 years' experience working as a consultant and advisor to companies worldwide, helping them to improve their supply chains. Just as the term suggests, it captures the idea of *dynamism*, or life, in the supply chain. Seeking *dynamic alignment* means treating your supply chain as a living being, rather than an inanimate mechanical beast. It's all about energy, execution and the dynamism of people and movement. If you can capture that you'll be in the type of 'zone' that top athletes achieve at their peak, only with a bottom line to match.

Again, let's look at the performance of some of the world's top brand names. Why is it that Nokia successfully transformed itself from a rubber boots and timber company in the early 1980s to become a world-leading electronics high-technology company? Or the way they are busy transforming themselves again, this time from a device manufacturer into a full-line personal communications solutions company. How can we explain the fact that a national icon such as Marks and Spencer can lose its way in the 1990s – and its customers – while others, such as Nestlé, continued to strengthen their position? Thankfully, Marks and Spencer has since gone a long way to recapture its former glory, owing to strong leadership by Sir Stuart Rose. We can see that it's possible for a company such as Dell to change a whole industry through innovations in its distribution channels and supply chain, while its competitors are still worrying about removing costs from conventional structures. And Daewoo's Korean shipyards can produce a supertanker every 36 hours. Clearly, some can reach 'the zone' while others languish behind them!

Before we explore *dynamic alignment* in detail, let's start by shedding the conventional definition of the supply chain. It is no longer all about technology, warehouses and distribution centres, or trucks, trains and planes. Agreed, they are all elements – the hard assets. But a modern supply chain is comprised of a lot more than that. We therefore must embrace a far more liberal view of supply chain configurations. In effect, the supply chain *is any combination of processes, functions, activities, relationships and pathways along which products, services, information and financial transactions move in and between enterprises, in both directions.* It also involves any and all movement of these elements from original producer to ultimate end-user or consumer; and *everyone* in the enterprise is involved in making this happen, a key point which is often overlooked.

Solving the problem of complex supply chains

If we accept this new definition of the contemporary supply chain, then every enterprise on earth has supply chain configurations of some sort running through them. These could be a manufacturer, a service company, a public sector agency, a private sector firm or even a non-government organization. Supply chains are omnipresent. They are out there! Most enterprises contain literally hundreds of supply chains that together look more like a bowl of spaghetti than finely tuned conveyor belts.

This has led to two key problem areas. The first is that many executives are largely blind to the presence of these supply chains in their midst. They can only see the physical movement of products and/or the capital assets involved. Complexity makes the true supply chain invisible. The second problem is that even if people recognize these complex supply chains for what they are, they start attacking their inherent complexity in inappropriate ways. Failure to see the full extent of supply chains in your company can be damaging. Seeing it, but then confronting it with the wrong solutions can be fatal.

If you are a service organization, companies in your sector are the most likely to suffer from supply chain blindness. They think that because their products are intangible, logistics and supply chain principles and practices don't apply. Wrong. If you are in the manufacturing or retail industries, companies in your field are likely to see the complexity but attack it with an operational sledgehammer. They are convinced the solution lies in reducing the internal operational complexity that they can see and have to manage. As a consequence, they are busily standardizing and re-engineering processes and installing new technologies, all designed to reduce complexity in the way they deal with customers.

However, these enterprises rarely become easier to deal with from the customer's perspective, quite the contrary. It would be much more productive if they were to accept and confront this inherent complexity head on, and then set out to master it. The tools and techniques are available, but only the conscious desire – or the understanding – to do so is in question.

Understanding will come from first accepting that the time has come fundamentally to rethink how we design and operate the supply chains that link our own enterprise with suppliers and customers, whether they are 'just around the corner' or around the world. For too long, there has been an unhealthy preoccupation with infrastructure and asset utilization, driven mainly by the obsessive desire to cut costs, mostly brought on by the relentless requirement for quarterly reporting to national stock exchanges. Unfortunately, even today many executives think of logistics and supply chains purely as areas for cost-cutting. While acknowledging that ever-lower levels of operating cost are important, achieving and maintaining future competitiveness demands more sophistication. You cannot grow the business by continuously cutting costs, a lesson learned the hard way by Al 'Chainsaw' Dunlap in the 1990s.[6] He relentlessly drove cost-cutting programs in every company that he led, because this delivered short-term improvement in performance. But he was incapable of taking the next step: growing the company.

Dunlap has a lot to answer for. Even today, senior executives in many major corporations continue to emulate his one-dimensional cost-cutting mindset. You may have seen this type of behavior. It almost always brings on a bout of *anorexia industrialosa*,[7] the excessive desire to be leaner and fitter, leading ultimately to total emaciation and death. In supply chain terms this approach has also encouraged senior executives to engage in endless benchmarking and process re-engineering exercises that go nowhere (witness the early efforts in Six Sigma), and innumerable on-going initiatives in the name of 'continuous improvement'. Cost-cutting, re-engineering, benchmarking and continuous improvement might have a place in the corporate arsenal, but they are not the answer to supply chain complexity. Seldom have these activities had the customer in the frame. In short, there has been a lot of effort and activity for relatively little gain.

What is required now is sustained investment in performance-enhancing supply chains. Look no further than a leading organization such as Nokia. It has delivered positive Cash Flow Return on Investment (CFROI) for more than two decades and this has underpinned its capacity to invest in competitive-building capabilities on a sustained basis.[8] If only we could all achieve this level of performance! Another challenge facing CEOs is the fact that so many people working in businesses think that systems technology is the one-stop shop for supply chain solutions. It's a mindset that started in the run up to the year 2000. No doubt you remember the Y2K phenomenon. Resources were poured into new information technology, affecting all areas of the enterprise, but for limited returns, and the world did not come to an end as some had predicted. The same mindset is now saying information systems will be the saviour of the supply chain and business generally – especially in this new age of terrorism, where the hope is that technology will magically make your business secure and manageable. Beware such prophets!

It's the people, stupid

In early 1997, Australia's largest processed food manufacturer, Goodman Fielder Ltd, had a rare opportunity to achieve a major transformation of its conglomerate-like business. It had business units in breakfast cereals, oils and margarine, poultry, food ingredients and milling and baking. David Hearn, the new Managing Director, had arrived from United Biscuits in the United Kingdom and was intent on boosting financial performance. He chose to start by transforming the existing logistics arrangements, which were messy and duplicated across several business units.[9] A new corporate strategy was devised and ready for implementation by mid-1997, but it never happened. In effect, David Hearn was overpowered by the managing directors of the business units, and the transformation simply limped along for a while before eventually fizzling out. Suffice to say, the financial performance of the company went the same way. This was a very powerful example of how internal resistance can slow down, or worse still, stop, what should have been a very successful change for good. A great opportunity was lost and the company has since struggled through ownership changes, privatization and, most recently, an attempt to re-list on the Australian Stock Exchange (ASX). In the meantime, the world has moved on from logistics to supply chain thinking and doing.

What do you think is the key ingredient in modern supply chains? The technology and the trucks? Or the people who design and run them? Supply chains may seem like uncontrollable, inanimate beasts, but they are in fact *living systems* propelled by humans and their behavior. However, it seems as though light might be dawning at last, in some quarters at least. *Harvard Business Review* convened an elite panel in 2003 to discuss future supply chain challenges and one member aptly concluded that '. . . despite years of process breakthroughs and elegant technology solutions, an agile, adaptive supply chain remains an elusive goal. Maybe it's the people who are getting in the way.'[10] Indeed. But what we are interested in is not how they get in the way, but how they bring the supply chain to life.

We can see the potent presence of human behavior, both inside and outside the enterprise. Customers, suppliers and third-party providers are driving the supply chain from the outside, while staff, managers and board members are seeking to manage and respond from the inside. If you can understand and correctly apply a more enlightened approach to managing this 'human presence' in the supply chain, you'll discover a primary source of performance improvement in the foreseeable future. It's all there for the taking.

It's best to stop thinking of supply chains as a 50/50 mix of infrastructure and information systems technology. Start thinking of the ideal mix as more like 45/45/10[11] – human behavior, systems technology and asset infrastructure. Whether we accept it or not, we are already shifting from Newtonian-like thinking to a more organic model. Once we accept this reality, a new world of performance improvement beckons, at every intra- and inter-organizational interface along our supply chains. Some more enlightened executives in adjacent fields have been on this wavelength for some time. David Smith, Head of Knowledge Management at Unilever, commenting in the *Financial Times* in 1998, mused that '. . . [organizational] alignment is 50 per cent of the game. Processes are 30 per cent. IT [Systems] no more than 20.'[12] He was referring to what goes on at the intersection between knowledge management and supply chains. More about this in Chapter 15.

If you need any more reasons, consider that during the next decade it will become progressively more difficult for enterprises to stand alone and compete successfully in their respective marketplaces. What we will see, and are already seeing, is the formation of supply chains made up of parties that consciously choose to work together in a preferred alliance (on either supply- or demand-sides), competing with other similar supply chain alliances or networks. The various airline alliances such as One World, Start Alliance and Sky Team are early examples of this phenomenon at work, sharing facilities, routes, reservation systems and maintenance among members in their own alliance, but competing with airlines in competitor alliances. In this world, you'll need to find and acquire completely new capabilities simply to stay competitive.

Talent will be at a premium, as will be the ability to select and manage new alliances and relationships with parties who bring specialized capabilities to help us 're-align' with customers, fast. At the same time, we will need to transform in other ways by embracing completely new business models.

Writer Thomas Friedman brings us some helpful insights in his book, *The World is Flat*.[13] He says that the 'connectivity' resulting from convergence of communications technology, computer technology and the explosion of software has led to the levelling of the global playing field, or a 'flat' world; and he cites what he calls 'supply-chaining' as one of the ten flattening forces that have caused this new phenomenon over the past decade. But even Friedman hardly acknowledges the underlying human forces at work in this massive transformation. He seems to be more concerned with all the **effects** rather than looking more deeply into what is driving them.

But give Friedman his due; his more recent writings and interviews are very insightful. In a television interview in Australia he reminded the audience of the words used by Roy Scheider in the 1975 blockbuster *Jaws*, when Scheider first catches sight of the great white shark that is circling his small fishing boat.[14] 'We're going to need a bigger boat', he says to his captain. The 2009 disaster movie 2012 echoes the same idea of how to deal with a seemingly insurmountable problem when its hero, played by John Cusack, looks at his map and observes, 'We're going to need a bigger plane.' Friedman was using this powerful metaphor to impress on his audience that the systemic failures and consequent global recession of the past few years will take a far bigger effort to correct than governments and businesses seem to comprehend. Witness what happened at the Copenhagen Climate Change conference in December 2009. Again, another good reason for fundamentally changing the way we do business.

Where did this transformation start?

To understand the current transformation of the supply chain, it's helpful to go back and see where it all began. Despite seminal articles by academics Robert Neuschel and John Stolle some 45 years ago, nothing immediate happened. Neuschel was one of the first to recognize that distribution activities stretched across a 'no man's land between functions' in organizations. He argued that any effort to reduce costs in logistics needed to be balanced with reaching the desired level of customer service and product availability.[15] Stolle observed that physical distribution was easier to analyze than to manage.[16] Logistics costs could be readily calculated; however, activities and tasks were scattered throughout the business and often under the control of divergent departments. The result? A fragmented approach to distribution – not unlike what a lot of companies have even today.

Businesses in those days focused primarily on managing finished product as it came off manufacturing lines. The production function of the enterprise was all-powerful. Product was stored in various places and then transported through a limited number of channels to consumers. At the time, with customers just starting to feel their buying power, it became obvious that the greater levels of service being demanded could not be sustained unless more was known about the in-bound side of the business. By the early 1980s, the demand and supply ends of the organization had been connected and the 'logistics' function formally established. Initially, logistics was structured only as a 'coordinating' role, but despite this other managers in the enterprise saw the new development as a grab for power by the fledgling function. Unhappily, even to this day, many senior executives are still confused about the distinction between 'control' and 'coordination'.

By the late 1980s, three important subsystems were clearly emerging in the enterprise. At the upstream end there was the in-bound logistics subsystem, consisting of procurement, in-bound transportation, inventory management, materials handling, facilities management and corresponding information systems. Downstream from production was the finished goods (or out-bound logistics) subsystem. This was a mirror image of the in-bound side, consisting of facilities management (including depots, warehouses and distribution centres), transportation links, inventory management, materials handling and information systems.

Where was production in all of this? It was caught firmly in the middle. While the production subsystem held out for an independent existence, it would gradually disappear in many enterprises over the ensuing decades. Indeed, these days production is effectively an integral part of the overall logistics effort in most forward-thinking enterprises. The combination of in-bound/out-bound logistics and production is sometimes called 'operations'. Meanwhile, service organizations have not even begun to think about any of these definitional matters; they don't even have them on their radar.

So for the enterprise to perform well, all three subsystems in this 'bow tie' organization structure have to be in synch. Once any one of them gets out of synch, the outcome is very predictable – either stock-outs or overstocks, both of which are expensive.

By the 1990s, events conspired to cause a great leap forward, like some accidental chemistry experiment. The 'discovery' of the Internet by commerce and industry opened up endless channels for humans to communicate, one-to-one. Coincidentally, a plethora of user-friendly software suites arrived on the scene. And the speed of telecommunications improved immeasurably. Now we could move forward from the previous preoccupation with internal integration and begin to link with parties upstream and downstream in a genuine network of supply chains. In almost a single stroke of genius (or good fortune), we had moved from talking about the concept of supply chain management to operationalizing supply chains, as depicted in Figure 1.1. The wavy lines in this diagram depict the many possible supply chains in which firms are implicitly or explicitly involved as they deliver their products and services to customers.

Let us consider what we mean by supply chain management, as it's a term bandied about today to cover all sorts of things. Supply chain management involves parties upstream and downstream agreeing to work together by joining their respective 'logistics' systems together. Simple? In concept, yes. But working together in complex chains, or networks, is quite difficult to achieve in practice.

In supply chain management, 'logistics networks' are a subset of supply chains, the key difference being the crucial interfaces between each supplier–buyer combination. Value is either created or destroyed through the management of these interfaces along the 'chain' or across the network. Given that a supply chain is the combination of multiple logistics networks, the potential to improve performance is much greater than within a single logistics system. In practice, all product, service and public sector enterprises have multiple supply chains running through them in a complex three-dimensional array.[17]

Another key difference in old and new ways of thinking is the approach to managing supply chains. We used to think of logistics as largely infra- structure- and operations-based, which led to an all-pervasive 'operational excellence' mentality that still prevails in some quarters even today. So management focused on costs and logistics was regarded as a cost centre. Not too exciting for those who worked in it! We now understand that managing *extended* supply chains involves far more than keeping costs in check (or working to reduce them). However, managing supply chains actually involves understanding the interaction between human behav- ior, information technology and infrastructure. Unfortunately, this is the antithesis of what actually happens in business today.

Since all types of enterprises have supply chains of various configura- tions running through them, you can see the extent of the oversight. How can we expect to start solving operational problems without first recog- nizing that the primary driver of goods and services moving through the supply chain pipeline is people? So far, there is only a small body of knowledge that goes beyond the hard assets of the supply chain – systems,

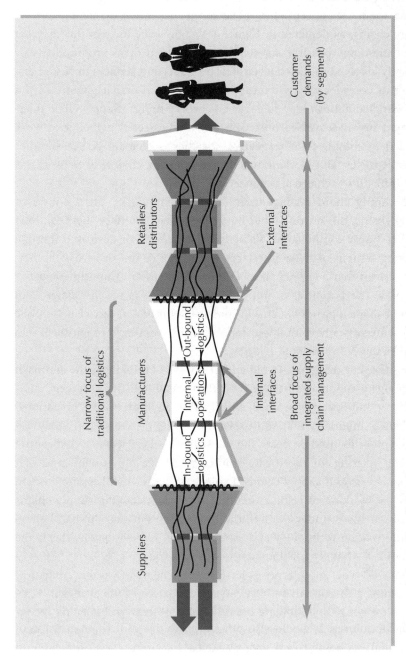

FIGURE 1.1 ◆ Operationalizing the concept of supply chains

Source: Adapted from Figure 1.1 in Gattorna (2006), p. 9

infrastructure and equipment – to get to what really drives performance: the soft intangible assets of human behavior and knowledge.

Watch the customer not the competitor

Management thinker Michael E. Porter caught everyone's attention in the late 1970s when he launched his quest for 'competitive strategy';[18] and he is still saying that '. . . every organization must have a clearly defined strategy to deliver superior profits'.[19] Competitive analysis and strategy are obviously critical to success, but we should not get things out of perspective. We know now that there is much more involved.

Do you not think it's time that companies start understanding what is going on inside their own businesses first? Porter's philosophy seems to have transfixed generations of managers into watching their competitors. The result? They have failed to develop the same degree of sensitivity towards internal resources and the internal dynamics of their own firm. They are even less aware of the interactions at the edges of their business. A myopic focus on competitors and the external environment can only limit understanding of internal cultural capability, which is so critical to executing strategy. With such a focus, it's not surprising there has been such a mismatch between strategy and implementation.

In reality, organizations can inflict much more harm on themselves by the very way they behave internally, than any external competitor is capable of inflicting. Maybe it would be more appropriate to adopt Maria Sharapova's philosophy in winning the 2004 Wimbledon tennis championship: 'I like winning. I love competition. But I try to be myself. I worry about what I want to achieve. Not what everyone else does.'[20] This is also a winning formula for business, because it avoids over-emphasizing external factors at the expense of internal factors. It has certainly worked for Maria Sharapova – she was ranked World No. 1 in women's tennis in August 2005.

If more enterprises were prepared to 'zero base', or go back to the fundamentals, rather than 'copy cat' their strategies, we would surely see fewer failures. It would also put a stop to the endless progression of new initiatives being rolled out in search of the next 'silver bullet'. Rob Murray, CEO of Lion Nathan National Foods, one of Asia Pacific's biggest food and beverage companies, expresses a similar philosophy: 'Right now, we're focused on trying to drive our own economic model and trying to make our own business work. You often end up losing if you obsess about what your competitors are doing. So I don't really care much what they are doing.'[21]

Can you see why we need to watch the customers, consumers and end-users of our products and services first and foremost? Unless all our energies and resources are focused on improving the 'alignment' between our business and customers (and suppliers too), then we are most likely wasting everyone's time and debilitating the company in the process. If we are sensitive to customer needs and buying preferences, it will be obvious what we have to do, and, like Sharapova, we won't have to worry so much about our competitors – they'll be worrying about us. The relevance of these insights to the design and operation of supply chains will become obvious in later chapters when we explain the inexorable principles that link an enterprise (internal cultural capability and leadership) with its marketplace, through operational strategy. All of these parameters interact in a multidisciplinary way, yet we continue to separate them into silos in the false hope that it will simplify the management task. Wrong. The paradox is that we're only adding further layers of complexity.

Internal 'forces of darkness'

Strategy is, in effect, just a set of *intentions*, which acts as a *bridge* between the enterprise and its marketplace. Until these words are brought to life and executed as actions, there is little difference between 'good' and 'bad' strategy. In fact, some would argue that an 'ordinary' strategy well implemented is better than a 'brilliant' strategy poorly executed. We can continue to debate this point, but we know from experience that 40 to 60 per cent of the original intentions articulated in business plans are dissipated or lost before ever being executed. While some of this loss is clearly a result of changing market conditions, competitor actions and the negative influence of government regulations, the biggest factor in the failure to execute the best-laid plans is the cultural resistance inside the enterprise itself. How often have we been in meetings where strategies have been presented by leaders on the assumption that their vision and accompanying instructions will be automatically followed by all present? Yet it's obvious that deep down some people, while appearing to agree with the implementation plan, are often quietly making up their minds to resist, or even opt out entirely. This is the insidious 'dark side' of culture at work inside the enterprise. The forces of darkness can undermine perfectly good strategies because particular people have different values to those needed to propel the strategies into action.

Organization design is the key

How can we anticipate and stymie negative and unwanted responses? Well, apart from the clues already provided, we need to consider the two factors that have perhaps most inhibited the development of business logistics and supply chain management as commercial disciplines over the past 45 years. The first is confusion around 'terminology'. Terminology is still an issue, as new terms are introduced on an almost annual basis, but we can at least be reassured by the fact that managers are becoming better educated and are more likely to understand what is really involved in moving goods and services, irrespective of the attached labels. The second is inappropriate organization design. We cannot dismiss its pervasive negative impact quite so easily.

The fact is that functional organization designs, which have seemingly served us so well for so long, together with matrix and partnership variants, are being rapidly marginalized. This is happening as increasing competitive intensity in many industry–market combinations drives customers towards more aggressive and demanding buying behaviors. The result is that while enterprises cling to these outmoded designs as markets move away, the degree of 'misalignment' is inexorably increasing. Worse still, it seems as if few enterprises have found ways of staying in *dynamic alignment* with their marketplace. New organizational formats are now urgently required to work in parallel with existing formats. More about this vexed topic in Chapter 6.

The four principles for designing more effective organization structures proposed by Lowell Bryan and Claudia Joyce provide a useful guide for the future.[22] In essence, they suggested that organizations need a 'portfolio' of coexistent structures that mirror the mix of dominant buying behaviors found in the marketplace. This means that successful organizations will blend all their disciplines in different configurations to match their various customer groups. Spanish fashion manufacturer-retailer Zara, does this perfectly. They form cross-functional teams for a merchandise category such as women's fashion, combining the efforts of design, logistics, production, sales operations and marketing. The result is a 'cluster' that can respond in close to real time, to a specific customer group, globally. Such customer-focused and flexible configurations are actually fundamental components of different supply chains. We are witnessing the early days of the way all enterprises will work in future.

Looking beyond conventional wisdom

To reach a new understanding of supply chains, we have to first leap ahead of another quest popular in the world of 'logistics', and that is the determination of academics, consultants and practitioners in the 1990s to extract the full potential of *internal integration*. Despite advances in technology that saw the introduction of Enterprise Resource Planning (ERP) systems, integration was always going to be a mirage. Why? No one during this period confronted the real blockage: the functional organization designs prevalent in most enterprises. Such structures set people to work in a straitjacket environment and offered little or no prospect of ever aligning with customers.

Indeed, the conventional functional style of organization design is still used by most enterprises in the world today, even though it is at least 90 degrees out of phase with the way customers prefer to buy. It was not until the mid 1990s, when the Internet arrived, that things moved forward again. The convergence of the Internet as a communications medium, and the coincidental development of a myriad of new software applications, brushed aside many of the internal and external obstacles to integration. This effectively connected and operationalized the supply chain for the first time. However, there was still something missing – an understanding of how the 'people factor' played out in all of this.

In search of *dynamic alignment*

As long ago as 1989 it occurred to me that 'logistics' as a field of management science lacked any substantive theoretical underpinning. Without this much needed conceptual foundation, it offered little prospect of further breakthrough developments, at least in the short to medium term. It seemed that we had hit a type of 'conceptual ceiling'. In response, I set out in search of ideas *beyond* the boundaries of conventional logistics thinking, in adjacent fields of management science. This proved to be an inspired move as it ultimately opened rich new avenues of thought that helped to inform us about the workings of modern logistics networks and supply chains. What we started in 1989, and continue to develop to this day, is a holistic view of how enterprises function, a type of 'new integrated theory of the firm'. The logic that underpins this approach was that casting a wide net could potentially produce new insights into how enterprises, and therefore *enterprise supply chains*, worked. And so it proved to be.

'Alignment' is not a new idea. In fact it has quite ancient origins. One of the earliest forms of alignment occurred in nature – the flight of wild geese.[23] Remarkably, a flock of geese flying in V-formation can fly 70 per cent further than a single goose on its own, so powerful is the aerodynamic effect in formation. A more contemporary example is the Australian 4,000 metre men's pursuit cycling team (pictured overleaf) competing in the 2008 Beijing Olympics, with all four riders in line astern, wheels millimetres apart, chasing around the oval race track at high speed.[24] That's alignment *par excellence!*

By applying the concept of alignment to the supply chain, I am seeking to emphasize the *dynamism* involved – the type of movement we can see and measure when it comes to a flock of geese or an Olympic cycling team. Alignment is a living (rather than static) concept that applies to the enterprise as a whole. We want to capture the underlying mechanisms in supply chains, which themselves are integral to all enterprises. We call this overarching concept *dynamic alignment*, because it holds true under changing conditions, and for the first time gives us an opportunity to design and operate supply chains that stay abreast of customers and consumers as they too evolve over time.

PHOTO 1.1 ◆ **The Australian 4,000 metre men's pursuit cycling team competing in the 2008 Beijing Olympics**

Source: Getty Images/Mike Hewitt

The economist R.H. Coase, in his 1937 essay 'The Nature of the Firm', first introduced the notion of 'moving equilibrium', where internal components interacted in such a way as to cause the firm to either expand or contract in size.[25] It is very likely that Coase was primarily thinking only of economic elements and did not consider the behavioral dimension, but this concept is very relevant to contemporary supply chains. Indeed, Robert J. Shiller, Professor of Economics at Yale University, has acknowledged as much in a recent TV interview when he remarked that '. . . we have been advocating going back to psychological fundamentals to try to understand macroeconomics, how economies move'.[26] Shiller is all for acknowledging the human effect in the economy! Some 60 years after Coase, Labovitz and Rosansky went part of the way towards redressing the situation with their dual concepts of vertical alignment (linking strategy and people inside the organization) and horizontal alignment (linking processes and customers).[27] They also introduced the notion of the self-aligning organization, but their work was based mainly on anecdotal evidence and as such lacked predictive power.

Perhaps the first indication that strategy and culture in an enterprise could be systematically linked came from Norman Chorn's doctoral research in 1987.[28] Subsequently, Chorn, myself and co-workers in our consulting firm[29] set out to study the leadership styles of individual executives. This led us to Carl Jung's seminal work on personality types[30] and ultimately to Ichak Adizes[31] and Gerard Faust,[32] who developed the 'P-A-E-I' coding system to categorize different management styles, encompassing 'Producer-Administrator-Entrepreneur-Integrator'.

Our collaboration during this period proved to be fortuitous, as we were able to combine this important research on leadership and personality types with my earlier work in customer segmentation and corporate vision development. It led directly to the first genuine multidisciplinary *dynamic alignment* framework that linked marketplace and strategy with internal cultural capability and leadership styles in the enterprise. The seminal framework is depicted in Figure 1.2.

We realized that the P-A-E-I behavioral coding methodology (or 'logics' as we referred to them) developed by Adizes and Faust to describe

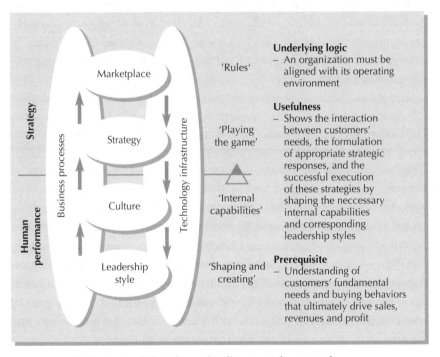

FIGURE 1.2 ◆ Elements of the *'dynamic alignment'* framework

Source: Adapted from Figure 1.2 in Gattorna (2003), p. xiii; also Gattorna (1998), p. 5; and Gattorna (2006), p. 16

different management styles of individual managers, **applied equally well at the aggregate level** – this was the step jump in logic we made at the time. In other words, *groups* of people inside enterprises with similar values could be identified and described as *subcultures*. Similarly, groups of people on the outside who shared similar dominant buying values for specific product or service categories could be identified and classified as *behavioral segments* (otherwise known as *external subcultures*).

We had indeed found the 'missing link', which turned out to be a behavioral metric (or logic) that could be used to describe (and measure) what was happening at all four levels of the emerging multi-disciplinary *dynamic alignment* model. This new behavioral metric is indeed the *DNA* of business and enterprise supply chains, a topic we will explore in more depth in Chapter 4. Just as important, this new coding regime facilitated comparative analyses of all four levels of our model in search of potential 'misalignments'. As engineers well know, you cannot make meaningful comparisons unless you express everything in a common metric. We had found that unique metric – something that had evaded previous researchers – mainly because no one had been looking across all the fields of management science, concurrently. No one had been eclectic enough or indeed mad enough.

Behavioral forces at work in supply chains

The behavioral coding system that we developed forms the foundation of the new insights on supply chains that I describe in later chapters. The roots of this system are firmly embedded in Carl Jung's theory of psychological types, which states that all conscious mental activity occurs in two perceptual processes: *sensing and intuition*; and two judgement processes: *thinking and feeling*. Adizes and Faust resolved and simplified Jung's original framework and identified four key behavioral types or 'logic sets' that might exhibit a dominant tendency. These are best represented as two pairs of counterveiling (behavioral) forces, which are always in *dynamic tension*, and are present in all human interactions, as depicted in Figure 1.3.

In the context of supply chains, we are particularly interested in the specific interaction between buyers and sellers. Adizes and Faust originally labeled these behavioral forces P-A-E-I as described above, but we later relabeled the 'E' to 'D' and defined them as follows:

P (Producer): the force for action, results, speed and focus.

A (Administrator): the opposing force to D, and represents stability, control, reliability, measurement, logic and efficiency.

D (Developer): the force for creativity, change, innovation and flexibility (originally labeled 'E' for Entrepreneurial by Adizes and Faust).

I (Integrator): the opposing force to P, and represents cooperation, cohesion, participation and harmony.

The four elements of the P-A-D-I coding system come together in different ways to produce 16 possible combinations, all of which are in *dynamic*

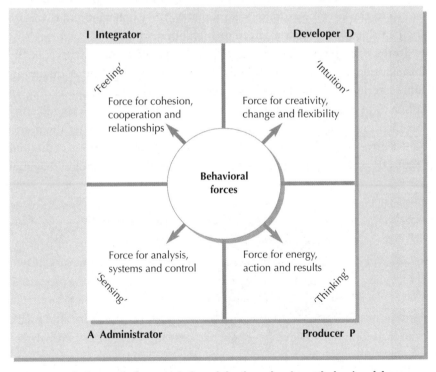

FIGURE 1.3 ◆ **General characteristics of the four dominant behavioral forces or logics**

Source: Adapted from Figure 29.1 in Gattorna (1998), p. 474; see also Gattorna (2006), p. 17

equilibrium; each dominant logic combination has a different '*centre of gravity*'. For example, if we are describing a particular buying style we may discern an overriding preference for speed, results and performance to specifications (P logic), and a lesser preference for reliability, consistency and price (A logic). There may also be some preference expressed for flexibility (D logic) and cohesion (I logic). So the overall summary of this particular buying behavior can be represented in shorthand code 'Pa', as depicted in Figure 1.4. Note that we have opted only to use 'primary' and 'secondary' parameters to describe the 'dominant logic', whereas Adizes originally used all four parameters in his descriptions of management styles. Our more abbreviated coding regime doesn't lessen the value of the approach, but has the advantage of making it simpler to use in practice.

The important insight to take on board here is that all customers have hierarchies of values. We are seeking to bring **the most dominant buying values to the surface** as these will ultimately drive behavior and therefore are the values with which we need to align our responses.

In the example in Figure 1.4, although the centre of gravity is in the P quadrant, and there is a secondary tendency towards the A quadrant, some overlap into the D and I quadrants suggests that there is also an influence of each coming into play. However, these forces are significantly less than the primary P logic and secondary A logic that defines the dominant centre of gravity. Horizontal and vertical logics can be combined (e.g., DI, or Di, Ia or IA, etc.) but it is impossible to combine diagonal

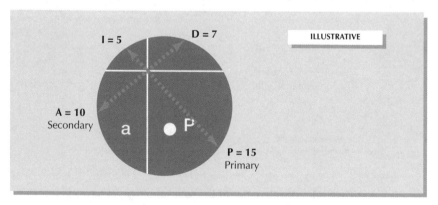

FIGURE 1.4 ◆ **Typical spread of attributes that define customers' buying behaviors; in this case 'P' is the dominant logic and 'a' is the secondary logic, making a composite 'Pa'**

logics, i.e., I and P logics or D and A logics, as they are at the opposite ends of a continuum. This is because the more a buyer moves along the diagonal towards one end of the continuum, the less the influence of the opposing logic.

The four elements of *dynamic alignment*

So let us consider the logic of the new model and see what impact it has on our thinking. The key driver in the marketplace is the dominant buying behavior or natural preference exhibited by customers for a particular product or service category in a specific marketplace. This is Level 1 in the *dynamic alignment* framework, as depicted in Figure 1.5.

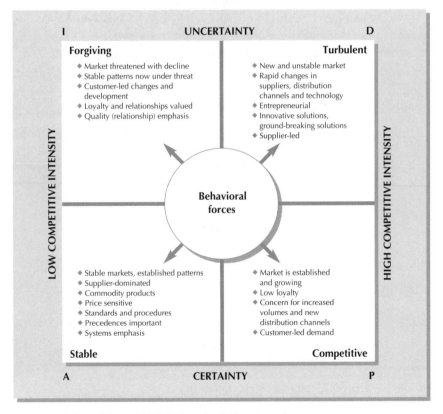

FIGURE 1.5 ◆ **Level 1 – Marketplace logic framework**

Source: Adapted from Figure 29.2 in Gattorna (1998), p. 474; see also Gattorna (2006), p. 19

Level 2 is the strategy element. This is the bridge that links the enterprise's internal cultural capabilities with the external marketplace, as shown in Figure 1.6.

Having an aligned set of subcultures (sitting on top of a set of enterprise-wide shared values, otherwise known as *corporate* culture) is crucial to the successful implementation of operating strategy. This is Level 3. Figure 1.7 shows this third level in the *dynamic alignment* framework.

Finally, Level 4. Effective leaders understand the aggregate values of their enterprise, and can mold from these the appropriate subcultures to align with the preferences being expressed by customers in the marketplace. There are four primary leadership styles identified: Visionary (D);

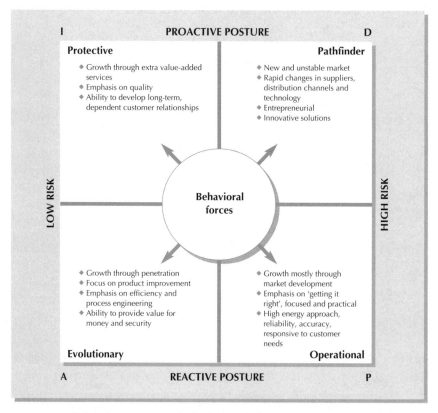

FIGURE 1.6 ◆ **Level 2 – strategy logic framework**

Source: Adapted from Figure 29.3 in Gattorna (1998), p. 476; see also Gattorna (2006), p. 20

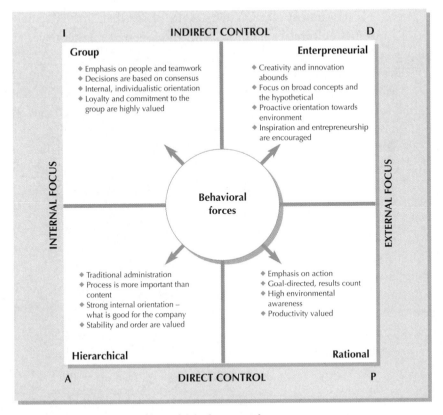

FIGURE 1.7 ◆ **Level 3 – culture logic framework**

Source: Adapted from Figure 29.4 in Gattorna (1998), p. 477; see also Gattorna (2006), p. 21

Company Baron (P); Traditionalist (A); and Coach (I). These different leadership styles are depicted in Figure 1.8 overleaf.

Time to re-invent the enterprise

Let us consider the need for organizations to adapt to new market conditions and the integral role that supply chains play in this change process. In 1996, Levi Strauss & Co. undertook what at the time was heralded at the time as the most dramatic change program in American business.[33] Despite solid growth in revenue and profits, Levi's management felt their customers were telling them they should change – and they were listen-

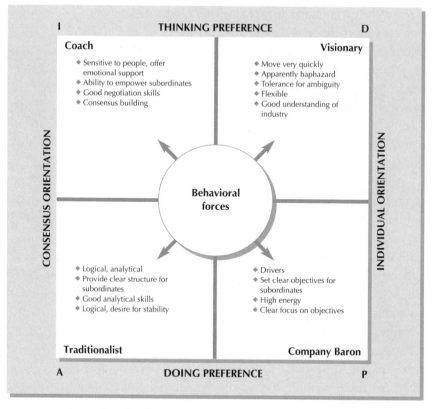

FIGURE 1.8 ◆ Level 4 – leadership logic framework

Source: Adapted from Figure 29.5 in Gattorna (1998), p. 478; see also Gattorna (2006), p. 22

ing. As the project unfolded it became very clear to team leader Thomas Kasten that Levi's customer service problems were deep-rooted and they involved the entire supply chain, from concept to end-consumer. The resulting transformation was timely for Levi's because it set up the company for strong growth for another decade. How many enterprises are as sensitive to the need for change as Levi Strauss? But how many either wait until the last moment or get lost in the change process itself? We have another less complimentary anecdote about Levi Strauss which we will relate in Chapter 2. You will be amazed that it is the same company!

The *dynamic alignment* model can make the difference. The model provides both a *map* and a *tool* to help you achieve superior performance across your corporate supply chains. It's a *map* to help you navigate your way through the increasingly complex network of supply chains out there today. And it's a *tool* because it helps to pinpoint how to align specific supply chains to particular customer behaviors. This is why it's such an important breakthrough for management thinking in general, and for the design and operation of supply chains in particular. It explains for the first time how the softer science of human behavior can be integrated with the more tangible – and generally better understood – world of infrastructure and technology.

The underlying logic of the *dynamic alignment* framework is that an enterprise needs to be aligned with its customers/markets in the context of the prevailing operating environment. The power of this framework lies in its ability to reveal the interaction between customers' preferences, helping to formulate appropriate response strategies, and successfully to execute those strategies through the shaping of internal cultural capabilities via the appropriate leadership. The essential starting point for successful *dynamic alignment* is a comprehensive understanding of customers' fundamental needs and matching dominant buying behaviors. This particular subject will be explored in depth in Chapter 2. However, it's not difficult to observe the difference between successful and unsuccessful enterprises as measured in terms of organizational effectiveness metrics, revenue and CFROI performance.

Successful organizations generally have a leadership that is in close touch with, and empathetic to, their customers and prevailing market conditions. Empathetic leaders tend to formulate relevant strategies and shape the most appropriate cultural capabilities to underpin and drive those strategies into their target marketplace. Tesco, IKEA, Cessna, Nokia, Nestlé, Caterpillar, P&G, Wal-Mart and Dell are just a few examples of successful *dynamic alignment* in their respective marketplaces. And the way Lord Coe and his bidding team dramatically won the 2012 Olympic Games for London is another example of superior *dynamic alignment*, beautifully conceived and executed to perfection. There is no real size limitation on the application and usefulness of *dynamic alignment* – it applies equally well to large and small enterprises. An example of the latter is the 14-strong chain or 'charm bracelet' (as she refers to her store group) of fashion retail stores developed by Belinda Seper in Sydney under her 'Belinda' branding. While there is clearly a common theme across all stores, each is different in its own way. Each store has its own personality in response to the lifestyle needs of women in each store's catchment area.[34]

Less successful enterprises, on the other hand, fall at the first hurdle. Their leadership appears to lose touch with customers and corresponding market conditions, and the strategies and underpinning cultural capabilities put in place become progressively more misaligned, until finally the responsible Board is forced to move and replace the CEO, and start the process all over again – often resulting in huge expense to the business with an accompanying negative impact on the share price. We saw clear evidence of this when IBM got into trouble in the early 1990s, and the subsequent much publicized demise of Carly Fiorina at Hewlett-Packard. Other examples of significant misalignment include such high-profile names as Enron in the US, Marks & Spencer and J. Sainsbury in the UK, Parmalat in Italy, and AMP and Coles in Australia. This phenomenon knows no borders. All of these organizations are working hard to regain their former glory through radical initiatives designed to overcome serious misalignments with their customers, which in turn led to progressively worsening operating and financial performance. But as they'll all tell you, it's very hard to come back.

This phenomenon occurs in all types of organizations, from religious to political and from public to private businesses. And they all have one thing in common: people and their behavior. Indeed, taking a leadership position these days is far riskier than yesteryear, because there is little or no time allowed for them to learn on the job. In many ways it's akin to what is known in aeronautical circles as 'fly-by-wire'.[35] We have to accept that the enterprise will be in a state of 'dynamic instability' all or most of the time, and therefore it is vital to learn fast how to manage under these most trying conditions. Aeronautical engineers learned to work with this 'dynamic instability' in aircraft as flight speeds increased exponentially. It's now up to managers and leaders in commerce and industry to do the same and increase the speed of their decision cycles. We will consider this notion further in Chapter 9 when we discuss the 'OODA' loop and *agile* supply chains.

Responsiveness at last

We did not set out to solve every problem in the world, but it's increasingly obvious that little or no progress can be made to improve corporate performance unless we take a more eclectic, albeit holistic, approach than is in vogue at the moment. By going well beyond the accepted boundaries of conventional management theory and practice, we can embrace a new approach to designing and managing enterprise supply chains, but this will always remain something of an art form. Fortunately, the more holistic *whole-of-enterprise* perspective offered by the *dynamic alignment* framework points to a new way forward. A fertile new world awaits if we pursue this line of thinking, a world where more value can be released and higher performance achieved, on a sustainable basis.

Indeed, logistics networks and supply chains (comprising multiple organizations in 3-D arrays) are largely driven by people power, either as customers, suppliers or employees. Systems are the next most critical area because these deliver information to people for visibility and decision-making, such as 'make or buy or act' in some way inside the enterprise. So it appears that the whole concept of *dynamic alignment*, when applied to logistics systems and the broader context of supply chains, is simply another way of expressing optimal cost–service effectiveness. This is the realm where customers are serviced appropriately, no more, no less, eliminating over- and under-servicing forever. At last we have a way around the service problem that confronts every manager every working day, epitomized by the words, 'We know we are over-servicing some customers and under-servicing others, but we don't know which is which.'[36]

Dynamic alignment principles bring with them a paradigm shift, away from conventional thinking which suggests that as service levels are progressively increased, cost-to-serve increases at a faster rate, approaching infinity at very high levels of service. This does not necessarily follow if resources are subtly re-allocated to align better, with and more accurately reflect, customer buying behaviors. Armed with a clearer understanding of the implications of improved alignment between an enterprise and its marketplace, the potential exists to move to a *best-of-both-worlds* strategy, where improved service comes at a lower overall cost-to-serve, at least up to a point, as depicted in Figure 1.9 overleaf.

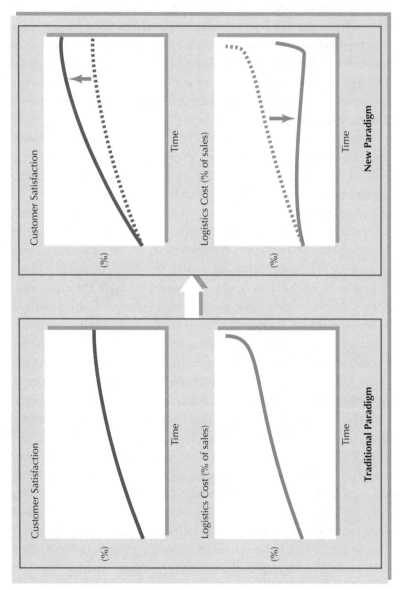

FIGURE 1.9 ◆ Paradigm shift to a best-of-both-worlds strategy

Source: Developed in discussion with Deborah Ellis, Carpenter Ellis, 2009

Building more responsive supply chains means building more responsive enterprises overall, because service means different things to different people, and customers do not split hairs between functions inside the enterprise. Indeed, supply chains *are* the business. Figure 1.10 illustrates in more detail the four primary customer service logics that result in at least 16 possible combinations; some types are more often observed than others, but they all exist in practice.

For one class of customer, good service means surprising them with an innovative response to meet their unique needs, at speed. This is the D logic. For another class of customers with a different mindset, good

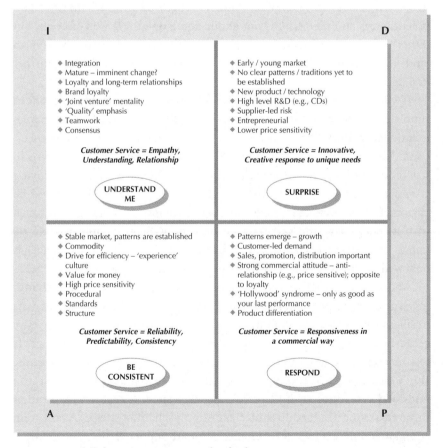

FIGURE 1.10 ◆ Primary customer service logics

Source: Adapted from Figure 2.4 in Gattorna and Walters (1996), p. 31; see also Figure 1.10 in Gattorna (2006), p. 27

customer service means delivering a reliable, predictable service, on a consistent basis. For this type of customer, consistency is essential. This is the A logic. For yet another class of customer, good service means being responsive to their demanding requirements in a commercial way. For them, straight out responsiveness and timeliness is paramount. This is the P logic. Finally for another group of customers, the opposite is true, as they seek service that is empathetic and understanding, generally delivered in a quietly consistent way. For them the crucial ingredient is having suppliers understand their special need for a close and sharing relationship, which ensures they are not taken out of their comfort zone. This is the I logic.

Following these logics leads us to conclude that the concepts of 'responsiveness' and 'flexibility' (much sought after by all supply chain practitioners and theorists) is not about doing one thing well after all, but rather having the capability to do *several* things well, concurrently. It is an 'and' rather than an 'either/or' world. We will explore this theme further in Chapter 2.

If you have any doubt about the importance of managing modern supply chains look no further than the example of some leading companies mentioned earlier. Why is it that one national icon, Marks and Spencer, could lose its way, while another, Nestlé, could move from strength to strength? Both had secure positions in their respective markets, enjoying a strong brand and loyal customer following. But one misunderstood its customers and made the wrong sourcing decisions; the other was in touch with its customers and was unfazed by supply chain complexity. Nestlé knows what *dynamic alignment* means. Meanwhile, Marks and Spencer is now well on the way back to alignment with its traditional customer base.

And why is it that retailer J. Sainsbury was rudderless in the changing world of supply chain and globalization, while Tesco expanded its business to capture the advantages offered by changing times? Sainsbury acted like a large steamer moving slowly through the market waters. It lost market share due to huge stocks-outs, high costs and lower margins. But Tesco navigated through changing times, expanding from food into non-food categories such as petrol and insurance. It secured its position through strong leadership and clear supply chain strategy. Again, one company could capture the benefits of smart supply chain management, while another was overcome by supply chain complexity. But things can change! J. Sainsbury's fortunes are now on the rebound.

Trying to navigate your way through the spaghetti bowl of today's supply chains is not easy for any enterprise, regardless of its age, experience, market penetration or financial resources. But some do it better than others and reap the rewards. Successful organizations understand that building more responsive, customer-focused supply chains is the key to the future. *Dynamic alignment* of supply chains means being able to see the life within those supply chains, capturing the energy and opportunity, and lining that up with the demands of customers. In the coming decade, little else is going to happen in an enterprise outside the domain of its supply chains. Supply chains **are** the business, and you better believe it!

Defining ideas

1 During the global recession, aligning your enterprise supply chains with customers, suppliers and third-party providers will give you the best chance of survival, and coming out the other side as a winner. And according to research by global consulting firm Accenture, '. . . winners pull away after recession'.[37]

2 Take a more liberal view of the definition and scope of contemporary supply chains – you will be well rewarded. We are in effect talking about the *central nervous system* of all business and commerce.

3 You cannot afford to let your market move away from you; stay connected and in synch.

4 Building more responsive supply chains means building more responsive enterprises overall.

5 **Challenge** for the reader: are you doing enough in your enterprise to engage with your customers and suppliers?

CHAPTER 2

Customer conversations

All pathways lead to customers

T he clear message in this chapter is that customers, and customers alone, are the ultimate frame of reference when you are designing and operating enterprise supply chains. To convert the rhetoric into action you inevitably have to start by re-segmenting your marketplace along behavioral lines. The myriad of other available techniques may be useful, but not essential. Behavioral segmentation, on the other hand, is mandatory.

Once the marketplace is interpreted in this way, we follow the behavioral thread back inside the organization, and the great news is that we only need three or four different types of supply chain configurations at any one time to cover up to 80 per cent of the market. This multiple-alignment, multi-dimensional format may on the surface sound complicated, but in fact, it's quite the opposite: it represents a significant reduction in operating complexity and, therefore, cost. This structure underpins the required dynamism in contemporary supply chains, and brings to life all the talk about 'flexibility' and 'adaptability'. Those relatively few global companies that have so far adopted *dynamic alignment* principles are already reaping the rewards of their first-mover advantage.

We have all been seeking the Holy Grail of improved operational and financial performance. The problem is we have been looking in the wrong places. The secret of designing a superior supply chain is to start by re-segmenting customers along behavioral lines and then reverse engineer from there. We need to shape specific *value propositions* and underpin these with supportive organization structures, processes, technology and other building blocks, highlighted in Chapters 7 to 10.[1] Indeed, something that we have known for some time – but have been denying – is that customers are the ultimate frame of reference. Mattias Holweg and Fritz Pil were adamant about this when they promoted the use of build-to-order strategies.[2] Dell has done it. Nokia has done it. Why not others? We believe introducing this type of genuine customer focus is critical to a breakthrough in supply chain thinking.

We shouldn't blame senior managers for failing to emphasize customers sufficiently because outdated organizational designs have not helped either. Rigid, hierarchical structures have often fragmented knowledge and responsibility into silos, leading to little information on customers ever filtering through to the people in back-office positions. What's more, most organizations have adopted erroneous and mostly irrelevant customer segmentation regimes. These include segmentation using Standard Industrial Classification (SIC),[3] industry sectors, geography, size, revenue, profitability, price points, product characteristics and an assortment of institutional parameters around which sales forces and logistics operations have been mobilized. Thomas Davenport and his colleagues were right when they observed that '. . . a firm needs more than transactional data to gain (customer) insight'.[4] Successful companies agree that the person behind the transaction must also be considered. We can better understand and predict customer behavior by examining behavioral data along with the corresponding transactional data.[5] Indeed, this is where knowledge management intersects with our interest in customer buying behaviors. Unfortunately, companies are relying too much on technology-driven transactional data, which leaves big gaps in their knowledge about actual customer behavior. Something else is needed to fill this gap.

Confusion around segmentation

The segmentation of customers, together with product differentiation, are perhaps the two most fundamental concepts in marketing. *Product differ-*

entiation is reasonably straightforward, but confusion is rife when it comes to the concept of *segmentation* and how it is operationalized. Essentially, the idea is simple: we need to group customers with common expectations together so that we can match service strategies to their unique (shared) needs. Each segment must be distinct, accessible and economically viable in size. Based on these guidelines your ability to dissect a market is only limited by the breadth of your imagination. But therein lies the problem.

One of the earliest forms of segmentation used by enterprises was the classic *one-size-fits-all* approach; this was not segmentation. This attempt to standardize all products and services was born out of a misguided desire to simplify internal processes for the sake of managerial convenience. A pity about the customers; alignment was not even on managers' radar! However, increasingly sophisticated customers soon forced big-brand companies to look for solutions that were more accommodating to their preferences. Unfortunately, some suppliers went to the other extreme and fell into the *over-customization trap*, where every customer was treated as unique. In turn, this led to further complexity and even higher cost-to-serve. In reality, the compromise (or '80 per cent' solution) lies somewhere in the middle of these two extremes: creating three or possibly four substantive behavioral segments, rather than one or many.

How do your sales and marketing people target their customers? Generally, sales and marketing managers have developed a myriad of ways to divide their markets and allocate resources, and in particular, to organize their sales forces and supporting logistics functions. But they have paid little or no attention to the consequent impact on back-office operations. Indeed, a real 'disconnect' continues between the way market-facing personnel view customers and the information they communicate back to non-market-facing personnel. Yet it's fundamental that everyone inside the enterprise who contributes to serving customers, directly or indirectly, should be on the same page. Despite advances in technology, we do not seem to have achieved this most basic level of common understanding. And while the search goes on at the front-end of organizations to find ever more subtle ways of understanding what customers want,[6] little or no work appears to be taking place to link this ever evolving understanding to back-office fulfillment operations. Sound familiar?

Most enterprises will ultimately adopt a segmentation method to guide the design and operation of their supply chains. Unfortunately, in many cases, you pay your money and get what you deserve! We have compelling evidence from many research and consultancy projects during the past two decades that there is really only one 'right' way to group customers. Perhaps one of the best attempts at arguing the case for behavioral segmentation comes from US strategic change researchers Phil Nunes and Frank Cespedes.[7] They argue that customers have 'escaped' from conventional channels, and this is certainly true. But then again, we need to find faster and better ways of keeping abreast of the evolving, learning customer. They identified four kinds of buyers, not unlike the 'straw man' I will present later in this chapter.

However, in some respects they go too far in attempting to describe how the buying behaviors of the four kinds of buyers vary across the five stages of a typical purchasing life-cycle. Of course, this can (and does) occur in practice, but their approach introduces an unnecessary layer of complexity, which paradoxically makes it more difficult to use in practice. Indeed, any new method of segmentation should be user-friendly, and this one is not. We agree with the notion that 'unfettered customer behavior is inevitable',[8] but this is not necessarily bad, or something we should openly resist. Quite the contrary. The solution is to accept that knowledge-rich customers will inevitably find ways to access products and services by selecting from the increasing number of pathways or channels on offer. We can achieve true alignment if the customers are satisfied with this process. However, to get to this point, we must first develop a much deeper understanding of the internal cultural implications for all of the parties involved along these channels and supply chains.

Moving away from one-dimensional solutions

Consider the supply chains that exist in your industry. How difficult would it be to shift towards using multiple supply chains to serve your different customer segments? And how effective? Where would you start? Let's look at several approaches investigated by academics and commentators since the mid-1990s.

Marshall L. Fisher was one of the first to define and explore the idea of multiple supply chains.[9] He proposed classifying products based on their demand patterns and devised two main product categories – functional and innovative – each requiring distinctly different supply chains.[10] He concluded that '. . . the root cause of the problems plaguing many supply chains is a mismatch between the type of product and the type of supply chain'. He suggested a matrix where functional products, such as everyday staples like bread, milk and petrol with mostly predictable demand, should be handled via an 'efficient' supply chain; and more innovative products, such as fashion apparel and electronic high-technology goods, would require what he termed a 'responsive' supply chain. In his estimation, problems arose when innovative products were processed via an 'efficient' supply chain configuration.[11] Does this thinking ring true for your organization?

We believe there are some weaknesses in Fisher's framework. He assumes the demand patterns for so-called *staple* products will stay constant under all market conditions. But demand for any product or service can be unstable at times, so it is incorrect to imply that supply chains can be designed around a broad product classification, a type of 'set and forget' approach. Changing market conditions can and do influence demand patterns and effectively change staple products into different types of 'products' that are bought in very different ways. For example, under normal circumstances, Fisher might classify petrol as a staple product, exhibiting relatively predictable demand patterns among consumers. However, if there is even the sniff of a refinery strike, or an accident interrupts supply, consumers are likely to rush to petrol stations and pay whatever price is being asked at the pump to fill their tanks. In such a situation, the supplying oil company has to manage the unpredicted spike in demand differently from everyday demand for petrol. The Coca-Cola Company is another example. Coca-Cola exhibits different demand patterns when sold in volume through a supermarket outlet compared to when sold in smaller quantities via the local convenience store or a vending machine; and the corresponding supply chains for each channel are configured differently too. Thus focusing solely on the product and its 'typical demand/supply characteristics' is not the answer. You have to consider the combination of product category *and* the situation in the market.

Hau Lee, the well-known Stanford University professor, attempted to develop Marshall Fisher's work in his paper, 'Aligning supply chain strategies with product uncertainties'.[12] He proposed four types of supply chain strategies, which look very much like my own taxonomy of four supply chain types, namely *efficient* supply chains (equivalent to my *lean*), *risk-hedging* supply chains (equivalent to my *fully flexible*), *responsive* supply chains and *agile* supply chains (which taken together appear to be equivalent to my *agile*). He does not suggest anything equivalent to my *continuous replenishment* supply chain type; some of these characteristics appear to be buried in his *efficient* supply chain type.

The framework he uses to develop his categorization of four supply chains involves matching supply uncertainty and demand uncertainty. This is a useful development, but in the end it proves to be insufficient to inform our decision-making. Why? Because it is based on categorizing products as either functional or innovative again – which is meant to characterize whether they experience low or high demand uncertainty. This is the weakness in the framework because we have already concluded that the same products and services can be subject to different customer buying behaviors, which in turn will change their demand and supply patterns.

Lee's model lacks the all-important *dynamic* capability that we will discuss in more detail later in this chapter. It is more of a static representation at a point in time, which although an approximation of reality, is not close enough when product-market situations are changing ever more rapidly. As an example, a small washer on a piece of capital equipment may be categorized as a staple item by Lee, but it could become critical if it fails, thereby causing the machine to fail or malfunction. In that circumstance, a customer's buying behavior for the humble washer would surely move (albeit temporarily) from staple product (involving an *efficient/lean* supply chain configuration) to an emergency requirement (involving a *fully flexible* supply chain configuration) – extreme opposites. Lee seems to acknowledge the need for a more dynamic approach when he says that '. . . because of shorter and shorter product life-cycles, the pressure for dynamically adjusting and adapting a company's supply chain is mounting'.[13] Perhaps this will be achieved, but in a somewhat different way to that which he originally envisaged.

IBM also has a view on this vexed topic of multiple supply chains. Bill Gilmour, IBM's global consumer product industry leader, argues that Fast-Moving Consumer Goods (FMCG) manufacturers need two supply chains to service their retail customers,[14] i.e., mass production push (equivalent to my *lean*) and something at the other end of the spectrum to handle unpredictable (pull) demand (equivalent to my *agile*). But he does not suggest how this might work. So there is no shortage of different viewpoints on the topic.

Another consultancy, Booz Allen Hamilton, proposes what it describes as 'tailored business streams' for its contribution to the debate on multiple supply chains.[15] Its view that '. . . the challenge for companies is not achieving a single point of focus, but rather about harmonizing multiple points of focus,'[16] is well made. Booz Allen Hamilton research found that 'Smart Customizers', companies that aligned their market-facing and fulfillment operations with customers, exhibited a 2:1 performance gap over those that did not. This is a significant finding and should accelerate the movement towards the multiple supply chain alignment that I am proposing in this book.

A third academic to offer insights into this topic is Jonathan Byrnes of MIT; he acknowledges that three or more supply chains may co-exist in and between enterprises.[17] Companies such as Wal-Mart, Procter & Gamble and Target are typical of those taking advantage of new supply chain information technologies, which are 'becoming more capable of dynamic management, assigning the right product to the right supply chain at the right time'.[18] His insights appear to be similar to those expressed by Fisher. But here too we should scrutinize where he places the most focus, and in this case Byrnes emphasizes what he calls '. . . an intelligent, precise supply chain IT system'.[19]

Like other commentators before him, Byrnes is close, but not quite close enough. He too is skirting around the more fundamental issue of *who* is actually *pulling* and *pushing* products through supply chains in the first place! If we factor this additional (human) dimension into the equation we will have the ability to explain a lot more about how modern supply chains really work and how they should be designed for peak performance. Byrnes is right about one thing though, that 'sooner or later, competitive pressures will force companies to employ dynamic, differentiated supply chains, because they will be accompanied by compelling first-mover advantages. The supply chain managers who start to create these systems now will lead their industries for a generation to come.'[20] That said, we are still left wondering about the underlying mechanisms that will bring about this most desirable outcome!

A fifth framework is provided by A.T. Kearney, which outlines a '. . . how-to approach for developing strategies that appropriately align with each supply chain'.[21] Their 2004 paper, 'How many supply chains do you need?', uses a combination of customer-related and product-related variables to segment supply chains. Unfortunately, any early promise is unfulfilled as they follow a similar path to that taken by Fisher, again categorizing the type of supply chain by product category. As discussed, this works some but not all of the time, because buying situations inevitably change for most products and services. The secret is to segment customers by their **dominant** buying behavior and **then** consider what this means for the design and operation of the corresponding supply chains (outside-in), rather than think in terms of segmenting supply chains from the inside out. A subtle but important distinction.

Another perspective is provided by Janet Godsell, a researcher at Cranfield.[22] Godsell introduces the notion of 'demand chain strategy' that links demand fulfillment (otherwise known as supply chain) with demand definition and creation (otherwise known as marketing). She sees demand chain management as 'the crucial missing link between business unit, market, and supply chain strategy – that creates alignment around a common set of demand chain objectives to ensure that the demand chain meets the needs of customers and shareholders alike in the most efficient and effective way'.[23] I am not too keen on the new terminology she has introduced, but that aside, Godsell proposes a useful four-step process for developing demand chain strategy, as follows:

1 Set demand chain objectives;
2 This will drive market strategy, comprising a) relevant segmentation and b) customer value segmentation;
3 This sets up the supply chain process strategy, comprising a) supply chain drivers and b) differentiated supply chain process strategy;
4 It also sets up process enablers, such as organization design, performance management, and systems.

This then feeds back into the demand chain objectives as an on-going interactive process. Her model is a useful introduction to alignment, with a few caveats; Godsell is primarily linking the market with supply chain processes. But I am proposing that there's more involved – culture and leadership must be addressed simultaneously if we are to align with our customers. More grist for the supply chain alignment mill.

Perhaps the most recent attempt at categorizing supply chains comes from Melnyk et al.[24] But here again, there is only a very indirect reference to customers; their framework is still very much 'inside-out' in orientation. They talk about a blend of six properties, rather than a combination of unique supply chain configurations or hybrids. It's just another dead-end in our search for enlightened design thinking which truly reflects customer expectations.

Disappointingly, none of the above perspectives seems to address the underlying influence and power of organizational culture in either supporting or resisting 'best laid plans'. In my view culture is the critical 'missing link' in our understanding of how supply chains really work in practice, and it is exactly this gap in current knowledge that we are addressing in this book.

Fittingly, Dave Anderson, a former colleague and Partner at Accenture, has the last word on the subject in his paper, 'Quick-change supply chains'.[25] He acknowledges that 'most of today's supply chains . . . are "hard wired"', which means 'they accommodate only standard service offerings and have no ability to meet fast-changing availability or delivery requirements. Yet business success in the 21st Century will increasingly demand quick-change supply chains.'[26] His 'quick-change' supply chains are equivalent to my multiple (aligned) supply chains. The only thing left to do now is agree how this new philosophy can be implemented on the ground. In this respect we are not too far away from success, and increasingly harsh trading conditions brought on by the global recession will provide the incentive for many enterprises to find a way to jump any final hurdles. In my experience (both advisory and research), those parties in supply chains under the most pressure are the first to innovate, simply to survive. If successful, these 'first movers' receive most of the benefits from leading, but very often the consequent costs of their innovations flow to the opposite end of the chain, depending of course on the balance of power at the time. This is 'survival of the fittest' in the business world.

Adding the missing behavioral dimension to supply chains

At this stage we should remind ourselves of an important point made earlier in Chapter 1: supply chains are not inanimate mechanical structures.

Products and services only move from raw materials and production sources to consuming markets because of human intervention. This can come from either outside the enterprise (customers, suppliers and third parties), or inside (company personnel). If it is true as we assert that a *one-size-fits-all* approach is no longer viable in a fast-changing world, we should be considering how many possible behavioral segments we need to organize our business around. Our fieldwork has led us to identify up to 16 possible behavioral segments, as depicted in Figure 2.1, which shows the most common segments highlighted by name.

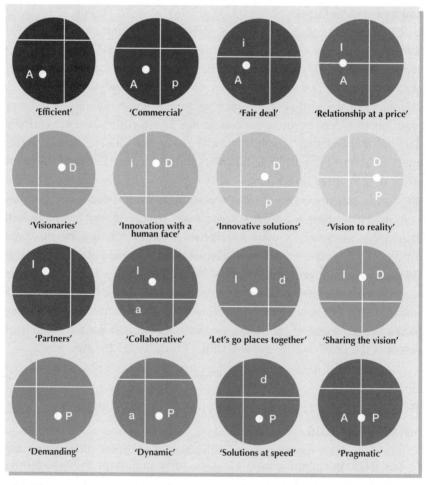

FIGURE 2.1 ◆ **The 16 possible dominant behavioral segments – demand-side**

However, while we have identified as many as 16 variants, we do not have to allow for all these segments operating at the same time. In fact, the empirical evidence we gathered not only confirms the importance of human intervention in supply chains, but brings to light some entirely new perspectives on customer buyer behavior. As such, the following four pivotal insights have the potential to revolutionize the way we do business:

1 Customers always exhibit a small but finite number of dominant buying behaviors for any given product or service category, usually no more than three, but four at most (to give an 80 per cent fit to the market).

2 The preferred dominant buying behaviors exhibited by customers can change temporarily under the pressure of changing conditions, such as lifestyle circumstances, government regulatory action, or the product life-cycle itself. But behaviors usually return to the preferred position when conditions return to 'normal'.

3 Where there is a permanent change observed, it is usually associated with a change in the customer's own internal decision-making group.

4 Finally, it is not unusual to observe more than one buying behavior inside a large corporate customer, where different groups are involved in buying different product or service categories.

The changeability of dominant buying behaviors is probably the phenomenon that Nunes and Cespedes were attempting to explain when they described how buying behaviors vary during different stages of the purchase life-cycle.[27] But changing behavior during a purchase is not equivalent to the observed phenomenon of changing buyer behaviors under severe market pressures. Significantly, they appear to agree with my position when they comment that 'buying behavior also depends on the shopper's particular circumstances (and) a buyer wears different hats at different times'.[28]

Coupled with these insights, there are two further observations that can be made:

1 People often exhibit a mix of preferred dominant buying behaviors depending on the product or service category they have in mind at the time. This means that an individual may display different buying behaviors for different product and service categories – a fact that has perplexed and confused market researchers and marketers for decades.

2 Customers do not distinguish between the outputs of different internal departments (or functions) inside a supplier organization; they don't say, 'the sales force is good but logistics fulfillment is poor'. Customers are very binary in their outlook and see service as simply good or bad – with little in between.

Can you now see why aligning with customers as they continuously learn and evolve their hierarchy of values is so difficult? Clearly, segmenting supply chains according to customer buying behaviors is a *dynamic* phenomenon. It is like trying to hit a moving target rather than seeking an all-embracing descriptor of a stagnant customer type, which is where previous efforts at aligning with customers have floundered.

From this point it is only a small step in logic to the concept and practice of *multiple supply chain alignment*, as depicted in Figure 2.2.

Leading enterprises are already using the idea of multiple supply chains in different formats. For example, Inditex has a multiple supply chain strategy based on its various store brands. Zara is the best known brand in its portfolio, but other companies in the Inditex portfolio that are aiming at specific layers in the market are becoming more familiar, e.g., Massimo Dutti, Pull & Bear and Berksha. The hi-tech firm Dell is developing a menu of supply chains to service each of its institutional markets, ie., Small Medium Business; Public; and Large Enterprises. Even health authorities are getting the message. In Australia, hospitals in Melbourne and Sydney have already started to separate emergency surgery cases from the more predictable elective surgery. Patients are no longer competing for beds, operating theatres, and staff.[29] Unilever North America has completely embraced the idea that multiple supply chains are essential for future success.

In its Supply Chain 2010 project, Unilever '. . . recognized that one size does not fit all, and that the 'right' supply chain model would require the integration of many supply networks linked through organizational structure, a common back-office infrastructure, and common ways of working'.[30] Interestingly, Unilever has also adopted the multi-functional customer-facing teams that I will be proposing in Chapter 6. Supply chains with different configurations start to emerge around the most commonly observed types of behavioral segments, as shown in Figure 2.3 overleaf.

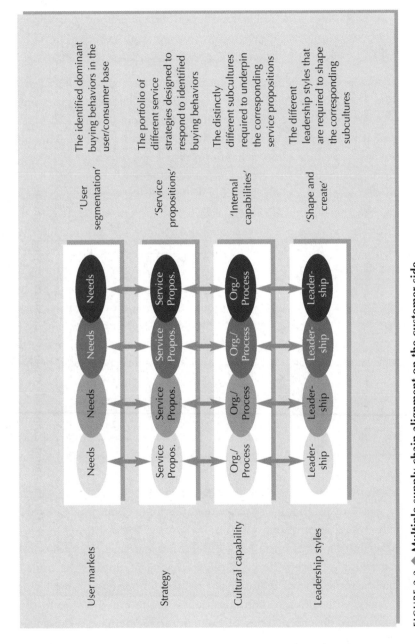

FIGURE 2.2 ◆ **Multiple supply chain alignment on the customer side**

Source: Adapted from Figure 4.3.2 in Gattorna (2003), p 459; see also Gattorna (2006) Figure 2.1, p. 40

Collaborative	Efficient	Dynamic	Innovative solutions
Close working relationships for mutual gain	Consistent low-cost response to largely predictable demands	Rapid response to unpredictable supply and demand conditions	Supplier-led development and delivery of new ideas
◆ Mostly predictable ◆ Regular delivery ◆ Mature or augmented products ◆ Primary source of supply ◆ Trusting relationship ◆ Teamwork/partnership ◆ Information sharing ◆ Joint development ◆ Forgiving ◆ Price not an issue	◆ Predictable demand within contract ◆ Regular delivery ◆ Efficiency low-cost focus ◆ Multiple sources of supply ◆ Little sharing of information ◆ More adversarial ◆ Standard processes ◆ Power imposed ◆ Transactional ◆ Very price sensitive	◆ Unpredictable demand ◆ Commodity relationship ◆ Time priority/urgency ◆ Opportunity focus ◆ Ad hoc source of supply ◆ Low loyalty, impersonal ◆ Fewer processes ◆ Outcome oriented ◆ Commercial deals based on pragmatism ◆ Price aware	◆ Very unpredictable demand ◆ Higher risk ◆ Flexible delivery response ◆ Innovation focus ◆ Rapid change ◆ Individual decision-making ◆ Solutions oriented ◆ Management of IP ◆ Incentives/ego ◆ No price sensitivity

FIGURE 2.3 ◆ **The four most commonly observed dominant buying behaviors**

Source: Adapted from Table 1.3.1 in Gattorna (2003), p. 32; see also Gattorna (2006), p. 41

Even though there are many combinations and permutations of possible behavioral segments, in my experience the four-segment supply chain combination depicted in Figure 2.4 overleaf is evident in markets as diverse as petrol, legal services, travel, dairy products, third-party logistics services and financial planning; note the equal emphasis on services as well as products. More examples are provided in Appendix 2A.

It is worth repeating that there are particular types of behavioral groupings where customers naturally reside, but customers can and do switch between all four buying behaviors according to situational pressures. Also, it is not uncommon in large complex organizations to find evidence of more than one buying behavior present, although mostly in different timeframes, e.g., the different ways Nestlé buys a range of dairy ingredients from its New Zealand supplier, Fonterra. For some product, Nestlé prefers to push on price; for others there is a preference for a particular product specification, at a premium.

At this stage we are in a position to make two more observations:

1 In segmenting customers, geography has little impact on the range of dominant buying behaviors; the only thing that changes is the proportional mix of these same buying behaviors.

2 Similarly for country (or national) cultures, the only change from country to country is again the proportional mix.[31] When you think about this it makes sense, unless of course we are dealing with extra-terrestrials! Often, too much is read into the potential impact of different national cultures, when really we should be emphasizing the similarities.

From spaghetti bowls to conveyor belts – a *dynamic* perspective

Can you see the result? Four discrete supply chains (or conveyor belts) run through most enterprises. Each has different configurations and operating characteristics, achieved by combining largely standard processes and activities in unique ways. The supply chains themselves may also combine in different ways, e.g., *agile* with *lean, continuous replenishment* with *agile*; but more about these subtleties in Chapter 13. The combination of up to four co-existent supply chains is depicted in Figure 2.4.

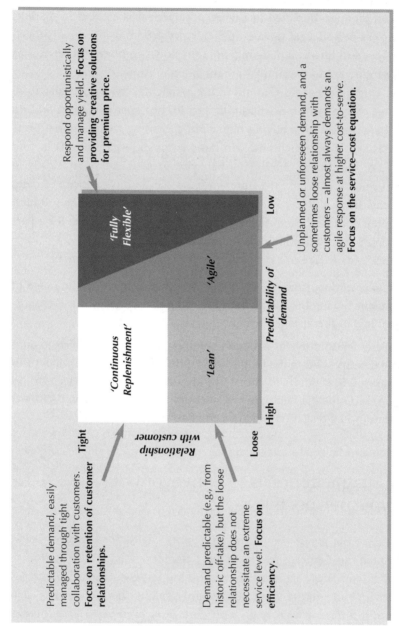

FIGURE 2.4 ◆ **The four generic supply chain types – demand-side**

Source: Adapted from Figure 2.3 in Gattorna (2006), p 43, supplemented by ideas from Marc Van der Veen, Dow Corning

Obviously, variations around these four 'generic' types can and do exist, but in my experience these are the ones most commonly present and therefore the most deserving of our attention.

A note before we go on. As much as possible, I've chosen to label the four generic supply chain types with existing names, e.g., in particular, *lean* and *agile*. Why? The literature already has too much different terminology without my adding further to the confusion. However, having said that, I need to briefly explain where my definitions of these terms vary from existing interpretations:

◆ *Continuous replenishment* supply chain: this one is quite straightforward. To work properly, it requires collaboration with customers, and suppliers, as simple as that.

◆ *Lean* supply chain: my definition of lean varies from existing usage in that I do not think lean necessarily involves collaboration with customers; that's why we have *continuous replenishment*. However, it may involve some pull component via collaboration on the supply side. But my definition of *lean* and the traditional definition both involve push into the marketplace, and a focus on efficiency by removing waste wherever possible. But lean still requires some external view in order to develop and align the appropriate value propositions with customers. However, we should not be trying to convert all customers to a collaborative buying behavior mindset – that is plain wasteful, and simply does not work. So the subtlety here is that *lean* is not completely internal in its orientation. Marks & Spencer misguidedly tried to go lean in the late 1990s, but this approach did not align with its customers' value set – so they got it wrong and failed. In fact, adapting to the customer's value set is a key consideration at all times. *Lean* works well when it fits the value proposition of customers with low cost and efficiency at their front of mind.

◆ *Agile* supply chain: this means responsiveness to customers in unpredictable demand situations; it is all about pull. Customer pull. And it can be achieved in various ways. However, the appropriate agile response almost always involves building in redundant capacity (or buffers) along the supply chain – in the form of inventory, labor, procurement, production and transport assets.

◆ *Fully flexible* supply chain: this is an extreme example of an *agile* supply chain. Indeed, some would argue that this is not a free-standing supply chain type in itself, but rather a 'must have' *competence* that can be brought to bear as and when customers require extreme solutions. Whatever your point of view on this, it is important to possess this competence for business continuity in crisis situations – and they do arise from time to time! As such, it might involve a small group of highly skilled and entrepreneurial people being available on a stand-by or emergency basis. General Electric has its product incubator which probably doubles, in part at least, as its *fully flexible* capability. The thing to remember about this type of supply chain is that the supplier always leads the market in search of the required innovative solutions; customers count on them for this. In every other situation, customers lead the way and have their say.

Can you see the internal capabilities that your firm needs to configure all these supply chains? The abiding challenge facing enterprises of all types is *flex*, i.e., the ability to have each supply chain capability compartmentalized inside the business, and have enough flexibility to change between supply chains in parallel with the shifting marketplace. Thankfully, this is not very fast. In fact, it is a bit like watching grass grow if you are alert to what is happening! So facilitating easy switches between the three mainstream supply chains, with the fourth on standby, is the type of dynamic we are suggesting. It's this more dynamic view of how supply chains serve the marketplace that differentiates the ideas in this book from other current literature on the subject.

Each of the four types of supply chain depicted in Figure 2.4 may be characterized as different 'laminar' flows, shaped by a combination of customer buying behaviors and internal culture-driven behavior. These flow types are illustrated schematically in Figure 2.5.[32]

The management of complexity will reduce significantly if the behavioral segment-driven regime suggested here is adopted. This is quite the opposite effect to that experienced where so-called standard processes (and standard technology) are implemented across the entire enterprise. This leads paradoxically to increased complexity and higher cost-to-serve – because of all the exceptions created along the way. If organizations are predominantly designed to deliver one type of value proposition, and the marketplace contains, say, three dominant types of customer buying behavior, then the degree of alignment will be very limited, and the organization will find itself continually making costly exceptions. The conclusion? Complexity is significantly reduced through superior *dynamic alignment*.

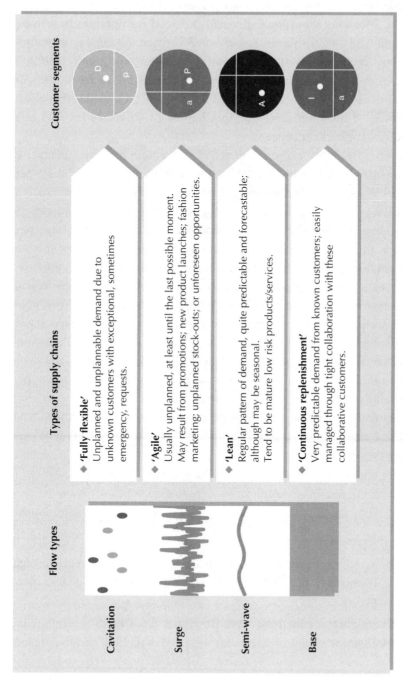

FIGURE 2.5 ◆ **Flow types and matching supply chain types**

Source: Adapted from Figure 2.4 in Gattorna (2006), p. 46

Flexibility is actually increased when alignment conditions are fulfilled. There is a lot said about flexibility and the need for organizations to be more agile and adaptive in the fast-moving world of the third millennium. However, flexibility is not about having one offer, and then creating a myriad of exceptions to achieve 'fit' with customers; that's far too expensive and does not deliver the required service levels on a sustainable basis. There will be more on this issue in Chapter 11 when we revisit Lee's 'Triple-A' supply chain concept.

Genuine flexibility can only be achieved through multiple alignment. The organization must be 'hard-wired' to a limited number of customer segments via a 'hybrid' organizational structure and a unique combination of processes and corresponding technology applications. Then, if customers change their buying behaviors under the pressure of new operating conditions in their respective markets, it simply means they move to another of the previously identified dominant buying behaviors for that particular product or service category. They are thereafter serviced in the pre-defined way for that segment. This is flexibility without the corresponding cost penalty. In business-to-business (B2B) situations, it is possible that a given customer organization will exhibit all four of the identified buying behaviors at different times; this is quite normal and relatively easily managed once understood. Figure 2.6 shows the details of each combination of supply chain–value proposition–customer buying behavior.

Alignment of the appropriate value propositions with customers' true needs and expectations significantly improves operating and financial performance for several reasons:

◆ It is easier to focus on consistently fulfilling customer requirements (better service).

◆ It is easier to charge appropriately for 'value added' supply chain services (improved margins).

◆ It allows advanced functional excellence to be brought to bear in high value segments, e.g., collaborative planning within the 'Collaborative' segment.

◆ It also facilitates functional excellence in lower value segments, e.g., reduced cost-to-serve.

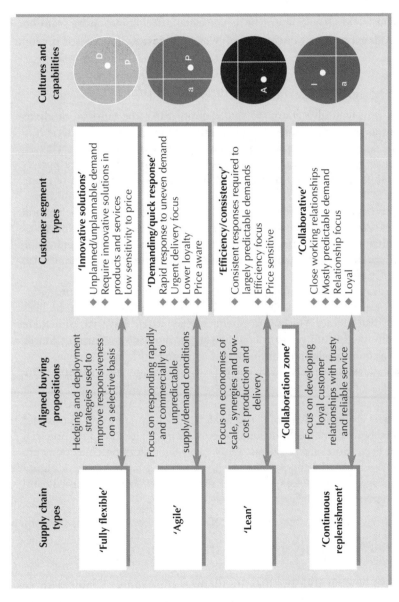

FIGURE 2.6 ◆ **Aligned supply chain 'value propositions'**

Source: Adapted from Figure 7 in Christopher and Gattorna (2004), p 120; see also Figure 2.5 in Gattorna (2006), p. 48

◆ It allows better management of opportunistic business in the 'Demanding' and 'Innovative solutions' segments, leading to increased revenue and margins.

◆ It allows the development of new service offerings resulting from continuous innovation across all supply chain types, e.g., increased revenue.

Zara – genuine *dynamic alignment* in practice

It is rare to find a company that demonstrates the benefits of alignment as well as Zara, the Spanish fashion retailer and manufacturer.[33] Zara is a superb example because its business brings almost every facet of alignment and supply chain principles into play. It is a powerful reminder that good performance flows from a combination of many factors. Of course, Zara mainly sells women's, men's and children's fashion apparel, a segment that will always be demanding in behavioral terms. Zara's decision to focus mostly on a segment with a single type of dominant buying behavior means it has an easier task in designing the appropriate supply chain configuration. And it has done just that with distinction.

Zara's amazing agility could even encourage it to move into adjacent, less fashion-oriented markets for apparel, competing with the likes of British retailer Marks and Spencer. Zara would have an immediate advantage if it did so, as it could easily work inside the current Marks and Spencer cycle time (from design to store shelf), in the process winning more customers for lower-priced, less fashionable apparel. The success of Zara's agility is demonstrated in its ability to move quickly from 'sketch to store' in 15 days, resulting in the customers' perception of their stores as always having fresh product. In contrast, Marks and Spencer has a more traditional supply chain for textiles and apparel, with cycle times up to a year. Only two major clothing collections are released by Marks and Spencer each year: Spring/Summer and Autumn/Winter, and consumers lie in wait for the inevitable mark-downs and clearance sales.

'Triple-A' supply chains are not here yet

The good news is that the idea of aligning your supply chains with customers, suppliers and third-party logistics providers (3PLs) is intuitively attractive and catching on fast.[34] In fact, we seem to be hearing all the right rhetoric lately. But no one has joined all the dots and fully understood what is involved in engineering an aligned supply chain. We are at best still in a world of experience and observation, and still some way from a comprehensive theory to guide us into the future. Hau Lee comments that 'most firms already have the infrastructure in place to create Triple-A supply chains. What they need is a fresh attitude and a new culture to get their supply chains to deliver Triple-A performance.'[35] By 'Triple-A' he is referring to the three properties – Adaptiveness, Agility and Alignment – that enterprises need to exhibit in their supply chains. We will examine these properties again in more detail in Chapter 11 and put a different spin on them.

Achieving superior performance is easy to say but difficult to achieve when most organizations still have such a poor understanding of how cultural capability underpins all action on the ground in some way or other. We must work to design and embed the appropriate subcultures in the organization to reflect the customer segments (otherwise called external subcultures) that are present in a particular market. It simply will not happen by chance. The ideal mix is the 45/45/10 we described in Chapter 1 – commit 45 per cent of your effort to human behavior, 45 per cent to systems technology and the remainder to asset infrastructure. Unfortunately, we still seem to be stuck in the 'old' 0/60/40 groove, with zero emphasis on human behavior and 60/40 on technology and infrastructure respectively. Other researchers have taken different routes towards alignment,[36] and some have even tried to use the alignment concept to help anticipate market trends.[37]

Beyond institutional segmentation in real life

One of the most common ways that enterprises segment their markets is along 'institutional' lines, because it is easy and convenient. Data is easily collected on recognizable institutions. Sometimes whole channels are built around specific institutions. For example, a recent reorganization at the Australian brewing company, Foster's Australia, resulted in the introduction of a new service model.[38] The sales force was split into dedicated teams servicing 14 different channels, made up of customers grouped by institutions such as hotels, nightclubs, five-star hotels and resorts, restaurants, national retailers and independent liquor stores. This institutional channel model, was expected to take three to four years to implement, and involve an overall increase in the number of staff serving customers, and reduce supply chain costs.[39] But will the lower costs necessarily follow? More importantly, will revenue climb faster than incremental costs?

Foster's has since divulged more about its plans.[40] It signalled to the market its intention to pursue a 'Blue Ocean strategy',[41] which involves making multi-beverage offerings to the 14 institutional segments identified in the Australian market. The better news, however, is that Foster's has gone further and reorganized the 14 into four behavioral segments – *Integrated, Destination, Local* and *Connect*. On the basis of available public information and previous work in the beverage industry, I've interpreted what each of these four new segments might look like. See Figure 2.7 for a summary of their characteristics. The Foster's strategy is truly break-through thinking, with dedicated customer-facing teams focusing on each of the four segments, and those in logistics fulfillment roles delivering differentiated service to match. Some method of coding customer behavior will be required to help people working in these back-of-shop operations to stay in synch with the responses required by customers. Fortunately, this level of management sophistication is well within reach with current technology. However, the success of the Foster's transformation has been significantly constrained by the company's well-publicized difficulties in integrating its global wine business into its overall beverage business, particularly in the US.

Ultimately it's all a question of 'packaging'. Customers in the different segments are all buying beer, but they are buying it in different ways with different product mixes, pricing, response times, quantities and relationship requirements. What the supplier must do is find correspondingly appropriate ways to align internal resources with these multiple customer requirements via a limited number of cost-effective supply chain configurations. Other examples of this phenomenon are provided in Figures 2.8 and 2.9. In Figure 2.8 overleaf we see where The Coca-Cola Company is selling and delivering to three types of customer (institutional) segments, all with differing service requirements. In terms of the fulfillment part of the operation, the logistics or supply chain infrastructure has to be capable of delivering an array of at least three discretely different responses.

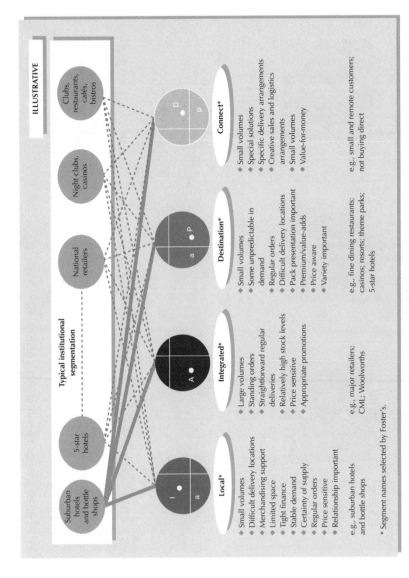

FIGURE 2.7 ◆ Foster's new behavioral-based segmentation in the Australian alcoholic beverage industry

Source: Adapted from Figure 2.6 in Gattorna (2006), p. 51

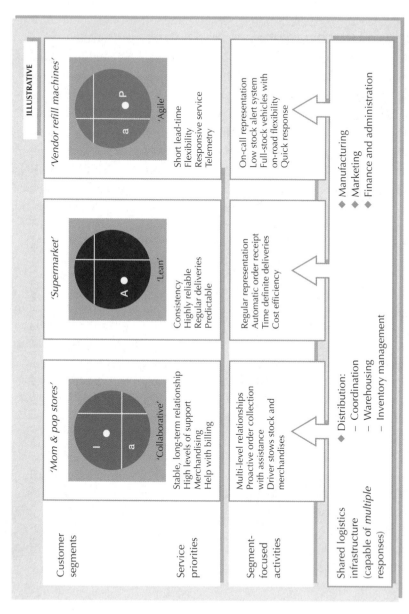

FIGURE 2.8 ◆ The three different supply chains at Coca-Cola, Japan

Source: Adapted from Figure 2.14 in Gattorna and Walters (1996), p. 44; see also Figure 2.7 in Gattorna (2006), p. 53

Figure 2.9 shows the customer segments used by Scholastic, a publisher of children's books. Here again, each of the three behavioral segments has distinctive service priorities, requiring correspondingly appropriate supply chain responses. Management must overcome conventional mindsets in order to deliver this multidisciplinary capability.

Two other examples of multiple supply chain alignment in different industries are provided in Appendix 2B. In the health care industry, four types of supply chains are necessary to carry all the supplies consumed in public hospitals. And, as already intimated in Chapter 1, major processed food manufacturer Goodman Fielder Ltd also needed a similar number of supply chains for its business in the Asia-Pacific region. Unfortunately, this design was never fully implemented because of a combination of internal resistance from business unit executives and subsequent changes in leadership at the top of the organization. So how do you undertake a behavioral segmentation of your customers? There are five possible approaches:

◆ *Top-down*. This is where your organization taps into its accumulated internal knowledge of customers to develop a detailed map of customer segments. You can start by conducting an internal workshop and quickly developing a first approximation. You can then refine the model progressively with other internal audiences, and finally validate the findings via primary research in the marketplace. When everyone involved is satisfied with the segment descriptors, another project team can allocate each customer to one of the pre-defined behavioral segments. After that it's a simple matter to calculate the size of each segment in terms of numbers, volume and revenue.

◆ *Bottom-up*. This involves your enterprise individually assessing each individual customer using the 'Quick' Behavioral Segmentation Diagnostic described in Appendix 2C of *Living Supply Chains* (2006). Staff would assess and code every customer in P-A-D-I terms and aggregate them into segments based on the similarities of their respective codes. While this bottom–up method can be somewhat time-consuming, the advantage is it provides an in-depth basis for segmentation from the start.

ILLUSTRATIVE

	'Facilitator'	'Fulfillment'	'Choices'
Customer segments	(I / A)	(A / P)	(D / P)
Service priorities	Partnership and collaboration High moral and ethical standards	Performance excellence 100% satisfaction Quality	Experience High expectations High service standards
Customer interface	Single point of contact Multi-skilled After sales service In-depth customer knowledge	Call centre Telemarketing eCommerce CRM capability	eCommerce Multiple outlets eCRM skills
Order processing	Uncomplicated order procedure Assistance with order process	High delivery accuracy Price availability Ease of order processing	Internet Quick response medium Order confirmation Real time availability
Physical fulfillment	Uncomplicated order procedure Assistance with order process Packaging by class/type	Planned in regular intervals Order status availability Incentives for economic ordering quantity (EOQ)	Next day delivery Quick response Highly streamlined returns process

FIGURE 2.9 ◆ **The three main supply chains at Scholastic, publisher of children's books**

Source: Adapted from Figure 2.8 in Gattorna (2006), p. 54

◆ *Direct interview method*: The other way of achieving the same result is to use the Interview Guide detailed in Appendix 2C in this book, initially using short telephone or face-to-face interviews. We used this method in our research into the way Taiwan companies preferred to buy 'express' services from suppliers such as DHL.[42] The interview file should be updated each time there is an interaction with a customer and made widely available to personnel on the company's intranet, ensuring customer tracking is ongoing.

◆ There is a fourth way, which involves undertaking *sophisticated market research* using conjoint analysis. In-depth investigation of the customer will deliver sound, timely and market-based information. However, except in special situations,[43] the additional time and expense is not warranted for the extra degree of accuracy it produces. The first two methods will provide sufficient accuracy for the initial segmentation, and the third method in particular is useful for tracking customers on a continuing basis. This 'continuous improvement' approach will ultimately lead to an accurate picture of your customer base.

◆ The fifth and final method being used by some retailers and their suppliers is to seek '*customer insight*' through the use of sophisticated data-mining techniques that involve analyzing POS data. Tesco (UK) and its suppliers are using this technique, combined with their loyalty card, Dunnhumby.[44]

Once you finalize a comprehensive re-segmentation of your customer base, it is important to take the opportunity to compare the '*value propositions*' and strategies **currently** in play with the 'ideal' strategies indicated by the new segmentation regime. More about this point in Chapter 3.

One final word on this topic of customer segmentation, channels, and supply chains. Very often suppliers, such as FMCG and pharmaceutical companies, have more than one customer or intermediary between them and their final consumer base. And it is more than likely that these will have different – even opposing – dominant buying behaviors at each level. Schering-Plough, the pharmaceutical company, faced such a problem when it launched an innovative product for treatment of hay fever in the mid-1990s. The consumer was attracted to the product through Schering-Plough's advertising and wanted the promised 'quick fix'. Many retail pharmacists, however, were not prepared to stock the product as they made less margin than on other competitive products. Area health authorities have a similar problem when building and operating hospital facilities. Patients (end-users), nursing staff, administrators, doctors, boards and government all have different 'buying behaviors'. So the task of reconciling all the different mindsets and expectations is a difficult one, even before operational fulfillment comes into play. We should not lose sight of this other dimension of the alignment problem.

Optimal pathways to customers

So what is your ultimate goal? You need to configure your total logistics network and wider supply chain relationships so that you have the capacity to deliver an array of supply chain responses that align with the dominant buying behaviors of your customers. And you must do this in an increasingly competitive operating environment. This objective is amply demonstrated by the case of Fletcher Challenge Paper, the major New Zealand based newsprint manufacturer, since acquired by Norske Skogg.

Fletcher Challenge Paper (now Norske Skogg)

In 1999, Fletcher Challenge Paper (FCP) was supplying 85 per cent of newsprint to a small number of major newspapers in Australia and New Zealand, and other users in Asia. Indeed, each of these individual customers was a market in its own right, with complicated end requirements. At the time, the company faced the threat of new newsprint capacity coming on-stream in Asia, which was threatening existing pricing arrangements and reducing margins. FCP decided to segment the relatively small number of major users of newsprint along 'buyer value' lines. The output of this buyer values segmentation is shown in Figure 2.10.

FCP also decided to model its entire supply chain network in order to understand the costs involved in servicing its major customers. The company used a sophisticated Network Optimization Modeling tool.[45] It was a complex undertaking which took six months to complete, but the results were beneficial. Figure 2.11 overleaf illustrates the complex supply chain model that was in place at FCP, from forest to newsprint user.

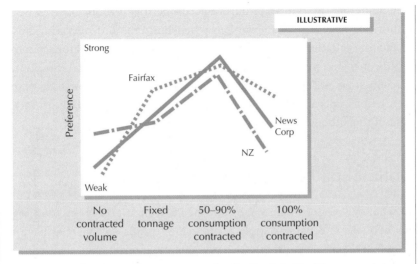

FIGURE 2.10 ◆ **Buyer values segmentation in the Asia-Pacific newsprint industry**

Source: Adapted from Figure 2.9 in Gattorna (2006), p. 57

Logistics network structure

The company sourced major virgin fibre from a combination of owned, managed and third-party forests, and sourced waste paper from more than 100 domestic suppliers. Production occurred at three paper mills on six machines. Seven major grades of paper were produced – representing more than 500 different stock-keeping units (SKUs) – and distributed through six distribution centres to more than 100 customers.

Business challenge

FCP's front-line challenge was to develop a comprehensive and transportable Decision Support System (DSS) to identify the benefits of supply chain optimization. But it also needed to use the system in conjunction with its buyer value and competitor analysis so that it could develop an optimal supply chain strategy. Why? FCP's ultimate goal was to increase market share and margins in an otherwise mature industry.

Approach

FCP developed an optimization model in sufficient detail that could test the validity and cost of current operating constraints in the supply chain, such as existing supplier and customer agreements and contracts. To cater for the multiple modeling objectives and provide the required detail, the model was designed to enable:

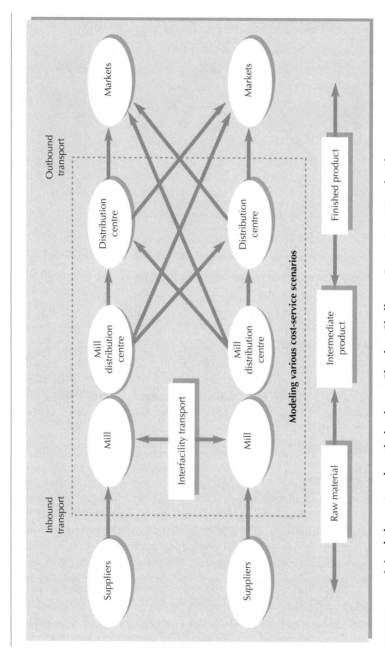

FIGURE 2.11 ◆ **Logistics network optimization at Fletcher Challenge Paper (now Norske Skogg)**

Source: Adapted from Figure 2.10 in Gattorna (2006), p. 58

◆ evaluation of benefits from closing specific items of plant;

◆ re-allocation of products to paper machines;

◆ evaluation of multiple cutting patterns on paper machines to minimize waste across the network;

◆ multiple production recipes for similar finished product; and

◆ alternative customer pricing structures.

Scenarios

The decision support capability of the model was integrated with customer and competitor analysis to model various scenarios, such as:

◆ major incursion by a competitor;

◆ new local entrant (i.e., new local mill);

◆ loss of 100 per cent of major customer business;

◆ gain of 100 per cent of major customer volume;

◆ increase in sales of specialties to commercial printers; and

◆ long-term change in newsprint demand (minus 25 per cent to 10 per cent).

The modeling prompted a range of possible responses. FCP could do nothing; use price as a deterrent; or choose to amend contracts or change capacity. It gained significant new insights into the differences between each major customer/market, which were subtle but important. The company was able to customize its product and service offerings for individual customers. Based on a deeper understanding of the cost of serving different customers/markets, each segment was served more cost effectively. Over- and under-servicing was eliminated. FCP achieved cost savings of around NZ$10 million a year and, just as importantly, improved its margins while enhancing its relationship with customers. Through all the changes, customers felt they were being better served. It was win–win all round.

Network Optimization Models of the type used by Fletcher Challenge Paper are very powerful, especially when linked to buying behavior segments in the target market. Every enterprise should build one of these models to enhance decision-making quality. Unfortunately, my experience is that relatively few companies understand the value of this type of decision support tool, and fewer still know how to build one. More detailed information on these network modeling tools can be found in John Gattorna (ed.) *Handbook of Supply Chain Management* and John Gattorna (ed.) *Strategic Supply Chain Alignment*.[46]

Now the picture is almost complete

By now you will understand why *dynamic alignment* of extended supply chains isn't easy to achieve. Clearly, a lot of pieces must be engineered into position if alignment of the various internal and external stakeholders is to occur, leading to the desired boost in performance. However, the good news is that we now know much more about what pieces are necessary for alignment, even if we haven't quite discovered how to orchestrate them to perfection. Chapter 4 will address this knowledge gap and help us move ahead to the implementation of alignment principles on the ground. Significantly, this is the area where most other commentators have not dared to go, but it's essential that we tackle implementation and understand more fully the cultural forces at work inside the enterprise. Success will raise our level of understanding several notches, from a descriptive albeit superficial level, to a more satisfying explanatory level. Taking that learning journey will give us far more predictive capability and get us closer than ever before to the Holy Grail – *dynamic alignment* of our supply chains.

Defining ideas

1   There is only one 'right' way to segment customers: according to their dominant buying preferences and behaviors.

2   Supply chain configurations that lack a dynamic capability to 'flex' between different service delivery propositions will inevitably lead to service failures and reduced operational and financial performance.

3   For the best outcome, link behavioral segments at the customer end, and suppliers at the source end, with a network optimization model that allows a clear line of sight on the best cost-to-serve pathways through the network to customers.

4 **Challenge** to the reader: what methods of customer segmentation are you using? If not the behavioral method suggested here, how effective is your adopted method in designing and managing your supply chains?

CHAPTER 3

Designing supply chain strategies

Formulating and delivering the appropriate *value propositions*

O nce we have identified the range of behavioral segments present in any product-market combination, it is a relatively simple task to develop the equivalent value propositions. These express in words what we are prepared to commit to and offer each customer segment. In effect each value proposition is a mini-vision for each segment. Once finalized, they become the springboard for operational strategy development.

We have identified 15 strategy dimensions, drawn from across all disciplines of the enterprise. These can be combined in various ways to produce unique strategy packages, which must be translated into action to deliver the promise to customers; and for this purpose we recommend using the OODA loop – *observe, orient, decide* and *act.* If we can complete this cycle faster than our competitors we will win every time!

A key question for supply chain design is what strategies we should use to get our products and services to the various customer groups we have opted to serve. And, most importantly, what method do we use to devise those strategies. In today's often-changing market conditions, our choice of supply chain strategy is critical to us being able to serve our customers faster than our competitors. Academic Martin Christopher and his colleagues, who conducted supply chain case studies in the clothing manufacturing industry, found evidence that '. . . the choice of supply chain strategy should be based upon a careful analysis of the demand/ supply characteristics of the various product/markets served by the company'.[1] Their analysis is correct. What's more, it's about as close as anyone has come to date in finding the correct fit for customers to supply chains! However, when they speak of characteristics they mean the degree of predictability on the demand side of the supply chain (the predictable versus the unpredictable) and the length of the lead-time on the supply side (long lead-times versus short). I believe this approach is too limiting. It excludes the most important dimension of all – human behavior which, as we have seen, influences both demand and supply sides.

Ultimately, there is only one valid basis for strategy formulation and that is a deep understanding of the range of customer buying behaviors that are present in any product/market situation. As we saw in Chapter 2, there are usually three or four main types of supply chains. Once we are clear about the precise types of supply chains needed for our particular operating environment, we can prepare the corresponding value propositions for our customer buying behaviors. In this chapter we will look at how the next step is to translate this understanding into action by developing strategy packages for each of our customer segments. In effect, these are just different combinations of the 15 standard dimensions listed in Figure 3.1.

Value propositions

For the purpose of this analysis, we will confine our attention to the four main supply chain types identified in Chapter 2: *continuous replenishment*; *lean*; *agile*; and the two variants of the *fully flexible* supply chain, 'business event' and 'humanitarian'. Let's examine each in turn.

For the customers in the 'Collaborative' segment (Ia), our value proposition is as follows:

> *We understand the importance to you of a reliable, effective and long-term supply chain solution that you can rely on at all times. We will stay close to you and your customers needs at all times, freely share information with you, and deliver a consistent service, hassle free.*

For customers in the 'Efficiency' (A) segment:

> *We will consistently provide you with the lowest cost product and corresponding service, delivered to your specifications.*

For customers in the 'Demanding/Dynamic' (aP) segment:

> *We will build sufficient capacity into our supply chains to be in a position to respond to your unique albeit unpredictable requirements as they arise, at speed.*

Finally the value propositions for the two *Innovative Solutions* subsegments are:
'Business Event' (Dp):

> *Our skilled resources, supported by specialist expertise as required will develop innovative solutions to your unique problems, very fast. We will also happily share the responsibility and risks associated with these solutions.*

and 'Humanitarian' (iD):

> *We will work in partnership with you to identify and implement innovative solutions to your unique, albeit unpredictable problems, bearing in mind that our resources are finite.*

Translation into hard strategies

As implied by the title of this chapter, strategies – or **how** we go about delivering our value propositions to customers – should never be classified as either right or wrong. Why? Because a strategy that is working well today may become obsolete in some future operating environment. And the corollary is also true: a strategy that has been tried and failed under one set of conditions at one point in time, may well be the best strategy under changed conditions in the future. So let's hear none of the old argument 'but we tried this strategy before and it failed' as an excuse for not trying it again! The trick is to avoid becoming too ideological and prescriptive about strategy formulation, and instead use the marketplace and customers as the compass to guide us in developing the most appropriate package for the specific conditions being addressed at the time.

With this in mind, let's review the possible combinations of strategy dimensions for each of the four generic supply chains addressing the corresponding four types of behavioral segments. We are calling these 'ideal' strategies because they are imputed directly from an understanding of each behavioral segment. Put simply, they are the theoretical best – what we all aim to achieve!

Later in this chapter we have replicated these strategy packages and also left a space for you to insert the 'actual' strategies you're using in your business. The difference between the ideal and the actual, of course, is a measure of the misalignment currently occurring between your business and its customers. Often it's not a pretty picture! Following in Figure 3.1 is a list of the 15 strategic dimensions that we've selected to develop strategy packages for each of the four generic supply chains.

You will note that the strategy dimensions included in the list are not confined to physical logistics considerations alone, but rather are a combination of **all** the variables that a business might want to bring to bear in order to deliver on the promise embedded in a particular value proposition. This approach is consistent with my view that *'supply chains, taken in aggregate, are the business'*. In addition, it is fair to say that customers don't look at a supplier's strategy and split hairs either, e.g., 'I like their product but not their service or fulfillment methods.' No, customers are very binary in this regard. Either a supplier satisfies them completely or not: there's not much in between. This point will be further reinforced in Chapter 6 when we push for developing a new type of organization that is multi-disciplinary in its design.

1. Product mix
2. Innovation emphasis
3. Marketing emphasis
4. Channels of distribution
5. Pricing regime
6. Promotional activity
7. Service emphasis
8. Product/sourcing approach
9. Production
10. Capacity considerations
11. Fulfillment emphasis
12. Relationship intensity
13. Systems/IT support
14. Resource allocations priorites
15. Strategic risk profile

FIGURE 3.1 ◆ **Strategic dimensions for formulating supply chain strategies**

Each of the above 15 strategic dimensions will be briefly explained below:

1 **Product mix.** The product or service is what a customer buys and has in mind at the point of purchase. It contains certain benefits that the customer is seeking. But there are products and products! Some are branded and carry with them a type of guarantee of performance and trust. Others don't carry any of these attributes and are bought on a different basis, perhaps price, or performance, or even convenience. A customer's particular mindset will determine what combination of attributes is being sought on any particular occasion. And this can change with the situation.

2 **Innovation emphasis.** Innovation means different things to different people in different mindsets and situations, and we have to choose the right interpretation.[2] For some customers who are loyal to their brands, they would only see innovation as useful if it led to product quality or delivery that is even more reliable. They buy safe, mature products and are not interested in taking any risks by switching to another, newer product while the one they are using is meeting their needs.

3 **Marketing emphasis.** Marketing is the sum of all the things you do with, and for, the customer in order to pre-condition him or her for a sale. But you have to know what your target market likes in this regard, otherwise you can waste a lot of money on things that cost you dearly but make little or no impression on the customer. So we have to consider what will help us better align with the target customers, and this means knowing their mindsets.

4 **Channels of distribution.** Channels are the pathways through which customers gain access to products and services. These channels are in effect the commercial arrangements we make with other parties to carry out some of the functions required to present our products/services to the target market. The physical pathways that products travel along as they make their way towards customers may not necessarily coincide with these commercial channels, and indeed, mostly don't. However, one observation we can make from experience is that it is rare that one channel is enough to cover our target market. In most cases we will need a combination of different channels, and the selection of these channels can mean the difference between success and failure.

5   **Pricing regime.** Pricing is perhaps the most underestimated strategy dimension of all. Yet it can impact heavily on the operational performance of enterprise supply chains, in both positive and negative ways. Pricing also drives the revenue line, so it's the other factor we must concern ourselves with when seeking to improve margins, apart from cost-to-serve. DHL did this in Taiwan when the incoming country manager realized that the company was trying to force all customers to buy their premium express service, but in so doing was driving away customers who were looking for a slightly slower, albeit reliable, delivery service at a lower price. By radically improving the alignment with the total customer base, DHL increased its revenue faster than its corresponding cost-to-serve, and so enhanced its margin.[3] Remember, not all customers want the lowest price; nor are they all prepared to pay a premium. We must work out which is which and include the right price emphasis in the strategy package.

6   **Promotional activity.** Promotional activity is expensive and needs to be carefully targeted. For instance, it is unlikely any such activity is required or even wanted by customers who are already brand loyal; for them it becomes a distraction and an annoyance. However, for customers in the 'demanding/dynamic' segment, it is essential to attract their attention.

7   **Service emphasis.** As in the case of innovation (point 2. above), service is something that takes on a different hue depending on the type of customer being addressed and their particular situation. For customers looking for a quick, creative solution to a major problem (Dp), customer service means 'just fix it, fast'. For a customer who is price sensitive and looking for consistency, service means we have to deliver just that, no more, no less. So it is a clear case of 'horses for courses'.

8   **Procurement/sourcing.** Selecting the best array of suppliers to source from and indeed to outsource to, is a vital consideration, and one that may well determine if we can honour our portfolio of value propositions to customers.

9   **Production.** For manufacturing that is kept in-house, we need to ensure it is configured to deliver the required range of value propositions. This may mean using straight production lines for products that are being produced in volume in order to drive down unit costs; or using postponement techniques and utilizing slack capacity in times of off-peak

demand; or it may simply mean using methods such as group technology, where small specialized batches are produced for either brand-loyal customers or customers that exhibit sudden and urgent demand for a product, for which they are prepared to pay. In any event, the production side of the business must be in complete synch with the demand and supply elements of the enterprise, upstream and downstream.

10 **Capacity considerations.** Capacity can come in many forms such as machine capacity, labor availability, inventories (all types), storage locations and transportation options. To counter any fluctuations in demand and potential problems on the supply side, both of which can cause disruptions, buffers can be designed into the overall supply chain as and where appropriate, as long as these are designed according to policies on stock-out tolerance levels.

11 **Fulfillment approach.** The physical delivery of products and services is what fulfillment is about. It can be designed on an agreed basis with the customer so as to drive shared costs down, or it may be more ad hoc to meet unpredictable situations. In any event, the type of customer and their expectations will largely drive the design and operation of fulfillment practices.

12 **Relationship intensity.** Some customers need to be recognized and provided with personalized service attention, and others want quite the opposite. Since providing close personal attention is costly, we must ensure it's only given to those loyal customers who genuinely deserve and appreciate such treatment.

13 **Systems/IT support.** While most contemporary enterprises will have modern Enterprise Resource Planning (ERP) systems installed, the exact combination of software applications that sits on top of this transactional system is largely determined by the type of customer being served, and their corresponding needs. The trick is to mix the right strategy package for each of the main customer types, rather than throw all available technology at every customer indiscriminately.

14 **Resource allocation priorities.** These are the three most important words in the vernacular for companies battling to survive in difficult trading conditions. Using shared forecasts will help when we are dealing with customers willing to share and collaborate; using sophisticated network optimization models may be necessary where this collaboration does not exist and we are trying to decide between different courses of

action. In the latter case we must decide whether to serve or not serve particular customers, with the aim being to maximize customer account profitability. It's interesting that some third-party logistics providers are culling their client base rather than taking on new clients, so that they can focus on long-term, mutually profitable relationships.[4]

15 **Strategic risk profile.** All strategies carry some element of risk (of failing), and we must manage these risks as much as we can. In a stable market in combination with a loyal docile customer who buys the same products and services all the time, the risks may be low. For a new customer coming on to the books and demanding new combinations of products and ways of being serviced, the risks are correspondingly higher. We have to assess these risks and where possible, make an early decision.

We will work through the list of 15 strategic dimensions for each of the four generic supply chains in Chapters 7 to 10, and offer advice on the best packaging of these dimensions to achieve optimal alignment with the corresponding customer segments being targeted.

Conversion of strategies into operational reality on the ground

In Chapter 4 we will consider the age-old problem of converting 'words on paper' into 'actions on the ground'. We know from experience that 40 to 60 per cent of intended strategies are never fully realized and we know why – the people inside the business passively resist the required changes. It is not the competitors we have to fear, but our own people.

However, for now it's appropriate to mention the operational arrangements necessary to bring the strategies to life. A useful check list is provided in Figure 3.7. This diagram shows a four-tier approach to operational strategy development, starting with the strategic level where the primary focus is on getting alignment with customers, and this of course means multiple alignment, then working down through the other three layers of structural, operational and support mechanisms. At each level pointed questions are raised, to which satisfactory answers must be found. This process is likely to involve a significant amount of further analysis, but at least we now know the boundaries of the conditions we are working with.

For the top two levels, development of a network optimization model would be very helpful as various cost-service scenarios can be posed and tested, without making any actual changes on the ground. I fail to see how any organization with more than $1billion in turnover can operate effectively without this type of Decision Support System (DSS) in place, interfaced of course with a standard ERP transactional system. Such a model would also provide useful pointers to the action that should be taken at the operational level. The fourth level is all about implementation, which we will investigate more fully in Chapter 4.

A comparative analysis of ideal versus actual strategies

Each of the behavioral segments we have identified requires us to develop a unique strategy package in response. In Figures 3.2 to 3.6 on the following pages, we have proposed what these various packages might look like if they were to exactly align with customers' expectations: the 'ideal' strategy. In the same diagrams we've also included space for you to insert the strategy you're currently using for each segment type in your business: the actual strategy. The comparative analysis will make it obvious where there are mis-matches in the best possible strategy and what is actually occurring. This new information will open the way for changes to be made.

Once it becomes obvious from the strategy comparison just where the misalignments occur, a detailed analysis of the customer segments and buyer behaviors should be conducted so that a plan for how to implement the necessary changes can be prepared. To guide this process, the organizational pyramid depicted in Figure 3.7 (page 85) will prove useful. It shows the types of questions that need to be asked at each of the strategic, structural, operational and support levels. It should be used in conjunction with the prioritization matrix shown in Figure 3.8 (page 86); this is designed to help set priorities based on the benefits that are likely to accrue from each of the initiatives as compared with their ease of implementation.

	Strategic dimension	Ideal strategy	Actual strategy
1	Product mix	Emphasis on mature, branded, and augmented products	
2	Innovation emphasis	Big emphasis on product quality; joint product development. Innovate to improve relationships	
3	Marketing emphasis	Build brand loyalty	
4	Channels of distribution	Either direct or via trusted outlets	
5	Pricing regime	Price according to strength of brand; moderate price sensitivity	
6	Promotional activity	Low promotional activity – simply not required	
7	Service emphasis	Empathy with local customers; consistency of service; trust	
8	Product/sourcing approach	Select suppliers on basis of relationships and capabilities	
9	Production	Low volume – high value add. Collaborate to reduce costs	
10	Capacity considerations	Maximum utilization achievable consistent with serving clients	
11	Fulfillment approach	Reliable/scheduled delivery; shared forecasts	
12	Relationship intensity	Mutual dependence between customer and supplier	
13	Systems/IT support	Emphasis on customer management; CRM essential	
14	Resource allocations priorites	Focus on supporting the relationship to retain customers	
15	Strategic risk profile	Low	

FIGURE 3.2 ◆ *Continuous replenishment* supply chain strategy – protective

	Strategic dimension	Ideal strategy	Actual strategy
1	Product mix	Stable product line; minimal variants	
2	Innovation emphasis	Focus on ways to reduce cost of inputs and processes	
3	Marketing emphasis	Lowest price; but reliable	
4	Channels of distribution	Wide distribution through multiple channels for maximum accessibility	
5	Pricing regime	Lowest price. EDLP where possible	
6	Promotional activity	Low, because margin too thin	
7	Service emphasis	Efficiency and process re-engineering	
8	Product/sourcing approach	Use automatic system if possible	
9	Production	High volume – low cost; commodity	
10	Capacity considerations	High utilization of existing assets	
11	Fulfillment approach	High reliability; predictable service and ready availability	
12	Relationship intensity	Low	
13	Systems/IT support	Emphasis on transactional system	
14	Resource allocations priorites	Focus on cost reduction at all times	
15	Strategic risk profile	Low	

FIGURE 3.3 ◆ *Lean* supply chain strategy – incremental

	Strategic dimension	Ideal strategy	Actual strategy
1	Product mix	Larger range; brand important; product performance critical	
2	Innovation emphasis	Seek product differentiation	
3	Marketing emphasis	Quick response to rapidly changing customer requirements	
4	Channels of distribution	Fewer, more direct channels to access consumers	
5	Pricing regime	Competitive; moderate price sensitivity	
6	Promotional activity	High; fashion-style approaches	
7	Service emphasis	Performance to specifications	
8	Product/sourcing approach	Market knowledge capacity to supply in volitile environment	
9	Production	Shorter runs; flexible scheduling; make-to-order. Use postponement techniques	
10	Capacity considerations	Lower utilization because of 'buffers' all along the supply chain	
11	Fulfillment approach	Short lead times; use postponement techniques	
12	Relationship intensity	Low and spasmodic	
13	Systems/IT support	Use modeling and analysis to support decision-making	
14	Resource allocations priorites	Build spare capacity to cater for volitile demand	
15	Strategic risk profile	Higher risk	

FIGURE 3.4 ◆ *Agile* supply chain strategy – operational

	Strategic dimension	Ideal strategy	Actual strategy
1	Product mix	Introduce new products/services on a regular basis	
2	Innovation emphasis	Extensive research and development; aim to be first to market. First with new solutions	
3	Marketing emphasis	Creative problem-solving capabilities	
4	Channels of distribution	Limited, and very targeted	
5	Pricing regime	Price appropriately for a creative solution; no price sensitivity	
6	Promotional activity	Target early adopters	
7	Service emphasis	Novel solutions	
8	Product/sourcing approach	Select suppliers with innovative capabilities	
9	Production	Prototypes; customization	
10	Capacity considerations	Low. Hedge and deploy resources as required. Form alliances to access capacity	
11	Fulfillment approach	Speed is vital at all times	
12	Relationship intensity	Intense but short term while problem exists	
13	Systems/IT support	Everything – whatever is required to solve the problem	
14	Resource allocations priorites	Hedge and deploy resources, sometimes ineffectively	
15	Strategic risk profile	High	

FIGURE 3.5 ◆ *Fully flexible* (Business Event) supply chain strategy – entrepreneurial

	Strategic dimension	Ideal strategy	Actual strategy
1	Product mix	New innovative products and services, developed through collaboration	
2	Innovation emphasis	Solutions are developed 'in situ', fast, and collaboratively	
3	Marketing emphasis	Some media activity seeking donors	
4	Channels of distribution	As many as needed in a given situation	
5	Pricing regime	Some price sensitivity, 'stewardship' of funds important	
6	Promotional activity	Low	
7	Service emphasis	Welfare of the human victims involved is paramount	
8	Product/sourcing approach	Seek suppliers who can deliver innovative solutions with a human face	
9	Production	The supply chain is the product itself – delivering services in emergency situations	
10	Capacity considerations	Build capacity very fast when confronted with a crisis. Hedge and deploy resources where possible ahead of time	
11	Fulfillment approach	Somewhat haphazard depending on conditions on the ground	
12	Relationship intensity	High	
13	Systems/IT support	Use whatever is available – beg/borrow/steal	
14	Resource allocations priorites	Reactive to events; somewhat inefficient usage is normal	
15	Strategic risk profile	High	

FIGURE 3.6 ◆ *Fully flexible* (Humanitarian) supply chain strategy – emergency response

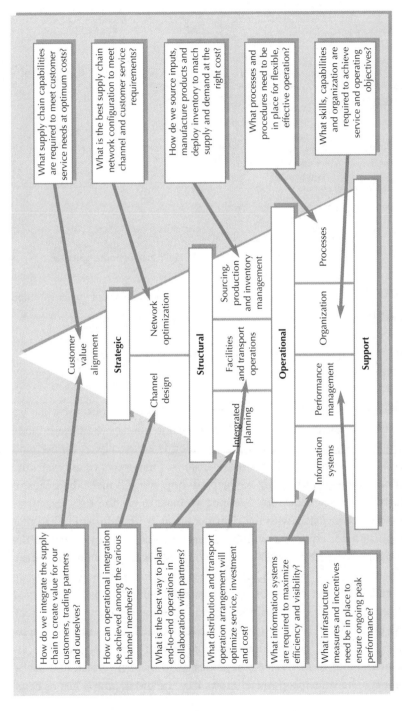

FIGURE 3.7 ◆ The supply chain organizational pyramid

Source: Adapted from Appendix 2D in Gattorna (2006), p 283

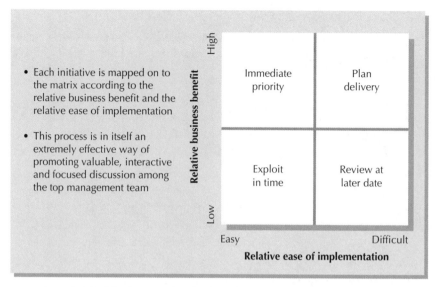

- Each initiative is mapped on to the matrix according to the relative business benefit and the relative ease of implementation

- This process is in itself an extremely effective way of promoting valuable, interactive and focused discussion among the top management team

FIGURE 3.8 ◆ **Prioritization matrix – business benefits versus ease of implementation**

Source: Adapted from Appendix 2D in Gattorna (2006), p 284

Getting your respective *value propositions* right is the key

It is all very well to laud the importance of value propositions but when we get to strategy development – or defining our intentions – we have to hone in on how we will deliver. A value proposition is essentially a promise, and delivering on that promise has two dimensions. First, we have to review the operational issues and identify any gaps in how we will meet the needs of our customer buyer behaviors. Second, we have to get the right organizational structure in place, with the right people and the right abilities so that the organization is equipped with the necessary capabilities to deliver on the promise represented by our value proposition. An example of how a strategy analysis might occur in the 'Collaborative' segment is depicted in Figure 3.9, highlighting the operational and capability-building issues involved in delivering the value proposition. In this case the organization, a Greek FMCG distributor,[5] is representing various branded goods manufacturers or principals, and selling to intermediaries downstream such as wholesalers, retailers, and food service companies, who in turn service end users/consumers. The value proposition shows that the distributor is just as com-

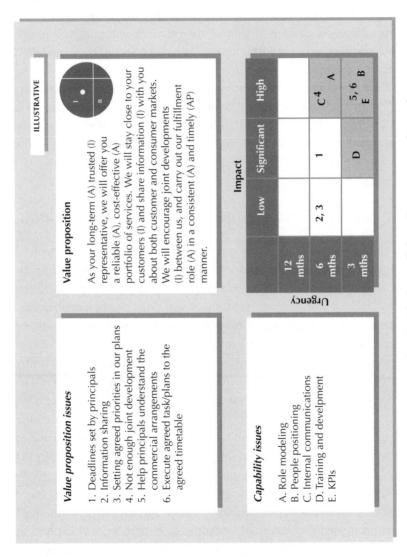

ILLUSTRATIVE

Value proposition

As your long-term (A) trusted (I) representative, we will offer you a reliable (A), cost-effective (A) portfolio of services. We will stay close to your customers (I) and share information (I) with you about both customer and consumer markets. We will encourage joint developments (I) between us, and carry out our fulfillment role (A) in a consistent (A) and timely (AP) manner.

Value proposition issues

1. Deadlines set by principals
2. Information sharing
3. Setting agreed priorities in our plans
4. Not enough joint development
5. Help principals understand the commercial arrangements
6. Execute agreed task/plans to the agreed timetable

Capability issues

A. Role modeling
B. People positioning
C. Internal communications
D. Training and develpment
E. KPIs

Impact

Urgency	Low	Significant	High
12 mths			
6 mths	2, 3	1	C⁴ A
3 mths		D	5, 6 B E

FIGURE 3.9 ◆ Strategy issues associated with the 'Collaborative' segment ('Ia' Logics)

mitted to the end consumer as it is to the other intermediaries in between: 'We will stay close to your (manufacturers) consumer customers and share information with you about both customer and consumer markets.' The value proposition ensures that everyone ultimately works together to serve the end consumer. The management of both firms work together on the value proposition issues such as sharing information, setting agreed priorities, joint planning and executing the agreed plans according to a shared timetable.

For further examples of similar issues that address value propositions for the 'Pragmatic' and 'Solutions' customer segments see Appendix 3A.1 and 3A.2. From this point it is relatively easy to extend these prioritized issues into actions and budgets using the template provided in Appendix 3B.

Getting inside your competitors' decision cycles

Increasingly in today's operating environment, enterprises have to find ways of getting their products and services to market faster than competitors, or adapting to changing market conditions faster than competitors. We now live in a world where customers will go with the supplier that is first to market or responds to their needs within hours or days rather than weeks and months. For this reason companies have been adopting the OODA loop, a process originally developed by the military as a way to penetrate the enemy's decision-making cycle and strike first.[6] OODA stands for *observe, orient, decide* and *act*. The desire, if not the necessity, to get inside your competitors' decision cycles and act first is something that applies equally as well to the commercial world. As one executive observed: 'If I can make decisions faster than my competitor, if I can get inside his decision cycle, then I've got him.'[7]

Clearly, formulating good strategy, fast, is important. But even more vital is having the capability to execute fast, and for this purpose you need the appropriate array of internal subcultures, a topic we will explore in depth in Chapter 4. In Chapter 9 we will give examples of companies that have mastered the OODA loop as a competitive weapon.

Defining ideas

1 We need to be very clear about which dominant buying behaviors are present in any given product-market combination. Only then can the corresponding *value propositions* be formulated.

2 *Value propositions* then break down into constituent strategies, and these strategies involve synthesizing up to 15 different strategic dimensions. We call these different combinations, strategy packages.

3 It is insightful to undertake a comparative analysis of 'ideal' strategies as indicated by the behavioral segments identified in a given market, and the 'actual' strategies a company is currently pursuing. The mismatches will surely become visible, as will the mis-allocation of precious resources.

4 The ideal strategies will be underpinned by bringing the real issues in play to the surface in a particular situation, and prioritizing these so that the downstream action is using scare resources in the best possible way.

5 To support and execute any change program, we refer you to the four-tier supply chain organizational pyramid depicted in Figure 3.7. It provides a systematic guide to implementing the various internal initiatives designed to extract maximum value for the enterprise as it improves alignment with customers.

6 You have to execute strategy fast if you are to stay ahead of competitors and make first contact with customers. For this purpose we recommend you embrace the principles of the OODA loop: observe, orient, decide and act.

7 **Challenge** to the reader: do you follow the suggested sequence in developing your supply chain strategies? And if so, are they truly multi-disciplinary strategies?

Implementing a multiple supply chain configuration

Aligning internal culture with customers to execute strategy

You have to build internal capability to execute the supply chain strategies that will transform your business. But to do this, you must enter the invisible world of the subconscious, and seek ways to shape the particular subcultures necessary to achieve the required change in behavior.

This chapter suggests how this delicate operation can be achieved by first understanding, then mapping the subcultures in your enterprise. Only then can you identity the best capability levers to use in the change process.

Unfortunately, few enterprises seem to understand just how the behavior of their people can lead to the transformation of their business.

'Who needs competitors when we have colleagues like this to work with?' I will always remember this telling observation in 1972 by my boss at the time, Don Johnson, a Vice-President of FMC Corporation's Petroleum Equipment Group, who was setting up divisional operations in Australia, based in Melbourne. The parent company, FMC Corp., was and still is a major United States-based conglomerate, with interests in many industries, from food machinery to defence. We had just come out of another interminable meeting, where very little had been achieved if you take out the politicking. Years later I came to understand what he meant, and unfortunately the same disease has continued to spread at geometric rates in many businesses! Nothing changes. Witness what happened to Carly Fiorina in her early days at Hewlett-Packard when she was trying to win over a sceptical workforce:

> *Mid-level managers and rank-and-file employees didn't openly attack her new ideas. They just meandered around them. In public forums, Fiorina appeared to win support. Then managers huddled privately to decide whether they liked what they heard. They softened goals, adjusted time-tables, made some exceptions. By the time they had finished, they had gutted whatever it was that Fiorina was trying to achieve. Resistance was so subtle and pervasive that she couldn't accomplish anything by getting angry. There was no obvious opponent. It was just the system.*[1]

Sound familiar? Louis Coutts, international management consultant and founder of the Hawthorne Academy in the United Kingdom, expresses much the same sentiments:

> *Whenever I hear the war cry, 'we need to change the culture of this organ-ization', I cringe. Culture cannot be imposed; it must be discovered. What is frequently overlooked is the fact that the culture of an organization is contained in the hearts and minds of the people it employs. It's already there, waiting to be expressed. To the extent that we allow that culture to be expressed, a range of benefits will emerge. If we don't allow that culture to be expressed, an organization will always fall far short of its potential.*[2]

No doubt you are familiar with this cultural war cry. From what I have seen over the past two decades, it seems that most, if not all, enterprises have problems converting stated intentions (otherwise called plans) into actions on the ground. Indeed, it's not unusual for 40 to 60 per cent of stated intentions and best-laid plans to go unrealized, for any number of reasons. Certainly, the changing operating environment comes into play here and can force a change in plans. But resistance from people within the enterprise is usually the biggest factor causing slippage of intended strategies. As observed in Chapter 1, enterprises can inflict much more damage on themselves than any external competitor will ever do.

The management literature has largely ignored the potential for self-wrought destruction; research normally focuses on competitors as the main source of concern. Most likely, this has been because the role cul-ture plays in driving action inside enterprises is not fully understood.

Ironically, if the culture is functional, it may be the organization's only key competitive strength because it is the only thing competitors cannot easily copy in the short term.

How often have you heard the same old mantra? Just formulate smart strategies (on paper), and the rump of the organization will automatically implement these in the marketplace, unquestioned and unmodified. Experience tells us something different! What we now know is that while the downward force of strategy on the organization to deliver plans is considerable, an even stronger force exists – the upward force exerted by the organization's culture. Quite simply, the resident culture selects those parts of the strategy it is prepared to support and put into action, and those parts which it chooses to resist – as Carly Fiorina discovered.

You can see why the 'cultures' in an enterprise are a major determinant of what plans get acted upon; we call this cultural force *cultural capability*. In this book I will refer to the various cultures that I identify as 'subcultures', as they are elements of the broader organizational culture, sometimes called 'corporate culture.' These have an ability to get things done within different supply chains. The refusal of managers and staff to deliver on intentions creates a hole which is mostly filled with a disparate array of other non-critical activities, often taking the organization off the critical path to high performance. This, in turn, leads to frustration among the senior executives, who have primary responsibility to shape the appropriate subcultures to get the job done in the first place. In this sense, the leadership has failed the organization, often because they are out of touch with their marketplace and their people.

Cultural mis-alignment hinders performance

So what is this mysterious phenomenon that has such an impact on the way enterprises perform? *Culture*, as depicted schematically in Figure 4.1 overleaf, is the intangible human force that sits **below** the surface of the 'performance iceberg.' It represents an organization's values, beliefs and deeply held underlying assumptions that people import into the enterprise over time. *Culture* represents the 'unwritten' rules about what is expected and valued in the organization. Edgar Schein defines culture as:

a pattern of shared basic assumptions that the group learned as it solved its external and internal problems, that has worked well enough to be considered valid and, therefore, to be taught to new members as the correct way to perceive, think, and feel in relation to those problems.[3]

The four-level alignment framework introduced in Chapter 2 provides an invaluable way to delve into the mysterious force of organizational culture. The key is to understand what is happening at the interface between each level, and particularly the **interface** between strategic response (Level 2) and cultural capability (Level 3). How many times have you seen internal culture derail the successful implementation of your plans? In short, the potentially damaging impact of mis-aligned or dysfunctional culture is a reality that has long been overlooked. And it's now time to address this oversight.

Of course, the invisibility of culture is in stark contrast to the tangible world of hard assets, infrastructure, systems, technology and observed behavior that fills the conscious world. Most people tend to manage what they can see, while either ignoring or remaining oblivious to what they can't see, touch or feel. This is the problem that has plagued not only the design and operation of supply chains, but all forms of human organizational endeavour over the centuries.

Expressed simply, *organizational culture* is the way of life within the enterprise's reality, often expressed as 'the way we do things around here'. Culture at the organizational level involves a shared understanding of how an enterprise perceives and responds to its operating environment. This explains how a company responds to market conditions and different customer demands. Enterprises express this as wanting to achieve a customer-focused culture. Culture also acts as the 'glue' holding the internal mechanisms together, making it capable of accomplishing what an individual alone cannot. Conversely, when culture is dysfunctional, it eventually leads to the demise of the enterprise. There are plenty of 'corporate shipwrecks' to support this latter point.

Pressure today on companies and governments to deliver shareholder value puts too much focus on cutting costs, which then creates inefficiencies in culture. For example, procedures are not documented or kept up to date because there are not enough people to do it, or people have left the organization and have not been replaced. Systems are not upgraded or are in a constant state of change. Employees avoid communicating with

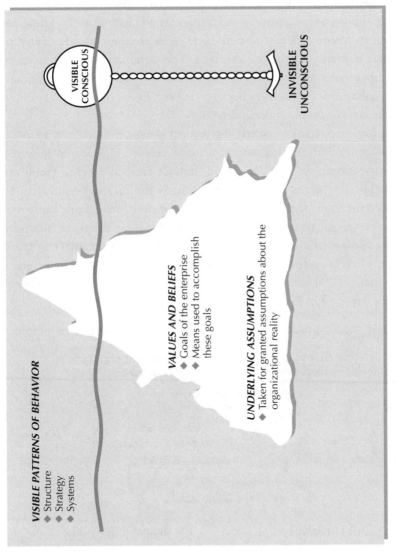

FIGURE 4.1 ◆ The 'performance iceberg'

Source: Adapted from Figure 4.3.3 in Gattorna (2003), p. 460

their manager as it usually means more work, adding to an already heavy workload. Customer service eventually suffers.

While there are common *corporate values* that apply across the entire enterprise, often referred to as *corporate culture*, other values can exist, forming subordinate cultures, sometimes termed 'subcultures'. These are essential to ensure different response strategies are there to meet different customer demands in the marketplace. The dominant logics that shape these subcultures are the same logics that shape and drive the dominant buying behaviors of customers because, in both cases, humans and human behavior are the common denominator.

It is also important to clearly distinguish *climate* from *culture*, to avoid confusion and misreading organizational culture. *Climate* is how the enterprise *feels* about itself, its mood, morale and the level of employee satisfaction at a given point in time. This is the internal equivalent to external customer perceptions of the organization, which are expressed as opinions about the relative performance of various suppliers. Both the internal climate and external customer perceptions are subject to rapid change, whereas culture and the dominant buying behaviors of customers are permanent features and cannot be easily changed. These fine distinctions are depicted in Figure 4.2.

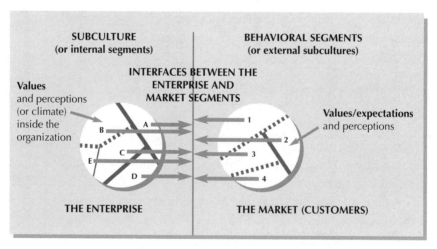

FIGURE 4.2 ◆ **The two sides of values, behavior, and perceptions – inside and outside the enterprise**

Can you see then, the pivotal role culture plays in implementing strategy, achieving superior performance in single enterprises and delivering performance along supply chains of linked enterprises? We need to achieve *dynamic alignment* between the internal culture and the expectations of external customers. Not an easy feat!

We learned in Chapter 2 that there are various combinations of the four primary subcultures forces present in all enterprises, and these are summarized in Figure 4.3 and detailed in Figure 4.4 (overleaf).

The opposing cultural forces are P versus I, and A versus D. The overall culture of an enterprise is the net outcome of the pull of the four forces, and is ultimately represented as the dominant force, with possibly a supporting secondary force.

Each of these four subcultures (and their various combinations) has particular strengths and limitations. These have to be factored into any change program that seeks to improve alignment between an enterprise, its strategies and the marketplace, since the four subcultures require very specific actions to shape and mold them.

However, there is also a bad or 'dark-side' of culture, which is the opposite to the ideal characteristics described in Figure 4.4 above. The 'dark-side' of culture occurs when an organizational culture becomes dysfunctional due to long periods of organizational stress or exaggerated, unchecked or undisciplined behaviors. The specific cultural characteristics displayed by the 'dark-side' are detailed in Figure 4.5 (page 100).[4]

Mapping internal values and cultures

Culture mapping is a way of profiling an enterprise in quantitative terms; it makes visible what is invisible. Some of the earliest work in developing mapping techniques was undertaken by Cameron and Quinn.[5] Their methodology proved to be very similar to our own, which had been under development since the early 1990s. A culture mapping questionnaire is distributed to all staff. The responses – which are usually a high proportion of the original number sent out – are sorted and mapped in any number of ways, e.g., by level, department, business unit, division, overall organization, etc. The culture mapping methodology is described in more detail in Appendix 4A.1.

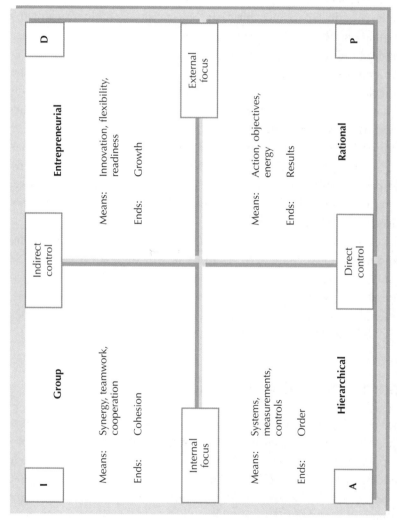

FIGURE 4.3 ◆ **The four generic enterprise subcultures**

Source: Adapted from Figure 4.3.5 in Gattorna (2003), p. 461

I	Group subculture	Entrepreneurial subculture	D

Emphasis on cohesion, teamwork, synergy and consensus

- Closed informal communication shared through groups and teams
- Control achieved by commitment to common values
- Management support emphasizes the *internal* climate, particularly cooperation, personal development and recognition
- Individuals' tasks are negotiated by consensus
- Rewards are based on informal standards and the ability to maintain internal cohesion – good team players
- Deviant behavior is tolerated – provided it adheres to consensus values

Emphasis on creativity, innovation and flexibility

- Open informal communication which is shared with whoever happens to be around at the time
- Control achieved by commitment to a common vision
- Management support emphasizes leading, inspiring, flexible and initiating behaviors
- Individuals are empowered to perform their roles
- Rewards are based on creativity and entrepreneurial behavior
- Deviant behavior is tolerated – provided it is goal directed

Emphasis on stability, order, systems and control

- Closed, formal communication which is shared only on a 'need to know' basis
- Control achieved by focus on processes
- Management support emphasizes procedures
- Individuals' tasks are established by precedence
- Rewards are based on formal standards and the ability to maintain internal control – good administration
- No deviation from approved processes

Emphasis on results, urgency and high levels of activity

- Open, formal communication by way of concise, timely updates using the most appropriate media for speed
- Control achieved by focus on results
- Management support emphasizes planning
- Individuals are given structural authority to perform their roles
- Rewards are based on formal standards and relevant results – analysis and action
- No deviation from plans or performance standards

A	Hierarchical subculture	Rational subculture	P

FIGURE 4.4 ◆ **Details of each generic subculture**

Source: Adapted from Figure 3.3 in Gattorna (2006), p. 74

I

Group subculture

Emphasis on cohesion, teamwork, synergy and consensus

Dark side …

- Favoritism and very cliquey environment (e.g., 'the boys' club')
- Information is shared with those in the 'inner circle'
- 'Corrupt' practices are tolerated – things are kept hidden in the 'family'
- Loyalty is rewarded rather than competence or talent
- Indecisive without consensus leading to a 'meetings culture'
- Difficult decisions regarding people and disagreements are avoided
- Internally focused, losing market focus and direction
- Focus on solving own problems without seeking external help
- Managers are highly political

D

Entrepreneurial subculture

Emphasis on creativity innovation and flexibility

Dark side …

- Initiative fatigue or exhaustion from too many projects and change
- High level of failure with going down blind alleys, starting and not finishing activities
- Brain freeze and spin out of control from too many ideas, options
- Can be too ahead in timing for developing products or services
- Enthusiasm lacking for strategy implementation
- Micro-managing and obsession with details
- Managers are defocused and disconnected from staff leading to employees avoiding their boss

A

Hierarchical subculture

Emphasis on stability, order, systems and control

Dark side …

- Bureaucracy runs rife, dogmatic about going 'by the book'
- Systems and procedures become cumbersome and slow
- Information is withheld to maintain power
- High blame element and people are not trusted
- People are treated as a number or unit of production
- People get ahead by not 'rocking the boat' or giving bad news
- Highly resistant to change, pessimism and inability to plan
- High focus on cost cutting leads to 'corporate anorexia'
- Managers are highly autocratic

P

Rational subculture

Emphasis on results, urgency and high levels of activity

Dark side …

- Burnout from a demanding environment and difficulty with work-life balance
- High competitive behavior amongst individuals
- Poor performance is not tolerated
- Analysis paralysis
- Rigid and arrogant, decisions made too quickly to get the job done
- Emotionally charged environment and impatience with drawn out solutions or involving people
- Managers are highly aggressive and prone to 'head kicking'

FIGURE 4.5 ◆ The 'shadow-side' of each generic subculture

Source: Prepared for John Gattorna by The Ryder Self Group, Sydney, 2004.

A typical array of output maps are provided in Appendix 4A.2. The *current culture* is represented by the black dot or the 'center of gravity'. It provides a consolidated picture of employee views on current values, beliefs and behaviors. The *preferred culture*, indicated by the open square, is where people would naturally like to be if there were no constraints on them or the business. Finally, to complete the picture, the *ideal culture* is superimposed over the two previous plots and represents the predominant behavioral segments present in the target marketplace. By comparing all three plots we are able to identify any significant 'mis-alignments' and decide what specific initiatives to take to improve alignment between the enterprise, its marketplace and current strategies. The comparative analysis gives us the ability to precisely identify mis-alignments.

The subcultures present in an enterprise are the collective set of values and beliefs held by staff and management; they influence the thinking and action of the organization. The techniques as described above have been developed to map multiple cultural dimensions by measuring the values present in relation to people's beliefs about the enterprise where they work.

Below is a list of nine cultural dimensions typically used in culture mapping. However, experience suggests that a minimum of five dimensions are required to produce usable results. The components of each of these dimensions are described in more detail in Appendix 4B. Note: the same P-A-D-I logics apply in each of the four quadrants of these factors. The nine dimensions are:

Autonomy/decision-making: indicates the extent to which individuals feel they are able to take the initiative and make decisions.

Change tolerance: measures employee assumptions about the enterprise's capability and willingness to change.

Communication: measures the nature and degree of information sharing going on inside the enterprise.

Conflict: assesses how and why conflict arises in the enterprise, and how it is resolved.

Control:	measures the way in which organizational effort is monitored and coordinated.
External coping:	assesses the values which influence the enterprise's ability to cope with external operating environment conditions.
Identity:	employee assumptions about the enterprise's effectiveness in the marketplace, and the extent to which they identify with this.
Internal organizing:	assesses the values which affect the way in which work is allocated, integrated and organized.
Performance-reward:	Measures employee assumptions about what constitutes 'good' performance.

These nine cultural dimensions represent the way an enterprise's culture can be dissected and analyzed to better understand what is happening within the organization. Ultimately they help us to determine which dimensions we need to focus on to improve alignment between strategy and the primary customer segments. It is much more precise than the seemingly brutal approaches used in the past, and that alone makes it infinitely more effective.

How does this help us? Through culture mapping, we can identify more accurately the most appropriate levers to use in the subsequent change process, thereby eliminating much of the guesswork that has previously plagued change management initiatives. Of course, the results from pulling any of these levers never occurs as fast as expected, but managers can now at least persevere with selected actions in the knowledge that they are on the right track, and therefore the action being taken should have the desired effect when the wheels stop spinning – and real traction is achieved.

In this process, the culture's appropriateness or inappropriateness, strengths and dysfunctional aspects are highlighted vis-à-vis the 'ideal' cultures identified through the array of customer behavioral segments. Managers are therefore in a much better position to understand how to communicate to staff, and predict how staff members are likely to handle and resolve conflict, change and cope with external pressures.

The most appropriate performance and reward system can then be more readily identified, and the recruitment process can be fine-tuned to attract people who not only have the necessary technical qualifications, but also bring with them into the enterprise a mindset that reinforces the desired subculture(s) and corresponding strategies. Culture mapping helps managers to improve individual and team performance. A 'quick' culture diagnostic which can be used to assess the current culture of your organization is contained in Appendix 4C. This should be overlaid with the market segments identified in the 'quick' behavioral segmentation diagnostic, and any mis-alignments noted.

Climate factors

The influence of the more transient climate factors at work in an organization should not be under-rated, because they provide a measure of the level of stress in the organization. This is depicted by the gap between the *current* and *preferred* cultures as defined earlier. The bigger the gap, the more the stress. So, in conjunction with undertaking a culture map, it is also important to gain some insight into the issues concerning employees about their work environment. The factors considered in assessing the climate or the mood of the organization are:

Physical environment: employee perceptions about the physical and aesthetic aspects of their workplace.

Job stressors: those factors which have a negative effect on employee performance.

Job motivators: those factors which stimulate individual performance.

Job rewards: employee perceptions about tangible and intangible aspects of reward and performance.

Corporate self-esteem: the extent to which employees believe the organization is successful.

Communication: employee perceptions about the style of delivery and the content and process of information sharing in the organization.

For the best results, climate and culture information should be analyzed together. Climate will signal the problem, and the clue to the root of this problem will be found in the culture data. For example, people may complain about poor communications inside the company. The corresponding culture map may reveal a predominantly 'A' type communication style, which means that information is only shared on a 'need to know' basis. In effect, this means that information is being withheld from people, leaving them with the feeling that communication is poor.

In summary, *culture* is the internal reality of the organization, while *climate* is the mood. *Culture* drives strategic capability, while *climate* reveals whether or not employees are satisfied or dissatisfied. *Culture* is a long-term capability embedded in the enterprise and difficult to change rapidly. *Climate* is a short-term issue because it involves perception and as such can be changed relatively easily. Ultimately, *culture* is the key to internal capability, and it informs *climate*.

Country cultures

The seminal work of Geert Hofstede[6] on cross-cultural management has helped immeasurably in understanding more about the differences in country cultures, and how these can modify the way individuals and organizations behave in certain situations.

As depicted in Figures 4.6, 4.7 and 4.8 (on the following pages), Hofstede's original work identified four major dimensions on which country cultures differ. He labeled these power distance, uncertainty avoidance, individualism and masculinity. Based on later research he added the short- versus long-term orientation dimension. Brief descriptions of Hofstede's five dimensions are described by Nadeem Firoz *et al.*:[7]

Power distance: the extent to which less powerful members of society accept that power can be distributed unequally.

Uncertainty avoidance: the extent to which people try to avoid situations where expectations and outcomes are unclear.

Individualism: the relationship between an individual and the group to which that person belongs.

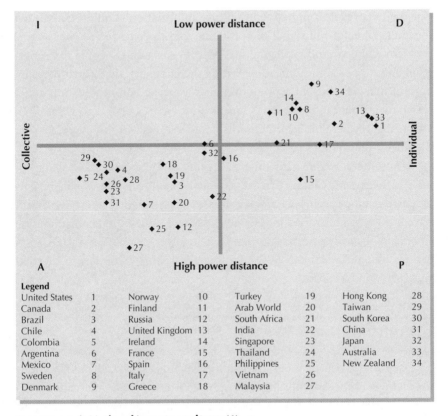

FIGURE 4.6 ◆ National/country cultures(1)

Source: Based on Geert Hofstede™ Cultural Dimensions (1980), prepared for John Gattorna by The Ryder Self Group, 2009

Masculinity/femininity: the 'masculinity' dimension describes societies where there is a polarization of the traits displayed by males and females. In a masculine society, traits such as assertiveness, strength and focus on material success are primarily considered male, while women are supposed to exhibit tenderness and a concern for quality of life. A 'feminine' society is one where both men and women exhibit traits of tenderness, modesty, etc., and there is less of a polarization between the sexes.[8]

Long-term orientation: the extent to which people within a culture have a long- versus short-term outlook on life;

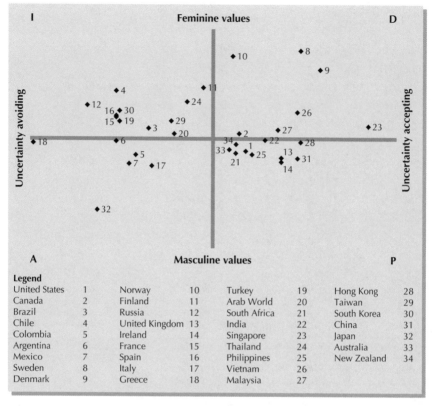

FIGURE 4.7 ◆ National/country cultures (2)

Source: Based on Geert Hofstede™ Cultural Dimensions (1980), prepared for John Gattorna by The Ryder Self Group, 2009.

So, the country cultures exhibiting different combinations of the above dimensions will have a pervasive influence on the way business is done in general, and on how supply chains operate in particular, across all source and consumption markets. Given that many of the world's major companies are now global in reach, this is a factor that requires more understanding and sensitivity as the search for ever higher performance continues.

Based on our own empirical work and the work of Hofstede, we can say that country cultures do **not** throw up previously unknown dominant buying behaviors in similar product and service categories around the world; nor do they reveal unknown subcultures and patterns of behavior inside organizations across the global terrain. The key insight here is that

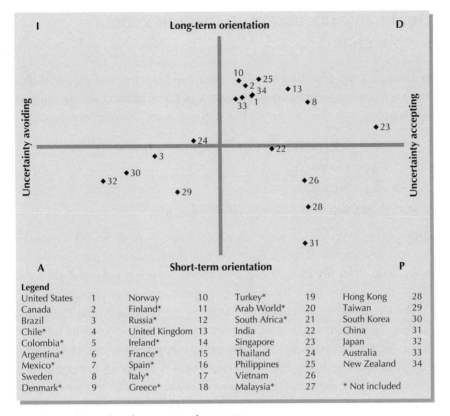

FIGURE 4.8 ◆ **National/country cultures (3)**

Source: Based on Geert Hofstede™ Cultural Dimensions (1980), prepared for John Gattorna by The Ryder Self Group, 2009

the prevailing values (or subcultures) in a given country appear to only have a modifying influence on the 'mix' of previously identified dominant buying behaviors for a particular product or service.

We were able to confirm this observation while undertaking a behavioral segmentation across global markets for the dairy ingredients division of New Zealand manufacturer Fonterra, involving 3,300 international B2B customers spread across more than 100 countries.[9] This is an important observation because it means that multiple supply chain alignment is a phenomenon which is valid in all countries or markets, and all the supplying enterprise has to recognize is the varying mix of previously identified dominant buying behaviors from country to country.

Dominant subcultures in the four generic supply chains

In Chapter 2 we identified the four most common types of supply chains that have been observed during the course of many projects during the past two decades; their corresponding P-A-D-I codes are shown in brackets:

Continuous replenishment supply chains (Ia);

Lean supply chains (A);

Agile supply chains (Pa); and

Fully flexible supply chains (Dp and Di variants).

Other configurations do exist and have been observed – for example, the *Fair deal* supply chain (Ai), which is a close variant of the *Continuous replenishment* supply chain type, and the *Commercial* supply chain type (Ap) – but the four types listed above are clearly the most common.

For the designer/operator of an array of supply chains, the important thing to know is the particular mix of the four most dominant types of buyer behavior evident in the marketplace being served, **and** the current prevailing culture inside the enterprise which is powering management's strategies into these behavioral segments. These are the two 'end conditions' that must be known at the start of any transformation program. Perhaps this gives a clue why so many transformation programs have failed so dismally in the past. Executive leadership has not understood that both of these end conditions must be known, and acted upon, to successfully implement a major change initiative.

Changing the enterprise to improve alignment

Figure 4.9 provides a quick insight into where the emphasis must be placed if the four generic types of subcultures (P, A, D, I) exist in the first place. Particular combinations of these subcultures must be present to underpin the four generic types of supply chains identified via our extensive fieldwork, i.e., Ia, A, Pa and Dp/Di (there are actually two variants of the *fully flexible* supply chain).

I

Emphasis on cohesion, teamwork, synergy and consensus

- Define 'What we stand for' statement
- Emphasise teamwork
- Consensus decision-making
- Define common values
- Joint-peer job design
- Informal standards for performance assessment of teams based on cohesion
- Reward team effort, loyalty and commitment
- Cash-based rewards for team (gain-sharing)
- Training emphasises personal interaction and team building
- Recruit 'I' people

D

Emphasis on creativity, innovation and flexibility

- Define 'our future potential'
- Allow people to work on their own to fulfill their potential
- Make individuals accountable for their decisions
- Formulate vision
- Job design to increase autonomy
- Informal standards of performance assessment for individuals based on creativity, flexibility
- Reward creativity of solutions, ideas, experimentation, lateral thinking
- Incentives for individuals, e.g., learning experience
- Open, informal communication for whoever is around at the time
- Training in creative thinking; creative problem-solving
- Recruit 'D' people

A

Emphasis on stability, order, systems and control

- Define 'how we do things' statement
- Centralise decision-making, especially for cost control measures
- Change guidelines to rules
- Define jobs by method
- Formulate policy and procedure manuals
- Set efficiency/productivity objectives
- Measure and reward conformance to systems and procedures
- Provide cash rewards based on productivity, 'sticking to the rules'
- Establish a formal, regular, structured, systematic communication process on 'need to know only' basis
- Training programs which emphasise planning, measuring, controlling and 'use of systems'
- Recruit 'A' people

P

Emphasis on results, energy and high levels of activity

- Define 'what we are fighting for' statement
- Decentralise decision-making; encourage staff to solve problems
- Specify clear guidelines, not rules
- Job design based on results, outputs
- Formalize position descriptions; individual performance objectives
- Measure performance against objectives
- Provide regular feedback on performance
- Reward achievement of objectives; speed of response.
- Provide incentives/merit-pay, based on results for *individuals*
- Establish a timely and speedy communication process
- Training programs which emphasise optimum use of time and resources
- Monitor competitor information and market conditions
- Recruit 'P' people

FIGURE 4.9 ◆ **The embedded emphasis of the four generic subcultures**

Source: Adapted from Figure 3.9 in Gattorna (2006), p.87

Change programs in the past have failed because of the lack of understanding about enterprise cultures, and the implications this has for the strategies being pursued at the time. This in turn has led to agitated staff and frustrated management, all for very little benefit. This phenomenon has been aptly named the *Canary syndrome*.[10] In this scenario, executives bang the cage every few years and keep the canaries (or staff) in a state of high agitation, without really achieving anything. The good news is that we no longer have to put up with this treatment. We understand what levers are available to create successful change, and more importantly, we know the right combinations to use. It is very similar to using X-rays to identify problems inside the human body. As long as the person conducting the analysis has an appropriate frame-of-reference, be it medical knowledge or as in this case an understanding of the mix of behavioral segments in the marketplace, it is possible to plot a systematic course of action to close any identified gaps. Behavioral segmentation techniques have emerged to provide the essential frame-of-reference for the external market. And new techniques to map the internal subcultures inside enterprises have coincidentally been developed over the past decades. It is now just a matter of comparing the two to gauge the degree of misalignment.

Change programs are either 'evolutionary' or 'revolutionary.' Evolutionary change occurs when change to the culture is incremental, and as such does not require an immediate alteration to the enterprise's 'subconscious.' Such change may be planned, but often occurs 'naturally,' as the organization adapts to its changing marketplace.

There are distinct modifications possible to strategies, organizational structures and management processes, such as expanding sales territories, changing product portfolios and entering new channels of distribution. Some logistics examples would include the move from hard-wired Electronic Data Interchange (EDI) systems to web-based communications, the use of network optimization models to rationalize supply chain assets, and strategic sourcing through the prioritization of suppliers.

Revolutionary change occurs when there are fundamental changes to underlying assumptions, values and beliefs, causing a significant change to manifested strategic behavior. It is usually planned, and often occurs when the enterprise is a 'victim' of rapid changes occurring in its own operating environment. Revolutionary change is almost always enterprise-wide, with radical shifts in strategy that may impact on the vision, organization structures, decision-making protocols, power distribution and status among the executive leadership. It is almost always accompanied by the import of new executives from outside the enterprise.

The suite of diagrams in Figure 4.10 defines the eight main change pathways that have been identified, four *evolutionary* and four *revolutionary*. In each case the so-called 'ideal' subculture has to align with the target market segment. Given that we have previously identified at least four types of predominant behavioral segments in most product or service markets, what are the implications? Well, it means that the executive leadership has to retain some parts of the current culture, while splitting

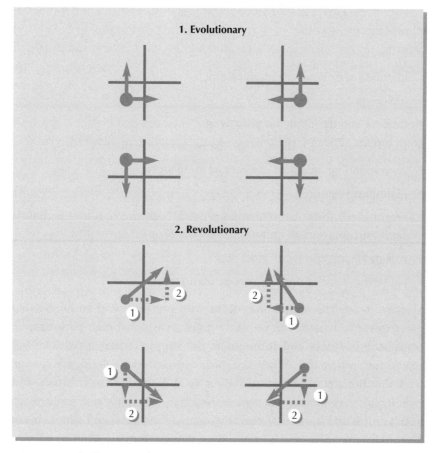

FIGURE 4.10 ◆ **Change pathways**

Source: Adapted from Figure 4.3.6 in Gattorna (2003), p. 463

off other parts and taking finely tuned initiatives to align with two or three other buyer behavior segments to achieve the desired multiple alignment. As the marketplace fragments, we have to reflect an equivalent fragmentation in the internal culture of the enterprise, albeit in ways that still make the enterprise manageable.

See also Appendix 4D for more detail on how *evolutionary* and *revolutionary* change is achieved.

In general terms, there are a limited number of change levers or *DNA building blocks* that can be used. For example:

◆ organization structure, reporting relationships and decision rights;

◆ positioning people in the organization according to their natural strengths;

◆ processes;

◆ IT systems;

◆ methods of internal communication;

◆ job design;

◆ training and development initiatives;

◆ Key Performance Indicators (KPIs)/performance metrics;

◆ corresponding incentive schemes or motivators;

◆ planning systems;

◆ recruitment from external sources with both the required technical skills and appropriate mindset to support planned initiatives;

◆ role modeling and mentoring; and

◆ leadership style of the top management team.

Manage these critical building blocks with precision and you inevitably move towards *dynamic alignment* – bringing sustained high-performance across the business and throughout the supply chains in which your enterprise participates. While the moves to achieve evolutionary change are either horizontal or vertical (i.e., A to P, P to D, D to I, I to A, and vice versa), *revolutionary* change is diagonal, but must also go through **both** vertical and horizontal moves along the way; you can't simply move diagonally! In other words, while the strategic thrust and ideal culture definition may shift from, say, A to D, P to I, and vice versa, actual implementation must follow a two-stage pathway, as shown by the dotted lines in Figure 4.10. Clearly, *revolutionary* change will take longer to bed down than evolutionary change, particularly if thousands of staff members are involved. For example, an enterprise with 10,000 staff can easily take three to four years to fully re-align with its marketplace, unless of course an accelerated approach is adopted as described in Chapter 14.

Culture as a powerful influencer of performance

If I were pressed to choose what were the two most powerful building blocks for change in the list above I would not hesitate to go for leadership followed by organization structure. So, if in doubt, start with these. If you think about it, all the recorded cases of successful change have started with the CEO as the prime mover and shaker. Jack Welch at GE comes to mind. As does Edward Zander at Motorola. He joined Motorola early in 2004 determined to bridge the gap with his main competitor, Nokia. His vision was to 'reinvent Motorola as a nimble, unified technology company', and his primary focus was on dismantling 'Motorola's debilitating bureaucracy and a culture of internecine rivalries [that were] so intense that Motorola's own employees refer to its business units as warring tribes.'[11] Have you heard that all before? Well, you will hear the same story and the same pattern repeated many times over in the years to come, unless of course senior managers in corporations adopt similar measures to Welch and Zander.

Nokia are not standing still either. Having been caught out by Apple's launch of the iPhone and the many associated services that it brings to the customer, Nokia are working hard in 2010 to transform their business model from a mass 'device manufacturer' to a provider of unique 'consumer communications solutions'. By moving away from their previous 'one-size-fits-all' mentality, Nokia's challenge now is to shape new subcultures so that they can successfully execute their new business model. A challenge indeed. However, given Nokia's record on transformation, they of all enterprises will understand the culture changes required.

Miller Coors, the giant US brewer formed through a joint venture between SABMiller and Molson Coors in 2008, is aggressively transforming its business into a more powerful and competitive brewer. The new company is working to create America's best beer company by building a winning culture shaped by its greatest asset – people. MillerCoors acknowledged that creating one cohesive culture out of the two former companies would be a challenge in its early days, but the company understands that to win in the beer business it cannot afford two separate and competing cultures. SAB Miller has more of a Rational (aP) culture, while Molson Coors has traditionally had the opposite, a Group (Ia) culture. In reality both cultures must learn to co-exist because that is what the market wants. Easier said than done!

The leading global PC and laptop supplier, Dell, is another giant enterprise on the move. They are currently transforming their hitherto successful 'direct' business model and developing a menu of supply chains for the market. This is requiring a corresponding re-vamp of their underlying subcultures, no small challenge in an enterprise of their size and reach.

Peter Widdows was appointed managing Director of Heinz Australia in 2003 and given just 12 months to turn around the ailing company. He succeeded by recognizing that culture was the root cause of the company's problems then changing it.[12]

Caterpillar is another organization whose *organizational DNA* became increasingly mis-aligned over its first 50 years of history, from the 1930s until its very existence was threatened in the early 1980s. Disaster was only averted by strong leadership on the part of CEO George Schaefer who took over in 1985 and instituted a radical transformation program to turn Caterpillar into a more resilient enterprise. Caterpillar went from a major loss in 1992 to sustained profits during the next decade.[13] The biggest factor in the transformation was the new organization structure, a decentralized and accountable business unit model introduced overnight on 29 January 1990. This changed everything once and for all, and put Caterpillar back in touch with its dealers and loyal users. The rest is history. So the combination of inspired leadership, knowing where to start and what to do is invaluable in today's corporations. We need more of this special ingredient, especially in those enterprises where the business is synonymous with the supply chain itself.

A prime example of a company currently suffering severe internal cultural problems is France Telecom. There have been 24 staff suicides reported in the past year – something is badly wrong with the culture in that company.

Another company that has distinguished itself in very negative terms is BP following the blast at its Texas refinery in March 2005. An investigation led by former US secretary of state James Baker concluded that '. . . weak leadership at BP and a lack of attention to effective safety, helped create a dangerous setting that led to 15 deaths at the Texas refinery'.[14] BP is now in even deeper trouble in the Gulf of Mexico.

Crucial influence of organization design and process

Among the levers for change mentioned above, leadership style of the top management team has the most impact, and organization design is not far behind. The performance management system, which measures and rewards the new behaviors, is the next most powerful lever for change.

Organization design refers to the way resources are configured inside an organization. It focuses the efforts of the organization and plays a major role in shaping its cultural capability. The functional capability of each major type of organizational design will be further examined in Chapters 7 to 10, but it is important to flag the importance of this key factor in organizational performance when discussing culture and implementation. In the scheme of things, **organization design** is so powerful because it is the springboard for strategies formulated by the business and deals directly with resource allocation and configuration issues. On the other hand, the **processes** that underpin each type of supply chain are more focused on ways of doing things. Ultimately, although both these powerful levers play pivotal roles in shaping cultural capability, organization design is a more powerful influence than process.

Organization design must always follow an understanding of both the marketplace and corresponding strategy formulation (in that order), not the other way around. This point was made long ago by the Roman Centurion Petronius when he said:

> We trained hard, but it seemed that every time we were beginning to form up into teams, we would be reorganized. Later in life I was to learn that we tend to meet any new situation by reorganizing, and a wonderful method it can be for creating the illusion of progress while producing confusion, inefficiency, and demoralization.[15]

Changing the culture – now faster than ever

In 1991, in the early development days of the *dynamic alignment* model, we worked with then CEO Bob Scott at General Accident (UK) in Perth, Scotland.[16] This 10,000-strong company had just suffered an appalling financial loss, and Scott, a New Zealander, was appointed to turn things around. Over the subsequent three years we systematically worked our way through all four levels of the *dynamic alignment* model: reviewing the competitive environment for GA's General and Life Insurance businesses in Britain; introducing a direct channel to consumers and rationalizing the domestic branch network; mapping and working on ways to change the legacy culture; and bringing new blood into the leadership team at all levels. It was a hard grind, but by the third year the results were beginning to show a substantial improvement in profit.

As it became clear that his strategy was working I remember asking Bob Scott what he would do differently if he were to do it all over again, and his answer: 'I would go much faster.' Changing the culture of a company the size of General Accident (UK) in three years seemed a fair result, but we now know a decade later that it is both possible and preferable to move faster when transforming an enterprise. Kurt Swogger, Research Director of the Polyolefins & Elastomers business at Dow Chemical Company, did it simply by choosing the right people and putting them in the right roles to find and launch innovative products at speed.[17] He grew a 'starter' culture that had key personnel working on concepts that potentially added value for customers, and he put 'finishers' in 'finisher' roles to ensure these were executed as promised. In the process, Swogger improved the degree of fit between a member of staff's personality and their roles from 29 per cent in 1991 to 79 per cent in 1995.[18] In addition, he worked on the 'recruitment' lever and consciously hired the most appropriate people for the job. In so doing, he increased the Myers-Briggs Type Indicator (MBTI®) based Creativity Index in his research and development (R&D) group (made up of both scientists and managers) from around 200 in 1991 to 260 by 1995, well above the national average of 235. His work showed that it is indeed possible to change the dominant culture in large organizations in a relatively short time through a deep understanding of the 'genetic nature of individual personalities and group cultures'.[19]

The same could be said of the more operational cultures commonly found in many corporate logistics and supply chain functions these days. It has always bothered me why a company like Philips, with such an impeccable pedigree for innovation and creativity in consumer and electronics products in particular, cannot seem to lift itself to the same creative levels when designing and operating its vital logistics networks and global supply chains. Why? Maybe its high time Philips switched some of its product R&D people to the task of thinking about new supply chain business models! The results are likely to be impressive if not unexpected.

There is certainly one chief executive intent on re-shaping the culture. Ken MacKenzie, the incoming CEO of the ailing Australian packaging group Amcor, was determined to tear down what he calls 'a silo mentality that is festering throughout the company and is hampering returns.'[20] So the message of the power of culture, for good or evil, is getting through to the highest levels at last. Let's hope that top management teams everywhere embrace the power of this hidden force and take advice on how it can be turned to the benefit of all stakeholders of the enterprise.

Helping culture formation with the built environment

One recent development has been the new focus on the built environment to influence the formation of the required array of internal subcultures. One of the leaders of this movement is Blackmores, an Australian company specializing in natural health products. They have created the Blackmores Campus in Sydney, Australia. It is a world-class facility 'that includes innovative features to minimize environmental impact, drive operational efficiencies, and importantly, provide resources and amenities to create a motivating, healthy happy place in which to work – so (employees) can do their best.'[21]

Indeed this emerging field has been called 'environmental psychology,' and it focuses on aligning company brand (values) throughout the organization, from customers to back-of-house operations. Blackmores seeks to engineer the built environment to have an impact on behavior in line with the company's brand position as a leader in natural health products and services. Other Australian companies in the vanguard of this Emerging trend include insurance firm AMP; St George Bank; Qantas travel; Toyota; Diageo; and the peak industry body, Standards Australia.[22]

Andrea Ehlers notes that

we (Watermark Architecture) started working on a brief from AMP in 2001 for a major overhaul of offices in NSW and Melbourne (over 40,000sq metres), and presented our ideas to the 10 AMP executives. After we presented the 'this is what you asked for scheme' we then presented a 'but this is what we think will benefit your future most'. Andrew Mohl was managing director of AMP Financial Services at that meeting and he was the one who took up the more innovative ideas we proposed about working styles, team versatility, information sharing, etc, and led the other directors to endorse the design which was very new thinking at that time. Andrew Mohl was appointed CEO in October 2002 and resigned at the end of 2007. We can say that operating earnings increased significantly during that period based on his simplified business model. The built environment was one tool to support Mr Mohl's model'.[23]

Defining ideas

1   It is the underlying cultural values that determine what gets done in organizations – not what you write down in business plans.

2   Now that it is possible to map *current*, *ideal* and *preferred* cultures in an organization, change management initiatives can be carried out with more precision and with greater probability of success.

3   The leadership group in an enterprise must take ultimate responsibility for shaping the various enterprise subcultures necessary to underpin and drive proposed value propositions into the marketplace – there is no escaping this responsibility.

4   Beer and Eisenstat sum things up well when they comment that 'between the ideal of strategic (dynamic) alignment and reality of implementation lie many difficulties.'[24] They list their six 'silent killers' and go on to say that 'Individually, the six barriers are troubling. Taken together they create a vicious circle from which it is difficult to escape.'[25] Actually I think there are more than six killers, more like 12 – and we have been at pains to identify these in this chapter.

5 **Challenge** to the reader: what do you understand about the culture and constituent subcultures in your own enterprise? Have you been actively trying to mold appropriate subcultures to underpin your supply chain operational strategies?

CHAPTER 5

Leading from the front

Converting customer insight into successful implementation

The older I get and the grumpier I get the more I come to realize that the most important thing in the life of any enterprise is 'leadership'. The fortunes of the enterprise rise or fall on the back of the leadership style of the C-level executive, as simple as that, and we have a myriad of examples to support this assertion. In this respect, Board's have a great responsibility, because they choose the CEO of the enterprise in the first place. After that, the appointed CEO will gather their team around and the task of re-aligning the enterprise with its various stakeholders begins. The best, most authentic leaders are those that fully understand their customers and the wider market, and put in place appropriate strategies to serve it. They also understand the nuances of their own organization, and move strongly to build the corresponding internal capabilities that will successfully propel their selected strategies into the marketplace. This chapter explores the 'leadership' issue in enterprises and their constituent supply chains. Everything is linked, but everything also depends on having the appropriate leadership in place at a particular point in the life-cycle of the enterprise.

How do you judge a good leader? Many of us can recognize good leadership when we see it, but it's harder to define. My experience tells me that successful leadership is not necessarily transferable from one organization to another – nor is one style necessarily right for a particular organization *through time.* Leaders and leadership styles need to be just as dynamic as the people they lead and the customers they seek to satisfy. Effective leaders will be able to shape the subcultures and implement the strategy needed in a complex supply chain environment. As John Kotter put it, 'institutionalizing a leadership-centered culture is the ultimate act of leadership'.[1] Kotter in fact was one of the first management writers to recognize that 'aligning' people around a vision, and its related strategies, involved far more than simply organizing and staffing.[2] Leadership and management are 'two distinct and complementary systems of action. Each has its own function and characteristic activities. Both are necessary for success in an increasingly complex and volatile business environment.'[3]

Politics gives us some telling examples of how different leadership styles are needed for different situations or challenges. Sir Winston Churchill was a strong and decisive leader as British Prime Minister throughout the Second World War, but he was unsuccessful during the ensuing peace time and was soon replaced. A more recent example is New York's Mayor, Rudolph Giuliani, who was heavily criticized before the 9/11 terrorist strike for his stance on race relations and civil liberties. But post 9/11, attitudes to Giuliani changed, even if his style did not. The Mayor's strong, energetic and hands-on style sent a consistent message to the city that he was in control and the 'right person' for the job at that time of crisis.

Deborah Ancona *et al.* take a very pragmatic approach to leadership when they suggest that '. . . no leader is perfect. The best ones don't try to be – they concentrate on honing their strengths and find others who can make up for their limitations'[4]. In their opinion, '. . . the sooner leaders stop trying to be all things to all people, the better off their organizations will be'.[5]

Leadership is about *authenticity*

The point is that good leaders are rarely cardboard cut-outs. Leadership is about *authenticity*, and the best leaders have the unique qualities of a genuine sense of self and the ability to inspire. According to Mike Hanley, 'in leadership circles, authenticity means "being yourself"'. Look at the likes of Jack Welch (GE); Richard Branson (Virgin), Terry Leahy (Tesco), Gerry Harvey (Harvey Norman), Michael Hawker (ex IAG), Philip Green (United Utilities) and Silvan Cassano (Benneton); all share a certain quality. Bob Goffee, the London Business School professor, claims that 'truly inspirational leaders are able to be themselves with great skill'.[7]

And about creating a winning mindset

I was impressed by Sir Clive Woodward, the 2003 England Rugby World Cup winning coach, when he spoke of 'leadership' as creating a 'winning mindset'.[8] He outlined five key elements of winning leadership as follows:

1 Lateral thinking: he gave the example of Paddy Lund, an Australian dentist who culled 95 per cent of his patients and continued to service only the 5 per cent he enjoyed working with. He was searching for a 'happiness-centred' business.

2 Critical elements: get the right people into the business; then get them into the right seat. Talent alone is not enough; you need passion, bordering on obsession among at least a few members of the top management team.

3 Critical non-essentials: look for something that sets you apart from your competitors. Woodward brought in Dr Sheryll Calder, a South African, as the Eyes Coach for the England Rugby XV! She trained the players' eyes to take in increased visual information.[9] This was unheard of in rugby circles up to that time.

4 Enjoyment: Woodward feels that it is important to have a happy and contented team that enjoys working together under strong direction. For this reason he conducted a climate survey on his players every six months. This may seem excessive, but it worked.

5 No compromise: in Woodward's view, no one remembers who came second, and he is right. Translated into commercial terms, analysts and shareholders are becoming increasingly demanding when it comes to financial performance, and if this is below expectations it is the leader or leaders of the business that are held accountable, including Board members. I share his belief that the difference between success and failure these days is marginal, so every initiative counts.

Joseph Grenny expresses a similar view about leadership when he says that '. . . leaders are responsible for intelligently and ethically influencing behavior in a way that creates value'.[10] He goes on to say that '. . . the most influential leaders- the 5 percent who succeed consistently at influencing profound and essential behavior change – spend as much as half their time thinking about and actively influencing the behaviors they know will lead to top performance'.[11]

Failed leadership

Failed or unsuccessful leadership can be demonstrated in a myriad of ways and leads inevitably to either the collapse of an organization or just poor performance. Can you think of some recent dramatic examples? The leadership triad at Enron produced an unhealthy 'group think' culture that ultimately led to the company's demise: they were Ken Lay (former Chairman and CEO), Jeff Skilling (CEO for six months after Lay retired), and Andrew Fastow (Chief Financial Officer, CFO). In Italy, the Italian dairy company Paramalat SpA almost collapsed after its former CEO, Calisto Tanzi, defrauded the company of more than €500 million. He is now in jail. Paramalat SpA's new CEO Enzo Bondi is working to restore the company, repay investors their lost funds and re-establish the firm's credibility within the financial community. An early step along that long path was taken on 6 October 2005, when the company stock was re-instated on the Milan Stock Exchange.

You might have also come across some of the poor leaders in large corporations that are now being characterized as 'workplace psychopaths'.[12] Exhibiting the same ruthlessness and narcissism as a criminal psychopath, these leaders somehow manage to stay under the radar as they rise through the ranks to senior levels in organizations. They cunningly manage upwards, while behaving vindictively towards their subordinates and creating a culture of mistrust. These are the worst kind of leaders because they leave a trail of destruction, the effects of which are often felt for a considerable time after they have either departed or been unmasked; I have personal experience of one of these corporate psychopaths, and it's not an enjoyable experience having to work under such a brute of a person. John Clarke quotes one such example in his book, *Working with Monsters*:

> *David worked for a large insurance company, and had a variety of techniques and devious strategies that helped him get promoted. Among other things, he would steal co-workers projects so he looked better than they did, and would spread false rumors about his boss. He lied to clients to make*

sure he got the contract, and then passed the work on to someone else who would get the blame when services were not delivered as he had promised. David was an up-and-coming star in the company. Most people had no idea that he had ruthlessly achieved his numerous promotions at the expense of the people around him.[13]

However we judge them, it is fair to say that today's C-level executives face several paradoxical situations that their predecessors were probably not even aware of. 'Chip' Goodyear, the ex-CEO of mining and resources giant BHP Billiton, summed up the predicament of today's leaders when he said that '. . . there are only two types of CEO, those that have been fired, and those that will be fired in the future'.[14] It's tough at the top, but the job has to be done and done well for the sake of all stakeholders. After retiring from the top job at BHP Billiton in 2007, he joined Temasek, the Singapore-based sovereign fund in early 2009 but lasted only a few months.

This challenge is being taken up by boards and CEOs around the globe. Sony, for instance, took the radical step of appointing Howard Stringer, a Welsh-born American, to the top job in an attempt to boost its flagging fortunes. Jeff Bezos is still driving Amazon.com towards the promised profitability in a business that looks more like a logistics fulfilllment operation every day. Sir Richard Branson's entrepreneurial and unconventional leadership style is helping him create one of the world's great brands in Virgin, and the reign of Sir Michael Rose as CEO at the UK retailer, Marks and Spencer, is helping to reverse its fortunes. Strong and successful leadership! The nirvana for many, but how do we identify, encourage, and sustain good leaders? Mark Hurd, the executive who took over HP after the demise of Carly Fiorina seemingly saved the company with brutal cuts and some fierce fiscal disciplines, but he now faces a fresh set of challenges. According to Ashlee Vance, the

most pressing is the concern that [he] has built an inflexible, solipsistic giant so obsessed with schematics and data-driven fiscal machinations that it has lost the ability to deliver that prized and perennial Silicon Valley trick: to surprise and astound. In short, what may be missing in the formidable intellectual and strategic artillery that Mr Hurd brings to bear at HP is creative inspiration.[15]

In many ways, Carlos Ghosn, the savior of Nissan faced similar challenges. Interestingly, his biggest test at Nissan was overcoming the deep denial inside Nissan about the company's true condition.[16] This is all about changing an engrained corporate culture as described in Chapter 4, and it's not an easy task, even when the enterprise is under threat of extinction.

And yet more complexities are coming the chief executive's way. Since the collapse of several high-profile companies around the world during the past decade, stringent new guidelines on corporate governance have been introduced by major corporations; and this was before the GFC of 2008/09! Martin Hilb's paper is the definitive work on this subject.[17] Boards and CEOs cannot afford to get this vital part of their corporate responsibility wrong in the future. Yet they continue to do so. Witness the wholesale collapse of banks and other financial institutions around the world over the past few years. Something must be done to raise leadership levels in the years immediately ahead.

And we need great leadership in times of crisis too. The recent Royal Commission into the bushfires on Black Saturday in Victoria, Australia, highlighted how Christine Nixon, the then Police Commissioner and therefore the person with operational responsibility for the safety of the State, didn't know what to do. She was just being 'busy busy' on the day, but totally ineffective.[18]

Creating leaders

Geoff Colvin in his article in *Fortune* gets it right when he says that '. . . your competition can copy every advantage you've got – except one. That's why the world's best companies are realizing that no matter what business they're in, their real business is building leaders'.[19] He goes on to describe how these companies do it. GE identifies promising leaders early, and makes leadership development part of the culture.[20] Eli Lilly chooses assignments strategically for its upcoming leaders.[21] Nokia takes the approach of developing leaders within their current jobs, and developing teams, not just individuals.[22] Whirlpool and Natura are simply passionate about the feedback and support they give aspiring leaders.[23] Hindustan Lever tries to exert leadership through inspiration.[24] And General Mills encourages its up and coming leaders to be active in their communities.[25]

So every company has its own particular formula, but the common theme in all these leading companies is the recognition of just how pivotal 'leader-ship' is to their on-going fortunes. This is entirely consistent with my own view that 'leadership' is the starting point in achieving *dynamic* alignment with your market: without which you will eventually fail as an enterprise.

Alexander Schieffer has the final word on the importance of leadership when he comments that '. . . the real fuel [essence] in leadership is understanding and believing in other people'.[26] He defines a good leader 'as someone who has faith in people's ability and who uses every opportunity to create the means for them to offer their creativity to the organization'.[27]

Identifying leadership styles

The P-A-D-I logic set first introduced in Chapter 1 can provide a useful tool to help you recognize leadership styles and match those styles with particular customer groups. If you recall, Figure 1.8 introduced the notion of four distinct leadership styles: P (*Company Baron*); A (*Traditionalist*); D (*Visionary*); and I (*Coach*). We identified these four primary leadership styles and up to 12 variants, all of which can be measured using the Myers-Briggs Type Indicator (MBTI®)[28] or a similar instrument[29] to assess preferred behavior. I suggest that you update your preferred 'Type' by undertaking the full-length assessment with a properly accredited MBTI® agency. To complete the puzzle you should then refer to Figure 5.1 to translate your MBTI® into P-A-D-I terms, thereby facilitating comparisons with the other three levels of the *dynamic* alignment framework.

Figure 5.2 describes each of the four pure leadership styles, and explains how each has both an upside and a downside. No single leadership style will be universally ideal in a multi-segment market, where the shaping of an equivalent array of matching subcultures is essential to achieve overall alignment.

Each primary leadership style will now be further explored on two levels, personal and management. In Personal, an individual's behavior is exhibited in personal settings, whereas in management we see the same person's behavior in a Corporate setting. A *coach*, for instance, is a person who is personally conscientious, respected for their principles and inspires people through the clarity and strength of their convictions. At a management level, these same attributes mean they like to develop the potential of their staff, they dislike change that could threaten the unity of the group and they prefer consensus-based rather than autocratic decision-making.

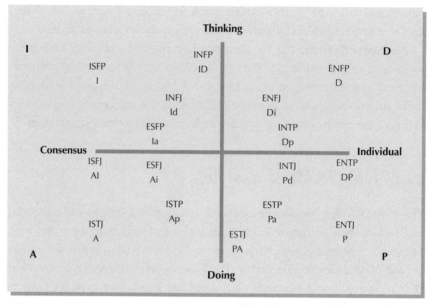

FIGURE 5.1 ◆ MBTI® overlay on P-A-D-I framework

Source: Adapted from Figure 29.6 in Gattorna (1998), p. 480

Company Baron (P)

Personal: Matter-of-fact, energetic, enjoys whatever comes along.
Tends to like mechanical things and sports.
May be a little blunt or insensitive.
Does not like long explanations by others.
Good with tangible things that can be worked, handled, taken apart or assembled.

Management: Comfortable with established procedures and rules.
Likes to work for change within the existing systems and structures.
Good at finding compromises.
Skilled at manoeuvring for increased personal power.
Uncomfortable with displays of warmth and openness by others.
Not always keen to put into practice ideas and policies that are considered new, unpopular or risky.

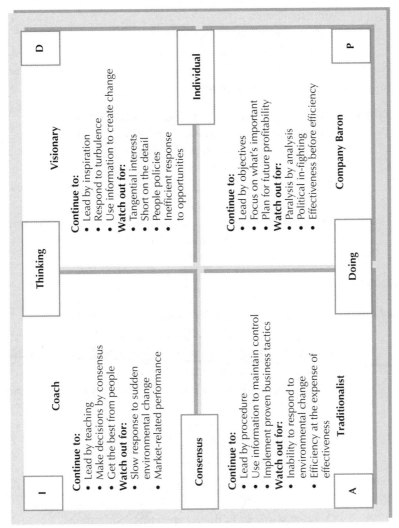

FIGURE 5.2 ◆ **Leadership styles**

Source: Adapted from Figure 4.2 in Gattorna (2006), p. 99

Traditionalist (A)

Personal:	Serious, quiet, achieves success by concentration and thoroughness.
	Practical, orderly, matter of fact, logical, realistic, dependable.
	Like to be well organized.
	Make up their minds as to what should be accomplished, and work steadily towards this objective, regardless of protests or distractions.
Management:	Likes to maintain superior/subordinate distance.
	Prefers clear standards and requirements for jobs.
	Comfortable with the supervision of well-structured tasks.
	Uses routines and procedures for getting things done.
	Prefers infrequent changes in work patterns or organization structure.
	Does not like too much discussion about new ideas and what the future might hold.

Visionary (D)

Personal:	Enthusiastic, high spirited, ingenious and imaginative.
	Able to do almost anything that interests them.
	Quick with a solution for deficiencies and generally prepared to help people with problems.
	Often rely on ability to improvise instead of preparing in advance.
	Can usually find compelling reasons for whatever they want.
	Sometimes impatient.
Management:	Likes to use personal influencing skills.
	Comfortable with criticism, confrontation and conflict.
	Good at working in poorly structured situations.
	Good change agent.
	Uncomfortable with details and routine.
	Does not like constraints and established procedures.
	Does not like to maintain group cohesion for its own sake.
	Does not like lengthy decision-making procedures.

Coach (I)

Personal: Success achieved by perseverance, originality and the desire to do whatever is needed or wanted. Puts best efforts into work and job.

Conscientious, concerned for others, quietly forceful.

Respected for their firm principles.

Often followed because of their clear convictions as to how to achieve for the common good.

Management: Likes to help develop the human potential among direct reports.

Prefers consensus-based decision-making.

Comfortable with changes in work patterns and flexible working hours.

Dislikes major changes that threaten the unity of the group.

Does not like autocratic patterns of decision-making.

Prefers to argue for changes in resource allocation.

Leadership in large enterprises means leadership at all levels, not just the top management team, so everything being said here applies to all levels. Clearly, in a large enterprise, the task of shaping the necessary sub-cultures can be allocated to different members of the management team. In a Small-to-Medium Size Enterprise (SME), this is usually not possible, and the task inevitably falls to just a few executives. Either way, it is a complex task, and one that is best undertaken by executives that have a preferred leadership style aligned to the subculture of the organizational unit that they have been allocated. If not, it becomes a change situation.

Ultimately, it falls to the Boards of enterprises to bear the responsibility for choosing the most appropriate CEO for the particular 'season' that an organization is in, and there are many examples of boards doing just that over the past few decades. Perhaps the most striking contemporary example is Hewlett-Packard. Carly Fiorina arrived as CEO in 1999 and set out a vision to rebuild the image of the flagging organization by trying to 'inspire employees with pleas to help her re-capture HP's lost glory'.[30]

In P-A-D-I terms, Fiorina represented something of a dichotomy. On the one hand she pushed hard for innovation (D logic) at the same time as she was seeking synergies (A logic) via an integrated sales force. This is a difficult combination to execute because of the opposing subcultures these two strategic philosophies represent, and in the end she paid the price. As *Business Week* commented, 'She's playing CEO, visionary, and COO, and that's too hard to do.'[31] Prior to her tenure at HP the culture had been characterized by teamwork and consensus. Her entrepreneurial, customer-focused, results-driven leadership style caused confusion and attracted progressively increasing resistance. Ultimately, she was replaced because the Board said it wanted more focus on execution.[32] Fiorina's successor, Mark Hurd, appointed in March 2005, opted for the more compatible logics of focus by separating the printer and PC divisions (P logic), while pursuing overall cost-saving efficiencies via a dramatic program to reduce staff across the company (A logic).

Change needs to be *led* not managed

How can real change be driven through an organization? Can you see the different potential and the different roles of leaders and managers? We believe that just as an army must be led rather than managed into battle, so enterprises also have to be led first and foremost, and then managed. Leaders will produce useful change while managers will focus on controlling complexity. Both are essential but very different capacities when it comes to change. Leaders will motivate, inspire and energize people; managers will develop the organization's capacity to deliver through organizing and staffing – they plan and budget. The differences between the two are significant and can be seen in Figure 5.3.

To put a finer point on the art of leading enterprises, various dominant coalitions within the top management team can be 'genetically' engineered to ensure the required cultural biases and corresponding cultural capabilities are embedded in the organization. These coalitions will ultimately be a mixture of the four generic leadership styles expressed in P-A-D-I code in Figure 5.2. Details of the characteristics of each type in the top management team are provided in Figures 5.4a and 5.4b.

Have you ever seen a universally ideal leadership or management style? Not surprisingly, no single 'ideal' style exists. Instead, as with other elements of the *dynamic alignment* model, multiple styles have to be formed and sustained, sometimes in spite of the natural conflict and associated

LEADERS	MANAGERS
PRODUCE USEFUL CHANGE	*CONTROL COMPLEXITY*
◆ **Make** the **change** occur	◆ Bring **order** and **consistency** – work within the current system
◆ **Set** the **direction** for constructive change	◆ Manage by **planning** and **budgeting**
◆ Relate to **what** the events and decisions mean to the people involved	◆ Relate to **how** things get done

◆ Focus on **aligning people**
  – communicate the direction
  – achieve common understanding of the vision
  – commitment to achieving the vision
	◆ Develop capacity to achieve through **organizing** and **staffing**

◆ Influence people to achieve **goals** and **objectives**	◆ Responsible for **performance** and **productivity**

◆ **Motivate, inspire and energize**
  – keep people moving in the right direction, despite obstacles to change
	◆ Ensure plans are accomplished by **controlling and problem-solving**
	  – rely on **systems** and **structures**

FIGURE 5.3 ◆ Leading versus managing

Source: Adapted from Figure 4.3 in Gattorna (2006), p. 103

tension brought about by having several styles coexisting. As expected, the natural style and value system of the CEO is vital. This is certainly the case at JetBlue, perhaps the leading low-cost airline in the United States. Here the founder and CEO, David Neeleman, and his executive team are consciously trying to preserve the airline's distinctive culture as it grows rapidly from a small to a big company.[33] I had recent experience of JetBlue in flights to and from Boston, and I found the service polite, efficient and certainly no frills.

However, perhaps the most outstanding example of contemporary leadership is to be found at Li & Fung, where Victor Fung and his brother William have transformed what was a small, Hong Kong-based trading company into perhaps the world's first genuine global supply chain company, using all the techniques and technologies you would expect of such a leading company. In many ways, Li & Fung epitomizes the concept of *dynamic alignment* in practice, because it has managed to remain aligned and attuned to its customers and suppliers for nearly a century. Why? Leadership! As we will see in Chapter 6, Li & Fung have overcome one of

I. REVITALIZERS AND INTEGRATORS	D. CREATORS AND BUILDERS
Shared values	**Shared values**
◆ Participation, cohesion	◆ Creativity, innovation
◆ Change	◆ Rapid response
Team style	**Team style**
◆ Sensitive to people	◆ Move very quickly
◆ Offer emotional support – have the ability to empower subordinates	◆ Apparently haphazard – guided by shared vision
Individual aptitudes	**Individual aptitudes**
◆ Consensus building	◆ Individualism, vision
◆ Good negotiation skills	◆ Flexibility
◆ Good conceptual ability	◆ Tolerance for ambiguity
Individual knowledge	**Individual knowledge**
◆ Group dynamics	◆ Technical
◆ Communications	◆ R&D
Conditions	**Conditions**
◆ Stable, traditional	◆ Turbulent, uncertain
◆ About to change	◆ Rapidly changing
Strategy	**Strategy**
◆ Developing long-term relations with customer	◆ Creation of a market
◆ About to change strategic direction	◆ New product development

FIGURE 5.4a ◆ **Characteristics of top management team (TMT) dominant coalitions**

Source: Adapted from Figure 2.9 in Gattorna and Walters (1996), p. 40

the biggest hurdles to sustained performance by adopting an organization structure which involves specialist teams ('tribes') of 40–50 multidisciplinary personnel, dedicated to each of its major retail customers. Surely there are some lessons in here for other corporations? For more information about the Li & Fung phenomenon I suggest you read their book, *Competing in a Flat World*.[34]

A. PRODUCTIVITY MANAGERS	P. GROWTH MANAGERS
Shared values	**Shared values**
◆ Control	◆ Objectivity, facts
◆ Analysis	◆ Results
Team style	**Team style**
◆ Logical, analytical	◆ Drivers
◆ Provide clear structure for their subordinates	◆ Set clear objectives for their subordinates
Individual aptitudes	**Individual aptitudes**
◆ Good analytical skills	◆ High energy
◆ Logical	◆ Clear focus on objectives
◆ Desire for stability	◆ Desire for clarity
Individual knowledge	**Individual knowledge**
◆ Accounting	◆ Marketing
◆ Production	◆ Sales
Conditions	**Conditions**
◆ Established, mature	◆ Settled down
◆ Margins under pressure	◆ Highly competitive
Strategy	**Strategy**
◆ Consolidation, fine tuning	◆ Gaining market share
◆ Improving profits, productivity	◆ Customer focus

FIGURE 5.4b ◆ **Characteristics of top management team (TMT) dominant coalitions**

Source: Adapted from Figure 2.9 in Gattorna and Walters (1996), p. 40

As you can imagine, if the mix of leadership styles and cultures is inappropriate, as so often happens, then damaging mis-alignments can occur, which ultimately will hamper performance. So what do you have to look out for? The respective flaws of different types of leaders are revealed in Figures 5.5a and 5.5b. Most likely you will recognize some of these: leaders who are inflexible, risk averse or fail to share the corporate vision. No wonder they are constraining growth at best, or worse, wreaking havoc!

'I' culture	'D' culture
The 'D' manager	**The 'I' manager**
◆ Failure to share vision	◆ Failure to achieve objectives
◆ Seen as maverick	◆ Protects subordinates from reality
The 'P' manager	**The 'P' manager**
◆ Insensitive to group norms	◆ Risk averse
◆ Desire for more internal control	◆ Misses the 'big picture'
The 'A' manager	◆ Subdues initiative
◆ Distance from 'real' decisions	**The 'A' manager**
◆ Development of conflicting subcultures	◆ Unnecessary controls
	◆ Inflexible decisions
	◆ Dismisses new ideas

FIGURE 5.5a ◆ **Culture and leadership style – what to watch out for**

Source: Adapted from Figure 4.5a in Gattorna (2006), p.107

'A' culture	'P' culture
The 'I' manager	**The 'I' manager**
◆ Undermines political forms	◆ Inefficient resource allocation
◆ Poor risk tolerance	◆ Climate of frustration
The 'D' manager	**The 'D' manager**
◆ Creates insecurity	◆ Loss of output control
◆ Leaves the rest behind	◆ Loss of strategic focus
The 'P' manager	**The 'A' manager**
◆ Systemic resistance to change	◆ System becomes an end in itself
◆ Mis-translation of objectives	◆ Lose sight of external change

FIGURE 5.5b Culture and leadership style – what to watch out for

Source: Adapted from Figure 4.5b in Gattorna (2006), p.107

Achieving multiple alignment via superior leadership

So where does this leave the corporation? The task of the senior executive is to select the top management team, along the way identifying the natural leadership styles and selecting the necessary technical disciplines. This has to be done in such a way that the embedded imbalance reflects the imbalance in the behavioral segments in the external market. This same imbalance or bias has to be embedded in the subcultures on the inside of the company so as to either consolidate or further improve alignment. Remember our goal? It's *dynamic alignment* in the supply chain. Through leadership we can also achieve multiple alignment with our customers.

Given the four generic supply chains identified in Chapter 2, enterprises have to decide how many of these they are prepared to support. The *Continuous Replenishment* supply chain requires a leadership that is empathetic and consistent in the way it manages customer relationships. The *Lean* supply chain requires a more conventional albeit steady style, with the emphasis on efficiency and reliability, and no particular emphasis on external relationships. The *Agile* supply chain must be driven by a leadership style which is predominantly results-oriented with an eye to responsiveness. Finally, the *Fully Flexible* supply chain requires a leadership style that is predominantly visionary, tinged with the reality that any creativity or innovation introduced must solve a particular problem for a customer.

You will see that we have come full circle since Chapter 1. Superior alignment, leading to superior sustained performance of the enterprise, always starts with the executive leadership being close to the market. The executive has to be close enough to customers to read and interpret *all* the signals being sent their way. Think again of Lord Coe, the Chairman of London's winning bid for the 2012 Olympics. Such was his deep understanding of all stakeholder interests, he led a reversal of fortunes in the 18 months leading up to the International Olympic Committee's decision to choose London.

When leaders and their key customers and consumers are aligned, there is more than an even chance that the most appropriate strategies will be formulated, and that the underpinning subcultures so necessary to drive these into the marketplace will also be taking shape under the guidance of the same management team. Lord Coe and his bidding team still have to deliver on this last part. Look for yourself and run a test on your own enterprise using the diagnostics already introduced in this and earlier chapters; success always follows superior alignment. Since supply chains permeate all enterprises, achieving multiple alignment across an array of supply chains embedded in the business is essential if significantly higher operating and financial performance is to become a reality.

Let us consider again the thoughts of management academic Hau Lee. When he described his idea of a Triple-A supply chain, he argued that several enterprises had achieved agility, adaptability and alignment to various degrees.[35] The companies he named were Lucent, Wal-Mart, Dell, Zara, Nokia, Cisco and Toyota, and especially Seven-Eleven Japan. But the closing comment in his article is most revealing: '. . . most firms already have the infrastructure in place to create Triple-A supply chains. What they need is a fresh attitude and a new culture to get their supply chains to deliver Triple-A performance.'[36] What he did not say is that it all starts with inspired leadership! Achieving Lee's 'Triple A' status is very difficult in practice, because we are dealing with the unseen cultural forces described in Chapter 4: the powerful force of human behavior that lies beneath the surface of the *performance iceberg*. More about Triple-A in Chapter 11.

We have sought to improve our understanding of the mechanisms at work here through the new *dynamic alignment* framework and the diagnostics that we have outlined to measure the mis-alignments that could occur inside and between the organizations along complex supply chains. We are now in a position not only to describe the visible outcomes of mis-alignment, but also to identify where the mis-alignments are, predict their likely impact and design precise counter-measures. At last some control over our destiny, and now is the time to discard the *mentality of denial*, which has plagued so many enterprises to date. We need to confront and harness the human behavioral forces inside our own enterprises, because this is where the seeds of success lie.

Leadership, vision and values

How clearly have you seen leaders articulate their vision and values? I believe great leaders invariably articulate a vision for their enterprise and then visibly live this vision day-to-day as an example to staff. This vision sets boundaries for everyone in the enterprise and helps to galvanize and focus the energy of the company on key customers, suppliers and other important stakeholders. And if you agree with my assertion in Chapter

1 that *supply chains* are *the business*, then it's vital that enterprises should clearly define the role that supply chains play in delivering the overall corporate vision. If you don't develop such a vision, then the old Hungarian proverb probably applies: 'If you are always trying to be like someone else, who's going to be you?' I believe vision formulation is so important that I've developed a four-part formula for constructing a meaningful statement to guide every level of the enterprise in its daily actions. You will find this described in detail in Appendix 5A, along with two examples of operating vision statements developed for large Asia-Pacific enterprises (Appendix 5B). You can also find a more detailed treatment of this topic in my 2003 handbook on the supply chain.[37]

But how do we bring the vision to life? All companies need to draw up a corresponding set of *values* to underpin the words in the vision statement. These are the corporate values that everyone in the enterprise must sign up to. If they don't, it's highly likely they will become part of the 'internal resistance' movement in the enterprise. It is good to see that increasingly companies are making these all-important values explicit. Xerox is a good example. Xerox CEO Ann Mulcahy attributes the articulating of corporate values, and living these values, as helping her to bring the company through some tough times.[38]

Leadership, vision, values . . . they are all critical to success in business, and because supply chains permeate every business, we need to have these qualities present in equal measure, embedded in the supply chain organization.

Peter Drucker, who died in November 2005, was a giant among management thinkers. Indeed, he was arguably the greatest management thinker of the twentieth century – his ideas were always years, and sometimes decades, ahead of their time. Let's hope the legacy of insight and foresight he leaves us in an otherwise thin terrain will be used to the full by future leaders to improve the performance of their enterprises and supply chains – for the benefit of all stakeholders.

Drucker once famously said that 'there are no more advantages to big business, only disadvantages'. Why? He continues that, 'once a company rises above a certain size, the head of the organization has to rely on subordinates for what is going on – who only tell him what they want him to know'.[39] He clearly understood how difficult leadership of major enterprises was.

Defining ideas

1 Leadership of organizations must be multidimensional and contain 'biases' that truly reflect the 'biases' in customer buying behaviors.

2 When leading collaborative initiatives, certain elements of the top management team who are charged with implementing this strategy should be prepared for other parts of the organization to be pursuing opposite strategies – it's called 'ambiguity', and we have to live with it.

3 Quite simply, great business leaders intuitively understand their marketplace and the internal cultural environment of their organizations – and have an uncanny knack of getting them to align!

4 **Challenge** to the reader: do you feel that the prevailing leadership style in your firm is appropriate for the markets that you serve?

CHAPTER 6

Designing responsive organization structures

Enabling enterprise supply chains

O f all the internal capabilities in an organization, organization design is perhaps the most important, after leadership of course. The structures that we set people to work in have a major influence on the responsiveness of the enterprise. Most contemporary enterprises have fallen behind in their organizational development, and consequently their organization structures are flawed and misaligned with increasingly demanding customers and consumers.

In this chapter we go in search of new organization designs to underpin the added dynamism needed to service modern customer segments. We start with the conventional wisdom and go on to critically review the designs of the past two decades. Finally, we propose a way forward that combines the strengths of functional structures with the embedded responsiveness of customer-facing, multi-disciplinary 'clusters'.

It is true that during the past four decades, and especially the past 16 years of growth, businesses and governments around the world have fallen into the apathy trap – apathy about their real operational and financial performance. Executives in many organizations have overseen high growth, bloated profits and correspondingly extreme remuneration packages. Everything seemed to work, no matter what was tried. But lurking underneath this façade were the seeds of failure.[1] In truth, we have learned little or nothing about managing enterprises and their supply chains for sustained profitability under volatile market conditions. In retrospect, the global financial crisis of 2008–09 was inevitable – an accident waiting to happen. The very growth we had all savored so much, because it brought such wealth, has been the very condition that hindered the development of the tools and techniques we now need so urgently in this new and difficult era. It's now time to change our ways and embrace new business models, because the old ones have clearly outlived their usefulness. In short, enterprises in their predominantly siloed formats are struggling to respond to customers who are demanding ever more responsiveness. The fault lies in the way we configure our enterprises and the supply chains within them.

Looking from outside in

It never ceases to amaze me how seemingly sophisticated enterprises go about their business. They develop plans and execute operations with only scant regard for their customers' expectations and wishes. To be brutal, many of these enterprises have been guessing for years and apparently getting away with it. Well, all that is about to change. The big banks have been the first to fail, and they will be followed by many other enterprises in the real economy.

> *If anyone is still in doubt, let's be very clear: you simply cannot conduct a sustainable business over time in a volatile operating environment unless you stay very close to your customers, and in some cases the consumers or end users served by those customers. Everything starts with the customer and/or consumer.*

During the past two decades I have been developing and refining, through field work, the *dynamic alignment* model described in earlier chapters. Its time has finally come. To recap, this is a holistic Business-to-Business (B2B) concept, which involves segmenting your marketplace along behavioral lines, and then linking these customer groups to the enterprise with the appropriate value propositions. It is no more, no less than this. Underpinning these value propositions there needs to be an array of equivalent subcultures that will be capable of, and willing to, propel these strategies into the marketplace in ways that meet customers' expectations.

And behind all this action a leadership team must understand and have empathy with the marketplace. It needs to develop the appropriate value propositions or strategies to serve customers and develop the corresponding subcultures inside the organization. This concept of *dynamic alignment* is one of the most significant emerging business models today. It is relevant to enterprise supply chains because businesses are in effect just an aggregation of all the supply chains running through them – and between the parties upstream and downstream. The full array of multiple supply chains can be seen in Figure 6.1.

Working back from the marketplace, through the enterprise and back to the supply base, and forward again is such a logical way of working, and yet it is seldom embraced by enterprises in practice. Little wonder that we have so much under- and over-servicing taking place, with all the attendant consequences of increased costs and lost revenue potential. Forget about taking the soap out of the bathroom and cancelling the papers in these tough times. Focus seriously on re-aligning your business (and its supply chains) with customers, suppliers and third parties and you will survive most crises.

Organization design as a major shaper of culture

I introduced the *dynamic alignment* concept in earlier chapters as a major new business model that will revolutionize the way we work. However, my main focus in this chapter is on just one facet of the model – organization structure – as we shape and mold the appropriate subcultures inside the enterprise to enable effective linkages with our customers.

Having discovered through rigorous empirical observations over many years that there are usually no more than three or four dominant customer buying behaviors in most markets,[2] we can extrapolate this finding into the equivalent three or four supply chain configurations. I have named these configurations: *continuous replenishment, lean, agile* and *fully flexible*. Other variations around these four types exist, as described in Chapter 2, but are not as common. Figure 6.2 depicts the characteristics of these four common supply chains.[3]

As explained in Chapter 4, these very different configurations require equally disparate subcultures to propel them into the marketplace, and

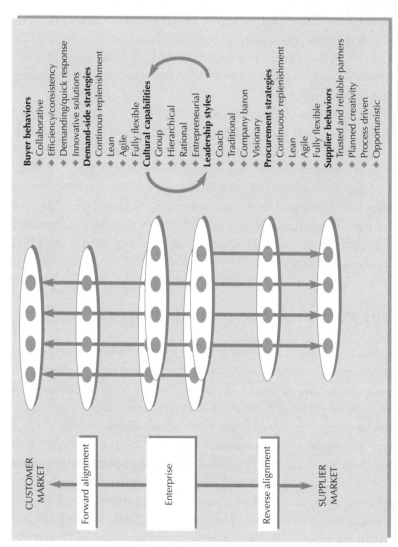

Buyer behaviors
- Collaborative
- Efficiency/consistency
- Demanding/quick response
- Innovative solutions

Demand-side strategies
- Continous replenishment
- Lean
- Agile
- Fully flexible

Cultural capabilities
- Group
- Hierarchical
- Rational
- Entrepreneurial

Leadership styles
- Coach
- Traditional
- Company baron
- Visionary

Procurement strategies
- Continuous replenishment
- Lean
- Agile
- Fully flexible

Supplier behaviors
- Trusted and reliable partners
- Planned creativity
- Process driven
- Opportunistic

CUSTOMER MARKET

Forward alignment

Enterprise

Reverse alignment

SUPPLIER MARKET

FIGURE 6.1 ◆ **Supply-side alignment – mirror image of the demand-side**

Source: Adapted from Figure 3.5.2 in Gattorna (2003), p. 346

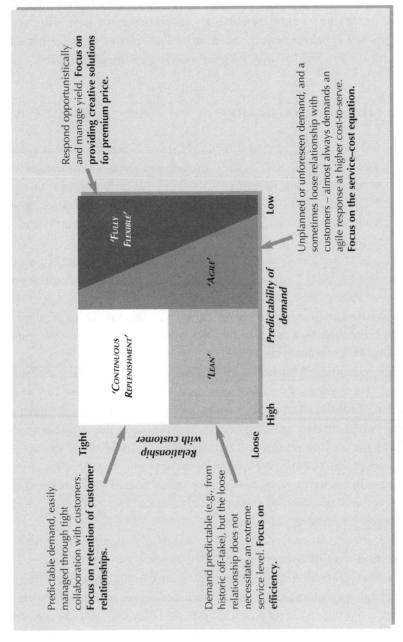

FIGURE 6.2 ◆ The four generic supply chain types

Source: Adapted from Figure 2.3 in Gattorna (2006), p. 43, supplemented by ideas from Marc Van der Veer, Dow Corning

one of the biggest factors in shaping the necessary array of subcultures is organization design. Why? Because to be truly effective and aligned with customers and suppliers alike, an enterprise must have different organizational capabilities embedded in it. The days of one-size-fits-all organizational structure are just as 'gone' as one-size-fits-all products!

From silos to silo busting

Perhaps the best recent historical review of the different types of organizational structures deployed in the logistics and supply chain arena is by Soo Wook Kim.[4] He identified five organization types as follows: the non SCM-oriented organization, the functional organization, the matrix channel organization, the process staff organization and the integrated line organization.

But none of these designs had the customer in mind; indeed, they were all internally focused. I am not interested in exploring these organization structures further because they are largely irrelevant to today's operating environment, which demands we move away from thinking of supply chain as a function and embrace the idea that it is more of an operating philosophy for the whole enterprise.

Ranjay Gulati goes further in his seminal paper on what he calls 'silo busting.'[5] He analyzes such companies as GE Healthcare, Best Buy and Jones Lang LaSalle, all of which have had significant success with organizational structures that are designed around customer needs rather than internally focused dimensions. The big mistake identified by Gulati is that 'many product-centric companies probably start out with a focus on customers. But after early successes, they institutionalize the notion that markets respond primarily to great products and services.'[6] Wrong! If ever that was true, it certainly isn't true now.

If we search more widely in the world of organizational theorists we find Gareth Morgan's work. His classic 2006 study *Images of Organization*[7] provides a much richer and more eclectic perspective using such metaphors as 'organizations as machines; organizations as (living) organisms; organizations as political systems'. Although not specifically directed at supply chains, his work provides useful insights into how we might re-conceptualize supply chain structures to do the tasks required of them today. It's a pity that designers of supply chain configurations have not invoked his work more widely. In any event we are left with the impression from Morgan that the way organizations should shape their supply chain structures involves integrating more into the overall business design, and I agree with this proposition.

Atomization of organizations

In the 1980s, I observed McKinsey & Company experimenting with a radical new form of organization design called 'atomization.'[8] This concept involved breaking up the organization into small groupings to force accountability across the conglomerate of which they were part. However, this led to unexpected inefficiencies and duplication, together with in-house competition and ultimately destruction of shareholder value. McKinsey tried the atomized configuration at BP, Fletcher Challenge (NZ) and Carter Holt Harvey (NZ), but the attempts failed to produce positive results. From a supply chain perspective, it is easy to see why. Supply chain management is about integrating processes **across** organizations, whether in real or virtual terms, and the atomization concept went in the opposite direction by fragmenting the organization, albeit for some sound business reasons.

More recently, McKinsey & Company has again broached the topic of organization design, but their focus has been on seeking ways to make people inside organizations more productive rather than seeking to satisfy customers, as can be gleaned from the following quote:

Today's big companies do very little to enhance the productivity of their professionals. In fact, their vertically oriented organizational structures, retrofitted with ad hoc and matrix overlays, nearly always make professional work more complex and inefficient. These vertical structures – relics of the industrial age – are singularly ill-suited to the professional work process. Professionals co-operate horizontally with one another throughout a company, yet vertical structures force such men and women to search across poorly connected organizational silos to find knowledge and collaborators to gain their cooperation once they have been found.[9]

I agree with many of these sentiments, but the point McKinsey & Company missed is that if you are able to achieve superior alignment with your customers, it's very likely that the internal processes by definition will be more productive.

The 'adaptive' organization

The Boston Consulting Group joined the debate in 2005 when it suggested that 'an adaptive organization that interprets and acts on new signals coming from the marketplace' was the way forward.[10] Interestingly, their suggested approach has undertones of my own *dynamic alignment* model.

Peter Robertson came next when he proposed the adaptive supply chain, involving a linked set of adaptive agents constituting a network.[11] Robertson suggested that 'supply chain actions are adapted in order to best achieve specified goals. A mix of top-down and bottom-up optimization principles aligns local goals with overall goals.'[12]

The customer drives the organization

However, George Day provided some prophetic insights back in 1999. He outlined four principles that he saw as essential to underpin his claim that the customer drives the organization. The principles are:[13]

1 *Firms will increasingly evolve towards a* hybrid *or hypertext form of organization, combining the best features of horizontal process and vertical functional forms – in order to get closer to their customers.* (Day's words are relevant as this is exactly what I will be recommending later in this chapter.)

2 *There will be a great deal of variety in the hybrid designs that are adopted, depending on the alignment of the value strategy and the core capabilities that are exercised in the processes. This will dictate the relative importance of staff groups, functional specialists and process teams.* (In my view, the variety is determined by the make-up of the customer groups being served, as defined by behavioral segments.)

3 *Advances in data networks will permit firms to link internal teams for better, faster decision-making, and to devise more interactive strategies that use information* from *the customer rather than about the customer* (using data mining techniques).

4 *As strategies become more interactive, leading to increased dialogue and collaboration with customers and (distribution) channels, there must be greater dispersion of information and decision-making throughout the organization.*

The idea of the customer driving the organization sounds a bit like my golf pro Gary Barter who is often heard to say during golf lessons, 'the left arm drives the company', meaning the left arm (for a right-handed player) leads the golf swing and is therefore largely responsible for the resulting flight of the ball! Certainly Day was spot on with all four of his principles, a decade ahead of this book.

Self-managed teams

One major experiment in how to structure the way people work was started by Ricardo Semler at Semco in Brazil some 15 years ago and reported in both his books in 1993 and 2003.[14] Semler believed in 'participative management' where the workers rather than management would devise strategies and execute them. His suggested organizational structure was unorthodox, akin to putting the inmates in charge of the asylum, but as noted author Charles Handy once commented, 'the way Ricardo Semler runs his company is impossible; except it works, and works splendidly for everyone.'[15] Semler's goal was to develop the creativity of his workers, which normally would have been suppressed in more conventional organizational models. Interestingly, Semco is still thriving today, but few if any other corporations have followed his lead and adopted a similar structure.

Drawing on similar principles the Irizar Group, a Spanish-based global bus/coach building company, has prospered during the past few decades. Here too, the company works 'through self-managed multi-disciplinary teams which are integrated into the main process (from thinking about customer/market at one end, to end of life of the supplied coach)'.[16]

Similarly one of the world's leading retailers, Best Buy, has already adopted this *modus operandi*, with local store employees being empowered to make decisions on the spot, leading to 'an agile, demand-driven supply chain that can react to decisions made at widely distributed localities, not just at centralized higher levels'.[17]

Fashion apparel companies first to break the mold

The first enterprises to break with convention were the fast fashion apparel companies. They had to survive in the hot house of near real-time competition and functional organizational models simply lacked the necessary agility in this environment. The fast fashion enterprises hit the 'unpredictability ceiling' well before most other industries. One name stands out – Zara.

Zara has achieved wonders in the fickle world of fashion by showing how an enterprise can become more responsive to its customers than any of its competitors. The Spanish-based company achieved this without any special new technology or hidden processes. In the end it has been all about the way Zara's management has mixed the recipe with otherwise known ingredients.

Zara has put in place cross-functional teams to manage the design, production and delivery of different apparel ranges to their target markets in women's fashion, men's fashion and children's wear. These teams work closely with store managers in the Zara retail chain and are co-located to facilitate rapid communications. The result: Zara is able to process a garment from sketch on paper to product in the store in 15 working days, while no competitor can get anywhere near that. Postponement techniques are invoked, coupled with *lean* supply chains on the in-bound side, but the result is an 'agile' response to the changing fashion whims of their consumers. It is a great success story, and one still in the making.

Organizing around brands

Vanity Fair, the US branded lifestyle apparel company based in Greenboro, NC, uses what it terms 'cross-coalition' teams to speed up its responsiveness to customers worldwide. In the process, VF Corporation has effectively transformed itself from a manufacturing business (owning machines) to a sourcing business (owning brands) in less than a decade.

Icon Clothing, a business unit within Pacific Brands, one of Australia's biggest apparel manufacturers, has adopted a similar approach. It was established in 1994 and has grown rapidly, positioning itself as a branded youth manufacturing, marketing and distribution company. The company describes itself as a 'house of brands', many of them secured under licence from VF Corporation.

The *dynamic alignment* model for the supply chain was introduced into the company at the instigation of Joint Managing Director Stephen Little and Operations Manager Kathryn Bolger. It had previously used a conventional, functional organization design, but following a pivotal workshop in March 2006 the company changed its structure from functions to 'brand clusters' once it established the customer buying behavior for each of its eight brands.

The new configuration, depicted in Figure 6.3, is working well, and has significantly increased the tempo of operations throughout the company.

Decathlon, a French company and leader in sports products in Europe has also adopted a cluster design around each of its brands, e.g., Tribord, Quechua, Inesis and Geologic. The company mixes designers with other functional specialists to improve the product innovation process, and has been very successful as a result. The company name has become synonymous with innovation, quality, design and performance.

The industrial world is doing it too

Aera Energy LLC is a self-sufficient, full-service oil and gas company based in California. Formed in 1997 using assets jointly owned by Shell and Exxon Mobil, the enterprise was established to extract oil from 'brownfields,' or old oil fields being re-charged so more oil can be extracted, and do so safely and at a low cost.

To achieve this objective Aera adopted a radically different approach to project management and a similarly different attitude towards its

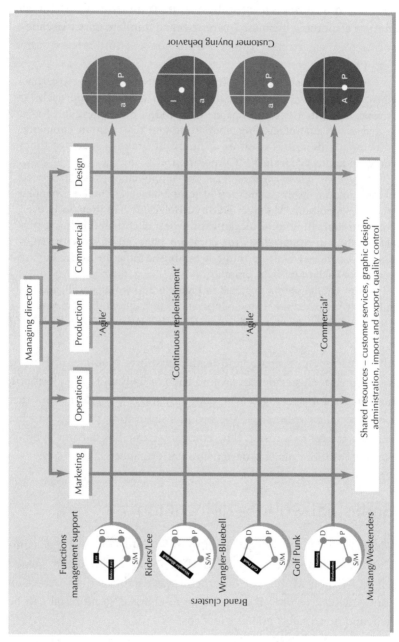

FIGURE 6.3 ◆ Organization design at Icon Clothing

Source: M. Nobhandhu, unpublished MBA research paper, MGSM, 2008

suppliers.[18] In particular, the company introduced a variant of the cluster organization design discussed above, which they called their 'daisy' organization structure. This structure focused and brought together all the processes in a particular project, from concept to implementation. Features of the daisy were:

◆ cross-functional teams;

◆ all team members focused on particular process outcomes; and

◆ suppliers included as accountable team members.

The results have been nothing short of startling. The on-site extraction project at Belridge in California produced a 47 per cent reduction in drilling and completion costs, while achieving a similar reduction in health, safety, and environment costs. Relentless execution led to these outstanding results, and the organization design was a prime reason for the success achieved in an otherwise difficult industrial operating environment.

Guidewire, a software company serving the global insurance industry, managed to gain a dominant position through the development of a new project management process called Scrum.[19] At the core of the Scrum methodology is the so-called Sprint team. Each team is small and nimble, with no more than nine members.

Every Scrum project starts with an understanding of the customer's vision – what outcome does he or she want? The customer and development team defines the requirements to deliver this vision. The development team works for 30 days (the Sprint) to meet as many of the stated requirements as possible. Meanwhile the customer continues to refine his or her vision to deliver the required business result.

At the end of the first and every succeeding Sprint, customer and development teams review progress to check if expected business value is being delivered.

Finally, at some point the customer will stop the development process and the software product will be refined and released for wider use in the business. In this way, the customer is able to steer cost date and business value on a continuous basis.

So is the US military

The United States military are seeking similar gains in responsiveness through a design they call 'jointness' or 'going purple'. These terms refer to the situation where two or more armed services seek to integrate their respective strategies, strengths and capabilities in ways that lead to effective synergies and improved performance in the field.[20] The inter-service operations are known as 'purple' operations because that is the color formed when the colors of the uniforms of the different armed services are combined. Now that is synergy!

Extreme organization design

Perhaps the best example of organization structures working at their maximum while under extreme pressure is in Formula One motor sport. Mark Jenkins espouses the principles that success in Formula One is built on:[21]

1 *Continuously improve in every way, every day, no let up.*

2 *Team work and integration . . . working together to drive down costs and enhance customer experience. It's not about the engine or the chassis – it's Ferrari.* (Here Jenkins is talking about Ferrari's success in particular.)

3 *The driver is just part of the team.*

You will see a telling picture of the Formula One pit stop in Chapter 9.

The 'common thread' in all these success stories

All the success stories of fast, responsive organizational configurations have a common thread running through them. They all involve some type of cross-functional team design, composed of personnel with interdisciplinary capabilities, all focused on a common objective, and given incentives through joint KPIs that hold the team together under pressure.

What has become clear is that (vertical) functional silos on their own do not work because they are at least 90 degrees out of phase with the way customers buy (horizontally, across functions). It is encouraging therefore that recent research is surfacing to suggest that companies are at last beginning to recognize the critical importance of cross-functional teams.[22]

This research found that 'the use of cross-functional teams will be an important supply management strategy because they provide a broader base of knowledge for decision-making and can lead to decisions that take into account the needs of all the stakeholders in the organization.'[23]

Fletcher Challenge Energy, a major New Zealand-based company came to the same conclusion a decade earlier, with the formation of 'market work teams'.[24] These work teams focused on operational issues and were comprised of key decision makers across several functions. These teams were charged with the shared responsibility of meeting customer service expectations, while maintaining optimum inventories. Most importantly, they were empowered to manage operating issues and consequently were very responsive to the company's customers.

On reflection it is obvious that, with a few exceptions, we became apathetic in the 1970s and 1980s, thinking we had all the answers. Then when organizations began to recognize functional silos were not the panacea after all, we tried what turned out to be a series of weak structural solutions that just did not deliver the desired results.

Perhaps the only enterprises that did 'get it' were management consulting firms. Enterprises such as Andersen Consulting (subsequently Accenture), have long understood that you need **both** the vertical functional specialties to build capabilities and competences **and** the horizontal teams of mixed disciplines with which to go to market and solve individual client problems. From their successes we can conclude that you need **BOTH** vertical silos of specialists **AND** horizontal teams of mixed disciplines focused on customers, with the exact mix being determined by a particular customer's requirements and/or situation. And this brings us full circle back to the business of enterprise supply chains.

The solution is more than just 'teaming'

Something else is going on here, and Henry Mintzberg understood this almost three decades ago when he defined his five organizational configurations.[25] According to Mintzberg, 'some organizations do indeed achieve and maintain an internal consistency. But then they find that it is designed for an (operating) environment the organization is no longer in. To have a nice neat machine-like bureaucracy in a dynamic industry calling for constant innovation or, alternatively, a flexible adhocracy in a stable industry calling for minimum cost, makes no sense. Remember that these are configurations of situation as well as structure.'[26]

Mintzberg goes on to say that

> *essentially, the organization has two choices. It can adapt continuously to the (operating) environment at the expense of internal consistency – that is, steadily re-design its structure to maintain external fit (for this read alignment). Or it can maintain internal consistency at the expense of a gradually worsening fit with its environment, at least until the fit becomes so bad that it must undergo a sudden structural re-design to achieve a new internally consistent configuration.*[27]

In my view there is a 'third way' and that is to hard-wire the business with three or four pre-prepared supply chain configurations that will provide sufficient coverage as customers change their buying behaviors. Each of these configurations will be explored in great detail in Chapters 7 to 10.

New supply chain organization designs: the *best-of-the-best*

What we sorely need at this critical time in history are fundamentally new supply chain organization designs: a new breed of designs that are capable of operating under volatile, sometimes extreme, market conditions. In this regard we have two role models to follow. In particular, the Li & Fung model is a good example because it embraces both demand-side and supply-side elements of the supply chain.

Li & Fung, the supply chain service company based in Hong Kong, is perhaps the consummate example of using organization design to power growth. The Fung brothers coined the phrase 'network orchestrator' in their book, *Competing in a Flat World*.[28] The Fungs transformed the original trading business through rapid acquisitions and by developing a completely new business model in the form of multi-disciplinary clusters, much as I am recommending. See what can be achieved if you break the old model!

Li & Fung created 300 customer-oriented multi-disciplinary clusters (variously called 'tribes' or 'little John Waynes'). Each of these clusters of 50 to 60 people focus on one or more customers and deliver revenue of $20 million to $70 million.

On the customer side of the supply chain they have developed a genuinely customer-centric organization structure; and on the supply side these clusters focus on managing and indeed owning the relationships with nearly 10,000 factories worldwide. Li & Fung, therefore, are effectively the largest manufacturer in the world – and yet they don't own a single factory! Victor Fung feels their success in this 'asset lite' business all boils down to managing the conglomeration of relationships at the front and back ends of their supply chains. The IT systems protect and nurture the relationships, and the 'rainmakers' create new relationships.

Victor Fung[29] believes that because these 'relationships' are so delicate, they can easily be destroyed. According to Fung, 'if the PH level (read culture) is wrong, it kills the relationship; it's as biological as that!' With a very strong focus on customers, and an equally strong focus on supplier relationships, Li & Fung effectively orchestrate hundreds, perhaps thousands of supply chains linking suppliers and customers to each other around the world.

More than anything else, the great success they are now experiencing comes from the organization design which by its very nature focuses personnel 'on business challenges instead of functional (issues) that dominate in so many large organizations'.[30] Each of these clusters is inter-disciplinary; full of self-starters; and highly incentivized through a remuneration package that is heavily weighted towards results achievement. Each cluster acts like the owner of their respective business, and is held to the central organization by a strong set of corporate values and financial disciplines. This is truly a success story quite unlike any other. But even here improvements and refinements are possible, and we will get to that discussion a little later in the chapter.

The other company to watch is Adidas. In the run up to the 2006 FIFA World Cup in Germany, management at Adidas decided they had to design and implement a more responsive supply chain to capture the value of being one of the major sponsors of the four-yearly event. Traditionally Adidas had needed a lead time of 120 days to supply replica soccer shirts from a standing start. Management knew that this would not be good enough for the 2006 World Cup.

Jay Pollard, Lars Sorensen and their teams set about breaking old business practices and replace them with a much faster, more responsive model.[31] Here's how they did it:

♦ set about to instill a mindset change;

♦ developed cross-functional, fully integrated teams involving representatives from all disciplines;

♦ co-located the newly formed teams in the same building, called 'the World of Football', three years before the 2006 event; and

♦ organized sourcing offices around the world into similar cross-functional clusters.

The new regime was road-tested at the 2004 European Cup, with incredible results. For example, 35,000 Greece replica shirts were produced in 20 days following Greece's unexpected win in the Cup final. This was an 80 per cent improvement over previous lead times!

Adidas found that the new organization design allowed it to scale up and down faster – providing much greater flexibility than previously thought possible.

Overall, the experiment taught them that by forming an end-to-end integrated supply chain with multi-disciplinary clusters of personnel (from design to shelf and into the customers' hands) and throwing out the old 'silo' system, the operational and financial benefits were immense. Adidas now plans to replicate this method at future major sporting events.

It comes as no surprise, therefore, that sales increased 52 per cent in 2006, to a record €10.08 billion boosted by the Soccer World Cup and the acquisition of Reebok.[32] However, Adidas will have to accelerate the roll-out of this new model if its 2008-09 fiscal results are anything to go on. The burden of absorbing the Reebok takeover is taking its toll.[33]

And the experimentation continues as we explore potentially new organization designs. Three more short case studies are described below;[34] all are examples of *fully flexible* supply chains, largely competing on the basis of their innovative products.

Oticon is a Danish hi-tech company and one of the world's leading producers of hearing aids. The company, established in 1904, exhibited a very typical hierarchical organization structure that included 'formal procedures, a conservative culture, employee loyalty, and consensus-seeking conflict-avoiding behaviors.'[35]

The company went through difficult times in the 1980s, and as is so often the pattern, a new CEO, Lars Kolind, was appointed in 1988 and given the mandate to turn things around.

He reorganized the company and replaced the old hierarchical structures with a project team-based structure. The enterprise effectively became two-tiered; top management decided which projects should be undertaken and appointed the project leaders. In turn, these project leaders took full responsibility for managing all resources, budgets and outcomes. Open communication and free exchange of ideas were encouraged under this new regime, and Oticon consequently earned the reputation for having a 'spaghetti' structure.[36] Interestingly, the physical layout of the office was changed to symbolize the change in philosophy, a new trend we have discussed in our chapter on culture formation and implementation, Chapter 4.

Wendy Sadler-Moyes is in no doubt why Oticon was subsequently so successful, and still is. In her words, the answer lies in 'the change orchestrated by Lars Kolind to a fully flexible organizational structure, so bringing the company into dynamic alignment with the needs if [its] customers.'[37]

Continuing the innovation theme, W.L. Gore & Associates is best known for its innovative and technically advanced products, particularly its GORE-TEX fabric. The company uses a similar spaghetti-style organization structure to that of Oticon, where the primary aim is to cultivate a work environment in which creativity can flourish and is rewarded. Multi-disciplinary teams of associates (not employees) are formed around opportunities, and leaders emerge naturally. The company founder, Bill Gore, was convinced that organizations should to be limited to 150 to 200 people arranged in clusters in close proximity to each other so they could at least share any 'expensive resources'.

Finally, Chaparral Steel was the tenth largest US steel producer before being acquired by Gerdau Ameristeel in 2007. Gerdau is a Brazilian steel company. Chaparral Steel's culture promotes problem-solving, innovation and experimentation; it has a horizontal organization structure that encourages its employees to innovate.[38]

All three of the above examples place an emphasis on innovation, which can be easily satisfied with a *fully flexible* supply chain. They do not, however, provide solutions for the other buying behaviors, and as such their usefulness is limited.

Contemporary designs now on the drawing board

If it is true that there are a limited number of variants in the dominant buying behaviors of customers, and that we mostly see the same three or four types irrespective of the product or service category, then the way forward becomes clearer. Now we can have the *best of both worlds*: strong functional specialism embedded in vertical silos, where specific capabilities are developed and reside, and customer-centric teams composed of representatives of all the appropriate functions or disciplines necessary to fully align with customer expectations. This is an 'and' world not an 'either/or' world.

So for those relatively few customers who we have identified as genuinely collaborative, we will engage the *continuous replenishment* supply chain, driven by clusters of personnel seconded from the vertical functions. And here is the twist. Not only will all the functions be represented in these clusters (or teams), but we have the opportunity to engineer the mindset of these clusters by taking into account the values of each team member recruited to the cluster. It is not simply a matter of having all the technical skills covered – the correct embedded bias in the team is just as important. This refinement goes beyond what Li & Fung is doing with its 'tribes,' but it is a necessary refinement to get maximum alignment with the customer's mindset, in this case driven by relationship values. See Figure 6.4 for a schematic representation.

Notice the solid line drawn connecting the customer-centric relationship clusters; they are accountable for meeting customer expectations, and the functions are there to provide support as required. The customer-centric clusters, however many there are, all report to a line executive, most probably the COO or Global Customer Solutions Director. No more dotted lines for the customer-facing teams!

However, to service those customers in the 'efficiency/ price sensitive' segment we need something very different. Here the emphasis is on refining the various processes involved to deliver the lowest possible cost-to-serve via the *lean* supply chain configuration. See Figure 6.5 overleaf for a schematic representation.

As in the case of the *continuous replenishment* supply chain configuration detailed above, multi-disciplinary clusters are formed. However, this time each cluster focuses on a major process rather than a customer, and

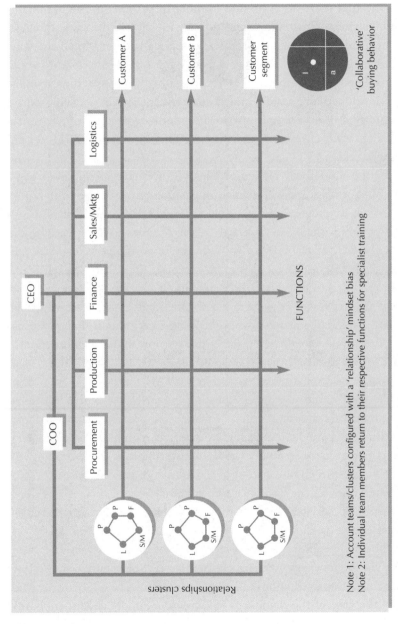

FIGURE 6.4 ◆ *Continuous replenishment* supply chain clusters

Source: Adapted from Figure 9.2 in Gattorna (2009), p. 140

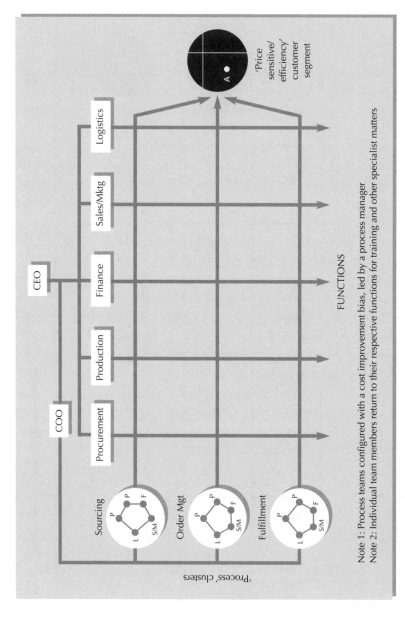

FIGURE 6.5 ◆ *Lean supply chain clusters*

Source: Adapted from Figure 9.3 in Gattorna (2009), p. 140

Note 1: Process teams configured with a cost improvement bias, led by a process manager
Note 2: Individual team members return to their respective functions for training and other specialist matters

the various processes come together to deliver the lowest cost and most consistent service possible for the particular target segment.

In order to satisfy those customers who demand a quick response in an otherwise unpredictable marketplace, we need something different again. In this situation the multi-disciplinary clusters are designed for speed, and the bias embedded in the *agile* supply chains serving these demanding customers is just that – absolute speed. It is very much like what Zara has done so successfully and the Formula One race teams. See Figure 6.6 for a schematic representation.

It is possible that there will be sub-sets of the 'demanding/speed' segment as depicted in Figure 6.6. For example Zara has to service the demand for fashion in three different sub-segments: women's, men's and children's wear.

Finally, in cases of unexpected events or crises, the *fully flexible* supply chain configuration is required to deliver innovative solutions, super fast. See Figure 6.7 overleaf for a schematic representation.

There may only be one cluster necessary to service the 'innovative solutions' segment and this could be composed of part-time members or volunteers, who only come together in times of an emergency. The individuals in this cluster are likely to be highly trained multi-talented personnel, capable of quick thinking and quicker action. There are plenty of examples of this type of structure in aid and military organizations around the world. A recent example is the voluntary fire-fighting crews that fought the large-scale bush fires in Victoria, Australia during the summer of 2009.

Bringing it all together

Based on all that we have said in this chapter, it is clear that any given supply chain has an upstream supply-side component and a downstream demand-side component, as depicted in different ways in Figure 6.1 earlier in the chapter and Figure 6.8 overleaf. The upstream or supply-side is focused on procurement and managing the inbound flow of materials into the production process. The downstream or demand-side is focused on sensing the type and levels of demand coming from consumers and customers in the target marketplace, and working out which supply chain type is best configured to satisfy such demand.

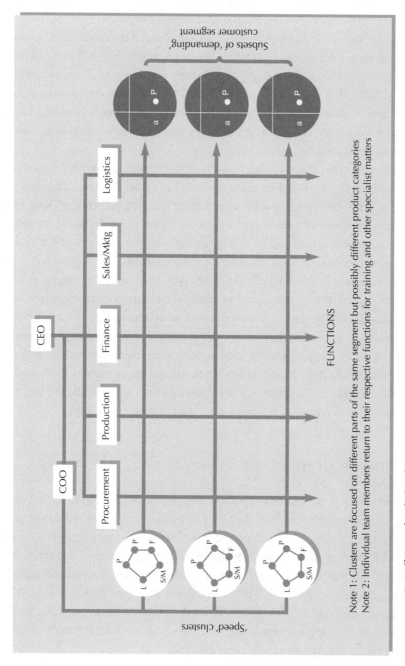

FIGURE 6.6 ◆ *Agile supply chain clusters*

Note 1: Clusters are focused on different parts of the same segment but possibly different product categories
Note 2: Individual team members return to their respective functions for training and other specialist matters

Source: Adapted from Figure 9.4 in Gattorna (2009), p. 141

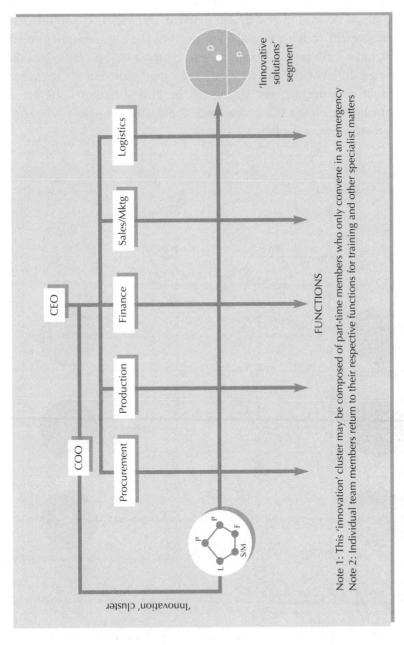

FIGURE 6.7 ◆ Fully flexible supply chain cluster

Source: Adapted from Figure 9.5 in Gattorna (2009), p. 141

The key is to have in place internal organizational clusters that power the different types of supply chain configurations (upstream and downstream) based on customer demand patterns and supply capabilities. It is also important to have in place internal linkage mechanisms to connect the various clusters in situations where supply chains are 'hybrid' in nature, i.e., different characteristics on the supply-side and the demand-side, which is quite a normal occurrence. This situation is depicted schematically in Figure 6.8 but we will explore this notion of 'hybrid' supply chains in more depth in Chapter 13.

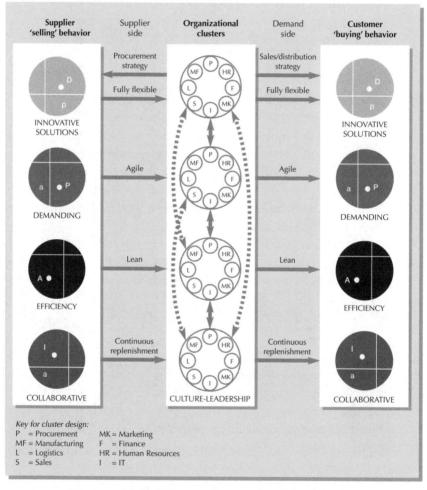

FIGURE 6.8 ◆ A new and dynamic organizational model for supply chains of the future

Source: Adapted from Figure 9.6 in Gattorna (2009), p. 143

And when it comes to implementation

It is one thing to design a new organization structure, and quite another to implement it with real people on the ground. Care has to be exercised, because what is being suggested is a whole new way of working and one that involves a big change to many of the individuals involved. We have found from experience that the following approach works.

1   **Select cluster leadership**
    - If possible, select a cluster leader with the appropriate experience and an MBTI which is aligned to the target customer segment;
    - If not available currently, you may have to either recruit someone or place strong emphasis on particular KPIs to drive the required outcomes;

2   **Build bias into cluster membership**
    - Satisfy functional and experience requirements first; but
    - Include people with appropriate MBTIs wherever possible to create a bias in the direction of the customer segment logic (but avoid the situation where everyone in the cluster has similar MBTIs);
    - Treat the first cut of the clusters as a Draft to be finalised after consequent operational and capability issues are explored, especially the balance between Focus and achieving Synergy; this matter can be openly discussed in a workshop;
    - In an SME, it is possible that some key personnel will have to play pivotal roles in more than one cluster, or in a cluster plus one of the shared services (such as IT, HR and Finance).

Defining ideas

1   Current organization designs for enterprise supply chains are fundamentally flawed, because they assume a one-size-fits-all world. They need urgent retro-fitting with more responsive configurations to keep pace with increasingly demanding customers.

2   It is impossible to separate overall enterprise organization structures and supply chain structures – they are one and the same thing.

3   The only successful way to design supply chain organization structures is to work from the 'outside in', i.e., to segment the marketplace along

behavioral lines (Chapter 2), and then try to mirror these segments with a corresponding structure on the inside of the enterprise.

4 Ultimately, it is necessary to have two structures that co-exist and support each other to properly service a disparate market. First are the vertical functions that train personnel in particular fields and build capabilities. And second are the multi-disciplinary and multi-functional customer-centric clusters, where personnel are seconded as needed to suit the particular customer group.

5 If this prescription is followed, organizations will make a successful transition from an inward-looking focus on individual silo productivity, to a broadly accepted philosophy where clusters representing all these silos will readily work together to align with customers, so satisfying all the key stakeholders, internal and external.

6 Conversion of the selected organization design into an actual structure on the ground requires sensitivity and openness by executive leadership, and is best undertaken in a series of workshops involving all key personnel. Co-location of personnel in each cluster is vital to ensure the mix of disciplines involved actually communicate in real time.

7 **Challenge** to the reader: do you think your organization structure is still appropriate for the customers/markets you serve these days?

CHAPTER 7

Continuous replenishment supply chains: demand-side

Where relationships matter most

This is the first of a quartet of chapters in which we describe the configuration of each supply chain type in detail; you will not be left guessing about what we think about collaboration and its corresponding supply chain type. *Continuous replenishment* supply chains are special, but they are not for everyone. Indeed, this chapter will help to de-bunk many of the myths currently going around about 'collaboration'. Above all, our advice is to identify those customers who deserve a special relationship and make sure you retain them. After all, they are your best and most sustainable source of revenue and margin. In this respect, make use of the available technology (CRM) to manage deserving customers in a consistent way, and in return be rewarded by their loyalty. Finally, we introduce the notion that emerging consumer concerns about sustainability and corporate social responsibility in enterprise supply chains are in effect a subset and indeed a subsegment of the 'collaborative' (Ia) customer segment; ignore their growing influence at your peril.

Can you spot a *continuous replenishment* supply chain at 100 metres? It is the type of supply chain where customers are loyal and, in return, expect a high level of commitment and service. The *continuous replenishment* supply chain has its highs and lows when it comes to demand, but all members of the supply chain seek to satisfy demand in the most cost-effective way.

Possibly the most distinctive characteristic of the *continuous replenishment* supply chain is that customers are truly collaborative in their buying behavior. You know you're in a *continuous replenishment* supply chain when all parties, including third-party providers, work as one to lower costs, meet demand and continuously improve delivery times and service. A happy end-customer for one is a happy customer for all!

Are we dreaming? No. Take a look at the Campbell Soup Company, which was one of the early innovators when it conceived and implemented its continuous (product) replenishment (CPR) program in the early 1990s.[1] Working with its main retail and wholesale customers, Campbell's worked to reduce the impact of demand fluctuations caused by its retailers' forward buying for promotional purposes. Such buying led to inefficiencies in Campbell's production and logistics processes and inflated the retailers' own costs for storage and handling. A later version of this program, CPR2, recognized that market conditions required a combination of *continuous replenishment* (low-cost production) and *agile* (promotional) supply chains, and the program was implemented mainly through changing pricing policies. We'll talk more about mixing supply chains in Chapter 13.

A more contemporary example can be found at Joe White Maltsters, a division of Adelaide-based ABB Grain (now Viterra), one of Australia's leading grain trading and handling companies. Every year, Joe White locks in more than 55 per cent of its production of 450,000 tonnes at the start of the year. Over time it has developed very collaborative relationships with six major Asian breweries, which take on average 50,000 tonnes of malt each per year, at negotiated prices, locked-in via firm contracts for up to four years ahead. These breweries provide updated forecasts three months in advance and re-set shipping schedules every two weeks. As a result Joe White knows exactly what to produce when, and ships a steady stream of malt in grain form by container to a regular, pre-agreed shipping schedule each year. Thousands of them! These are dream customers, and a superb example of a *continuous replenishment* supply chain in action.[2]

Customers are forgiving – up to a point!

First, let's look at the customers in the *continuous replenishment* market in more detail. They are largely predictable in their buying behavior; they demand regular delivery of mostly mature products and services. These customers normally like to buy from one or two suppliers only, and loyalty is taken very seriously. This is not a market that easily embraces risk taking. Trust is uppermost in the supply chain relationship. Members of the *continuous replenishment* supply chain readily enter into partnerships and joint-development projects, and freely share information that will help the common cause of improved performance. Collaborative buying behaviors also tend to be very forgiving, and customers with this mindset will put up with a lot, including being ignored at times. But they will only do so for a limited time, after which they are likely to go to the opposite type of behavior and become adversarial and very demanding.

How can you capture the potential of these customers? The most important thing is to discover which of your customers are truly 'collaborative' and then look after them with all the care you can muster. Unfortunately, that is easier said than done. Companies rarely get a second chance to restore their relationships in a *continuous replenishment* supply chain without spending a tremendous amount of time and money. Enterprises are often poor at differentiating which customers deserve their priority attention and, as a result, have lost some of their best long-term (and profitable) customers. Some don't even realize it at the time. Leading credit card companies such as American Express and Diners Club are prime examples of this phenomenon. They don't appear to follow up customers and ask them why they are no longer using their card or other services. It seems extraordinary that this should happen, but it's not actually that surprising. Companies lose their focus on collaborative customers because these customers are not overly concerned about price, their cost-to-serve is relatively low and margins are generally good. In other words, they are easy to take for granted! All that these customers crave is recognition, and preferential treatment based on strong personal relationships. They are prepared to trade off other service parameters to achieve this. But ignore them at your peril.

Why else do you think companies lose their focus on important collaborative customers? It's not only that these customers are easily overlooked. It's because enterprises become preoccupied with the **other** categories of customers, particularly those who are especially demanding and time consuming. You could call these customers the Exocets of the commercial world, because they suddenly appear from 'out of the blue' and are highly destructive on contact. We will talk more about their behavior in Chapter 9, but suffice it to say that companies seeking to avoid an Exocet strike will often provide erratic over- and under-servicing of these difficult customers. However, the result is deteriorating performance for customers overall. Unfortunately, suppliers respond inappropriately to customers every day. The trick is to recognize who are your most important customers and therefore who deserves the most attention. Fonterra, the New Zealand-based world number four dairy ingredient company is a case in point.

In 2001, when global dairy ingredients company Fonterra segmented its 3,300 business customers across 100+ countries along behavioral lines, it found that 25 per cent of its customers by number, and 40 per cent by volume, were exhibiting collaborative buying behavior tendencies. But no one at Fonterra was aware of this, and the revelation came as a shock. Consequently, many of its best and most loyal customers were not being given the appropriate attention, and previously good business relationships were souring.

You want what, when?

Of course, leading companies sometimes don't mind being asked to deliver on challenging requests. Demanding customers can stretch their performance and create new standards – for the better. But you have to know when and at what point the extra response is justified. The characteristics of *continuous replenishment* supply chains (or base flow, as defined in Chapter 2) are the mirror image of customers' collaborative buying behaviors; it's as simple as that. The whole emphasis is on gradually building deep and sustainable relationships with customers that exhibit genuine collaborative values. Reliability and trustworthiness are essential ingredients for success in this type of supply chain, because customers greatly value these qualities. You need to respond in a requisite way: not too much or too little, but just enough. I call this *requisite collaboration*.

The customers see value in entering into long-term strategic partnerships because they can secure the certainty and stability for which they are always yearning. Information is freely exchanged in both directions when this relationship is established. The customers provide forecasts of specific requirements, well into the future, and update these on a rolling monthly basis. It's important that the staff you select to serve these customers share their values and their commitment to a common goal. Without shared values, you are likely to lose these customers and their future revenue streams.

A company that appears to have all the appropriate characteristics for genuine collaboration is vehicle parts manufacturer Unipart, which has enjoyed a 21-year relationship with Jaguar worldwide. These two companies act as one. Unipart participates in every facet of Jaguar's business, from design of the car and the manufacture of its component parts, through to worldwide distribution. It's a uniquely successful relationship that has endured the test of time. Jaguar and Unipart are truly in the 'zone of collaboration'. Has your company ever been in this zone? Would you be able to recognize it if you were? I suggest the only way you can come close to such an intense partnership is by only collaborating with the enterprises who really want to collaborate, and exhibit genuinely collaborative values. Unilever's former Chairman Anthony Burgmans made this point strongly when he said, 'If retail customers want to collaborate, we will collaborate with them. But if they want to fight we are ready to give them a good fight too.'[3] This is an important distinction because it provides guidance on the priority for allocating scarce resources. For some, servicing customers has become an art form in that both collaborative and adversarial behaviors are practised in the same marketplace. The former CEO of Woolworths Australia, Roger Corbett, put it plainly – if you 'get too cozy with your suppliers . . . you're in trouble'.[4] During his time at the helm Corbett was constantly spilling the trading arrangements he had with suppliers. Yet independent field research found that a small number of key suppliers were (and still are) collaborating intensely with Woolworths, so why fracture the relationship? Upon reflection this double game makes sense, because true collaboration is very relationship-intensive and, therefore, can only be practised on a selective basis. Corbett's approach may appear to send mixed signals to the supply base, but in reality it's a cunning strategy based on the idea that it is best to collaborate only with those parties who are really vital to your business. The rest simply have to take their chances. The Australian 3PL, Linfox Logistics, is following a similar principle by culling its client base.

But collaborative responses do not happen by accident. Companies will need to carefully design strategies and manage the operations that underpin this special form of 'alignment' between suppliers and their customers. Certain conditions must be present inside supplying companies for this to occur. Let's talk about the strategies first.

Get your intentions right from the start

In Chapter 3 we discussed the various different value propositions and corresponding strategy packages that should be formulated to align with the customers' buying behaviors identified in any given market. As we said earlier, the marketplace is the starting point for strategy formulation, but so many enterprises ignore this fundamental tenet.

For the best operation of the *continuous replenishment* supply chain, we will now explore in detail the appropriate combination of the 15 strategic dimensions introduced in Chapter 3; a short version of this is provided in Figure 7.1.

1 **Product mix.** Customers in a collaborative mindset tend to buy mature or proven products, perhaps augmented with additional services. They are not in the habit of exploring new products because they are innately conservative and slow to change. In essence this type of customer is a 'laggard' and just wants the same product-service experience repeated over and over.

2 **Innovation emphasis.** This type of customer likes quality and is not afraid to pay for it. Indeed, paying a premium is in effect their 'insurance' that they will receive what they expect. They are happy to collaborate with suppliers in joint developments that lead to incremental improvements in the product and/or service experience. They share information, and in particular forecasts that will help the supplier. They are also keen to work with suppliers to improve processes and take cost out. Most of all, they will embrace any innovation that will lead to a material improvement in the relationship.

3 **Marketing emphasis.** The marketing effort with this type of customer is quite simply one of building brand loyalty with existing customers, i.e., market penetration. There may even be some product development, where other products in the suppliers' range are bought on trust.

	Strategic dimension	Ideal strategy
1	Product mix	Emphasis on mature, branded, and augmented products
2	Innovation emphasis	Big emphasis on product quality; joint product development. Innovate to improve relationships
3	Marketing emphasis	Build brand loyalty
4	Channels of distribution	Either direct or via trusted outlets
5	Pricing regime	Price according to strength of brand; moderate price sensitivity
6	Promotional activity	Low promotional activity – simply not required
7	Service emphasis	Empathy with local customers; consistency of survice; trust
8	Procurement/ sourcing approach	Select suppliers on basis of relationships and capabilities
9	Production	Low volume – high value add. Collaborate to reduce costs
10	Capacity considerations	Maximum utilization achievable consistent with serving clients
11	Fulfillment approach	Reliable/scheduled delivery; shared forecasts
12	Relationship intensity	Mutual dependence between customer and supplier
13	Systems/IT support	Emphasis on customer management; CRM essential
14	Resource allocations priorites	Focus on supporting the relationship to retain customers
15	Strategic risk profile	Low

FIGURE 7.1 ◆ *Continuous replenishment* supply chain strategy – protective

4 **Channels of distribution.** Channels are the commercial pathways along which products and services are sold; but they do not necessarily move along the same pathways between the various agencies and intermediaries that share the functions and tasks of getting products and services into the hands of the final end user/consumer. For customers in a collaborative mindset, they will use trusted outlets to access the products and services they desire, so the channels are relatively few. The other fast growing channel is of course the e-channel.

5 **Pricing regime.** Pricing is not a big issue with this customer, so, as long as we are consistently meeting their expectations we should not be overly concerned about cutting prices or costs unless of course there is a significant reduction in the cost-to-serve through improved processes and practices. Remember, it is better to keep up the personal service and keep the price at a level to support this, rather than cut the service in an attempt to reduce costs. That is foolhardy and quite unnecessary in this situation.

6 **Promotional activity.** Customers in this segment know what they want and how they want to be serviced. There is usually no need for anything exceptional by way of promotions. Indeed, promotions are the last thing they are looking for. Save the money and invest it in relationship and brand building activities.

7 **Service emphasis.** The service that this segment yearns for is to be recognized as important by the supplier; and given the necessary priority to ensure consistent and reliable service at all times. They want their trust in the supplier reciprocated.

8 **Procurement/sourcing approach.** In order to provide the consistency required by this customer segment it is important to ensure the same consistency on the supply side. This means selecting suppliers who share 'collaborative' values and will treat us as the buyer with the same respect as our customers expect of us as their suppliers. If this means outsourcing so be it. But we should never lose control of the overall supply equation.

9 **Production.** As the products this customer segment buys get towards the end of their life-cycle we can expect volumes to drop, but in turn we have to find ways to add value to these same products to extend their life-cycle. Here again, the collaborative segment will work willingly with preferred suppliers to take cost out of the system.

10 **Capacity considerations.** Consistent with delivering a reliable product/service, we should be trying to reach and maintain high levels of capacity utilization, especially as the forecasts we are working to are likely to be highly accurate – as they are updated regularly in close consultation with our customers in the 'collaborative' segment.

11 **Fulfillment approach.** Here again, uppermost in the customers' minds is a reliable delivery schedule, with no surprises. Shared forecasts will also help to achieve this mutually desirable result.

12 **Relationship intensity.** True collaboration between buyer and seller involves trust and a high degree of interdependence. We must recognize this and seek to use this to our mutual advantage. In no circumstances should we allow non-collaborative customers to receive a higher priority than this segment when it comes to product allocation and service delivery. This segment will comprise our most profitable customers, and if necessary they should be protected from interference by other parts of our own organization in the service of less loyal customer segments.

13 **Systems/IT support.** We will talk more about this dimension when we address cultural considerations later in this chapter, because technology is a major shaper of cultural capability. Suffice to say here that it is essential to use whatever technology available that assists in the smooth management of loyal customers, e.g., Customer Relationship Management (CRM) systems, of which there are several.

14 **Resource allocation priorities.** As indicated, this segment should receive top priority in terms of product allocation and corresponding service attention. This idea can be reinforced by conducting regular Customer Account Profitability (CAP) analyses which will surely confirm that this segment, and the individual customers in it, is our most profitable and therefore most valuable. Lose them and we lose not just the corresponding margin on the sale, but we lose a profit stream that would have continued into the future for some years at least.

15 **Strategic risk profile.** As the over-riding emotion in this segment is loyalty to the supplier and the brand, there is low risk – but only if we remain empathetic to these customers. If we ignore them they will surely leave, and the risk levels increase significantly just before this occurs.

So having laid out all the dimensions that we have to work with in couching our specific strategies for the *continuous replenishment* supply chain, there remains just one more thing to get right – shaping the underlying culture so that our best laid plans are delivered as intended. Unfortunately, 'there is many a slip between the cup and the lip'! We will now describe how to shape the most appropriate subculture for propelling this type of supply chain configuration into the marketplace.

Didn't you know – it's all about culture

Perhaps the most definitive research in this vexed area of collaboration was undertaken by Mark Barratt, at Arizona State University.[5] He identified 83 *enablers* of supply chain relationships in coffee supply chains between a major manufacturer and a leading retailer in the UK grocery industry. On inspection, most of these enablers are related to culture and have underlying values that are clearly *collaborative*, such as commitment, mutual benefit, openness, jointly defined processes and timely exchange of information.[6] The 34 *inhibitors* to supply chain relationships that Barratt observed also showed a bias towards culture-related factors.[7] Interestingly, both the *enablers* and *inhibitors* were evident at strategic, tactical and operational levels within the manufacturer and retailer organizations participating in the research. The majority of *enablers* and *inhibitors* appeared to occupy the inter-organizational space in the supply chain **between** the supply chain parties.

This is a significant finding given the current efforts by suppliers and retailers, particularly in Fast-Moving Consumer Goods (FMCG) globally, to achieve collaboration and make it a source of competitive advantage. Yes, it can be, but only under very specific conditions. If these are not present, all the technology in the world won't cause parties in supply chains to act in a genuinely collaborative way towards each other. Barratt's *enablers* and *inhibitors* are detailed in Appendices 7A.1 and 7A.2 respectively.

Of course, this suggests that all parties in supply chains now require a new array of competencies in areas such as customer relationship management, continuous improvement, multi-level communications, management of joint KPIs, and many others. But collaboration on its own is not a 'silver bullet' for all occasions.

Getting the subculture right

So how do we attempt to create a subculture to support collaboration? I've heard 'culture' described as trying to hold a fistful of sand: inevitably it defeats you! We found in Chapter 4 that nothing gets done unless the values of the people working in the enterprise support making it happen. Indeed, the fact that so many business plans never materialize is evidence of this phenomenon, although some would argue, quite wrongly, that such slippages are due to the actions of competitors. Actually, both factors impact implementation, but I'm convinced the insidious resistance that often lurks just beneath the surface of organizations is the major reason. On the flip side, the positive force of people behaviors and beliefs is a critical key to success. Barratt's work on *inhibitors* and *enablers* also supports the idea that 'culture is key'.

Has your business ever sought to generate a particular work culture through change management processes or human resource management? You wouldn't be alone. My experience tells me culture-shaping activities in isolation do not work: there are many factors that can influence and shape a desired subculture in an organization. For *continuous replenishment*, our emphasis needs to be on building a predominantly Group subculture inside the enterprise. This subculture is characterized by people-focused values such as a commitment to customer relationships, a teamwork style of working that embraces and rewards participation, aversion to risk and the pursuit of synergy through developing cohesive and loyal relationships. A bias towards these values should be evident in all functions that contribute to delivering products and services to collaborative customers. In turn, this means that suppliers and customers need to be open and respectful of each other.

But where do we start? I have chosen 13 of the most critical *capabilities* that can help you to form a Group subculture and have described how they are relevant to collaborating in *continuous replenishment* supply chains; see Figure 7.2 overleaf. None alone is a silver bullet, but putting in place elements of the 13 capability areas listed below will help you to influence the success of your supply chain strategy.

MARKET SEGMENT	COLLABORATIVE	CLOSE WORKING RELATIONSHIPS SOUGHT WITH SELECTED SUPPLIERS
FULFILMENT STRATEGY	VALUE PROPOSITION	**STRATEGIES** ♦ Share information ♦ Seek *strategic partnerships* ♦ Seek long-term stability ♦ Build mutual trust
INTERNAL CULTURAL CAPABILITY	CULTURAL LEVERS 1. Org design 2. People positioning 3. Processes 4. IT/system 5. S&OP 6. KPIs 7. Incentives 8. Job design 9. Internal comms. 10. T&D 11. Role modeling 12. Recruitment	**GROUP SUBCULTURE** ♦ Relationship cluster ♦ Ensure bias in cluster is towards personnel with 'F' in their MBTI profile ♦ Standard processes, e.g., Customer Account Management ♦ CRM; VMI; ECR; CDP; CPFR ♦ S&OP processes relatively simple in this collaborative environment ♦ Emphasis on loyalty and retention ♦ Encourage participative schemes ♦ Authority/autonomy negotiated by consensus ♦ Consultative; face-to-face ♦ Team building ♦ Managers with ESFP/MBTI profile are ideal ♦ Recruit team players
LEADERSHIP	13 LEADERSHIP STYLE	**COACH** ♦ Conscientious ♦ Lead by teaching ♦ Concerned for others ♦ Loyal, committed, politically astute ♦ Seeks agreement by consensus

FIGURE 7.2 ♦ *Continuous replenishment supply chain configuration – demand-side*

Source: Adapted from Figure 1.1 in Gattorna (2009), p. 48

1. Organization design

Let us start with the big picture – the organization's design. Developing the Group subculture necessary for a *continuous replenishment* supply chain means installing a design that is a combination of specialist vertical functions and horizontal, customer-facing clusters. Since I have covered this topic in detail in Chapter 6 I will simply recap the main ideas behind the proposed new model for supply chains of the future. You will note that my thinking has moved beyond the matrix structure suggested in the first edition of this book.[8] It has taken three years of work, but I am now convinced you need to have **both** the vertical functions and horizontal clusters co-existing in an enterprise; one without the other is insufficient, because they perform different albeit complementary roles. The reality is that vertical functional organizations are always going to be 90 degrees 'out of phase' with the way customers wish to buy. While this has been conceded to some extent by the introduction of dual-reporting matrix structures, when push comes to shove in a conflict between the two, the vertical function inevitably comes out on top, and the customer-facing account management element loses, so everyone loses! Quite simply, we need a fundamentally new model, and some leading enterprises have already moved in this direction, as seen in Figure 6.4.

2. People positioning

Call centres in the financial services and tourism industries often have technology with caller identification software so that employees can identify the customer and update their information on a real-time basis. When the customer calls, a reference list of facts and preferences is readily available to employees so they can tailor their conversation to put the caller at ease – or feel special.

One example of this is the Royal Bank of Scotland in Britain, which operates several insurance companies, e.g., Direct Line, Privilege and Churchill. These entities are all aimed at different segments. Incoming calls all go to the same call centre, but the system tells the operators which company the customer is seeking so that they can respond accordingly.

A more manual system is used by veterinary surgeons who often refer to pets by their first name and give the pet the owner's last name. They chat about the animal with the owner and ask how things have been going since their last visit. All the information is contained on a card or computer note, but the vet gives the impression of knowing and caring about the much-loved pet.

Whether your system is technologically sophisticated or simple and manual, the fundamental requirement is for the customer to feel important and wanted. The use of empathy and listening skills are essential in the process of these interactions. This has been recognized by those companies that tend to hire customer-facing staff with good people skills (e.g., ex-teachers or actors). This type of process is made or broken by the manner of the staff and their ability to exhibit good interpersonal skills, supported by technology that will provide adequate information and help in the delivery of the required processes. Some (but not all) people with 'F' (Feeling preference) in their Myers-Briggs Type Indicator (MBTI) profile are essential in this cluster.

3. Processes

It is important that the processes followed in the *continuous replenishment* supply chain are participative, internally and externally, and, of course, standard and replicable. Leading companies will always put customer account management processes at the forefront, as well as joint-development processes. Everything about these processes is unambiguously focused on the long term. The aim is to maintain and deepen existing relationships with nominated customers in every facet of service; and this is what they expect and demand.

4. Systems/information technology

Information technology may not seem like a culture shaper but it is important to get the right systems in place to overlay and institutionalize key processes. There is no point in seeking collaboration in a *continuous replenishment* supply chain when your IT systems are designed for the opposite effect. IT systems in various combinations provide a 'view' of the business, and this can help you to align your business processes and activities to match the profiles of your customer segments. Point-of-sale systems can provide daily information on the purchasing profiles of your customers. In turn, this information materially assists the replenishment process. Data warehouses and business analytics are vital facilities now readily available to modern enterprises.

In *continuous replenishment* supply chains, transactional intensity is relatively low and systems complexity is likewise low because collaboration flourishes best when the operating environment is relatively predictable and stable. This means Enterprise Resource Planning (ERP) systems are useful but not essential. However, additional systems applications that assist in managing customer relationships are important. The Kanban scheduling mechanism (more commonly associated with lean activities) is useful, as is Vendor Managed Inventory (VMI), although this is usually an in-built capability of most contemporary ERP systems.

Operational environments with more demanding VMI specifications will benefit from the advanced capabilities offered by some of the major supply chain management software vendors, e.g., Manugistics, i2 and Aspentech. The distinction between these providers is that Manugistics and i2 are geared towards more discrete product industries, while Aspentech is a process industry leader. Every Day Lower Prices (EDLP), which is essentially a pricing strategy, is also important in this operating environment, as are Collaborative Demand Planning (CDP), Efficient Consumer Response (ECR) and Collaborative Planning Forecasting and Replenishment (CPFR).

The processes and systems applications for Customer Relationship Management (CRM) are progressively being integrated into a portfolio of systems that combine to jointly service customers, and if used in this way they are extremely valuable in providing access to good customer information to support fulfillment. However, if used in isolation, CRM, while still useful, loses a lot of its potential power. We strongly suggest that a CRM system be used where a 'collaborative' customer segment is being served, and that the P-A-D-I coding method be used to keep everyone in the firm abreast of a customer's buying behaviors, and in particular any changes occurring in their usual behavior brought on by either internal or external pressures. In our view, a CRM system becomes less effective in the other three generic supply chain configurations because of a general lack of collaboration between parties. Additional systems on the 'customer end' of the supply chain include support systems such as Point-of-Sale (PoS), Radio Frequency Identification (RFID) and the increasingly utilized Global Data Synchronization Network (GSDN).

Figure 7.3 is an attempt to depict the ideal systems configuration for the *continuous replenishment* supply chain, using the Oracle suite as an example. I will build this diagram progressively as we discuss each type of supply chain in following chapters.

5. Sales and Operations Planning (S&OP)

Sales and Operations Planning (S&OP) is at the heart of matching supply and demand, and is one of the most critical activities inside the company, bringing all parties together for discussion of their respective forecasts and ultimately agreeing a single demand plan. The *continuous replenishment* supply chain, serving collaborative customers, is a natural sweet spot for S&OP, and consensus is relatively easy to achieve.

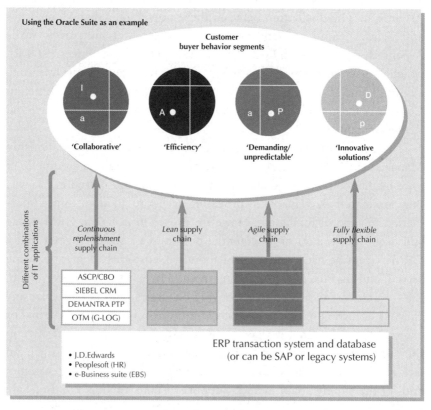

FIGURE 7.3 ◆ **Requisite technology for *continuous replenishment* supply chains**

Source: Adapted from Figure 1.5 in Gattorna (2009), p. 55

6. Key Performance Indicators (KPIs)

Don't we all love performance measurement? Unfortunately, this important area of management is often poorly understood and misused and abused as a result. Too often companies compile long lists of KPIs across a broad spectrum of functional areas without realizing that specific KPIs apply to each type of supply chain, or combination thereof. Early versions of the balanced scorecard approach developed by Robert Kaplan and David Norton[9] proved both a blessing and a blight on the landscape; while bringing new disciplines to the monitoring and management of performance in practice the scorecard did not always identify clearly enough the need to align different KPIs with particular customers. Instead, the impression was that an arbitrary list of financial, customer, internal operational processes and market KPIs selected by management, applied equally well across all customer buying behaviors in the marketplace. This is simply not the case. The oversight has now been partly redressed with Kaplan and Norton's latest insights on balanced scorecards.[10] In any event, we would prefer to use the term 'biased scorecard', meaning that we select *only* those KPIs that are relevant to each type of dominant buying behavior in a particular marketplace – and for a specific combination or types of supply chains. The mix of these buying behaviors is particularly important, because it will guide us in the selection process and the subsequent allocation of efforts in data specification, data collection, and monitoring of the selected portfolio of KPIs.

For *continuous replenishment* supply chains, our emphasis should be on measuring customer retention and loyalty, the length of individual customer relationships, and our business's percentage of the customer's overall spend in the particular category. Other measures such as the amount of information sharing and insights to drive customer service improvement are also relevant. Measures such as service reliability, Delivery-In-Full-On-Time-Error-Free (DIFOTEF) and parameters that reflect the way we are managing the all-important relationship with selected customers are also useful. In addition, Customer Account Profitability (CAP) measures indicating strong profitability from this customer segment are extremely helpful. This just reinforces the need to isolate and focus on 'collaborative' customers – as a conscious priority.

CRM systems are often used in implementing KPIs that focus on the relational measures commonly used in call centres, health insurance and financial services, and brand-oriented companies. In addition to customer retention rates, cost of customer retention, as well as the 'cost effectiveness' of tactics used to achieve high rates of customer retention, is monitored, e.g., Toyota measures a range of KPIs that track customer loyalty and retention.

Without a doubt, KPIs are a major shaper of culture in organizations, because people tend to do what is measured, irrespective of whether it is correct or the most appropriate thing to do in the circumstances. The world is full of examples where particular KPIs set in place inside the enterprise are driving dysfunctional behavior. This could be an urban myth, but I once heard of a US airline that ostensibly found a 'motivator' for its pilots to reduce fuel wastage and so encourage more energy efficient flying practices. Pilot bonuses were linked to the reduction of fuel use. This was a very effective motivator for a behavior change and resulted in considerable reductions in fuel usage. It also lost them customers! The pilots were turning off the air conditioning while queuing for take-off clearance on the tarmac, which saved fuel, but in the tropics the passengers were sweltering in the heat.

Call centers modify their KPIs according to the type of calls – in-bound or out-bound – and whether they are seeking to gather information, generate sales or build a relationship. Compare the likely KPIs used for a crisis counseling centre with those for a directory assistance service at a telephone company. Both services are provided by telephone, but the type and level of service is very different indeed. An extreme example maybe, but it illustrates the point. In call centers today, the time taken on a call is less important if the operator is trying to convert the caller into a customer. However, the duration and number of calls per day are still important when the aim is simply to deliver information, and not necessarily establish a relationship.

7. Incentives

Incentives are useful in encouraging staff to do what the organization wants them to do, and they go hand-in-hand with KPIs. In the case of *continuous replenishment* supply chains, we need incentives that encourage participative and team behaviors. For a Group subculture, any schemes that recognize performance, in a public way are appropriate, e.g., honor boards, team rewards such as dinners out or bonuses. These types of incentives need to carry a real level of achievement with them and not be something that is inappropriate or seen as irrelevant – otherwise they don't work.

Examples of incentives in this category reflect a participatory emphasis. Until the 1990s, McDonald's used honor boards to acknowledge excellent customer service and exceptional levels of staff performance. Symbols were put on employees' name badges to indicate the level of customer service they had achieved. IKEA, on the other hand, uses departmental sales targets rather than individual ones, encouraging their sales staff to perform as a team rather than compete for customers.

8. Job design

Job design and job descriptions in *continuous replenishment* supply chains need to focus on teamwork and cooperation to satisfy customers. Ideally, any activities involving authority, autonomy or control should be decentralized and negotiated by consensus. Getting the line and customer-facing staff to agree on 'who will do what' in serving customers is especially effective, as it emphasizes how best to manage the relationship.

The type of job design that supports this situation is descriptive rather than prescriptive. If employees are given both responsibility and authority commensurate with the level of their duties it tends to empower them to make more relationship-based decisions. However, this should occur under the guidance of a coach who uses meetings to discuss scenarios and their possible resolutions.

9. Internal communications

Internal communications are a critical factor in shaping the required responses to customers from inside organizations. But this importance has not been fully recognized. Suffice it to say that a Group subculture tends to flourish in an environment where internal communications are highly consultative, and the underlying theme is 'we care'. Fortunately, this type of communication works well in a relatively slow-moving and stable operating environment, which is what the collaborative buying behavior is all about. However, as will be seen in later chapters, this style of internal communications does not suit a fast-moving world characterized by high levels of uncertainty and unpredictable demand.

The best vehicle for good internal communications in the Group subculture is team-based, and face-to-face, hence, meetings, and lots of them! However, this can be slow and cumbersome and can sometimes become cliquey – in which case certain individuals and groups purposely withhold information from other individuals and groups. But the strength of the team approach is that staff turnover is relatively low, otherwise the subculture is lost.

10. Training and development

Training and development efforts are too often unfocused and undifferentiated, and as a result much of the budget provided for this purpose is wasted. Then it is indiscriminantly cut during difficult trading conditions such as in recessions, just when we should be singling out certain talent for further development and retention. Such is the world of one-dimensional management. Remember, it is not essential to train **all** personnel in **all** skill areas. In order to foster a Group subculture, training and development activities should focus on team-building, and emphasize the value of relationships and the synergy that is derived from them if applied appropriately, both inside and outside the enterprise.

The most effective vehicles for promoting the rapport so necessary to this type of subculture are small work groups and a 'hands-on' style. Fact-based negotiation skills and a thorough understanding of group dynamics are also important. The Group subculture is supported very strongly by the 'buddy' system, as used in many businesses that adopt project teams. In this case, the responsibility for a person's own work and the development of another person becomes the norm, and results in successful team-building, e.g., consulting teams comprising a combination of senior members, consultants with a medium level of experience and a few junior associates. The junior associates work in quite directed environments, while still learning the culture of the organization.

11. Role modeling

This is a little used lever in the cultural formation process, but nevertheless a very influential one if you can get it working effectively. Having 'leaders' in the *continuous replenishment* cluster that demonstrably live the values of empathy and respect for staff and customers alike is a powerful shaper of behavior among subordinates and fellow workers. For this cluster you would expect to find such role models exhibiting a lot of 'F' in their MBTI profile.

12. Recruitment

Too often, personnel are recruited into organizations and selected for positions solely on the basis of a combination of their technical qualifications and previous work experience. Little if any consideration is given to the *microculture* that they bring to the organization as they enter, and the impact this could have on their performance and on the performance of those around them. If only it were recognized how this particular factor could be used to 'genetically engineer' organizational subcultures, we would see correspondingly more effective implementation of plans, across the board.

What we are seeking to grow is a subculture that is personal, has people with good relationship skills, is team-oriented and empathetic, and above all, is focused on delivering personalized service to key customers – on a continuing basis.

13. Leadership style

We now turn our attention to the most vital factor of all in shaping subcultures in organizations – leadership style. You only have to look at the myriad of examples of successful and unsuccessful organizations over the past few decades to realize the impact that particular leadership styles can have on their ultimate fortunes. The case clearing houses in Europe and the United States are full of salient examples. The reality is that successful organizations tend to display an array of leadership styles consistent with the mix of dominant buying behaviors in their marketplace. This is a fundamental requirement for success in today's world.

In turn, the top management team in successful organizations tends to formulate strategies that are appropriately aligned to the needs of their customers or markets, because they are close enough to know what they want. They then develop and manage a corresponding array of subcultures inside the organization to drive these intended strategies into the marketplace. The key is this 'alignment' with customers, but it all starts from the leadership team recognizing their customers' buying behaviors. Such recognition sets up the conditions for ultimate success. Without it, there is little chance of sustained alignment with customers (and suppliers) and therefore superior operational and financial performance.

So the real conundrum facing today's top management teams is how to develop and (coincidentally) maintain a mix of diverse subcultures inside the organization tasked with under-pinning particular strategies – especially when some of these subcultures have fundamentally opposing values. Few enterprises have yet found a workable solution to this problem.

In the case of a Group subculture, it is important to have someone in the management team who has a predominantly *coach* leadership style, and ensures that the values required to form and deliver genuine customer-emphatic strategies are in place. A *coach* leads by example and teaching, is very conscientious and shows genuine concern for others. He or she likes to help, is loyal to subordinates and superiors alike, and remains committed to the vision espoused by the leader of the enterprise. The *coach* is also politically astute, seeking to lead by agreement and consensus. In Myers-Briggs terms, this leadership style is epitomized by an ESFJ (or extrovert-sensing-feeling-judging) type. IKEA is a company that has consistently embraced the *coach* style of leadership. This Swedish firm has a very Group-oriented culture and aims to have a fairly flat organizational structure. Using Geert Hofstede's classification for country cultures (see Figure 4.6), the characteristics for Sweden are high individuality, small power distance, low uncertainty avoidance and, like the rest of the Scandinavian countries, highly feminine.

Real or artificial 'collaboration'

Genuine collaboration appears to occur when the parties in a particular supply chain have similar power, and hence their relationship is by definition more interdependent. Where a power imbalance exists, genuine collaborative behavior is less likely to occur. Some companies achieve a 'pseudo collaboration' effect through the very power they exert on their suppliers, e.g., Wal-Mart flexing its muscles with its suppliers. Despite these aberrations, the original principle remains true, i.e., seek to collaborate only with those parties in the supply chain who have collaborative values and genuinely wish to collaborate. Only in that way will truly *win–win* experiences be sustained over time. Andrew Humphries and Richard Wilding have developed an evolutionary approach to gaining trust and achieving collaboration, namely cooperation, coordination and finally collaboration.[11]

I have found that strategic relationships between pairs of enterprises, ideally in *continuous replenishment* supply chains, can take two forms:

- Supplier–supplier: these are horizontal relationships, which we will refer to as 'alliances'.

- Buyer–seller: these are vertical relationships, which we prefer to call 'partnerships'.

Both types of relationship can be explained using the *dynamic alignment* framework introduced in earlier chapters and depicted in a different way in Figure 7.4. Within each of these types there are at least four subcategories of relationships that closely parallel the types of customer behavioral segments that we identified in Chapter 2. These are: *loyalty*-driven relationships (*continuous replenishment*); *cost*-driven relationships (*cost/efficiency*); *performance*-driven relationships (*demanding/quick response*); and *innovation*-driven relationships (*innovation solutions*). However, irrespective of the type of strategic relationship, potential conflict can arise as a result of:

- different priorities caused by unclear focus;

- incompatible long-term objectives, e.g., cost minimization (supplier) versus profit maximization (distributor);

- different cultures;

- lack of communications/information;

- traditional 'zero-sum' negotiation strategies; and/or

- incorrect pricing.

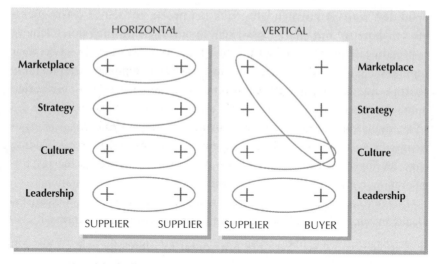

FIGURE 7.4 ◆ Critical alignment interfaces in horizontal and vertical strategic relationships

Source: Adapted from Figure 13.1 in Gattorna and Walters (1996), p. 191

Given the experience with conflict as noted above, the priorities for achieving effective strategic relationships must include the following initiatives:

◆ Develop a common/shared vision.

◆ Recognize each company's independent objectives, e.g., ROI, budgets, market share.

◆ Develop common objectives that are as compatible as possible with independent objectives, but which ultimately optimize the mutual benefit to the parties involved.

◆ Get to know each other's marketplace as this affects the interaction.

◆ Get to know each other's culture, possibly by placing personnel inside each other's company or by creating strategic project teams with employees from both companies.

Strategic partnering is most relevant to our discussion of *continuous replenishment* supply chains because of the preferred collaborative values present on both sides. Indeed, the ability to select and manage successful partnerships is fast becoming a required competency. The unique *strategic partnering* methodology described in more detail below has been developed and refined through extensive fieldwork; it focuses on fostering growth in trust and shared information, through **joint action**. This in turn naturally leads to the development of joint competitive advantages for members in the same supply chain. The desired outcome is integrated business plans for the collaborating parties and subsequent sustained operating success.

Corporations that have 'collaborative' values and practice *strategic partnering* usually have a number of 'partners.' However, while relationships between partners should be unique, they need not be exclusive. The nature of the strategic relationship forged with one company may be quite different from that forged with another. The essential ingredient for success is that the partners are culturally compatible. Our definition of *strategic partnering* is detailed in Figure 7.5 overleaf, along with the features and implications of this unique relationship type.

Along with others who have worked in this area,[12] we have developed a one-day workshop-driven *strategic partnering* program, which is fully detailed in Appendix 7C, and comprises of two stages. In Stage 1, **each** executive management team attending the event completes a purpose-designed 'quick' *dynamic alignment* diagnostic questionnaire. The primary aim of Stage 1 is to assess the degree of *compatibility* between the cultures and leadership styles of the two parties. In Stage 2, the proprietary workshop-driven *strategic partnering* technique is used. Significant success has been achieved with this accelerated workshop-driven technique, but for best results a preliminary screening process should aim to ensure that only parties with genuine collaborative values (and therefore part of the *continuous replenishment* supply chain) are invited to participate.

The ultimate outcome of the *strategic partnering* workshop is to enable agreement between the two parties on the joint issues they feel need to be resolved. The real-time process in getting to this point creates the required early momentum and creates pressure for action. However, it is important that before the inaugural meeting breaks up, the senior executives from both buyer and supplier organizations in the room appoint joint project teams to prepare detailed work plans for consideration at a subsequent workshop, approximately one month later. On the assumption that the recommendations are accepted all round, implementation of a range of joint initiatives can proceed immediately after that. There is no better

Strategic partnering develops enduring corporate relationships based on understanding and shared knowledge. The process gets its name from developing and maintaining a strategic fit between an organization's goals and capabilities and its changing marketing opportunities.

FEATURES	IMPLICATIONS
Businesses develop a profound understanding of each other's business operations	The parties develop an approach to business which resembles a 'good times, bad times' attitude allowing for greater flexibility and ultimately control.
Two parties in a given supply chain commit to a unique, though not necessarily exclusive relationship.	Sometimes we work to develop relationships with customers only to lose them just before they start to become ardent supporters, or 'advocates' of our company
This relationship is mutual and becomes part of the corporate structure.	Conflict is resolved quickly between the parties because they have similar objectives in the partnership.
The intention to commence strategic partnering is initiated at the highest managerial level.	This results in increased commitment to the technique and greater understanding at all levels in the organization.
A 'meeting of minds' is achieved by intra-company communications downwards, and horizontal inter-company communications.	Problems between parties can be pre-empted or solved quickly.
Mutual business plans and shared objectives may be a feature of the partnering.	Companies are in a superior position to their competitors due to their superior knowledge. Gains are achieved by the 'two heads are better than one' maxim

FIGURE 7.5 ◆ Definition of strategic partnering

communication process than having buyers and sellers working together on joint initiatives for mutual benefit.

After all that, how does your enterprise measure up as a collaborative partner in the various industry supply chains you participate in? In fact do you need to be collaborative at all? Or do you have a mix of collaborative and other types of relationships in your supply chains? Keep an eye out so you can spot the opportunities as they arise.

And then came sustainability and CSR

Just like the Exocets described in Chapter 15, the two related Exocets that have come quickly over the horizon since publication of the first edition of this book in 2006 are sustainability and Corporate Social Responsibility (CSR). The reason I raise these issues in this chapter is because they both have relationship (or Ia) undertones, and are starting to look like a sub-segment within the classic 'collaborative' segment as defined in Chapter 2. In the case of sustainability, this is mainly to do with the environment. Corporate social responsibility can relate to social, ethical and environmental concerns. Either way these new considerations are influencing customer and particularly consumer buying behavior, so they cannot be ignored. We will talk in more detail about both in Chapter 15.

Defining ideas

1. 'The conventional view that business is all about competition is being challenged by the idea of collaboration, as companies look to find ways of exploiting the power of partnership.'[13] But by the same token, collaboration is not the solution for all customer strategies.

2. Know who your truly collaborative customers are, and focus on them first and foremost.

3. Only collaborate with those supply chain members who genuinely display collaborative values. Relationships take a lot of time and energy to develop and nurture, so don't squander this effort.

4. Use CRM technology to manage your special customers in the consistent and proactive way that they expect – and you will be rewarded with their loyalty.

5. Be aware that some situations will require a combination approach, e.g., maybe *lean* on the supply-side with suppliers, and *collaborative* on the customer-side. More about these 'hybrids' in Chapter 13.

6. Sustainability and corporate social responsibility are newly emerging issues that are closely related to the logic of *continuous replenishment* supply chains in that they both carry relationship undertones. Be prepared to treat these situations with the appropriate responses.

7. **Challenge** to the reader: how many of your customers (in numbers or a percentage) can you say truly exhibit *collaborative* values? And do you reward them for this loyalty?

CHAPTER 8

Lean supply chains

Focusing on efficiency and lowest cost-to-serve

Much is spoken about 'lean' because it seems such an obvious solution to achieving ever lower costs and prices. But there is more to it than meets the eye. In this chapter we explore the origins of lean principles and practices and make some fine distinctions between the early concepts of *lean* manufacturing and the more contemporary lean supply chains. They are not the same thing. *Lean* is also very difficult to implement successfully because it is more of a philosophy that has to be adopted unquestionably throughout the enterprise rather than a prescription that can be applied by rote.

And then there are the dangers. If you do happen to succeed in removing costs, but take the leanness too far, the resilience of the enterprise will surely suffer when unexpected disruptions occur. We will find out how to tread this tightrope.

How lean is your business? It's the magic question, as being 'lean' is often seen to be the cure-all approach to lowering costs. It's not so much how low can you go, but how lean can you be? Japanese car manufacturer Toyota got us hot under the collar in the 1980s when it introduced lean manufacturing into its factories. Organizations have been applying lean concepts to corporate logistics systems and the wider domain of supply chain management ever since. However, as so often occurs when new concepts are applied to supply chain thinking, we can start to have unreasonable expectations about the actual benefits. We can also get confused about what we mean by the concept itself. We can probably agree that lean principles are focused on eliminating waste in materials, processes, time and information. But can we expect all of this, **plus** creativity, flexibility and adaptability as Kate Vitasek and her colleagues seem to suggest in *Harvard Business Review*?[1]

I want to differentiate between two separate supply chains, *continuous replenishment*, as discussed in Chapter 7, and *lean*. It might seem like splitting hairs, but you cannot simply roll them into one, at least not in this brave new world. Why? Because not all parties involved in *lean* supply chains are going to be collaborative – and that's a fact! In contrast, parties in the *continuous replenishment* supply chain will share information and help each other to eliminate waste; put simply, they collaborate. I see the classic *lean* supply chain as one where low cost is achieved by ensuring customers are not over-serviced, especially in recessionary times. Low costs are achieved by doing only the very basic processes, but doing them well. In *continuous replenishment* supply chains it will always be a case of customer 'pull' combined with some informed 'push', but in the classic *lean* supply chain, if customers are not willing to share their demand projections, we will naturally have to 'push' product downstream using the best available forecasts in what is hopefully a fairly stable environment.

So we are all agreed that lean is basically a 'push' strategy that is underpinned by supply values rather than customer 'pull' as is predominantly the case with *continuous replenishment* supply chains. However, to work most effectively, *lean* supply chains require collaboration with suppliers on the supply-side. Having said that, it is worthwhile understanding where the original *lean* concept and practices originated from.

Origins of lean manufacturing

Toyota triggered the quest for lean production when it decided in the early 1980s that American-style mass production would not work in Japan. In the United States, companies were still using the assembly line approach in production that had been so successfully introduced decades earlier by Henry Ford. The mass production of cars was still in vogue, and this required a large market with fairly standardized manufacturing systems – resulting in a limited range of vehicle models.

In contrast, the Japanese market was restricted due to international trade barriers limiting the importation of Japanese cars into Western nations. This market restriction was reinforced by the ban on Foreign Direct Investment (FDI) by the Japanese Ministry of International Trade and Industry (MITI). The ban effectively curtailed the development of any highly capital-intensive industry, such as the automotive industry, in a country which, just after World War II, had relatively no available capital. Although the size of Japan's domestic market was small, the demand for variety from the Japanese consumer was very high. The Allied occupation forces also introduced labor unions into Japan, which led to demands for higher wages and restricted the ability of managers to lay off employees when the economy turned down, as they were accustomed to doing in the past. The Japanese labor market also had no temporary migrants to work in the nation's factories (unlike in the United States, where migrant groups formed the bulk of the workforce). Consequently, Japan's automotive factories had a higher wage cost compared to that of other nations.

Toyota recognized the impact of these factors and developed the Toyota Production System (TPS), now more commonly known as lean manufacturing. The two major features of lean manufacturing that distinguish it from mass production are: increased efficiency through the reduction of errors; and reduced carrying costs of inventories, achieved by manufacturing in relatively small 'batches'. The key ingredient to these improvements was Japan's highly skilled workforce. In lean manufacturing, skilled workers manage each section of the assembly cycle, which contrasts markedly with the equivalent mass customization processes. US automotive factories use primarily low-skilled labor on the shop floor and restrict knowledge on a 'need-to-know' basis. The combination of increased human capital in the Japanese workforce, increased individual responsibility, the practice of systematically and consistently tracing problems back to their source and rectifying the root cause (thereby eliminating errors and reducing waste – called *muda* in Japanese), along with reduced inventories, has resulted in considerable competitive advantage in the Japanese supply chain.[2]

The relentless customer

You can guess what happened next. The Japanese customer – and customers globally – soon took to the product diversity and lower costs made possible through lean manufacturing techniques. But are all customers lean customers? How do you recognize the customer in what I'm calling the *lean* supply chain? One buying behavior found in most – if not all – markets to some degree or other is the desire for efficiency or consistency. In the *lean* market, this behavior is paramount. While loyalty and service are a premium in the *continuous replenishment* supply chain, in the cost/efficiency customer segment, it is price and predictability that is most valued. With such stability in demand, forecasting on the supply-side becomes both feasible and necessary.

Customers in the *lean* market will often shop around and use multiple sources in the search for steady supply and lowest prices. But in doing so, they can be impersonal or even adversarial, with few if any loyalties developing. This is a very transactional style of marketplace, where information is power and little or no information sharing occurs between buyers and sellers. For suppliers, it's a hard relentless market to serve; with customers so price-sensitive that there is little or no opportunity to differentiate value propositions. If you are looking to compete under these conditions, you must strive to be the lowest-cost producer, and sustain this advantage over time, using whatever techniques at your disposal.

The Virginia Mason Medical Center in Seattle, Washington fully embraced the Toyota Production System and adapted it for use in the hospital,[3] across all its campuses. Virginia Mason introduced the initiative in 2000 after recognizing that the hospital's infrastructure was designed around the hospital's needs, not the patients'. Sound familiar? They set out to identify and eliminated waste in the system and build patient satisfaction. Significant results have been achieved over time – an 85 per cent reduction in the wait time for the return of laboratory results is just one benefit. Facilities have been redesigned with the patient in mind, and temporary labor expenses have been decreased by more than US$500,000 per year.

Dr Gary Kaplan, the Chairman and CEO of Virginia Mason, comments, 'we have more than enough resources in health care . . . we just need to stop wasting it and only do what's appropriate and value-added and we'd save millions.'[4] Make that billions if only other health care systems around the world would follow their example!

In a further initiative launched in 2005, Virginia Mason joined with local employers Costco, Nordstrom, Starbucks, King County and insurer Aetna to improve the quality of patient care and reduce the cost of treating common medical conditions such as back pain. By arranging same day appointments for various treatments, and reducing the number of patient visits, the cost of care dropped, and patients returned to work more quickly. So there is real potential in embracing lean disciplines, but it takes leadership to initiate and follow through.

Response strategies

The value proposition in the 'efficiency/consistency' customer segment is that of a standard and reliable service – so customers **know** what they are getting. The offering may still have some bells and whistles, but the offer is supplied in such a way as to standardize the different components to ensure lowest cost. The notion of innovation is still important here as it is really used to drive manufacturing standardization rather than product innovation *per se*. The Zara, Benetton and Toyota stories all demonstrate value-add and clear value propositions – and used innovation to minimize waste, which is where *lean* principles re-emerge.

The best and only way to service the low-cost and reliability-seeking marketplace is via a *lean* (or semi-wave flow) configuration of the supply chain. The primary focus is on efficient operations offering high volume and low variety, and mostly producing goods and services to forecast. This is the classic Make-To-Forecast (MTF) operating environment, compared to the Make-To-Order (MTO) type of response that we see in *agile* supply chains, explored in more detail in Chapter 9. Customers being serviced by *lean* supply chains are offered the value proposition that: 'you will benefit from low-cost production and efficient logistics achieved by using all available synergies and economies of scale'. The ability to forecast demand more accurately is a big advantage, and the fact that we are usually dealing with mature products with predictable lead-times makes the situation all the more manageable. However, these parameters come at the cost of reduced agility and resilience, and are best achieved when system capacity is not under pressure, and production is occurring under regular lower priority schedules.

Get your intentions right from the start

In Chapter 3 we discussed different value propositions and the corresponding strategy packages that should be formulated to align with the customers' buying behaviors identified in any given market. The marketplace is the starting point for strategy formulation, but so many enterprises ignore this fundamental tenet.

For best operation of the *lean* supply chain, we will now explore the appropriate combination of the following 15 strategic dimensions (see Figure 8.1).

1 **Product mix.** Customers in a 'price/efficiency' mindset tend to buy mature, proven products. They are innately conservative and slow to change. In essence this type of customer is a 'laggard' and just wants the same product-service experience repeated on a consistent basis, and they will shop around to get it. The lowest possible cost to drive the lowest-price offer to customers is essential.

2 **Innovation emphasis.** This type of customer puts price and consistency before product-service quality. The supplier must therefore find ways to continually reduce the cost of inputs, and seek to refine processes.

3 **Marketing emphasis.** The marketing effort with this type of customer is to sell the message of reliability of supply at lowest prices.

4 **Channels of distribution.** This is a low price-volume business, so the widest possible array of channels should be sought to give customers every chance to easily access the product.

5 **Pricing regime.** To succeed in this segment the supplier should ideally be the lowest cost producer in order to drive prices lower than competitors. The effort by Wal-Mart to introduce Every Day Low Prices (EDLP) was primarily designed to drive costs down in its supply chains by introducing more predictability, thus allowing it to offer lower prices to consumers.

	Strategic dimension	Ideal strategy
1	Product mix	Stable product line; minimal variants
2	Innovation emphasis	Focus on ways to reduce cost of inputs and processes
3	Marketing emphasis	Lowest price; but reliable
4	Channels of distribution	Wide distribution through multiple channels
5	Pricing regime	Lowest price. EDLP
6	Promotional activity	Low
7	Service emphasis	Efficiency and process re-engineering
8	Procurement/ sourcing approach	Outsource standard products to gain lowest cost production
9	Production	High volume – low cost; commodity
10	Capacity considerations	High utilization
11	Fulfillment approach	High reliability; predictable service and ready availability
12	Relationship intensity	Low
13	Systems/IT support	Emphasis on transactional system
14	Resource allocations priorites	Focus on cost reduction
15	Strategic risk profile	Low

FIGURE 8.1 ◆ *Lean* supply chain strategy – incremental

6 **Promotional activity.** Customers in this segment know what they want and how they want to be serviced. There is no need for anything exceptional by way of promotions. Indeed, promotions are the last thing they are looking for. Save the money and invest it in reducing costs and prices even further.

7 **Service emphasis.** The service this segment is looking for is quite simply 100 per cent reliability, at lowest cost-to-serve.

8 **Procurement/sourcing approach.** If lower cost of production is available through outsourcing, then it is best to outsource, but usually the standard part of the range and only if high reliability can be maintained.

9 **Production.** Emphasis is on seeking lowest cost-to-serve for the high volumes involved. The products are usually in the mature stage of their life-cycle, so margins are under pressure and little differentiation is possible.

10 **Capacity considerations.** The demand forecasts are usually fairly reliable so high capacity utilization is sought when serving this segment, which in turn reduces unit costs.

11 **Fulfillment approach.** Uppermost in customers' minds is a reliable delivery schedule, with no surprises. This has to be achieved without the benefit of shared information from the customer, who nevertheless expects low price and consistency.

12 **Relationship intensity.** This type of customer does not want or expect the supplier to try and develop a close relationship. For them it is a distraction and not values, even though it costs the supplier in the attempt. Simply accept that this segment does not require close working relationships and find other ways to overcome this void.

13 **Systems/IT support.** We will talk more about this dimension when we address cultural considerations later in this chapter, because technology is a major shaper of cultural capability. The emphasis in this type of supply chain is on transactional (ERP) systems, although Network Optimization Modeling (NOM) applications can prove useful working in tandem with the ERP to remove cost by finding optimal pathways to customers.

14 **Resource allocation priorities.** This segment, because of its high emphasis on price and consistent service, can significantly erode margins. Using Customer Account Profitability (CAP) techniques it is

possible to make decisions about what priority should be given to this type of customer, especially in situations where product supply is limited.

15 **Strategic risk profile.** Because we are operating in a customer-market segment where demand (and supply) patterns are relatively predictable, risk is low. But on the other hand, these customers will quickly move away if alternative sources are found that have lower prices and reliable delivery.

So having laid out all the dimensions that we have to work with in couching our specific strategies for the *lean* supply chain type, we can now turn our attention to shaping the underlying subculture necessary to implement these strategies.

Getting the subculture right

What sort of subculture do you think will work best in a *lean* supply chain? These supply chains need security and predictability to satisfy their customers: nothing too flashy or risky. The relentless cost-driven customers are best served by a Hierarchical subculture, described in Chapter 4. This is a subculture characterized by policies and procedures, systems, stability and order, control, logic and economy, to name just a few attributes. It is best staffed with people who enjoy working under relatively repetitive conditions. But it can prove frustrating for staff members who prefer variety and creativity. As in the previous chapter, I have chosen 13 of the most critical levers (capabilities) that can help you to form a Hierarchical subculture and have described how they are relevant to driving low-cost and consistency in *lean* supply chains, see Figure 8.2. None of these levers alone is the 'silver bullet', but the correct combination will help you to influence the success of your supply chain strategy. Let's look at the various parameters needed to formulate this type of subculture.

1. Organization design

The ideal organization structure for shaping the Hierarchical subculture are the 'process' clusters depicted in Figure 6.5.

In this design, employees are organized in multi-disciplinary clusters around several *core processes* in the enterprise that are replicable on a con-

MARKET SEGMENT	'EFFICIENT'	**REQUIRE RELENTLESS FOCUS ON COST AND EFFICIENCY**
FULFILLMENT STRATEGY	VALUE PROPOSITION	**STRATEGIES** ◆ Seek economies of scale ◆ Low cost production and distribution ◆ Forecast demand; mature products; predictable-lead times
INTERNAL CULTURAL CAPABILITY	**CULTURAL LEVERS** 1. Org design 2. People positioning 3. Processes 4. IT/system 5. S&OP 6. KPIs 7. Incentives 8. Job design 9. Internal comms. 10. T&D 11. Role modeling 12. Recruitment	**HIERARCHICAL SUBCULTURE** ◆ Organize clusters around core processes ◆ Ensure bias towards personnel with 'S' in their MBTI profile ◆ Standard processes; emphasis on cost ◆ Replace legacy systems with ERP system ◆ Effective decision framework in a relatively predictable operating environment ◆ DIFOTEF; forecast accuracy; productivity ratios ◆ Conformance to policies ◆ Centralized control – rules and regulations apply ◆ Regular; structured on 'need to know' basis ◆ Emphasis on analysis and measurement ◆ Managers with ISTJ (A) MBTI profile are ideal ◆ Recruit players with deep analytical skills
LEADERSHIP	**13 LEADERSHIP STYLE**	**TRADITIONAL** ◆ Leads by procedure; precedent ◆ Implements only proven business practices ◆ Cost controller; efficiency focus ◆ Uses information to control ◆ Seeks stability ◆ Is risk averse

FIGURE 8.2 ◆ *Lean supply chains – demand-side*

Source: Adapted from Figure 1.2 in Gattorna (2009), p. 49

tinuous basis. Teamwork is the key, both within and between the clusters. Shared responsibilities and decision-making emphasizes teamwork in this type of organization design, and risk-taking is not readily embraced. A good, if novel, example of this situation is the Russian Eye Hospital. Here, operating tables are mounted on a slide arrangement that allows them to move sideways from one operating point to the next. This means that specialists at each station can carry out different steps of the eye operation on each patient.[5] Another striking example of this type of organization design is the phenomenon of the Dabbawallahs of Mumbai in India.

Supply chains do not have to be incredibly complex to be efficient, effective and appropriate to the culture. The Dabbawallahs of Mumbai are from a particular caste in India who developed a daily delivery service for more than 150,000 home-cooked lunches in a round metal container called a *dabba*. They arranged the delivery of these lunches from home to work and then the return of the lunch container – all to a level of accuracy far greater than Six Sigma.

In Mumbai, due to cultural traditions from early last century and overcrowding on the public transport system, employees generally do not take their lunch with them to work. However, buying lunch is an effort because workers would have to leave their air-conditioned offices for the crowded, polluted and hot streets of Mumbai, only to buy food of dubious quality. Home-cooked food has until recently been the preference, and an efficient industry has grown up over the past century to resolve the problem of delivery of lunchtime meals from the home to the office, on a daily basis.

The Dabbawallahs have established a network of distribution routes to collect lunches from workers' homes. The *dabbas* are delivered to sorting points at the railway stations, loaded on to dedicated carriages on the normal commuter trains, sent throughout the city, then distributed to offices and ultimately to their owner. One hour later the *dabbas* are collected and returned to the home – following the reverse route taken earlier. This is achieved by a largely illiterate group of people who have developed a very efficient (albeit manual) system at an incredible level of accuracy – no more than one mistake in every 15 million deliveries![6] In addition to this efficient regular service, the Dabbawallahs will collect a lunch that is not on the agreed weekly route or a late delivery – and deliver for an additional price. But even this foolproof system will fail when heavy rainfall similar to that experienced in July 2005 disabled the train network!

▶

The Dabbawallahs have organized themselves around specific tasks and processes. There is also an element of hierarchy based on age. The more senior/older Dabbawallahs work at the various distribution points where they load and unload the trains. The younger, less experienced Dabbawallahs do all the running around, usually along pre-defined routes, each and every day.

2. People positioning

The ideal people to distribute liberally throughout the 'process' clusters are those who thrive on consistency and repetition. In terms of the Myers-Briggs Type Indicator (MBTI) profile, this translates to people who are ISTJs (Introvert-Sensor-Thinker-Judgers) or ISTPs (Introvert-Sensor-Thinker-Perceivers). In my P-A-D-I code this means A and Ap respectively.

3. Processes

When certainty and stability – at lowest cost – are paramount, transactional-type processes are critical. *Lean* supply chains are all about replicating standard processes to produce a standardized product. The unerring emphasis is on minimizing cost and achieving optimization in all key production and logistics processes. Most famously, McDonald's led the way in its global application of how to produce and serve a hamburger. Another lesser known but telling example is Domino's Pizza in Australia, which remodeled its business model to suit the Australian market.

For Domino's Pizza to successfully compete in Australia where the marketplace is already crowded with individual pizza restaurants and takeaway shops, it had to modify its business model. In North America customers tend to eat fast food in restaurant-style outlets, while Australians usually purchase 'takeaway' food to eat elsewhere; either at home or another venue. This cultural difference, along with some other contributing factors, has resulted in the following changes to the Domino's Pizza model in Australia.

Labor costs for fast food outlets in Australia are higher than the United States, due to the lack of immigrant labor and a higher minimum wage. The cost of real estate, especially in state capital cities, is also relatively expensive, with few locations available for the typical large fast food restaurants commonly seen throughout the United States. All these factors have an impact on the cost of goods sold. The solution for Australia was to develop shop-front pizza outlets (without dining areas) that used most of the store space for food preparation and the remainder for a comparatively small waiting area for customers. This type of store reduced the level of labor required in the stores, and eliminated the floor space needed for dining rooms (thereby reducing building and land costs), making Domino's a very competitive fast food provider in Australia.

To compete well in the low-cost market sector, Domino's Pizza follows a strategy of reduced price promotions that 'bundle' the sale of pizza, drinks and extras (e.g., garlic bread). The pizza production processes are all standardized, resulting in a rapidly produced and relatively low-cost product, so although Domino's may 'lose' money during its promotions on individual pizzas it makes money on the 'total' sale. Even with heavily discounted specials it has a policy of 'not reducing the quality or quantity of ingredients used in the pizzas, as customers notice when the pizza doesn't taste as good as the last time'.[7] Domino's also offers the option of extra toppings and changes from the 'basics', although it charges more for the service.

Staying on the retail side, Factory Gate Pricing (FGP) trading terms are gathering momentum in FMCG markets around the world. Here, instead of the supplier making the delivery arrangements, the (retail) customer arranges collection from the supplier's factory. Payment for transport is either by the supplier to the customer's carrier, or, by charging the customer a lower price for the goods supplied. It is just another reflection of the imbalance of power that exists today in the FMCG industry – and it is here to stay as there are benefits for large organizations with regular suppliers. However, it is unlikely to provide the same benefits for irregular seasonal categories such as apparel.

4. Systems/IT

The systems that support *lean* supply chains, such as Enterprise Resource Planning (ERP) systems, generally involve significant capital investment. While these systems are essential to underpin low-cost processes, they are also useful as a foundation for all four generic types of supply chain.

On top of the ERP system, you can install other non-optimal systems such as Materials Requirements Planning (MRP), Production Planning and Distribution Requirements Planning applications, as depicted in Figure 8.3. It is ideal if you can cap this off by interfacing a free-standing Network Optimization Model (NOM) with the ERP system. This will allow you to test new network and operational scenarios from time to time to ensure that the overall network is meeting agreed service levels, at minimum total (system) cost. The SCOR® model[8] also fits into this section as a useful tool for analysis; but it has its limitations.

In terms of staffing, *lean* supply chains tend to work best with largely permanent staff that are very experienced in their particular roles and enjoy the inherent routine. Labor Management Systems (LMS) may also

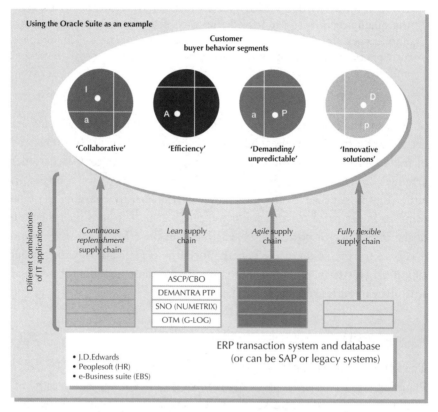

FIGURE 8.3 ◆ Requisite technology for the *lean* supply chain

Source: Adapted from Figure 1.5 in Gattorna (2009), p. 55

be used in scheduling staff on shift work, estimating crew size, sorting out changeover of skill-sets as the type of work changes, and mapping skills, all designed to maximize labor resources within given constraints; even constraints as micro as 'employees with fork-lift truck tickets'. In this type of supply chain, Point-Of-Sale (POS) and radio frequency identification (RFID) are valuable as they are able to automatically trigger re-ordering processes as goods and services are sold (POS) or move 'off-the-shelf' (RFID), in real-time if required.

5. Sales & Operations Planning (S&OP)

The S&OP process fits well in the relatively predictable operating environment of the *lean* supply chain. It provides an effective alignment and decision framework for enterprises that are generally organized as silos. The focus is on aggregating forecasts into agreed demand plans for the short to medium term.

6. Key Performance Indicators

Measurements that track accuracy, quality and predictability are the most relevant metrics for *lean* supply chains. Such metrics include logistics cost per unit, forecast accuracy, forecast/plan variances, utilization factors in storage facilities and transportation modes, Delivery-in-Full-On-Time-Error-Free (DIFOTEF), and variance from established quality standards. These are what really matter. The measurement of relational factors is definitely not relevant in this type of supply chain configuration.

7. Incentives

The most appropriate incentives in *lean* supply chains are those that encourage behaviors to conform to pre-set policies, procedures and rules. Incentives in this category include a retirement bonus or annuity payments, long-service leave and status symbols such as a large office on the executive floor.

8. Job design

Job design in the *lean* supply chain environment focuses on adherence to process specifications. Authority/autonomy is established by precedent, and control is centralized by way of predefined rules and regulations with which everyone is expected to fully comply.

9. Internal communications

The style of internal communications is formal, regular and structured to reflect the type of operating environment that is being formed, and the underlying message is that 'we are efficient'. Information is communicated on a 'need to know' basis, and is mostly in hard copy format. In any case, communications in this type of subculture are very directive and staff generally react to such directions; being proactive is not a quality that is valued here. Because 'information is power' in the Hierarchical subculture, it is often used as a weapon, which leads to a further reduction of trust in the lower ranks as individuals feel patronized. But this is not a subculture for individuals anyway, and the prevailing feeling is that there is safety in numbers. Taking any form of risk at the individual level is avoided at all costs.

10. Training and development

The training component of this subculture stresses the use of systems and compliance to rules and procedures. There is a real emphasis on measurement and measurement systems. The style of learning is practical and involves workshops, use of workbooks and the teaching of standard procedures. Competences in analysis, planning, scheduling and communications are mandatory, as are skills in continuous improvement regimes and root cause analysis.

11. Recruitment

To solidify the Hierarchical subculture, you need to seek out people with deep analytical skills and attention to detail. You should value highly a commitment to accuracy and process skills. Personnel coming into this operating environment should ideally enjoy and indeed thrive on routine. Many organizations already have long-established Hierarchical subcultures simply because of their longevity, and there is nothing wrong with that. However, we are observing a distinct shift in customer demand characteristics away from the predictable to the unpredictable, and under these conditions Hierarchical subcultures struggle to keep up with the speed of response increasingly demanded by an increasing number of customers.

12. Role modeling

The role model in this cluster is the 'cost controller' who lives by this creed in full view of others.

13. Leadership style

Leaders who thrive in this type of supply chain are *traditional* in that they lead by a combination of consensus and action. They regularly invoke procedures, and tend only to feel comfortable when implementing proven business practices. However, that said, they tend to be very well organized, practical and efficiency focused, although sometimes at the expense of effectiveness. They embrace the values of reliability and productivity, and often use information to control. Their whole life is about maintaining internal company stability and order, a classic ISTJ (introvert-sensor-thinker-judger) in the Myers-Briggs categorization, or A in our P-A-D-I code.

A revolution is on the way

We need to say a bit more about the importance of processes, especially in this type of supply chain configuration. Is your company prepared for the coming revolution? The revolution is coming in the form of *business process innovation and management* and it could potentially envelop all four generic types of supply chain and their variants. Unfortunately, business process improvement – a vital area of management – has largely been underestimated in the past, as evidenced by the numbers in Figure 8.4. But we believe it is *fundamental to sustained alignment* and, by implication, *future competitiveness*. Business processes must endure for the life of the enterprise, and evolve as the enterprise transforms to stay in *dynamic alignment* with its customers and operating environment.

Unfortunately, we have not yet seen enough of this more enlightened approach. Indeed, conventional wisdom has been to create a radical once-and-for-all process improvement. Put the ERP system in and then . . . what? It has been a bit like the old 'set and forget it' approach to production. But making radical changes implies accurate knowledge of emergent conditions in the future, and there is also the lag in implementing new processes and systems that has to be taken into account. So-called 'best practices' are really only best practices under specific market conditions. And contemporary ERP systems can only handle a limited menu of 'best practice' processes anyway. All this has connotations of a cat chasing its tail. The fundamental issue is that current ERP systems embody business processes in software applications and are by definition limited in their flexibility. A new way must be found to meet the flexibility requirements of increasingly turbulent markets. The solution lies in accepting the principle of 'multiple alignment' outlined earlier in Chapter 2.

Benefit category	'System replacement' No fundamental business changes (%)	'Re-engineered' Key processes re-engineered (%)	'Transformed' Processes and organization aligned with strategy (%)
Revenue uplift	0	1–3	5–10
COGS reduction	0–1	1–2	3–8
Overhead reduction	0–1	1–2	3–5
Inventory reduction	(30)–5	5–20	25–50

FIGURE 8.4 ◆ **Benefits flowing from different degrees of process re-engineering**

Source: Accenture; Adapted from Table 1.1.3 in Gattorna (2003), p. 8

In this environment, we move away from trying to hit a moving target with constant and costly exceptions, and instead hard-wire into the enterprise up to four unique combinations of standard processes, each supported by the appropriate systems applications and underpinning organization structures and subcultures. Then, as operating conditions in the marketplace change and cause customers to move to alternative dominant buying behaviors, we are likely to have these covered already. The pre-canned responses will already be embedded in the enterprise. 'Flexibility' takes on a new meaning under these circumstances, and most importantly, it becomes feasible at a lower cost. I will refer again to this 'flexibility' in Chapter 11 when we revisit and refine Hau Lee's Triple-A concept of supply chains.

Using price to modify buyer behavior

I am sure your customers know what a 'special' is. But what about Every Day Low Prices (EDLP)? The idea behind EDLP is simple: retailers promise to pass on discounts to customers so that the supermarket consistently offers 'low price'. The aim is to deliver a *lower total cost per shopping event, every time* – surely, better than a special! The concept, which gained prominence through the example set by Wal-Mart in the 1990s, is superbly tailored for the *lean* supply chain. *Lean* supply chains are primarily about delivering efficiency across their length and breadth. This is made easier if the products are standardized and have relatively long life-cycles. At every stage, *price drives costs* rather than *costs driving price* in *lean* supply chains. Companies will need economies of scale, considerable experience and relatively smooth demand so that capacity utilization can remain high most of the time. Coincidentally, suppliers are selected primarily on a price basis, sometimes with an eye to value, which we will define as 'quality at a price', but contrary to the conventional definition of *lean*, there is little loyalty in this marketplace.

In the *lean* supply chain, forecasts are made at the generic product category level rather than at the individual Stock-Keeping Unit (SKU) level, and everything that can possibly be done to smooth the flow of product through supply chains is embraced. Hence the emergence of EDLP. Wal-Mart and Procter & Gamble joined forces so that they could smooth the flow of product and take out costs incurred in demand surges associated with promotional activity.[9]

There was some collaboration in this arrangement as well, that is if you can collaborate with a gorilla. EDLP has since been implemented in various forms by many retailers around the world, especially supermarkets, to increase their market share. Often the promotion of EDLP is to 'roll back the price' and pass the savings on to the consumer. Unfortunately, the price reduction is often due to an imbalance in the supply chain that allows powerful retailers to 'shop around' and select cheaper suppliers, or through coercive tactics that force suppliers to reduce their sale price or lose the contract.

While logically the low-cost/reliability-driven consumers should be responding well to the lower prices offered by EDLP, it seems they are a little confused. Many still view the EDLP's reduction in prices (which is often identified with a yellow ticket) as a 'special' rather than an ongoing approach that delivers lower prices for each and every visit to the supermarket. Their confusion is perhaps unsurprising because supermarkets continue to offer specials in parallel with EDLP pricing. It will take a while before shoppers understand EDLP. In the United States and elsewhere, EDLP has apparently worked for Wal-Mart. However, employees can find it difficult to manage the inherent conflict between promotional activities (P logic) and EDLP (A logic). Businesses in the *lean* supply chain need to explain EDLP better to consumers – an educational campaign, for instance, could be useful. EDLP works best when the offer is aligned with buyer behavior. It can have a significant impact when the customers are 'trained' to expect more for less.

The Wal-Mart experience raises a number of *lean* issues that are retail specific, e.g., leverage on suppliers; standard products versus 'own brand'; wide SKU range reducing dependency on a supplier; local and national market dominance impact on rivals' competitive strategies; vulnerability to monopoly legislation; vulnerability to suppliers' cartels for protection, or as a way of balancing the power equation. And finally, the EDLP strategy simply doesn't work with monopoly suppliers.

The manufacturing equivalent of Wal-Mart is of course Ford, whose demand for yearly supplier price reductions has had a similar effect. However, the underlying difference is that Ford will 'help' its suppliers to achieve these price reductions, whereas Wal-Mart pushes the responsibility on to the suppliers entirely. Wal-Mart's recent foray into RFID is a good example of its unilateral approach, telling suppliers what standards have to be met, and then leaving them to foot the bill for systems development. This strategy has led to several state law suits.

In pursuit of *leanness*

Can you imagine the complexity involved in managing supply chain networks spreading out from national to regional and – in many cases – to global markets? Such scale is difficult, but not impossible, to manage. The example of the newsprint company outlined in Chapter 2 gave us an insight into how to alter the business to compete internationally. But we need to revisit this important issue from a *lean* supply chain perspective – how to minimize the total costs of running large networks and keep them sustainable. This leads us to the topic of Network Optimization Models as foreshadowed earlier. In a complex supply chain network, strategic and tactical decisions about network design and the optimal use of the network go beyond the scope of experience-based or spreadsheet-assisted decisions. In these situations, where there are a myriad of trade-offs and interdependencies to be considered, sophisticated decision support is essential. For this task the Network Optimization Model has become the accepted tool. Indeed, I can't imagine how you can effectively manage a complex network, especially one of global proportions, without using network optimization models.

Building a Network Optimization Model (NOM) involves capturing all relevant costs, capacities, volumes and constraints in a particular supply chain network. The result is a very large data set. The data set is used to populate a model 'shell' containing literally thousands of equations. This algorithm is then 'solved' to satisfy an objective function, usually either to minimize the cost of operating the network or (if revenue has been included in the model) to maximize profitability. Although the backbone of the model is usually off-the-shelf software with a mathematical 'optimizer', the characteristics of each supply chain need to be carefully configured and entered into the model's data sets to ensure it accurately reflects what is happening in the enterprise. A base 'validation' model is built to match a period of sales and operations – typically using a period of a year. Next, a set of scenarios are identified by the organization and the impact of these different strategies on the performance of the network can be assessed by running the data in the NOM.

The model is a strategic view of the supply chain. In order to produce results which make sense at the strategic level, aggregations of the key elements are usually required. Thus products, suppliers and customers are typically aggregated into logistically meaningful groups. For product 'groups,' the *key driver* is typically handling characteristics. For customers and suppliers, location is, of course, a *key driver* as it determines transport time and cost. This alone, however, is rarely sufficient to capture different service requirements, and therefore determine the cost of servicing different types of customers. It is in this aspect of designing a supply chain model that alignment principles have been used to significantly enhance the power and efficacy of the results. This is amply demonstrated in the following example.[10]

CSR Gyprock, is a major Australian building products supplier with a broad customer base, ranging from distributors and large commercial building contracts to large and small end-user installers. These customers were buying the same or very similar products, but their service expectations, buying patterns and underlying needs were very different.

When an optimization model was developed for this business a critical aspect was to capture the key buying differences in the customer groupings and to factor in the format of the order and 'service package' that was purchased. The customer groups for this NOM were developed using behavioral segmentation based on the customer's purchase preference (project or non-project) and the level of direct support required from the supplier. On one end of the spectrum were distributors (including all formats of resellers) who ordered regularly for stock and whose priority was for reliable and consistent service. 'Commercial project' and 'residential project' were segments of customers identified as having long-term relationships with the supplier and ordered for one-off projects with specific requirements. Their priority was responsiveness and flexibility. At the other end of the spectrum the 'commercial' and 'residential support' customers were generally (but not always) smaller end-users who required delivery to site, but also often needed easy access for last minute requirements. These customers valued technical support and day-to-day relationships with their supplier who they saw as the 'hub' of their trade network.

The service and product packages these customers purchased were defined for modeling as: bulk (larger, stock orders picked up or delivered); crane-ups (deliveries, with narrow delivery windows to meet crane schedules); house lots (larger mixed orders picked up or delivered); standard orders (smaller mixed orders picked up or delivered); and immediate orders (pick ups with no advance notice). Many of these packages were purchased by more than one type of customer.

Product groups were determined by the product's weight, handling characteristics and manufacturing characteristics (as manufacturing was also considered in the model). The network developed using these parameters, and evolved by trying various management scenarios and model runs, is illustrated in Figure 8.5.

The resultant Metropolitan Distribution Network (MDN) features three major pathways to the customer. The *bulk* pathway is in effect the same as our *lean* supply chain, and is designed for high-volume, regular activity and includes supply to facilities in the other two pathways. The *pick* pathway, or *agile* supply chain, is more responsive, capable of shorter lead-times and geared for a less predictable workload. There would be one or two of these facilities to support each metropolitan area. The *trade centre* pathway, or *continuous replenishment* supply chain, is a multi-facility network located close to the end-user's home or site location, providing not only small-volume and top-up products but also technical support and the relationship aspect of the tradesman's service needs.

The strength of combining the decision support capability of the Network Optimization Model with the concept of *dynamic alignment* is the ability to minimize cost within the context of a focused and appropriate service network. By bringing together the physical aspects of the business and its products, and the dominant buying behaviors of customers, the natural 'pathways' through the complexity of a supply chain network start to emerge. See Appendix 8A for a description of the phases involved in building a NOM.

A good example of a company that is endeavoring to become leaner yet more responsive to its markets is BlueScope Steel (BSS), a global leader in adding value to commodity flat steel products to produce branded products used in the building sector. BSS has revenues of US$4.3 billion and a network of steel manufacturing and processing facilities in 16 countries. BlueScope's progress on the project is described below.[11]

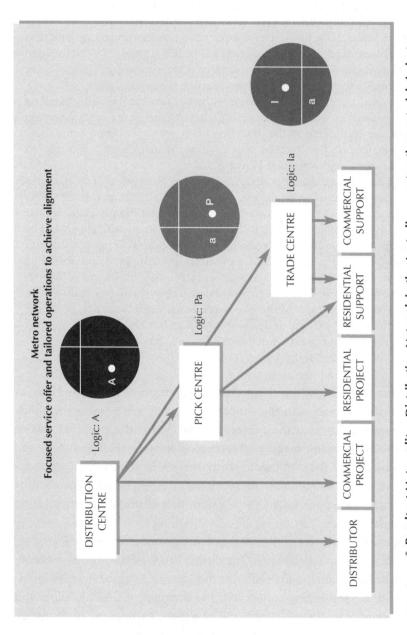

FIGURE 8.5 ◆ **Resultant Metropolitan Distribution Network in the Australian construction materials industry**

Source: Carpenter Ellis, 2006; Figure 6.4 in Gattorna (2006), p. 153

In Phase 1, BlueScope re-segmented its customers and aligned its key value propositions to match the new segments. It aimed to reduce order lead-times using Vendor Managed Inventory (VMI) and other methods. On the manufacturing side, BSS focused on identifying and managing the controllables and sought to standardize processes wherever possible.

In Phase 2, the company emphasized aligning key supply chain processes in manufacturing, distribution, planning and scheduling, and performance measurement. It introduced a 'supply chain velocity' program across the organization with the aim of developing and implementing lean manufacturing.

Phase 3 involved focusing on reducing and managing variation, as it became obvious that the key to achieving more responsiveness in the delivery to customers was to have the ability to 'flex' capacity to follow more closely forecast demand and supply variations.

Overall, improvement in delivery performance as measured by DIFOT has so far proved elusive, despite all the initiatives. However, external customer surveys have revealed a steady increase in customer satisfaction. The project remains 'unfinished business'.

Lean works

So, approached in the right way, *lean*, low-cost, reliable supply chains can be designed and operated to provide the efficiencies, predictability and low costs desired by customers. But, as the examples highlight, it's not simply about reducing freight rates, or squeezing the providers of third-party services; it is much more creative than that. It is about smoothing product flow, reducing errors and producing goods to forecast right across the supply chain. And, just as importantly, a *lean*, low-cost supply chain will only deliver value when aligned with the appropriate buyer behavior. Indeed, *lean* protocols will be quite dysfunctional in an operating environment where customers demand high levels of responsiveness in unpredictable trading conditions. This is your great challenge: 'go *lean*' where it is appropriate, but recognize that other pathways to customers with different requirements must also be working in parallel, or in series, and above all, in synch. That is what it's all about: *dynamic alignment* with all segments of your supply chain. In summary, perhaps the most critical element of lean is the ability to collaborate with suppliers on the supply-side in order to smooth out inventory holding and associated costs as you grapple with customers on the sales-side who sometimes treat you and your product like a common commodity.

Beware the 'dark side'

It is possible to take lean practices too far and in the process reduce the resilience of your supply chains; this tendency should be avoided. In any lean program, the 'continuity challenge' in the face of unexpected disruptions must always be considered, e.g., a fire in a key supplier's factory or an earthquake that disrupts supply of a key component. These types of events have happened in the past and will happen again. More about this phenomenon in Chapter 10.

Tenacity is required

The principles of lean production and management have been around long enough to be understood, but the difficulty of putting these into practice is also well known and documented. Indeed, many companies have found to their cost that the gap between the underlying philosophy of the original Toyota Production System and the prevailing system of management in the enterprise is just too big to bridge. As Liker comments, '[Western company] leaders are either unable or unwilling to grasp one essential lesson: that they should first understand the Toyota principle, then build their own capabilities using these principles. And they must be willing to do it slowly, step by step.'[12] It is painstaking work, and you can't simply leapfrog this learning phase with software.

Liker concludes that making the deep cultural changes required to implement lean systems is a tall order for many Western companies.[13] But it can be done if done right.

Defining ideas

1 Original *lean* concepts developed for the manufacturing environment do not easily translate into the more unpredictable supply chain operating environments of today.

2 Hence there is some confusion between *lean* ideas extrapolated from manufacturing, which seem to assume the presence of collaborative relationships between all members of supply chains. As we have seen, this is not necessarily so. At best we can shoot for collaboration on the supply-side.

3 A lower cost-to-serve is achieved primarily by ensuring that customers are not over-serviced. Our term is *dynamic alignment*. It is critical to focus on customers to ensure your standard offerings remain relevant. You can invoke *lean* principles as much as you like, but not at the expense of giving the customers what they expect!

4 To resolve complexity in global supply chain networks you will almost surely require the help of a Network Optimization Model to guide you to where costs can be cut without endangering service.

5 A special type of subculture is required in order to effectively design and implement lean practices, and this involves the combination of several capabilities. Even so, it is a relentless task, and one which Western companies have not been up to.

6 **Challenge** to the reader: have you gone overboard with the application of *lean* ideas and principles in your firm? Or are you using it only where it will clearly add value?

CHAPTER 9

Agile supply chains

Where quick response is paramount

T his chapter is all about developing a capability to service customers, at speed. However, to be in a position to react quickly requires spare capacity located throughout the system, and this comes at a price. So it may be necessary to select those customers you want to deal with, and cull the rest. It's a choice you have to make because resources are not unlimited. To achieve speed also requires breeding a subculture which will support fast decision-cycle times, and here the OODA loop, borrowed from the military, comes into play. To get the desired results it is necessary to configure your organization for speed, and populate it with individuals who are comfortable with working fast and prepared to take measured risks. This is not a place for consensus-seeking individuals.

It is the third millennium. We all want to be better, cheaper and faster. Let's make that faster, faster and faster. Stop the planet, I want to get off! A new breed of enterprises is certainly demonstrating what is possible when it comes to responding to customers in a fast-moving operating environment, where life-cycles are short and variety reigns supreme. Apparel companies Zara, Adidas and Staroup; technology companies Dell, Nokia, Apple and Cisco; medical appliance manufacturer Cochlear; and supply chain service company Li & Fung are among these leaders. The winners in this environment are those that can respond urgently and effectively. Think of the ultimate example set by the pit crew during a pit stop in a Formula One car race as depicted below. The highly skilled individuals in the crew work in perfectly executed harmony, racing against the clock and doing so in a confined space. This is a world where milliseconds count, where we worry about speed of execution first and the spare capacity required and the cost involved, a distant second. Races have been won and lost during pit stops. But good planning also underpins a quick response. Many pit stops are scheduled and therefore predictable – planned to the lap. It's the unplanned pit stops where you see the difference between success and failure, winners and losers.

The world for businesses operating in *agile* supply chains is similar; the only thing is we have neither the budget nor the capacity of an F1 team standing-by on alert 24/7, 365 days a year. Yes, speed is paramount in this twenty-first-century world. But in keeping the roving, foraging customer firmly in our sights, we need to deliver in a cost-effective way; otherwise we will find ourselves careering off the track in a high-cost, high-speed wreck. Possibly, we are getting a little carried away. But the point is: is such an extreme response necessary for **all** our customers? As

PHOTO 9.1 ◆ A Formula One pit stop

Source: © Schlegelmilch Photography

with the *continuous replenishment* and *lean* supply chains, there is a time and place for everything. The focus in *agile* supply chains is on being fast and also on being smart about how to align with demanding customers. Sometimes the answer may be that we don't want to even attempt to serve them, or at least some of them. It's called culling your customers. Often high responsiveness requires an ability to forecast capacity accurately, rather than predicting the next hit product, and being prepared to switch into high-priority production when the time comes. The challenge for companies is to know how to satisfy their customers as they migrate from predictable to unpredictable operating environments, knowing when to scale-up, and especially, when to scale-down as many enterprises are having to do during the current recession. This is another reason why we should know our customers so well.

Watch out, they are hostile

We thought the customers were relentless in *lean* supply chains. Now they are virtually hostile, or at least the operating environment is. You might have a customer who is absolutely chaotic, but still expects lightning service, at a discount. Or else you are dealing with a business whose customer is just plain disorganized. Sometimes it's justified – their behavior could be driven by uncertainties caused by world oil prices, terrorism-related demand changes or new government regulations. The unpredictability is not so much the result of one customer causing chaos; it's the combined effect of an uncertain world rippling up and down your supply chain. Often the longer the supply chains, the more complexity and increased potential for the 'bull-whip' effect.[1] To combat this, 'some companies are establishing supply chain "war rooms" to make fast decisions across functions . . . populated by leaders from production, procurement, logistics, and sales – these teams meet weekly or even daily to devise near-term operational plans'.[2] Sound familiar? Indeed, we are now under increasing pressure to respond to the demands of all categories of customers, from consumers and end-users through to the most sophisticated corporate enterprises. You know when fast response is important when a company such as IBM uses a television campaign to promote its 'on-demand' supply chain capabilities.[3]

In industries such as fashion and consumer technology, the plethora of products seems to increase exponentially while at the same time life-cycles are forever contracting.

Remember, though, that sometimes the urgency is needed, and sometimes it's not. We need to work out when the demand is genuine and therefore absolutely necessary, and if so, respond in quick time. And we need to know when the customer does not absolutely need the product immediately, or if they do, there is a price premium involved. Perhaps the best solution is the fast (and regular) *rhythms* used by Spanish retailer Zara to replenish its global network of retail stores, which it does at least twice a week. This is a best-of-both-worlds strategy: predictable yet fast, very fast. This is exactly what fashion-loving customers demand, and get. Other enterprises with similarly perishable products going to a known network of customers would do well to replicate the example of Zara. However, you also have to do all the other things that make this a great strategy; more about this later.

It will come as no surprise to you that the dominant buying behavior of customers in an *agile* supply chain is 'demanding/quick response'. These customers seek a rapid response to unpredictable supply and demand conditions, but all too often this is a response designed to compensate for a lack of prior planning rather than an essential requirement. However, where market conditions are genuinely unpredictable, high priority is placed on getting an urgent response from suppliers, and there is little time for relationship development. The exception is if the relationship between a buyer and seller has been in place for some time, or the parties agree to collaborate to achieve a fast response, as is the case with Ericsson and some of its telecom customers.

There is usually an opportunistic edge to the 'demanding/quick response' buying behavior. Suppliers may be treated as an ad hoc source of supply where loyalty is relatively low, overshadowed by an almost obsessive quest for a particular outcome. In some ways, this is simply the commercial real world: one tinged with pragmatism and driven by a focus on results, but not to the point that lowest price is essential. People who live and work in this world understand that trade-offs sometimes have to be made between high-performance responsiveness and the corresponding cost.

Can you predict what the inherent problem will be with these customers? It's not so much the 'need for speed', but in a similar way to the 'cost/

efficiency-driven' customers discussed in Chapter 8, it's the impact on the rest of your customer base that is the real concern. The 'demanding/quick response' buying behavior of these customers requires an *agile* response and they can very easily derail your efforts to deliver consistent and reliable service to the rest of your customers. This is particularly the case for loyal customers, simply because your organization could be swamped by surprise demands from other powerful customers. The resulting disruption as the enterprise attempts to satisfy *all demands from all customer types* is one of the fundamental reasons why the resolution of complexity in supply chains has fallen short of early expectations. Indeed, it is not too far-fetched to suggest that if 'demanding/quick response' customers are given free rein, they would create chaos across the business. This is not to say they are not valued, but rather to suggest that they must be managed carefully and with a plan in mind, rather than on an ad hoc or reactive basis. The use of Decision Support System (DSS) applications can help immeasurably in these tight situations, and an overall awareness of the particular customer's contribution to the business is mandatory for quality decision-making.[4]

In some situations it may be prudent to embargo parts of production, or even an entire factory or production line, to reduce the negative impacts caused by customers placing random demands on your enterprise. As indicated in Chapter 7, global dairy ingredients manufacturer Fonterra recognized the negative impact of demanding customers on its loyal customers in 2000, and took steps to protect the latter.[5]

Being quick *and* cost-effective

How can we respond to the growing band of 'demanding/quick response' customers without being overwhelmed by them? Quite aptly, the *agile* supply chain is also described as a surge-flow supply chain because demand surges during unpredictable, high-variety market conditions. We need to focus on embedding responsiveness in the extended enterprise to match uncertain business conditions into the future. I think it's safe to say these markets are not going to go away. If we get it right, we can capture significant new business. Surges through supply chains may also be the result of our own commercial practices, e.g., pricing policies, payment terms and promotional activity, so to some extent the solution is in our own hands.

Make-to-Order (MTO) or Assemble-to-Order (ATO) capabilities are critical for quick response to customer demands. Hewlett-Packard has long adopted the practice of postponing final assembly of its printers when the exact country or market and configuration are known; manuals are then added, with the power plugs and leads at the last possible moment. Likewise, Vision Express meets delivery deadlines for prescription spectacles measured in hours by assembling frames and custom lenses at the last moment. And Dell Computer is a past master at assembling-to-order and delivering a customer order within days – but they get paid even quicker! However, responsiveness comes at a price unless you are very well organized.

BMW are also getting into the act. According to Rich Morris, VP Assembly for BMW Manufacturing Co., 'flexibility is defined as the ability to shift production of different models among plants as demand shifts in different global markets [or] within the same plant where BMW offers a wide array of factory-installed options . . . the way individual customers order them'.[6] 'The real battle,' says Morris, 'is the race toward efficient flexibility'.[7]

Typically, high responsiveness cannot be achieved for minimal cost. Customers (and suppliers) have to make a choice. Otherwise the business becomes unmanageable and unprofitable. There is always an incremental cost associated with servicing demanding customers, but those who genuinely need urgent service will pay a premium, albeit grudgingly at times. They have already done their sums, made their own internal trade-offs and decided it is worth it. Of course, in practice we often see a mix of Make-to-Forecast and Build-to-Order processes. Companies will Make-to-Forecast for high-volume products that are subject to predictable demand; they will also build low volumes of unpredictable product configurations to meet specific customer orders.

The unique value proposition of *agile* supply chains is that they can and do respond rapidly and with high priority in unpredictable supply and demand conditions. To do this sometimes means holding spare or redundant capacity aside to cope with unpredictable surges in the pipeline, but that is part of the price you pay to be in that market. Anyone who knows about fluid mechanics is familiar with the essential role of surge tanks in absorbing rapid changes in flow volumes through pipelines; the same is true for supply chains. For instance, Zara has two very large Distribution Centers (DCs) at La Coruña and Zaragoza in Spain which at times may only be 50 per cent utilized. This is a conscious strategy rather than an oversight. Zara management understands the cost of redundancy, but they also know the benefit and indeed the necessity of having adequate transient capacity available to support their rapid-fire replenishment business model. So this is yet another example where the previous one-dimensional emphasis on incessant cost reduction for its own sake is flawed. Going back to the Formula One pit-stop analogy, the team's success is partly due to in-built redundant capacity being kept on high alert for the duration of the race, ready for action at a moment's notice, at speed. Maintaining this capacity on stand-by pays off.

Agility and the OODA loop

A vivid example of agility occurred in the immediate aftermath of Hurricane Katrina, which swept through the US state of Louisiana in September 2005. One of the most affected companies was a major oil company, which lost all of the computing equipment in its service centers. The company contacted Hewlett-Packard, its regular hardware supplier, with a priority request to replace 1,000 specially configured PCs as quickly as possible. HP got back a few days later with a commitment to deliver the replacements by Christmas – Christmas 2005! This was not the answer the oil company wanted to hear, so it called Dell, which had not previously been a preferred supplier and asked the same question. Back came the answer almost immediately: 'Is Monday okay?' Dell got the business and won a new customer as well. Obviously the story improves with the telling, but the essentials remain: one supplier could meet an urgent request and the other could not.

How could Dell deliver in such a short time? Probably a combination of lots of spare capacity built into their network; power over their suppliers; and good scenario planning. Clearly, Dell demonstrated the more responsive culture on this occasion. And all that accompanies this, including an *agile* supply chain for new product. Dell's embedded agility enabled it to respond inside Hewlett-Packard's cycle time with a faster OODA loop.

The OODA loop was originally designed for the military by Col. John Boyd for use in combat operations to out-think the enemy.[8] It stands for observe, orient, decide and act. According to Baker, speaking in a business context, 'if I can make decisions faster than my competitor, if I can get inside his decision-cycle, then I've got him'.[9] And the best enterprises are applying this principle to their supply chains.

Staroup, an apparel company based in Botucatu, Brazil, was forced to launch what they called their 'survivor' project in January 2007, when their major customer for jeans, Levi's, announced it was shifting its sourcing to China. Up to that point Staroup had supplied all Levi's women's jeans sold in the United States.

Staroup CEO Vicente Moliterno responded by visiting the US and studying the behavior of American women who bought branded jeans. It emerged that American women were in fact buying jeans every 30 to 45 days, depending on whether they were on the west or east coast. Levi Strauss & Co had not picked up this nuance because they had thought of themselves as wholesalers of the Levi brand of jeans; essentially, they had lost touch with their ultimate consumers – women.

Moliterno acted to radically change his supply strategy. He hired European designers to design a succession of new jean designs for American women, and sent these into 12 pilot stores in the US that Levi had agreed to let him experiment with. The results were startling. Sales grew faster than other stores not in this arrangement. As a result, Levi's adopted Staroup's strategy for some of their range and allowed Staroup to continue as a supplier. Production of the less time-sensitive part of the range was shifted to China, but Staroup had saved their business by getting close to their ultimate consumers, and then using innovation and the OODA loop to produce and supply new designs faster than any Chinese competitor could copy, produce and supply.

And innovation plays a further role

Others have found ways around the after-sales service problem. Michelin has been highly innovative in its approach, introducing e-tires for its customers. The e-tire is a device like a RFID (Radio Frequency Identification) chip, inserted at the time of manufacture; it monitors air pressure in the tire when in use. With the right air pressure, tires perform optimally and last longer; correctly inflated tires also reduce fuel consumption, which is a significant cost in the transportation business. In this case 'service' has been added to the product itself, and becomes a source of differentiation for Michelin compared to its competitors. And this agility does not necessarily mean higher cost.

Companies such as Haier, the giant Chinese domestic appliance company, combine low production costs with rapid innovation to devastating effect. An example of this 'quick-cycle' mindset came after the company discovered the reason for an unusually high incidence of service calls to repair failures in some of its washing machines – customers in rural China were washing their vegetables in their machines! Haier rapidly re-designed the valves in the affected models to accommodate this unusual application and the level of service calls reduced significantly.[10]

It seems that in the harsh environment of the emerging markets of Brazil, Russia, India and China, the so-called BRIC countries, companies learn survival techniques fast. These markets are characterized by high volatility in demand, low disposable incomes and high consumer expectations. According to Donald Sull,[11] there are perhaps 10 to 20 companies in the emerging markets today that are potentially category killers, and in a decade there will be ten times this number.[12] Maybe such threatening news will at last prod Western enterprises into accelerating their own transformations. The alternative is to be swamped by companies with access to relatively low-cost labor, and the ability to adapt and innovate faster than their Western counterparts. A frightening thought.

Superior agility doesn't just happen by accident. It is the result of combining specific processes and techniques with a responsive mindset. Techniques such as strategic sourcing and postponement play a central role in the scheme of things. Everything must align if a quick and cost-effective result is to be achieved without plunging the enterprise into uncontrolled and costly chaos. *Agile* success is also dependent on the ability to 'compartmentalize' lean activities into modules, and have the in-built flexibility to recompile (or reconfigure) the modules in ways that provide the desired responses. This requires quick decision-making cycles, and absolute clarity regarding the roles, responsibilities and level of empowerment that is available to the personnel involved, i.e., what staff are able to commit to the customer. This becomes part of having the appropriate subculture in place to underpin the strategy. But first we must revisit the issue of the most 'appropriate' strategy package needed to serve the 'demanding' customer segment.

Converting value propositions into strategy packages

For best operation of the *agile* supply chain, we will explore in detail the appropriate combination of the 15 strategic dimensions introduced in Chapter 3; a short version of this is provided in Figure 9.1, and is followed by more detailed explanations of the individual strategies in the package.

1 **Product mix.** Customers in a 'demanding' mindset tend to like choice and convenience. Choice means a greater variety in the product range, but the emphasis on meeting the quality specification is strong nonetheless.

2 **Innovation emphasis.** This type of customer is seeking differentiated products and services, and will pay a premium if necessary. The challenge for suppliers therefore is one of 'continuous improvement'.

3 **Marketing emphasis.** The marketing effort with this type of customer is to keep up with the rapidly changing tastes of end consumers, and launch new products in the marketplace before competitors. It is another example of the OODA loop at work.

4 **Channels of distribution.** This type of customer is looking for easy access to products and services, i.e., convenience. So, as volumes grow, the channels of distribution should be widened to accommodate this desire.

5 **Pricing regime.** Pricing in this segment does not have to be the lowest, just competitive with other equivalent products and services. And to cover the extra effort and cost when responding quickly to customers in unpredictable environments, the pricing has to be higher to avoid margin erosion. This is the world of deal makers!

6 **Promotional activity.** A lot of promotional activity occurs in this segment as suppliers attempt to attract customers. This higher level of promotions inevitably pushes costs up, so the pricing regime must cover this additional cost. Where possible, efforts should be made to anticipate and smooth the peaks in demand that flow through the system.

	Strategic dimension	Ideal strategy
1	Product mix	Larger range; choice important
2	Innovation emphasis	Seek product differentiation
3	Marketing emphasis	Quick response to changing customer requirements
4	Channels of distribution	Provide easy access to consumers; convenience
5	Pricing regime	Competitive; moderate price sensitivity
6	Promotional activity	High; fashion-style approaches
7	Service emphasis	Performance to specifications
8	Procurement/ sourcing approach	Market knowledge and distribution
9	Production	Shorter runs; flexible scheduling; make-to-order
10	Capacity considerations	Lower utilisation because of 'buffers' in the system
11	Fulfillment approach	Short lead times; use postponement
12	Relationship intensity	Low
13	Systems/IT support	Use modeling and analysis
14	Resource allocations priorites	Build spare capacity to cater for volatile demand
15	Strategic risk profile	Higher risk

FIGURE 9.1 ◆ *Agile* supply chain strategy – operational

7 **Service emphasis.** The service required is timely response to the customer's sometimes unreasonable demands, and these customers can be impatient!

8 **Procurement/sourcing approach.** It is important to have a selection of suppliers available who have spare capacity in order to respond to our unforecast orders, quickly.

9 **Production.** This supply chain will most likely use a combination of in-house production and outsourcing to get the required capacity in the short lead-times involved.

10 **Capacity considerations.** this supply chain has to cope with wide fluctuations in demand patterns, so it is essential to build in spare capacity, or 'buffers', along the way; these can be in the form of additional suppliers, more production capacity, additional inventories and extra manpower etc.

11 **Fulfillment approach.** This segment demands quick response to orders, so postponement techniques combined with the 'buffers' are essential to meet their expectations.

12 **Relationship intensity.** Members of this segment are more interested in outcomes than processes or smooth relationships. So accept that the relationship intensity will be low and avoid over-servicing.

13 **Systems/IT support.** The emphasis in this type of supply chain is on achieving a quick response to sometimes unreasonable demands. For this purpose it is essential to have a Network Optimization Model available to run scenarios and decide on allocation priorities.

14 **Resource allocation priorities.** Focus on forecasting and building additional capacity in order to cope with volatile demand. Using Customer Account Profitability (CAP) techniques it is possible to make decisions about what priority should be given to this type of customer, especially in situations where product supply and capacity are limited.

15 **Strategic risk profile.** Because we are operating in a customer or market segment where demand (and supply) patterns are relatively unpredictable, the risk is high. On this basis contingency plans should be prepared to mitigate some of the risk of disruption in supply to key customers.

With these dimensions set in place in our strategy package for the *agile* supply chain, we can now turn our attention to shaping the underlying subculture to implement these strategies.

Getting the subculture right

It is beginning to sound as if we are going to need employees with roller-blades on! It would be very handy indeed to have all the cross-directional momentum made possible by roller-blades in order to serve some of our unpredictable customers. The subculture embedded in agile supply chains is the Rational subculture: it's action-oriented, competitive and, above all, driven to perform. It is a subculture that values achievement and promotes a sense of urgency. High levels of activity can sometimes disguise less than optimal effectiveness, but brute energy makes up for this. Maybe we should trade the roller-blades for hockey sticks and ice-skates! In this subculture the focus is predominantly on the external operating environment. The policies and rules so evident in the internal-oriented Hierarchical subculture are replaced by softer guidelines, where individual employees are expected to behave proactively, guided by the principle that you do what is best for the customer. We will now look at what conditions are necessary for a Rational subculture to develop in the first place. Having said that, look at what is happening with many leading US-based companies, e.g., Dow Chemical and Exxon Mobil, who are reducing headcount in their global organizations and bringing key decision-making back to the center. Where is the flex in that? Decision-making speed, action orientation and solution-based logical thinking are all key elements of this vital subculture. I have chosen the same 13 critical capability levers as used in the two previous supply chain configurations; this can be seen in Figure 9.2 overleaf.

1. Organization design

Who needs structure anyway? This is the point where we again diverge from convention and use a dual design already explained in Chapter 6. However, in this case the 'clusters' are designed around speed, and focused on individual customers or groups of customers with quick response as their individual and joint expectation. The cluster will have all the various functions represented, but the embedded bias will be one of speed. It is a harsh, unrelenting work environment and team members will rotate on a reasonably regular basis back to their functional specialties to refresh and receive additional training. It is almost essential for

...where quick response is paramount

MARKET SEGMENT	'DEMANDING'	RESPONSE REQUIRED TO UNPLANNED OR UNFORESEEN DEMAND
FULFILLMENT STRATEGY	VALUE PROPOSITION	**STRATEGIES** ♦ Fast decision-making ♦ Fast delivery ♦ Rapid response in unpredictable conditions
INTERNAL CULTURAL CAPABILITY	**CULTURAL LEVERS** 1. Org design 2. People positioning 3. Processes 4. IT/system 5. S&OP 6. KPIs 7. Incentives 8. Job design 9. Internal comms. 10. T&D 11. Role modeling 12. Recruitment	**RATIONAL SUBCULTURE** ♦ Clusters designed for speed and focused on specific subsegments ♦ Ensure bias towards personnel with 'N' in their MBTI profile ♦ Process short-cuts; fast response; postponement techniques ♦ Software applications: SCP; APS; network models ♦ Keep S&OP at aggregate capacity planning level ♦ Absolute speed of response ♦ Achieve targets; cash and in-kind bonuses ♦ Authority/autonomy established by clear and published limits ♦ Formal; regular; action-orientated ♦ Problem-solving; resource allocation and management ♦ Managers with ENTJ MBTI profile (or P code) are ideal ♦ Recruit personnel who are results-drive
LEADERSHIP	**13 LEADERSHIP STYLE**	**COMPANY BARON** ♦ Leads by objectives (MBO) ♦ Embraces change ♦ Goes for growth ♦ Focuses on what's important ♦ Analytical; fact-based negotiations

FIGURE 9.2 ♦ Agile supply chains – demand-side

Source: Adapted from Figure 1.3 in Gattorna (2009), p.50

individuals in this type of cluster to be co-located physically near each other, but where this is not possible they can operate virtually, with team members spread across geographies. Whatever the case, the essential values of this cluster can be summed up in two words – *collaborative individualism*. Companies such as Zara, Li & Fung and Sears Canada have managed to breed this type of responsive culture into their organizations, as have Virgin Atlantic and South West Airlines. In all these cases their success to date, and continuing success, depends on the responsiveness they are able to produce from **inside** their organizations, mirroring their customers' desires. Dow Chemical, especially in Europe, evolved from a narrow but successful product flow function in the early 1980s, to materials management in the late 1980s, to a strong integrated supply chain management function by the mid-1990s. These were all functional organizations, with loose business alignment, until 1998 when the pendulum swung back in favor of individual business units and perhaps went too far. Dow's full-blooded business alignment resulted in a loss of leverage, lots of duplication, and did not deliver the uplift in earnings before interest and tax (EBIT) that was expected. So the story continues to unfold today with perhaps some misgivings. The company still cannot find the right formula, and this is one of the world's best chemical companies. What hope is there for the rest?

In real life, however, pure examples of particular business models seldom exist. We live in a hybrid world, which brings with it dangers for the unsuspecting. Charles Fine, the renowned MIT professor and management writer, highlights just what can happen when two business models come together, as was the case with the acquisition of Chrysler by Daimler-Benz in 1998 to form DaimlerChrysler AG.[13] A 'modular' supply chain in Fine's terms is roughly equivalent to *agile* in my terms, displaying 'relatively flexible and interchangeable relationships among suppliers, customers, and partners'.[14] This was Chrysler pre-takeover. Daimler-Benz had a much more integral product and organization architecture, equivalent in my terms to a cross between *collaborative* and *lean* supply chains, underpinned by a functional organizational structure. In this case, the two architectures were like oil and water, which is one reason why the merged entity has struggled to perform ever since, culminating in Chrysler going into Chapter 11 in May 2009.

Fine highlights the imperative to align the supply chain and product architectures because 'they have a powerful impact on each other'.[15] He uses three companies to exemplify this point – Toyota Cars, Dell and Nokia:

> *Toyota cars, known for their reliability and flawless performance, have an integral supply chain and product design. Dell's renowned modular designs match its standardized multi-vendor supply chain. Nokia employs a deliberately designed hybrid approach, with a modular semiconductor and software core, highly integrated components for the rest, and a complementary supply chain design.*[16]

Zara's business model uses cross-functional teams known as 'commercials' to manage the design and production of clothing lines in specific fashion ranges, for women, men or children. These teams work closely with the store product managers and travel extensively to observe purchases and communicate with the local store managers. Employees are given a high level of autonomy to make decisions within their business. However, a note of caution is also appropriate here, because there is increasingly too much rhetoric on company websites and in company reports about how they are shaping a more 'responsive culture', and in the same breath they claim to be cutting costs and becoming leaner. The two can coexist – but such precision, call it a 'coalition' if you like, is still relatively rare. In effect, what has to happen is that individuals are empowered to pull together the appropriate modular components to make things happen the way the customer wants them to happen, fast.

2. People positioning

The ideal people to sprinkle liberally throughout this cluster are those that thrive on speed and reacting quickly to hitherto unknown situations. This is typical of the ENTJ (Extrovert-Intuition-Thinking-Judging) or INTJ (Introvert, Intuition, Thinking, Judging) profiles in the Myers-Briggs Type Indicator (MBTI®) profiles, which translate to P (Producer) or Pd (Producer-developer) in my P-A-D-I code.

3. Processes

The further we move to the right along the continuum of supply chain types, the less we need formal *processes*. But you still need good processes, and plenty of them, to cover the more predictable side of your business. This is not an 'either/or', but an 'and' situation. In the *agile* supply chain, processes are still necessary, but they are by definition fewer. Any process that slows down response time is dispensed with via creative process re-engineering. Short-cuts are invoked and the risks increase, but not to the point where safety is compromised. Ways are found to work around regulations, and there is generally an opportunistic flair embedded in the remaining processes. However, we are not talking about creating a myriad of costly exceptions. Quite the contrary, the processes that drive and support *agile* supply chains are mostly *unique combinations of standard processes*. This is the key to containing costs while delivering rapid bursts of obsessive service over short periods of time.

4. Systems/IT

Agile supply chains are best underpinned by an ERP system similar to those used in other supply chain types, but that is where the similarity ends. We need to invest in an array of additional systems applications designed to optimize capacity and reduce the risk of interfering with the more standard regimes in the *continuous replenishment* and *lean* supply chains. See Figure 9.3 overleaf. In particular, capital should be invested in applications that support scenario development and analysis, e.g., the broad category of supply chain management systems which include Supply Chain Planning (SCP); Advanced Planning and Scheduling (APS); Supply Chain Event Management (SCEM); supplemented by postponement methods. Because of rapid obsolescence, and the changing nature of the marketplace, one wonders if many of the tools being offered by the ERP providers are just too cumbersome. MySAP and Netweaver seem to aim for more modularity, flexibility and, most importantly, value.

The uncertain nature of demand on the *agile* supply chain type means there is significantly more management involvement. Experienced, multi-skilled staff members are preferred because the complexity that has to be resolved is greater than in the *continuous replenishment* and *lean* supply chains. Above all, you should remember it is fruitless to go in search of ever more forecast accuracy in unpredictable demand situations, when forecasting is not really possible at any level. The guiding principle here is to *plan for capacity . . . and execute to demand.*

Companies such as Zara follow this principle to perfection, sourcing raw materials and components in distant low cost markets in the Far East, pre-booking manufacturing capacity in advance in locations closer to consuming markets and using postponement techniques and *agile* organizational formats to rapidly produce up-to-the-minute fashion for swift delivery to regional markets. The formula has not been successfully replicated to any significant degree by competitors to date, and Zara has the capacity to enter other apparel markets at will and work well inside

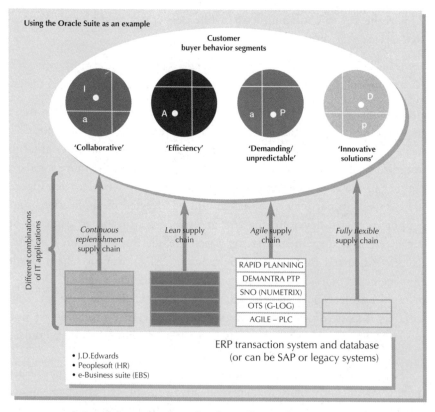

FIGURE 9.3 ◆ **Requisite technology for the *agile* supply chains**

Source: Adapted from Figure 1.5 in Gattorna (2009), p.55

the delivery cycle times of more traditional retailers such as Marks and Spencer; there's that OODA loop in action again! If Zara chooses to follow this route it will be bad news indeed for their new direct competitors. Benetton is probably in a position to do likewise.

A strong component of systems in this type of supply chain is the decision-support and analytics capability, which helps you understand the cost of doing business with various customer accounts. Indeed, Customer Account Profitability (CAP) analysis should be undertaken for all major customer accounts that fall into the 'demanding/quick response' category of buying behavior.

Zara's ability to achieve responsiveness in the fashion industry has been due to its determination to monitor constantly *both* what is popular in the marketplace and what sells well in its stores, in close to real-time. There are formalized (and well proven) communication links between the store network and its designer 'commercials', which provide daily updates of sales information, including customer comments. This gives Zara accurate information not only for product re-orders but also of 'what the customer wants', so it can produce designs within very short lead-times. Of course, the ultimate example of postponement that provides almost infinite agility is the mixing of paint colors at the point-of-sale. In the automotive industry it is at the point-of-application.

The other sizable global enterprise that follows the same principles is Li & Fung. Typical is the case when Li & Fung heard that Levi Strauss was planning to order one million garments – style and color unknown.[17] Since the specifications would only be revealed four weeks before delivery, Li & Fung went ahead on trust with both customer and suppliers to reserve un-dyed yarn while coincidentally locking-up production capacity at mills and the downstream manufacturer of the finished garments. Li & Fung orchestrated the lot and achieved the relatively short delivery cycle required by Levi's.

Finally, for this type of supply chain it is almost mandatory to develop and maintain a Network Optimization Model, because this has the capability to materially improve the quality of decision-making at the executive level when key issues need to be resolved, e.g., should we close a particular distribution centre? Will we continue to use a particular third-party logistics provider (3PL)? What part of the product range should we produce in particular plants throughout our production network, including outsourcing? With a NOM facility available to undertake intense analytical work, the chances of achieving optimal alignment between the enterprise and its various customer segments, including the 'demanding/quick response' segment, are significantly enhanced. Point-of-sale and RFID systems also help drive the required responsiveness.

5. Sales & Operations Planning (S&OP)[18]

In a demanding and volatile operating environment, the S&OP process has to become an effective capacity management tool that can be acted upon within a short cycle-time. There is no longer the luxury of long meetings and time to reach a consensus.

6. Key Performance Indicators

In the Rational subculture, the key performance metrics are absolute speed of response to customer enquiries and firm orders, and the ability to be first into the marketplace. Measurements such as elapsed time from concept to launch of new products, including delivery lead-time to customers, are a fundamental indicator of good or bad performance. Another good indicator is optimization of capacity at different points along the supply chain, and overall optimization of the entire supply chain in terms of the service/cost equation. Frankly, this area is one of the biggest challenges facing the supply chain community. You have to get it right.

7. Incentives

The most appropriate incentives are those that encourage results-oriented behavior, such as achieving budgets and stretch targets. Rewards come in the form of cash bonuses, increased salaries and fringe benefits. The achievement-oriented Rational subculture is motivated by tangible rewards and recognized performance. But here again, be careful to choose the right incentives for your company. Many would argue that these types of cash incentives can have the opposite effect, and destroy agility – because the business becomes self-centered rather than customer-centric. Maybe this is one reason why Dow Chemical has not performed up to early expectations?

8. Job design

Job designs that help shape the Rational subculture focus on clear output requirements. Authority and autonomy is established by clear structural limits, and control is centralized by setting clear guidelines and principles for action.

9. Internal communications

Competing in an *agile* supply chain, you will do best to adopt internal communications that are relatively formal, regular and very action-oriented. The underlying theme to all communications is that 'we respond'. Communications are open and preferably face-to-face, although emails, text messages and mobile telephones are used for convenience and time efficiency. With the emphasis on results, the tone is impersonal and business-like. The risk you need to watch out for is that staff will withhold information; if this happens silos will start to form within the business. In a cost-saving exercise Dow Chemical had eliminated most of the cell phones in the company, only then to face some significant communication problems after Hurricane Katrina. A false economy if ever we have seen one!

10. Training and development

Your training and development programs should emphasize resource management. Staff should study rational models of subculture and undertake challenging assignments on problem-solving and resource allocation. The aim is to develop competencies in areas such as time optimization, communications and influencing skills. Staff will not just be participating in the process – the backbone of this culture is results, results, results.

11. Recruitment

Your business should be eagerly seeking personnel with a 'driven' personality and a desire to achieve results. Decisive, analytical, energetic and objective are words to describe the people who are most appropriate and indeed essential to shaping a Rational subculture. The ideal recruits will have a pragmatic mix of operational and strategic mindsets, be very customer-focused and prepared to take measured risks.

12. Role modeling

The role model in this cluster is the *Company Baron* who sets objectives and drives himself/herself and his or her subordinates relentlessly to achieve same. Sometimes these people drive their people too hard and cause physical and mental exhaustion – this behavior is not condoned.

13. Leadership style

The members of your top management team should exhibit the leadership styles that mirror the subcultures you need to drive your company strategies into the marketplace. A *Company Baron* leadership style is the most appropriate for shaping a Rational subculture and realizing value in an *agile* supply chain. *Company Barons* lead by objectives; they enthusiastically embrace change, go for growth and focus only on what is important. They are challenging individuals, practical, analytical and seek fact-based commercial solutions. Above all they get their way through force of personality; they are a typical ESTP (Extrovert-Sensing-Thinking-Perceiving) in the MBTI® profiles or Pa (Producer-administrator) in my P-A-D-I code.

Changing times

So while leanness is important in difficult trading environments like the current recession, so also is capacity, which is going to cost. However, we should beware, whatever the trading environment, of going too far in blind pursuit of leanness and cost reduction. This philosophy was a major factor in Marks and Spencer's fall from grace in the late 1990s. According to McKinsey & Company:[19]

> . . . *while many companies benefit from sending work to places where labor is cheap, manufacturers [and retailers] often over-rate the value of wage savings and underestimate the inventory, obsolescence, intellectual-property, and currency risks of off-shoring. Some also overlook the benefits of producing goods close to their markets so that customers can get them in days instead of months.*

Both points raised by McKinsey are relevant in today's fast-moving global trading environment. One wonders if Australian apparel supplier Pacific Brands factored in any of this thinking when the CEO decided in 2009 to move the manufacturing operations offshore.[20]

McKinsey found that Californian manufacturers that had adopted lean practices would only realize marginal savings if they moved to Asia: 13 per cent for apparel; 6 per cent for plastics; and less than 1 per cent for high technology products.[21] Given the declining importance of direct labor, which according to McKinsey may now only represent 7 to 15 per cent of cost of goods sold,[22] some manufacturers are questioning the logic of going offshore. Consider the case of a Los Angeles-based fashion apparel company, described below.

The US fashion apparel manufacturer referred to above had 1,500 workers making casual wear in a dilapidated multi-storey building in Los Angeles. The workers were paid above-award labor rates. However, labor costs only represented 3 per cent of retail price, and were on the decline. If production was moved offshore, the additional logistics costs would certainly overshadow any savings in labor. But just as importantly, responsiveness, and therefore sales, would suffer as the lead-time blew out from days to weeks because of the greater distance from consumer markets.[23]

This is exactly why appliance and electronics manufacturer the Haier Group is expanding its manufacturing base to the United States, and forsaking the lower production costs in China. In the words of CEO Zhang Ruimin, 'our strategy is to satisfy consumers as quickly as possible'.[24] So the world is full of contradictions. While many manufacturers are racing to source their manufactured goods in China, a Chinese company is going in the opposite direction! At least it is doing so for part of its production. Those companies moving their production to China are also changing the nature of their business at the same time. Consider the case of Redan, a Polish textiles and apparel company.[25] It has moved from producing and selling its own goods, to creating its own brands at the retail level and leaving the sewing to others. This is the early phase of Redan's defense against Chinese manufacturers flooding its home markets in Poland with low-priced apparel.

Shades of things to come

Are you inspired by finding examples of what the future may look like? Igus, a Cologne-based company, is a hive of constant innovation. It makes 28,000 different industrial products, most of them customized. The plant layout is flexible and can be rapidly changed as demand shifts across the product range. And the workforce has a culture that embraces change, every working day. This is the ultimate *agile factory* where everything is designed for speed and responsiveness.[26] They are being smart and fast in how they deliver to their customers. A bit like a Formula One team, only better! The competitive edge used to be about superior product, now it's about the quality product together with the capacity to customize and deliver. All we need now is to re-create the same formula in the rest of our supply chains.

The other development coming through the pipeline is the phenomenon of Rapid Manufacturing (RM), which 'involves the economic manufacture of low-volume products on demand at multiple locations near the point of consumption'.[27] This agile production strategy enables a truly distributed supply chain, where manufacturing can take place concurrently at multiple locations close to the consumer.[28] Leading companies already using RM include Boeing, Airbus, BAE Systems, Renault and Honda. It seems that the best will just get better!

The epitome of agility and speed

Perhaps the image that we can leave you with that epitomizes agility and speed is that provided by the Italian climber, Reinhold Messner.[29] He climbed all 14 of the world's highest peaks using a radically new climbing technique – the direct alpine approach – which uses minimum equipment and no oxygen to reach the top!

Conventional mountaineering practice is based on massive amounts of support, including extra oxygen, thought essential over 25,000 feet. Men like Sir Edmund Hilary and Sir Christopher Bonington relied on hundreds of helpers to carry food, oxygen and other supplies.

Messner on the other hand argued that 'slowest man sets the pace'. His goal was speed of execution – sound familiar? Although assisted by guides up to base camp, Messner usually made the final assault by himself, or with one other person, in a single day. He scaled the north face of Mt. Everest solo, without oxygen! That's speed and agility personified. Let's hope many of our contemporary businesses find the same formula works for them.

Defining ideas

1. Forget about forecasting at the product/SKU level – just forecast the capacity you require at different points along your supply chains, and lock it in with your suppliers.

2. Accept that you will almost always need to add 'redundant capacity' in the form of inventory/labor/factory space when operating in a volatile environment.

3. You can only participate successfully in a fast unpredictable market if you have developed a Rational subculture in your business. If this is not possible, forget it – you won't succeed.

4. It is essential to understand and apply OODA loop principles in order to get inside your competitors' decision cycle-times, just as Zara and Staroup do so successfully.

5. **Challenge** to the reader: do you use 'agile' practice at the appropriate times in your company?

CHAPTER 10

Fully flexible supply chains

Where nothing is impossible

Here come 'extreme' supply chains in the form of the *fully flexible* type. This is an entirely new category of supply chain configuration, which has always existed but never previously identified formally. There are two distinct types. The 'business event' *fully flexible* supply chain occurs in industry and commerce when enterprises are faced with completely unexpected and unplannable situations. Such is the scope and impact of the disruptions to this supply chain, we almost need catastrophe theory to understand it! And then there's the *fully flexible* 'humanitarian' supply chain; it comes into play when natural disasters occur and human lives are at stake. In both cases an enormous effort is involved, with abundant personnel and financial resources needed to devise and deliver creative solutions, very fast. The military and non-government organizations manage this supply chain, supported by major corporations, so there is an opportunity to learn from each other in the face of adversity.

With new-breed companies leading the pack in winning difficult customers in fast-moving environments, we all thought the ultimate had been achieved. Agility to match the unpredictability! But there's always a new Himalaya to conquer when we are tackling the supply chain, and today it's the emerging phenomenon of 'emergency supply chains'. Increasingly, organizations are finding themselves at the centre of unforeseen, indeed, unplannable events – emergencies, breakdowns and other critical events that interrupt and threaten their global supply chains. We thought we had it all figured out when we mastered the conventional logistics systems, making it lean and mean and delivered straight to the customer. But such systems are not good at coping with unplannable crises, on any scale. The post-9/11 era, including such incidents as the Iraq war, the London bombings, SARS and swine flu, has focused attention on the need to develop new capabilities that can be rapidly deployed when necessary.

Can you see times when your business might need a fast, flexible response to unexpected conditions? The *fully flexible* supply chain is pursuing the ultimate quest for a **creative solution** to an unusual, and seemingly low probability event, happening somewhere along one of your supply chains. Often this occurs when non-government and government organizations are coping with a disaster on a massive scale. But there are also times when businesses like yours might need the capability to manage an unexpected event, to avoid serious disruption and damage to your competitiveness. We will say more about the negative impact of such disruptions in Chapter 15. You can incorporate some of the strategies you use during a crisis into your supply chain in the long term, or adopt the strategies you learn from other agencies as they find solutions to incredibly complex problems. *Fully flexible* supply chains – wherever they occur – are designed to find a solution, and find it **very fast**. If this requires creative thinking, innovative behavior, intense flexibility, and high costs, then so be it. The final result is paramount.

In general, this is a costly supply chain to configure for just routine business, but you will need the capability anyhow to mitigate risk and ensure business continuity. This capability could be regarded as a required competence and positioned within the business development function. The Entrepreneurial subculture that underpins this type of supply chain is ideal for start-ups and incubation of fledgling businesses. Indeed, it is essential for any activity that is at the edge of the core business, or is subject to imminent market discontinuities through competitive, regulatory or other external forces – with unpredictable outcomes.

Two types of *dynamic* flexibility

In our *dynamic alignment* model, *fully flexible* supply chains share common features, but they also fall into two distinct categories: the 'business event' and 'emergency response/humanitarian' supply chains.[1] Important features such as the purpose of the supply chain, its life-cycle, and where and how funds are sourced can vary; this means the organizations managing them need to approach these two types of *fully flexible* supply chain in different ways.

'Business event' *fully flexible* supply chain

Have you ever had to contend with a situation that demanded full-frontal flexibility in your supply chain? Did you have the money to do it? The 'business event' supply chain is normally found in the business sector, as its name suggests, but unlike most business projects the supply chain is not overly cost-sensitive. Managers in this supply chain already have adequate supply chain options for everyday business. But when an unexpected problem arises, and an innovative solution is needed, they will make available substantial – almost unlimited – funds. The attitude is often 'just do it', the implication being, 'to heck with the cost'. Funds are normally provided by the customer, who has a clearly defined focus and pre-determined timeline. An example comes from the oil company mentioned earlier in Chapter 9, which sought to have 1,000 PCs replaced urgently in the aftermath of Hurricane Katrina. The 'business event' supply chain is necessary to solve a transient rather than on-going business problem. So we are looking at a solution to a one-off 'event' that is supported by substantial funds and people resources.

'Emergency response/humanitarian' *fully flexible* supply chain

Unfortunately we all recognize the large-scale emergencies that prompt the need for an 'emergency response/humanitarian' supply chain. The 9/11 terrorist strikes in 2001 and the Bali bombings of 2003 called for an immediate, crisis response on a large scale, as did the natural disasters such as the Indian Ocean tsunami of 2004, the Pakistan–Afghanistan earthquake of 2005[2] and the 2008 Cyclone Nargis crisis in Myanmar.

The 'emergency response/humanitarian' supply chain differs from the 'business event' supply chain largely because of the source of its funding and its sensitivity to cost. Funds are limited because they are often provided by donations from a wide mix of third parties: national governments, the United Nations, individual donors and Non-Government Organizations (NGOs) such as charities, and community and aid organizations. The groups who build this type of supply chain also have an extra factor to consider – governance. They need to be highly accountable for all the funds they collect and apply to disaster operations. This supply chain is not only price sensitive, but is accountability sensitive too.

In many emergencies, the normal supply chains that underpin business and community activities are completely disrupted or destroyed. Urgent help is required to save lives or, in environmental cases, to protect the natural environment. After the initial critical response period, the 'emergency response/humanitarian' supply chain usually develops into longer-term humanitarian aid and/or environmental 'restoration'. Examples include on-going aid in war-torn areas (e.g., United Nations aid in Afghanistan 2001–02; Niger in mid-2005) or rebuilding communities after a natural disaster, such as the Iranian earthquake of 2002, the Indian Ocean tsunami in 2004 and Hurricane Katrina in the United States in 2005. In each of these situations there is an initial event (or series of events) that dictates the requirement for a *fully flexible* supply chain, although the characteristics of the supply chain can evolve dramatically as the situation develops from the critical response phase into the on-going rebuilding phase.[3]

'Life-critical' variant of the 'humanitarian' supply chain

Another variation on the supply chain types needed in extreme (life-saving) situations is emerging from studies of diabetes patients in developing countries.[4] In this situation the supply of a core product (insulin) and the complementary products and services to enable its effective use (e.g., syringes, test strips and accompanying training) are so life-critical that an interruption to availability of even a few days can mean the death of a patient. Unlike the supply chains needed in emergency relief situations, this supply chain does not need to re-configure itself and respond differently to each new event. Instead this *steady state* supply chain needs to be built around absolute reliability. How to achieve this level of reliability, particularly in a resource-poor setting, is a complex question. The levers for high availability are usually spare capacity (such as very high inventory levels), but in these settings more creative cross-channel solutions such as the centralized multi-country holding of back-up stock may be more cost-effective and sustainable. This is essentially an *agile or fully flexible* supply chain being used in a contingency role for a day-to-day *lean* operation.

A similar situation exists in the treatment for HIV/AIDS. The Clinton Foundation has launched initiatives to expand access to life-saving medicines and help developing countries to systematically treat HIV/AIDs victims.[5]

It's urgent, and we mean it

I can hear you asking, 'So who is the customer?' *Fully flexible* supply chains are unlike most supply chain types because 'the customer' varies from normal market environments and market behaviors. The customers in the 'business event' supply chain are the everyday customers of the enterprise who start behaving in a radically new way, generally under pressure. They seek *innovative solutions* to rare and seemingly intractable problems; they are trying to avoid the problem taking on crisis proportions – unless it's a crisis already! Customers in the 'emergency response/ humanitarian' supply chain are not only the end-consumer – the survivor or victim of a tragedy or natural disaster – they are also the many organizations within the supply chain demanding emergency services and assistance for the affected population. They could be local authorities, domestic national governments, community groups, emergency service organizations and local arms of non-government organizations.

'Business event' *fully flexible* supply chain

The customer in this supply chain will normally display one or more of the other three buying behaviors: collaborative; efficiency/low-cost; or demanding. But they will *move* into an 'innovative solutions' behavior for short periods when a crisis occurs. They are likely to return to their preferred or natural buying behavior when the crisis subsides, as shown in Figure 10.1.

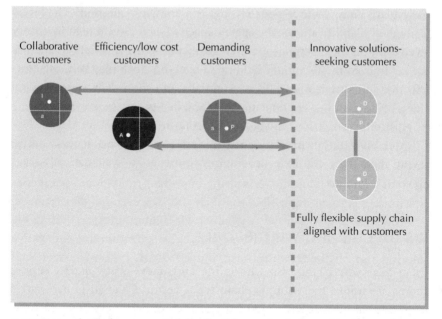

FIGURE 10.1 ◆ 'Business event' *fully flexible* **supply chain and its innovative solutions-seeking customers**

Source: Taken from Figure 8.1 in Gattorna (2006), p. 183

In September 1992 the international airline Qantas, then owned by the Australian government, acquired the domestic airline Australian Airlines. To ensure the merger of the two airlines was successful, Qantas urgently needed to integrate the Australian Airlines' legacy IT systems with its own within 90 days. Up until that point Qantas had been very price sensitive in its dealings with systems integration providers. But the airline quickly shifted to a 'fix at any cost' mindset because the task was so vital. Suddenly it demanded a *fully flexible* response to its problem. Once the task was completed, Qantas returned to its former *lean* buying behavior for subsequent transactions involving systems technology.

Occasionally, due to extreme external pressures this innovative solution becomes a new 'innovative solutions' supply chain incorporated into the on-going operations of the company. The government bus authority in Israel, Egged, operates about 70 per cent of public bus services. This company operates under incredibly difficult conditions – as a target of terrorism. Company chairman Arik Feldman sums up the resilient attitude of the company's culture when he says: 'Drivers and managers have learned to adapt to the realities of the situation . . . if a bus blows up, it doesn't stop us from running public transportation . . . it gives us more courage to continue.'[6] Such an on-going *flexible* type of supply chain as that developed by Egged is extremely rare. How often do you hear of a company continuing to offer its customers service under such extreme conditions? They are still operating the bus service today.

DHL has made an art form of handling extreme challenges on an almost daily basis. Request for replacement equipment following a breakdown at a remote mine site, or moving important exhibitions for galleries and museums to an impossible time schedule, or even handling dangerous goods, all fall within the company's capabilities, albeit requiring the intensive focus of those creative personnel skilled in finding innovative solutions for customers, ultra-fast. Indeed, DHL has now established an Asia Pacific Quality Control Center (APQCC) in Singapore. One of its roles is to act as a 'crisis centre', which attempts to anticipate and/or respond to dramatic and destructive events in the region.

'Emergency response/humanitarian' *fully flexible* supply chain

Humanitarian crises demand two essential ingredients – good leadership and the right people on the ground to direct and co-ordinate disaster relief operations. Yet, we are seeing a distinct lack in both. Despite an increase in reported disasters of over 60 per cent in the past ten years, the humanitarian response is simply not keeping pace.[7]

Emergency or humanitarian situations usually involve both customers/buyers of services on the ground and consumers/survivors who are caught up in a disaster; natural or man-made. The immediate aim is to quickly provide life-saving essentials to the survivors, who often have no choice of buyer behavior. Instead, the buying behavior in the initial phase following a crisis is a response to 'whatever is provided'; required initially by individuals who rapidly move into community clusters as people try to re-establish what was familiar. In the next stage, when basic living requirements are restored, and later as the community is rebuilt, survivors will exhibit a greater range of buyer behaviors as the situation permits.

This situation occurs when an entire complex of supply chains need to be created from scratch because of a major disruption to normal living and business operations due to situations such as war, terrorist attacks, famine and natural disasters like earthquakes or tsunamis. The third parties providing the funding – and normally there are multiple parties involved – often have conflicting objectives. These groups may become temporary partners at best, or competitors at worst, all working in a situation where there are no straightforward answers to the short- and longer-term issues involved. Sarah Murray outlined some of the difficulties faced by humanitarian agencies in her article in the *Financial Times*, including the many lessons learned on the ground from having to bring essential supplies to people in the worst-hit regions of the world.[8]

The singular focus in the 'emergency response/humanitarian' segment is on finding a solution to the problem, and very often the customer has no idea what that solution might look like. Indeed, it is one of those rare occasions where customers look to their suppliers for a supplier-led solution involving an abundance of innovation and creativity. There is a corresponding risk involved, but customers are usually quite prepared to take risks (in the case of the 'business event' supply chain) to get to a solution, or have no choice but to take whatever is offered (in the case of survivors at the end of 'emergency response/humanitarian' supply chains).

So, the demand characteristics in this market are very unpredictable, much more so than in the 'demanding/quick response' customer segment. There is relatively higher risk involved for all parties and a desire for an innovative, flexible response by customers/consumers. A genuine solutions mindset is prevalent for the time that the crisis exists, and price sensitivity is nowhere to be seen. As such, this type of buying behavior represents a real opportunity for suppliers with the capacity to respond appropriately. Sometimes a solution in this situation can be the breakthrough to a new longer-term relationship with the customer involved.

The complex sequence of events that occurs in a humanitarian disaster was first proposed by Kate Hughes as distinct phases.[9] I have adapted her work as shown in Figure 10.2. In reality, these phases don't follow each other in a neat sequence, but almost always blend and overlap in time and space.

In the Prequel phase,[10] before a catastrophic event, governments, aid agencies and private donors are increasingly trying to hedge and deploy by prepositioning supplies at strategic locations around the world. This strategy is designed to speed up the subsequent response to any disaster.

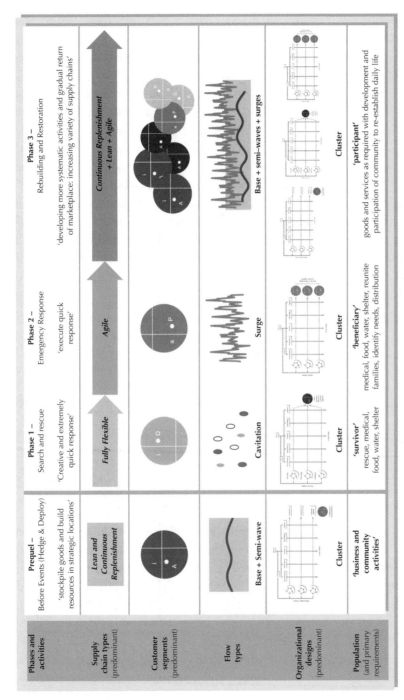

FIGURE 10.2 ◆ **The phases – and corresponding types of supply chain configurations – in humanitarian disasters**

Source: Adapted from Figure 5.1 in Gattorna (2009)

In the Search and Rescue phase,[11] the demand for food, water, and life-saving essentials is extreme, so the supply chain has to ramp up very quickly, with participating aid organizations responding at short notice. This is the *fully flexible* supply chain at work.

This soon transitions into the Emergency phase[12] as the full extent of the disaster becomes evident and aid organizations on site seek to deliver creative solutions to save lives in very fast time. This is the *agile* supply chain operating in the face of extreme disruption. Finally, there is the Re-building and Restoration phase designed to help re-establish the affected communities, and this may stretch over months and years.[13]

The London bombings in July 2005 were a good example of what can be achieved in terms of providing fast response to the victims and maintaining and restoring service during a crisis. Interestingly, the British government and its agencies have already started a thorough review of the old plans to see what lessons can be learned for the future.[14] Scenario planning is an important tool for anticipating what skill sets might be needed in all sorts of possible disasters.

Response strategies

Now this is where it gets really difficult. How do you respond in such extreme, changeable conditions? *Fully flexible* (or cavitation flow in Chapter 2) supply chains are configured around hedge and deploy principles that seek to provide maximum responsiveness on a selective basis, for short periods. The value proposition is aimed at meeting unplanned and unplanable demand with fast, effective, customer-centric solutions that are usually unavailable under normal operating conditions. The 'emergency response' supply chains are a good example, and are activated to meet sudden humanitarian crises anywhere around the globe. In the same way, the 'business event' supply chain is activated quickly and demands urgent attention from suppliers to unforeseen and unexpected events. DHL was requested to transport a replacement mast from Sydney to Newport, Rhode Island, during one of the America's Cup races in the 1980s. The Australian team had broken a main mast on its lead boat. DHL took on the challenge and managed to load the 100-foot mast by removing the front cockpit window and threading it down through the plane and then replacing the window.

The reverse process was performed at the destination end. This is a living example of a 'business event' *fully flexible* supply chain!

Another more contemporary example is the way Dell responded to requests for help following the Haiti earthquake of 2010. The first call came on 16 January 2010. The Dell team worked through the weekend to process orders and assure readiness for production the following Monday. Delivery to Miami occurred on Tuesday 19 January, for immediate transshipment to Haiti. This was an example of super-agility on the part of Dell in the face of a crisis.

Emergency supply chains, whether in response to a natural disaster or the outcome of war, are extreme examples where the *fully flexible* supply chain configuration comes into its own. It has to be created quickly, often from a zero base, often under extremely difficult conditions to service thousands, sometimes millions, of people, who are subsisting under extremely poor conditions. Whether for reasons of distribution of food and clothing, medical aid and treatment, or security and safety, these supply chains are generally highly complex.

Coincidentally, they face huge impediments such as substandard or zero infrastructure, limited capital, multiple partners, language difficulties and usually the involvement of more than one political group. Beyond this initial mission there are always added demands for assistance that can cut across the original task of distributing food, aid and evacuation services as has been the case in Afghanistan.[15] And, of course, political complexities are involved in dealing with the host and donor nations, who often place divergent demands on the supply chain network and so stretch human and financial resources to the limit. The people who work in extreme situations are often highly motivated; some will volunteer their services, work for lower salaries than normal, or work for extended periods without recompense. It takes special people to work in these conditions.

Converting the *value proposition* into operational strategies

To achieve the best operation of *fully flexible* supply chains, we will now explore in detail the appropriate combination of the 15 strategic dimensions introduced in Chapter 3. These provide the individual elements of the strategy package needed for *fully flexible* supply chains, which is shown in summary in Figures 10.3 (overleaf) and 10.4 (on page 264). First, the *fully flexible* 'business event' supply chain.

	Strategic dimension	Ideal strategy
1	Product mix	Broad changing product line
2	Innovation emphasis	Extensive R&D; aim to be first to market
3	Marketing emphasis	Creative problem-solving
4	Channels of distribution	Limited
5	Pricing regime	Price appropriately for a creative solution; no price sensitivity
6	Promotional activity	Target early adopters
7	Service emphasis	Novel solutions
8	Procurement/sourcing arrangements	Product; technology; innovation
9	Production	Prototypes; customisation
10	Capacity considerations	Low. Hedge and deploy resources
11	Fulfillment approach	Speed is vital
12	Relationship intensity	Intense but short term while problem exists
13	Systems/IT support	What is required to solve the problem
14	Resource allocations priorities	Hedge and deploy resources; sometimes ineffectively
15	Strategic risk profile	High

FIGURE 10.3 ◆ 'Business event' *fully flexible* supply chain strategy –

1 **Product mix.** Draw on any and all products and services to get a successful solution to the problem being faced.

2 **Innovation emphasis.** We are looking for extreme innovation to help a particular customer in a particular predicament. And it is generally only the supplier that has the capabilities to help the customer

and lead them to a solution – the customers can't help themselves, because they are not aware of all the available options.

3 **Marketing emphasis.** Customers should be made aware that we can help them in these extreme situations.

4 **Channels of distribution.** Channels should be kept very narrow and specialized.

5 **Pricing regime.** Price is not an issue – customers simply want solutions at any price, because the alternative is costing more.

6 **Promotional activity.** No promotional activity is needed or indeed relevant.

7 **Service emphasis.** This segment is looking for immediate attention to their extreme problem.

8 **Procurement/sourcing approach.** Seek alliances with external parties who can help with innovative solutions in extreme situations.

9 **Production.** Prototypes must be developed fast.

10 **Capacity considerations.** This is a world of 'hedge and deploy'. So, lack of capacity should never get in the way of finding a solution to the problem at hand. Draw on in-house and external parties for resources in this regard. And it will be costly!

11 **Fulfillment approach.** Do anything for speed.

12 **Relationship intensity.** No real on-going relationship is needed in the usual sense, but at the time of the crisis there is an extreme relationship, with both company's fortunes seemingly tied together.

13 **Systems/IT support.** Whatever systems and technology are needed to solve the crisis will be used; nothing is left to chance.

14 **Resource allocation priorities.** A crisis in the customer gets top priority in terms of resources, all types.

15 **Strategic risk profile.** This is very risky for both parties, but the downside of failure is even worse. So sometimes new and untested solutions have to be tried.

For the *fully flexible* 'humanitarian' supply chain, there are different strategies required as summarized in Figure 10.4 overleaf.

	Strategic dimension	Ideal strategy
1	Product mix	New innovative approaches as required by the problems faced
2	Innovation emphasis	Solutions are developed 'in situ', very fast
3	Marketing emphasis	Some media activity seeking donors
4	Channels of distribution	As many as needed in a given situation
5	Pricing regime	Some price sensitivity; stewardship of funds important
6	Promotional activity	Low
7	Service emphasis	Welfare of the humans involved is paramount
8	Procurement/ sourcing approach	Seek alliances with suppliers with major innovation capabilities
9	Production	The supply chain is the product itself – delivering services
10	Capacity considerations	Very high. Hedge and deploy resources
11	Fulfillment approach	Somewhat haphazard depending on conditions on the ground
12	Relationship intensity	High
13	Systems/IT support	Use whatever is available – beg/ borrow/steal
14	Resource allocations priorities	Reactive to events; somewhat inefficient
15	Strategic risk profile	High

FIGURE 10.4 ◆ 'Emergency response/humanitarian' *fully flexible* supply chain strategy – Emergency response

1 **Product mix.** Use any combination of products and services required to 'solve' the problem(s) faced on the ground.

2 **Innovation emphasis.** Solutions are developed 'in situ' to stay ahead of an unfolding emergency situation, very fast.

3 **Marketing emphasis.** Engage in some media activity to keep stakeholders informed and to attract new donors to fund operations.

4 **Channels of distribution.** Nothing is fixed, so use whatever channels that can provide help and assistance in the critical situation – in the form of funds and in-kind assistance.

5 **Pricing regime.** Some sensitivity is needed because these operations usually work to a budget from the UN. There is also a sense of 'stewardship' of the UN funds and other funds given by donors to support the relief operation.

6 **Promotional activity.** Keep promotional activity low, other than for news to the outside world.

7 **Service emphasis.** Service intensity is high because the welfare of the victims is paramount.

8 **Procurement/sourcing approach.** Seek alliances with suppliers of products and services, especially those that have significant capacity and also innovation capability.

9 **Production:** The supply chain network at the disaster scene is the 'product' itself – delivering services to the needy in a life-saving situation.

10 **Capacity considerations.** Capacity must be very high. Hedge and deploy resources ahead of potential disasters as much as possible. Then seek additional sources with available capacity during the actual disaster.

11 **Fulfillment approach.** This can be somewhat haphazard, depending on the conditions on the ground at the time. It is influenced a lot by prevailing weather conditions.

12 **Relationship intensity.** This is high, between all stakeholders.

13 **Systems/IT support.** Use whatever technology that can be seconded to assist relieve the disaster situation.

14 **Resource allocation priorities.** By definition setting priorities is fairly reactive because the exact location of the next emergency is unknown. Some advanced deployment may help if lucky.

15 **Strategic risk profile.** The risk is very high in these operations, and a lot is at stake, not the least of which is human life.

So having laid out all the dimensions that we have to work with in formulating our strategy package for both *fully flexible* supply chain types, we can now turn our attention to shaping the underlying subculture necessary to implement these strategies.

Getting the subculture right

The subculture needed to underpin the *fully flexible* supply chain is seldom found in commercial enterprises. It is an Entrepreneurial subculture: entrepreneurial in the sense that it is a place for unpredictability, opportunity, and corresponding high levels of risk. Entrepreneurial individuals who are attracted to working in *fully flexible* supply chains are highly creative and innovative; they embrace risk and change like no other behavioral group in the quest for satisfactory solutions, and deliver these at speed. Entrepreneurial leaders have a proactive leadership style. If you have a 'business event' supply chain, you will need to encourage the Entrepreneurial subculture while also protecting it against other opposing subcultures in your enterprise. You need to protect the subculture so that it will be available if and when the need arises. In the initial stage of setting up an 'emergency response/humanitarian' supply chain the Entrepreneurial subculture is often the only one present, and the issue is not so much protecting this subculture, but being able to phase in other types of subcultures as the situation stabilizes and more stable processes evolve.

There are, however, some important cultural differences between the two types of *fully flexible* supply chains. The 'business event' supply chain tends to foster individualism and autonomy. In contrast, the success of the 'emergency response/humanitarian' supply chain relies on cohesion of the team, and the ability of the individuals within the team to work with widely divergent groups – who often have very different or conflicting ideologies – for the purpose of the greater good. We will again examine the 13 capability levers for change that must be present and used in appropriate ways if the required subcultures are to be shaped into delivering the necessary actions. Figure 10.5 provides an overview, while a detailed explanation of each lever follows.

...where nothing is impossible			CREATIVE SOLUTIONS REQUIRED, VERY FAST
MARKET SEGMENT	**'INNOVATIVE SOLUTIONS'**		
FULFILLMENT STRATEGY	**VALUE PROPOSITION**		**STRATEGIES** ◆ Meet unplanned/unplannable demand ◆ Innovative solutions, delivered fast
INTERNAL CULTURAL CAPABILITY	**CULTURAL LEVERS** 1. Org design 2. People positioning 3. Processes 4. IT/system 5. S&OP 6. KPIs 7. Incentives 8. Job design 9. Internal comms. 10. T&D 11. Role modeling 12. Recruitment		**RATIONAL SUBCULTURE** ◆ Small multi-disciplinary cluster, usually on standby, but can be full-time ◆ Ensure bias towards personnel with EN in their MBTI profile ◆ No standard processes; use local initiative at the time ◆ Low systems requirements; event management applications ◆ Focus on aggregate capacity planning in the short-term ◆ Emphasis on finding creative solutions, very fast ◆ Reward individualism and risk-taking behavior ◆ Autonomy through empowerment ◆ Spontaneous and informal · Lateral thinking; brainstorming ◆ Managers with ENFP (MBTI profile) and D (P-A-D-I logic) are ideal ◆ Recruit enterprising, resourceful personnel
LEADERSHIP	**13 LEADERSHIP STYLE**		**VISIONARY** ◆ Leads by inspiration; is authentic ◆ Informal ◆ Decisive ◆ Cares about ideas ◆ Values innovation

FIGURE 10.5 ◆ *Fully flexible supply chains – demand-side*

1. Organization design

The classic organization for the Entrepreneurial subculture is a loose structure that involves small clusters or project teams. Unlike the clusters formed for the other generic supply chain types, this cluster can be either temporary or semi-permanent, as already depicted in Figure 6.7. There are few, if any, hierarchical elements to the cluster structure, with most emphasis placed on innovation and self-reliance. People will work in a highly cooperative manner either as individuals or in teams of different combinations.

The Special Air Services (SAS) in the armed forces of several Western nations is the ultimate example of this type of cluster organization. The team comes together for a specific mission, and is composed of individuals who each have specialist skills and competences. Despite this accent on individual skills and flair, the team functions as a unit and under pressure has the capability to adapt to changing conditions with the individuals concerned taking on other roles as required. Indeed, multi-tasking is mandatory for individuals in this type of cluster.

It is no accident that modern armies have adopted an array of different organization structures to fight under varying battlefield conditions. The large-scale, slow-moving standing army takes time to position and build up for the main attack. For example, it took the coalition forces six months to prepare for the first Gulf war. The smaller 'quick reaction' force adopted by the European Union moves faster and can be rapidly deployed to regional trouble spots at relatively short notice. This is an agile type of response. The SAS (Britain and Australia) or the Green Berets (United States) and Brigade des Forces Spéciales Terre – BFST (France), can deploy in small groups within 24 hours to undertake key missions practically anywhere in the world; these were used extensively during the second Gulf war, and continue to operate in Afghanistan today. This is the *fully flexible* supply chain organization par excellence.

We are likely to see more of this organizational configuration in the commercial world as operating environments become even more turbulent and unpredictable following the 2008/09 recession imposed by the global financial crisis. The downside is that they are, by definition, costly to develop and maintain. This is a primary example where extreme flexibility comes at a high cost. As you've heard before, 'You get what you pay for'. The classic hedge and deploy strategy, where capabilities and especially capacity is held in reserve for unforeseeable situations, is only worthwhile if the stakes are high enough to warrant the cost. In the commercial world this means having customers who will pay for such a high-powered response. And they do exist. Indeed, the major international courier companies such as DHL, UPS and FedEx all have customers who demand this type of 'express' response from time to time, and each of these providers has developed internal capabilities to meet their customers' exceptional demands. Other businesses that foster innovation and high responsiveness using a cluster-type of organization are Apple, 3M and Google – often offering solutions before the customer knows they need them.

The most commonly recognized enterprises that have this type of supply chain organization structure are usually government-supported emergency services, such as ambulance services, fire brigades and search and rescue teams. Another group comprises the voluntary (yet highly trained and organized) organizations such as surf lifesaving clubs and bushfire brigade services in Australia. They raise funds through a combination of donations, government grants and industry partners to support their operations. A third group is the global cluster organizations such as the United Nations Joint Logistics Centre (JLC) that is a consortium of the World Food Program (WFP), UNICEF and the World Health Organization (WHO).

2. People positioning

In this cluster as we have stated, it is vital to have an embedded bias towards P (perceiving) in the Myers-Briggs Type Indicator (MBTI®) profile or D (developer) in our P-A-D-I code. Again, it's only the bias we are talking about; other individuals with less entrepreneurial profiles will be present, but in a minority.

3. Processes

Processes? How can these be planned for? Perhaps not surprisingly, there are practically no **standard** processes in the Entrepreneurial subculture. But there are some processes – the most basic and the most complex. The point to remember is that you are in uncharted waters and you step in where others fear to tread. There are no road maps; you are 'making it up as you go along'. The trail blazer, however, may reap huge benefits and could uncover new approaches to business problems in the future. Or, you could devise a one-off solution. Organizations will embrace the processes that work best locally in the midst of an emergency. The teams can operate either virtually or in physical proximity to each other. Autonomy is paramount and the ability to operate as separate unconnected 'cells' for extended periods is mandatory. Australia's SAS uses 'scenario dreaming' to achieve high flexibility and reduce reaction time to events that *may* happen in the future. Unfortunately, due to the constraints placed on resources in businesses today, there is little opportunity to invest time, money, or labor in scenario development. The potential here is huge, though the benefits are unpredictable.

Despite the challenges, process design is not impossible in this type of supply chain. I am indebted to the late Chris Morgan of Cranfield University for providing the following insights into process design:[16]

- Establish clear overarching goals (and update in real-time consistent with emerging situation).

- Break goals into manageable subgoals (and update in real-time).

- Establish a communications framework (robust technology for remote communications; internal and external structures).

- Establish key milestones and collective review (international vectors and review in line with goal variations).

- Recruit people who can cope with evolutionary project iteration and risk evaluation.

4. Systems/IT

The requirement for high-cost transactional systems/IT in the *fully flexible* environment is relatively low, and consequently there is an equivalent lower requirement for capital investment. However, contrary to practices in *collaborative* and *lean* supply chains, there is a heavy emphasis on management intervention, coupled with the presence of highly skilled and experienced permanent staff. Web technology is embraced as required, and some form of enterprise profit optimization (EPO) system is used to gauge the 'profitability' of any innovative solutions that are applied to customer problem situations. Investment in high-technology applications may be necessary from time to time. Figure 10.6 provides an insight into how applications in this supply chain may be configured.

Overall, the main systems used in *fully flexible* supply chains can, and do, vary across the full spectrum, from those required for financially and time-limited humanitarian supply chains, to those needed to deliver high-cost creative solutions. The key is to apply the **appropriate** degree of systems sophistication and avoid unnecessary over-engineering. Indeed, it is not unusual for manual systems such as Gantt charts to be used at one extreme and online rules-based ordering systems of the type developed by Cisco Systems at the other. Originally, Cisco, which produces complex modular products and components to meet its high-tech customers'

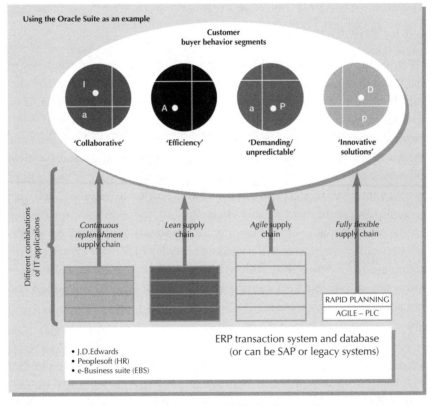

FIGURE 10.6 ◆ Requisite technology for the *fully flexible* supply chain configuration

specifications, found it was reworking many of its products because it failed to meet customers' demanding specifications. Now customers order for themselves through an online ordering system that provides parameters around what they are likely to want. So Cisco, working with its partners on this novel solution, has become a world leader in this particular technological space. Scenario analyses, using say Monte Carlo methodologies, are also likely to be a required business modeling capability.

5. Sales & Operations Planning (S&OP)

In both types of emergency supply chains the focus of S&OP activities is on short-term capacity planning, and sensing and responding to rapidly changing circumstances in real-time. In each case all planning should be kept to the aggregate level.

6. Key Performance Indicators

KPIs in this area of the business emphasize finding creative solutions in the very short lead-times demanded, and in the case of 'business event' supply chains, measure customer satisfaction with the solutions. The 'emergency/humanitarian response' supply chain can be more complex because of the number of parties involved – normal business style measures may not suffice when issues such as governance and political expectations, not to mention saving lives, can all be part of the mix of 'performance' in this critical supply chain. Suffice to say that little else is important in the heat of this operating environment save for getting results. Risk-taking is encouraged and mistakes are not punished, unless of course they are repeated. Basically the standard KPIs for an aid organization are to 'get there fast and save lives' with an eye on expenditure of funds due to increased accountability and greater expectations of responsible behavior in this arena.

7. Incentives

Rewards for individuals who lead or contribute to the development of creative solutions and new ideas that meet the required KPIs can be tailored to the particular individuals and teams involved; whatever they prefer is what they are given. Usually, the rewards are 'in kind' rather than monetary, e.g., research grants, industrial sabbaticals, further education and overseas travel to investigate advanced practices or the satisfaction of achieving more altruistic goals. In the 'business event' supply chain, personal development and personal challenge is uppermost in the minds of the individuals involved, and this is one of their main motivators. In the 'emergency response/ humanitarian' supply chain, self-development and challenge can be overtaken by the personal and emotional benefits of supporting a humanitarian cause and helping people, animals or the environment.

8. Job design

Do you like job descriptions? That's going to be difficult. To foster an Entrepreneurial subculture you need to have loosely defined **roles** rather than tight job descriptions. Your focus should be squarely on encouraging flexibility and rapid response – nothing should be allowed to get in the way of achieving your objective. The vision of the organization, to which everyone agrees, provides the broad boundaries for individual and team action. You can empower people to perform various roles within those boundaries. Control is achieved through adherence to this vision and an agreed set of values. This is a very self-regulating subculture, but it is important to have boundaries in place. Empowerment without boundaries is a recipe for chaos at worst – and inaction at best.

9. Internal communications

The style of internal communications is spontaneous and ad hoc. If you are not around, you will not hear what is going on inside the organization. The underlying message is that 'we participate in the search for creative solutions'. The method of communications is mostly face-to-face, and is usually very open and informal. This is not a place for hidden agendas. However, there are downsides; including the haphazard nature of internal communications leading to confusion and a lack of information reaching the right people at times. This is the 'business event' situation. In the 'emergency response/humanitarian' situation, where armed forces or emergency response teams are involved, the level of communications is necessarily much better because of the life and death situations usually involved.

10. Training and development

You can expand and reinforce the skills of individuals who work in the Entrepreneurial subculture by providing training in lateral thinking and problem-solving, and by enabling them to gain cross-industry experience. This is a very cerebral if not conceptual world, where techniques such as brainstorming are used to surface and extract ideas. Individuals have their communication skills developed through training and are taught how to build rapport in team environments. The reason for risk-taking is explained and risk-management skills are further developed and refined.

11. Role modeling

Managers with the ENFP (extrovert-intuition-feeling-perceiving) Myers-Briggs profile are ideal; or 'D' (Developer) in my P-A-D-I code. They generally display the type of behaviors that you want the rest of the cluster to adopt. These are self-starting people who are prepared to take risks and back themselves in critical situations.

12. Recruitment

People with special qualities are required to work in *fully flexible* supply chains. You should be looking for recruits who are comfortable with taking risks and are highly intuitive and flexible in their working style. This category of employee needs to have an almost contradictory combination of independent thought coupled with a team-orientation. They also need to be self-confident, passionate, have good listening skills, be good networkers and resilient in order to maintain their ability to function in extreme 'business' environments that would challenge most other human beings. Your recruits should be the type to challenge the status quo, be strategic in their orientation, resourceful and original. These are rare and talented individuals indeed.

Generating and retaining an Entrepreneurial subculture in the appropriate locations in an enterprise is not easy. Some enterprises have found it impossible to do so as they seem inevitably to become dominated by a more operational mindset. They are not alone. This mindset pervades too many businesses today. However, an operational focus will only take the

enterprise as far as operational excellence – the **first** level in the performance and capability continuum. Going to higher levels of performance
requires entirely different capabilities and competencies, some of which
require the more risk-taking Entrepreneurial subculture. But for this to
occur, a necessary pre-condition is to already have in place leaders in the
executive who are naturally *visionary*.

13. Leadership style

Visionary leaders lead their enterprises by inspiration. They tend to
be informal yet decisive, and they genuinely care about ideas generated
by others as well as themselves. They are not people who feel threatened by subordinates, and they certainly don't curtail talent that has the
potential eventually to challenge their position. Such leaders are inherently strategic, and they ooze innovation and creativity: leaders such as
Richard Branson (Virgin) and perhaps even Carly Fiorina (ex Hewlett-
Packard). Their Myers-Briggs Type Indicator style is usually INTP
(Introvert-Intuition-Thinking-Perceiving), ENFJ (Extrovert-Intuition-
Feeling-Judging), or thereabouts. Branson, in particular, stands out. He
has a very unconventional leadership style nurtured since he was very
young; he invariably challenges conventional wisdom. For instance,
Branson believes strongly that employees matter most, and if you create
an exciting workplace environment for staff, this will motivate them to
serve their customers. As a result, shareholders also do well. I can vouch
for this approach having flown Virgin Atlantic on the Shanghai–London
sector in June 2005; it was a much more enjoyable experience than flights
I have previously taken on many other airlines. Branson is a living example of alignment. He has been quick to see opportunities and understand
exactly what customers want in all sorts of diverse markets. But that's not
the end of the story. He has been able to develop value propositions that
match customer buying behaviors and find ways to breed appropriate subcultures in these businesses to drive his strategies into the marketplace.
The results are there for all to see, as the Virgin group, established only 20
years ago, is now one of the world's biggest brands; the group boasts more
than 270 branded companies, all doing well in their respective markets.
Branson exemplifies what can be achieved when the natural energy **inside**
the enterprise is harnessed to serve customers.

Collaborative individualism

The combination of autonomous independence and the ability to work in cohesive teams is rare; these are usually individuals with a strong team commitment, epitomized by the descriptor, *collaborative individualism*. They can either be individuals with the ability to move from one extreme to the other on the I–P axis of the P-A-D-I framework, as outlined in Chapter 5, **or** they are in balance and are able to select 'appropriate' ways to respond along the axis given the requirements of any particular situation. The preferred mode of behavior would be Dp (Developer-producer) in the P-A-D-I code for individuals working with 'business event' supply chains and more towards Di (Developer-integrator) for the 'emergency response/humanitarian' supply chain. If a Myers-Briggs assessment was to be undertaken on individuals working in *fully flexible* supply chains this group would probably yield widely divergent personalities. However, we could expect a high degree of similar characteristics in the individuals who are leading both emergency variants of this supply chain configuration.

In an '*emergency response*' supply chain, the first thought is a rapid response to save lives and help stabilize the situation (Phase One – *fully flexible*). This will evolve over time into a more scheduled re-building program as routine is restored (Phase Three). And underneath this, you are receiving cooperation from NGOs and the government(s) involved – the 'collaborative' subculture. As normality is restored, this will morph into an array of supply chains that reflect natural buying behaviors in the affected community.

Defining ideas

1 Don't be afraid to 'walk on the grass'. Anything goes. Rules are there to be broken.

2 The key to success is speed, innovation, flexibility and passion.

3 Everything in the *fully flexible* supply chain is assessed the *instant* it happens, and the 'most appropriate' responses are framed and launched in real time – this is decision-making on the **run**, without apologies. Only decisive thinkers need apply!

4 Lead by inspiration.

5 **Challenge** to the reader: has your enterprise developed a *fully flexible* response capability for use in emergencies? Was it effective in past emergencies?

CHAPTER 11

The triple-A supply chain revisited[1]

What is really going on under the covers?

The notion of the Triple-A supply chain has been around since 2004. But is this a phenomenon we see in practice? The more you look under the covers of the concept as originally described by Hau Lee, the more unlikely it looks. Certainly, some confusion is created by the definitions he uses. When these are redefined in a more liberal way to reflect reality, we find that Agility and Adaptability (or extreme flexibility if you like) are at the same level in the conceptual hierarchy, and represent two quite separate supply chain configurations. My concept of *dynamic alignment* is at a higher level in the conceptual hierarchy – it is the over-arching organizing principle under which the other two operate in this multiple supply chain world. And it is the *dynamic alignment* concept that brings the notion of flexibility alive, allowing different patterns of demand and supply to be serviced by discretely different configurations. The idea is designed for the reality of a plural world, rather than a world where a single supply chain contains all three qualities. The single supply chain state just won't materialize any time soon!

Hau Lee's highly acclaimed seminal article[2] on the Triple-A supply chain has been in the domain for six years now, during which time our understanding of how supply chains function has increased exponentially. So it's high time to revisit the ideas in that article, discerning some helpful nuances and adding some refinements.

Lee gives many interesting examples to support his definitions of each of the A's – Agility, Adaptability and Alignment – but while these are quite descriptive, lingering questions remain about exactly what is going on under the surface. Indeed, Lee himself admits as much in the last paragraph of his article when he muses that 'what they [firms] need is a fresh attitude and a culture to get their supply chains to deliver Triple-A performance'.[3] He is right, of course, and in this extension to Lee's article I will endeavor to introduce that missing ingredient – the internal cultural perspective. Without it, I'm afraid the story, while instructive, remains purely descriptive and consequently lacks explanatory power.

By better understanding the human dimension of supply chains, it becomes possible to move from a purely reactive to a more predictive level. In other words, if you know what subcultures are in place and what supply chain strategies are being proposed, you're in a better position to predict the likely outcomes in the all-important implementation phase.

Unfortunately, in my experience, more than 40 per cent of intended strategies written into business plans fail to be fully executed, and it's mostly due to a misalignment between those strategies and the values of the people inside respective organizations and their partner organizations in the supply chain. When the chips are down they tend to do what they 'prefer' to do. That's human nature all over and we better get used to it.

Lee posits that 'only those companies that build Agile, Adaptable, and Aligned supply chains get ahead of the competition'.[4] I agree with his overall thrust, but we need to explore and refine his definitions of the three A's to better understand why this might be so.

Redefining the three key properties

Lee's first 'A' – Agility – is becoming increasingly critical in today's volatile markets. But you pay a price for it. You can't be agile and lowest cost concurrently – something has to give. In truth, you will find customers in your markets that want one or the other or, at times, both responses. If the latter, you have to try to understand which they want more. To give an agile response at lowest cost-to-serve is, in effect, rewarding customers who are often behaving badly. This conundrum was one of the main factors that drove me to develop the *dynamic alignment* model described in this book. Now we have a systematic way of looking at supply chain design and operations, and doing so from the customer's perspective by better understanding their dominant buying behavior.[5] When I segmented markets for a wide range of product/service categories, I observed patterns which could be used to reverse-engineer matching supply chain config-urations. Specifically, I seldom found more than three or four dominant buying behaviors present in any market for any product or service cate-gory, which means that a small number of supply chain types are capable of covering up to 80 per cent of the market – no more, no less. And, although customers have a preferred way of working (based on their deep-rooted values), situations can still arise that cause them to change their behavior (but not their values) for short periods. This inherent dynamism requires different supply chain solutions. My broad concept is depicted in Figure 11.1 overleaf.

As we have seen in earlier chapters, in order to align with the four main behavioral segments identified in my fieldwork, there are four cor-responding discrete types of supply chain configurations – *continuous replenishment, lean, agile* and *fully flexible.*

For those customers who genuinely seek **lowest-cost** product (acquisi-tion and fulfillment), *lean* is the solution for them. By definition, we are dealing with a relatively predictable market environment – a risk-averse customer with a transactional mindset – so there is a lot of emphasis on making and fulfilling to forecast, creating scale and using process improve-ment techniques such as Six Sigma to lower costs. Cost-efficiency is the dominant value shared by both customers and the supplying organization in this type of operating environment. More importantly, the underpin-ning subculture essential to successfully execute a low-cost solution for the customer is one that demands removal of all waste and involves rou-tine processes, backed up by a 'cost-controller' leadership mentality. But the more you cut costs the more brittle your supply chains become, and the less the ability to flex and respond rapidly to sudden changes in demand. Fortunately, there is always likely to be a sizable segment of customer/ market combinations that demand a consistent low-cost response.

On the other hand, for those customers (it can be the same cost-driven customers albeit in a different situation) with values that are dominated

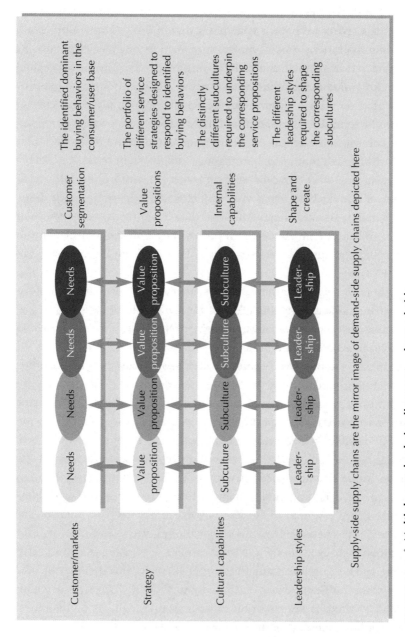

Customer/markets

Customer segmentation — The identified dominant buying behaviors in the consumer/user base

Strategy

Value propositions — The portfolio of different service strategies designed to respond to identified buying behaviors

Cultural capabilities

Internal capabilities — The distinctly different subcultures required to underpin the corresponding service propositions

Leadership styles

Shape and create — The different leadership styles required to shape the corresponding subcultures

Supply-side supply chains are the mirror image of demand-side supply chains depicted here

FIGURE 11.1 ◆ **Multiple supply chain alignment – demand-side**

by a requirement for speed, taking risk, a low emphasis on relationships, and time sensitivity, we need something very different in this case – an *agile* response. I largely agree with Lee's definition[6] of Agile and the six rules of thumb he proposes for the development of this type, although it's difficult to see how collaborative relationships can flourish when dealing with such demanding customers who come and go on an ad hoc basis. Some customers may exhibit a degree of loyalty, but for most it's just hard-nosed commercial pragmatism. However, there is a better chance of collaborating with suppliers on the supply-side (if you wish to do so) because in that situation, you are the buyer/customer!

Lee also provides examples[7] of major unpredictable and unplannable disruptions that have occurred – 9/11, SARS and other natural disasters. Here, I think we are dealing with a special case of 'super-agility', which requires an **additional category** of market segment and corresponding supply chain configuration. In my work in this area, I and my co-workers have discovered what I describe as the *fully flexible* supply chain.[8] It has two variants for emergency situations – 'business event' and 'emergency response/humanitarian' supply chains. We have covered both these variants of *fully flexible* supply chains in detail in Chapter 10.

In a more recent presentation,[9] Lee uses Shanzhai Mobile Phones as an example of a super-agile supply chain, where the time taken from concept to mass production is just 40 days. To achieve this result everything must come together in perfect unison – design and manufacturing; use of postponement techniques in assembly; knowledge of the mass market for cell phones; skilful outsourcing; and innovation at every stage.[10] But what about the human dimension? And how do organization design, specific processes and particular KPIs play a part in this? While inferred, these are not spelt out in Lee's description, and yet they are central to making Agility happen.

Adaptability is Lee's second 'A' and the one that I am having the most difficulty with in the Triple-A nomenclature. Lee seems to restrict his meaning to the idea of adaptive versus static supply chains. But this is really what *dynamic alignment* is all about. I see the concept of adaptive being applied to the situations where there have been sudden and unpredictable interruptions to enterprise supply chains that require extraordinary efforts to overcome. It might be a fire in a key facility; or destruction of a factory due to an earthquake; or the sudden failure of IT systems. All these situations are covered by my concept of a *fully flexible* supply chain configuration as depicted in Figure 11.2, which has embedded resilience to facilitate a very fast response to save the day. So Lee's Agility and Adaptability (and my *fully flexible* supply chain type) are at similar levels in the conceptual hierarchy. Alignment is something else.

In my vernacular, the third 'A' of Alignment is the overarching organizing principle that needs to be applied to drive business success – that is, aligning your strategies, internal subcultures and leadership styles with customers, suppliers and third-party providers in the marketplace. It is the only way to achieve sustained operational and (therefore) bottom-line performance. So, I see alignment as a much broader concept than Lee in his definition, where he confines his attention to the 'differential' interests of multiple players in the chain. In Lee's understanding, alignment is more about collaboration, common incentives and joint KPIs. This view is okay, but insufficient to capture the potential of true alignment – across **all** aspects of multiple supply chains.

Under my more liberal definition of alignment – *dynamic alignment* – the related concepts of agility and adaptability, as used by Lee, are simply constituent components at a different (lower) level in the conceptual hierarchy. This differentiation is clearly depicted in Figure 11.2. Indeed, taken together, the latter two properties provide the dynamism in *dynamic alignment*, which explains a lot in the context of how supply chains must actually work in the real world.

Dynamic alignment, therefore, goes well beyond Lee's narrower interpretation of 'Alignment', which focuses mainly on aligning the interests of all firms in their respective chains. I agree with this too, but we must also align the **internal** resources of the firm as well to have any chance of delivering high performance on a consistent and sustainable basis. And when it comes to aligning with customers downstream in the chain, we need different value propositions to address the range of buying behaviors evident in the target market. The same applies upstream when we are the buyers, seeking products and services from our own source markets.

In truth, the missing link in Lee's article is a comprehensive explanation of **how** the internal culture of the firm plays such a pivotal role in executing these value propositions. That's really why so many of the firms he uses as examples have been successful – internal cultural considerations are at the root of their success, but we only see the tangible results

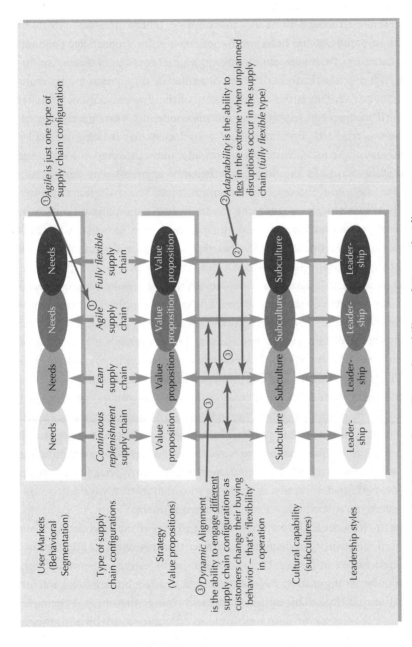

FIGURE 11.2 ◆ Revised definitions for Agility, Adaptability and *Dynamic Alignment*

that ultimately emerge on the bottom line. But then we should not forget that financial success is a lagging rather than leading indicator.

If there are structural shifts in a marketplace, which in turn are likely to drive the reshaping of the behavioral segment mix for a particular product/ service category, then you simply engage a different supply chain configuration. This is the flexibility that is *embedded* in my dynamic alignment construct. Indeed, that is the simple beauty of the *dynamic alignment* model – you hard-wire several supply chain formats and simply engage the appropriate one as required. For example, if a loyal customer is being served by the *continuous replenishment* supply chain, and that customer, for whatever reason, shifts across to the 'low-cost/efficiency' segment, you simply recognize that fact and engage the *lean* supply chain lever. Or if a customer in the 'low-cost/efficiency' segment experiences a major disruption (as in the case of Nokia and Ericsson quoted by Lee),[11] then the customer effectively moves to the innovative solutions type of behavioral segment and we engage the *fully flexible* supply chain configuration. Indeed, irrespective of whether you call it 'adaptability' or 'flexibility', or 'resilience', what you have to do in essence is shift gears from one type of supply chain configuration to another – fast. This is the 'quick-change' supply chain in action, and it requires some clever organization design. The good news is that some of the world's leading enterprises have clearly cottoned on to this *modus operandi* and are in the midst of rolling it out across their operations.

This is a key discussion point because the word 'flexibility' gets bandied around a lot in the supply chain vernacular, and you have to ask yourself: what does it really mean in practice? In my view, it does **not** mean bending and squeezing your current 'one-size-fits-all' supply chain configuration so that it fits every customer demand coming your way. That would create hundreds, perhaps thousands, of exceptions, which in turn would drive the cost-to-serve up, just when you're trying to get it down!

What it does mean in an operational sense is to have your business hard-wired with three, perhaps four, different supply chain configurations as depicted earlier in Figure 11.1, and you simply engage customers with the particular configuration most appropriate to their buying behavior (or mindset) at that time. This approach doesn't change the original principle of no more than three or four supply chain configurations. Indeed, this is the very essence of *dynamic alignment*,[12] something we have been seeking to understand and explain in the marketing arena for a long time.

To be fair, Lee gets close when he remarks that 'smart companies tailor supply chains to the nature of markets and products'.[13] However, I disagree with his observation that 'they usually end up with more than one supply chain, which can be expensive'.[14] Quite to the contrary, if we are able to eliminate over-servicing in *lean* and *agile* supply chains, then recognizing under-servicing in *continuous replenishment* supply chains and being paid the appropriate prices in each case, then margins overall will improve significantly. We found as much at DHL Taiwan.[15]

The examples that Lee mentions, where companies develop different supply chain strategies around their different brands, is valid and quite consistent with my view that you use only the appropriate supply chain configuration in each market or customer segment. In the end, it's all about keeping your eye on the marketplace and your customers within. Amazingly, and contrary to popular opinion, if you do that, things seem to move very slowly and you rarely get caught out. Try watching grass grow – it's quite slow. But take your eye off the back lawn and go away for the weekend, and look at the grass when you return!

Architecture

In his most recent presentation,[16] Lee introduces the notion of a fourth 'A' – Architecture, to bolster his original Triple-A concept. Architecture was originally part of his 'Adaptability' property, but he has now pulled it out and made it a free-standing property in its own right. According to Lee, 'Architecture' is about having the right supply chain strategy – right product, market and time. However, although this new addition goes part of the way to cover some of the short-falls in the original concept, it is still not enough, for the reasons we shall explain in the following section.

Understanding the real driver of successful supply chains

So let's step into where all these forces of darkness live and operate. My field research indicates that there are at least 13 levers to pull to shape a particular subculture, all of which are well known in their own right –

no mysteries there. However, the 'secret sauce' is in knowing which ones to pull, and in what sequence. Or if you want another metaphor, think of different *recipes*. And, of course, you need some point of reference to guide you in this process – namely, an understanding of the structure of the marketplace and the particular mix of dominant buying behaviors present there. For best results the internal structure has to be a mirror image of the external structure – that is what alignment is ultimately all about! The 13 levers are as follows:

> *organization design; positioning of individuals within the structure; processes; IT systems; S&OP process; internal communication styles; job design; KPIs and their corresponding incentives; training and development; role modeling; recruitment; and leadership style.*[17]

All of these component capabilities are well known in their own right, but the potentially different recipes that can be achieved by mixing and matching the capability levers is understood by very few executives, and that is why we have seen few successful business transformations during the past two decades. The problem is that reconfiguring the prevailing corporate culture in an organization into say three or four subcultures in order to properly underpin newly configured supply chains takes time. To give you some idea, it took three years to achieve full alignment in a service organization of 10,000 people. You can change the strategies on a Saturday afternoon, but it takes much longer to get the required subcultures in place and in a fit state to propel these strategies into the target market. Indeed, it is no coincidence that the best-performing enterprise supply chains in the past decade have come from firms which did not exist a generation ago. Hence, they were able to start with a clean sheet and design their supply chains from a zero-base, without legacy cultures to hinder progress. The old 'bricks and mortar' companies have mostly struggled for this very reason, and this reason alone. And they will continue to struggle unless new leadership cuts through the old conventions that are so deeply embedded.

Clearly, based on their respective records, companies like Zara (Spain), Li & Fung (Hong Kong), Adidas (Germany), Apple (US), Dell (US), Nokia (Finland) and 7-Eleven (Japan) have discovered how to mix the 'secret sauce' of culture. They know that, in the end, it is people and their leadership that matters most if the enterprise is to deliver ever-improving operational and financial performance.

Defining ideas

1   Agility is just one of several possible supply chain configurations in a multiple supply chain alignment format; it specifically addresses those situations where there is uncertainty and volatility in demand (or supply).

2   Adaptability is the ability to flex in the extreme when unplannable disruptions occur in enterprise supply chains, and is the quality embedded in my *fully flexible* supply chain type.

3   *Dynamic* Alignment, my broader concept of alignment, is the ability to engage different supply chain configurations as customers change their buying behaviors due to changes in their situation. It is the overarching organizing construct and is multi-dimensional. This is genuine flexibility in practice, using different configurations that have been hard-wired into the design – rather than seeking to go 'duck shooting' with one type of supply chain for all situations.

4   A deeper understanding of what is going on in the subterranean of the enterprise – the 'human engine room' – is what provides a predictive capability to guide management decision-making in an otherwise incoherent world, and leads directly to improved performance. There are no mysteries, except for ignorance of how internal subcultures can influence and drive the execution of strategy.

5   The three A's as re-defined in this chapter appear on the supply-side as well as the demand-side of the enterprise; and they can come in different (hybrid) combinations as further discussed in Chapter 13. Lee's definitional scope does not seem to allow for this reality.

6   And where is *lean* in this scheme of things? This is another entirely different supply chain configuration that often works in parallel with *agile* and *fully flexible* supply chains. As do *continuous replenishment* supply chains. It is not possible to discuss one without the other. They co-exist for a purpose – the markets contain customers that require different responses.

7 Ultimately, the three A's could be redefined as **Align, Align, Align** – and that takes care of everything, including Lee's fourth 'A', Architecture!

8 **Challenge** to the reader: have you ever seen a 'Triple-A' supply chain as originally defined by Lee?

CHAPTER 12

Supplier conversations and the four generic supply-side supply chains

The mirror image of the demand-side

This chapter is about reconnecting the supply-side to the demand-side of enterprise supply chains. Each is vital to the other as we seek a full and uninterrupted view of what is going on along our multiple chains. Because we are customers of the supply base in this situation, it's even more important to listen to our suppliers. Mostly because we will benefit handsomely!

Not surprisingly, we find that it's possible to align with the supply base in much the same way as with our customer base, and this means we can translate many of the lessons learnt on the demand-side directly to the supply-side.

The two come together in the cluster organizational designs already described in Chapter 6. They are the pivotal points of our enterprise supply chains!

With these new insights, we are also able to see the possibilities for improved 'reverse' supply chain pathways, a topic that deserves more attention given the growing concerns of consumers about environmental sustainability.

The whole area of supply-side sourcing is coming back into focus once again as the world recovers from the global financial crisis and seeks to reduce its impact on the real economy. Since the turn of the new millennium, multi-national corporations in particular have been pursuing global sourcing strategies in the relentless search for ever lower cost inputs to manufacturing. Research by M. Christopher and his colleagues at the Cranfield School of Management found this has had the effect of 'making supply chains longer and more fragmented, and this is exposing firms to greater costs and risks'.[1] The same research also found that most firms were still largely basing their procurement decisions on a minimum price approach rather than the more sophisticated 'total cost of ownership'[2] concept. Finally, global trade appears to be significantly contributing to the emission of greenhouse gases because of the added transportation sectors involved, and this flies in the face of the growing global effort to reduce carbon dioxide emissions. Maybe we will see a change back to regional and local sourcing as a result of the community's growing concern about the impact of climate change. Indeed, from our own work we see a clear trend towards a *sub-segment* within the overall 'collaborative' customer segment emerging, which appears to be very empathetic towards sustaining the natural environment and consequently is demanding corporate social responsibility. This sub-segment will surely penalize suppliers along the supply chain who do not take sufficient measures to minimize their carbon footprint.

The task ahead in this chapter is to re-connect the supply-side to the demand-side. I hear some of you say, 'But it's never been connected!' And you're right. The disconnection is part of the problem. It is hard to imagine how an enterprise can successfully procure the raw materials, components, sub-assemblies, packaging and other inputs for its business if there is not a live connection with the customer-facing side of the business. But that is what has been going on for generations and, sadly, continues to this day in many enterprises.

Listening to suppliers

Just as we set out in Chapter 2 to understand customers' dominant buying behaviors, we must do something very similar at the supply-end. This means listening to our suppliers and engaging them on their terms, not ours. This may seem strange given that we are arguing the case from the customer's point-of-view, but it is a necessary reversal of convention if we are to achieve genuine *dynamic alignment.*

Suppliers are the largely ignored element in the human system that propels contemporary supply chains, along with customers at the front end and employees inside the business. According to A.T Kearney,[3]

Companies that take the time to listen to their suppliers can eventually realize rewards beyond cost savings. Often, they can generate new ideas and concepts, determine how their performance stacks up against their best-practice competitors, and identify areas and processes on which to focus attention. In short, they are well positioned to embark on major supply chain management initiatives.

But how do you categorize your suppliers? That is the key question! We believe that you must start by segmenting them along behavioral lines.

Supplier segmentation

You rarely hear of this methodology being used these days, and the few attempts at segmenting suppliers have revealed the same flaws as similar attempts at customer segmentation revealed at the consumption end of the chain. In 2006 Diane Bueler presented a paper on segmenting suppliers, but she used the characteristics of the product/service being purchased as the basis of her segmentation framework.[4] The four categories she identified – 'commodity', 'strategic', 'standard' and 'key' – provide useful statistical data, but contribute little to our understanding of the way suppliers prefer to supply, or their 'selling behavior' as I call it. See Figure 12.1 overleaf for details of the characteristics in each quadrant of Bueler's framework.

Jeffrey Dyer and his colleagues[5] see strategic supplier segmentation as a necessary precursor to achieving best practice in supply chain management; and they are spot on! Their work identified two very different supplier management models, i.e., the traditional 'arm's length' approach, which deliberately sets out to avoid any kind of commitment or interdependence. This view is consistent with my 'efficient' buying behavior at the customer end. 'In contrast,' Dyer and his team wrote, 'the success of Japanese firms has often been attributed to their close supplier relationships, or 'partner model' of supplier management'.[6] Clearly, in order to get close to their suppliers, trust had to be developed over time, and it's very likely suppliers were carefully selected for their collaborative values. This is the equivalent segment to 'collaborative' customers on the demand side, and we will label the equivalent segment on the supply-side as 'trusted and reliable partners'.

COMMODITY	STRATEGIC
◆ High Spend	◆ High Spend
◆ Low Switching Costs	◆ High Switching Costs
◆ Multiple Sources of Supply	◆ Few Sources of Supply
◆ Short-Lead Times	◆ Typically Long-Lead Times
◆ Low Complexity / Items on Shelf	◆ Critical Performance Characteristics
◆ Low Item Costs	◆ High Item Costs
◆ High Volume	◆ Variable Volume
STANDARD	**KEY**
◆ Low Spend	◆ Low/Medium Spend
◆ Low Switching Costs	◆ High Switching Costs
◆ Multiple Sources of Supply	◆ Few Sources of Supply
◆ Short-Lead Times	◆ Typically Long-Lead Times
◆ Standard, on Shelf Items	◆ Critical Performance Characteristics
◆ Low Item Costs	◆ High Item Costs
◆ Volumes Vary	◆ Variable Volume

FIGURE 12.1 ◆ Supplier segmentation based on a combination of product and supplier characteristics

Source: Adapted from Diane Bueler (May 2006)

Examples of both types of segments can be seen in the automotive industry, where General Motors has traditionally applied arm's length and largely transactional methods with their suppliers, while Toyota (and more latterly, Chrysler) has employed the partner or 'trusted and reliable partners' model. I will leave it to the reader to decide which has been the more successful.

Dyer and his team conducted extensive research into supplier-automaker relationships in the United States, Japan and Korea, and they found that 'firms should not have a "one-size-fits-all" strategy for supplier management'.[7] Sound familiar? However, it should be said that while Dyer and his colleagues were on the right track (towards multiple supplier segments), they were mainly thinking about how each 'supplier's product might contribute to the core competence and competitive advantage of the buying firm'.[8] They were not thinking of behavioral segmentation per se.

In summary, it appears that most buyers in the market have been focusing on finding suppliers who have the required array of supply *capabilities*, and then the relationship approach adopted has been one of the two described above. Not very sophisticated, and quite one dimensional.

We have seen enough evidence in our field work to suggest that supply-side alignment is generally the mirror image of the demand-side. This means at least 16 behavioral segments on the supply side as depicted in Figure 12.2.

Of these we can be confident that the most prevalent segments seen in practice will be similar to the demand-side as depicted in Figure 12.3.

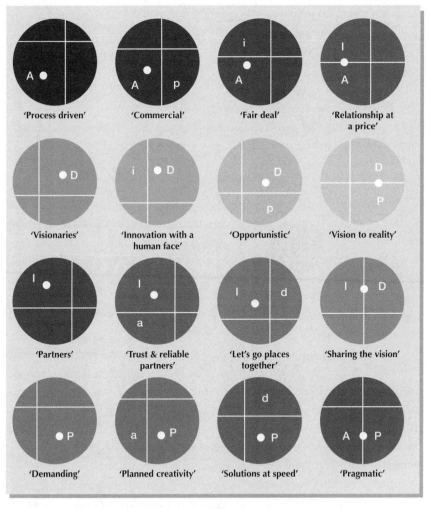

FIGURE 12.2 ◆ The 16 possible 'selling behaviors' in source markets

TRUSTED & RELIABLE PARTNERS	PROCESS DRIVEN	PLANNED CREATIVITY	OPPORTUNISTIC
Close working relationships for mutual gain	Consistent low cost response to largely predictable demands	Capability to provide rapid response in irregular demand situations	Capability to create innovative solutions, very fast

TRUSTED & RELIABLE PARTNERS
- Like predictability
- Prefer regular orders
- Prefer producing nature products
- Like to be treated as an exclusive source
- Seek trusting long-term relationship
- Enjoy partnership/ teamwork
- Prepared to share information
- Engage in joint development
- Expect fair margin

PROCESS DRIVEN
- Prefer tight contracts
- Regular order/delivery schedule
- Offer lowest cost-to-serve
- Don't wish to share information
- Can be adversarial at times
- Adopt standard processes
- Impose power where possible
- Very transactional mindset
- Sensitive to low price demands

PLANNED CREATIVITY
- Have capacity to meet volatile demand
- Prefer not to enter close relationships
- Can respond to urgent demands
- Use as few processes as possible
- Outcome oriented
- Very commercial
- Require price premium

OPPORTUNISTIC
- Have the capacity to cope with unexpected situations
- Can provide creative solutions as required
- Innovation mindset embedded
- Very solutions oriented
- Prefer to charge a significant premium

FIGURE 12.3 ◆ **Supply-side behavioral segmentation characteristics**

Reverse (supply-side) multiple supply chain alignment

Based on the segmentation of the supply base as depicted in Figure 12.3 the supply-side (reverse) multiple supply chain alignment will look as depicted in Figure 12.4 overleaf. Clearly, up to four different procurement strategy packages will be required to achieve full coverage in support of the demand-side supply chains discussed in Chapter 2.

The Royal Australian Navy (RAN) and the Logistics Support Agency-Navy within the Defence Materiel Organization (DMO) have been testing the use of alignment principles to guide the procurement of diesel engines (and subcategories) for a component of its destroyer fleet. A pilot project was undertaken with a major international supplier and produced promising results. Not unexpectedly, the buying behaviors exhibited by the Navy/DMO for main engines/rotatables, component and service spares, and routine maintenance were quite different to the selling behaviors of the supplier, in each of the three subcategories examined. This highlighted the need for different procurement strategies and correspondingly aligned responses from the supplier. So much for the old one-dimensional tender process!

The overall alignment diagnostic we conducted between the RAN/DMO as a customer of the major international supplier identified a similar mis-alignment in all of the diesel engine subcategories tested. This amounted to the supplier endeavoring to sell and service their RAN/DMO client using 'trusted and reliable partner' values, but facing a customer that was mostly driven by what I would call a 'pragmatic' buying behavior, with little room for relationships. This mis-alignment led to on-going issues between the supplier and the customers as clearly evidenced in Figure 12.5 overleaf.

Another interesting case arose in the bovine meat industry in Brazil. JBS Swift, one of the major processors in the market wanted to obtain a greater share of the available live cattle for slaughter, and set out to understand what needed to be done to more closely align with ranchers' selling expectations and corresponding supply behaviors. The conventional wisdom espoused by the procurement department in the particular processor was simply to pay more for live cattle and in that way secure additional head.

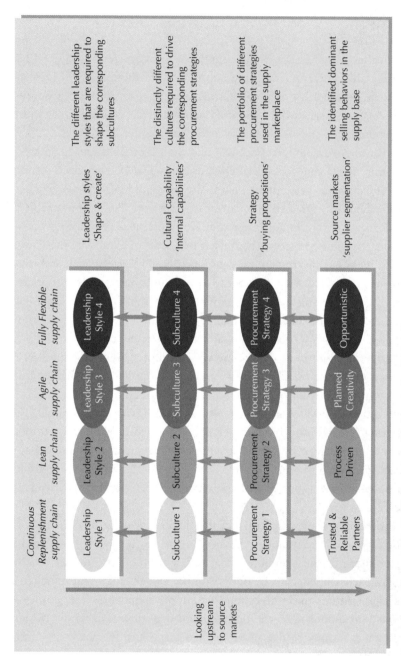

FIGURE 12.4 ◆ Supply-side (reverse) multiple supply chain alignment

Source: Adapted from Figure 2.12 in Living Supply Chains (2006), p.62

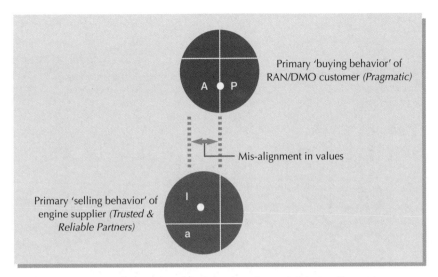

FIGURE 12.5 ◆ Alignment diagnostic between the Royal Australian Navy
and the Defence Materiel Organization, and a major supplier of diesel main
engines for the RAN surface fleet

Source: Primary research by Gattorna Alignment Pty Ltd (2005); unpublished report

The subsequent selling behavior research conducted among a large sample
of ranchers in a region of Brazil delivered a completely different answer
as depicted in Figure 12.6 overleaf. In fact, 81 per cent of the sample was
found to have a relationship (or I logic) element in their selling logics, and
only the residual 19 per cent were straight out driven by yield and price. This
finding allowed the processor to fine-tune its offerings to the various rancher
segments, and include significant non-price relationship components, which
had the effect of simultaneously satisfying the ranchers, and delivering more
head of live cattle at cost-effective market prices to the processor.

Adidas is another great example of a company that changed its
business model and profited from closer alignment between its global procurement and logistics operations during the 2004 FIFA European Cup
in Greece, and the 2006 FIFA World Cup in Germany. We have already
used Adidas as a case study in organization design in Chapter 6. A study
by Rudy Puryear and his colleagues found,

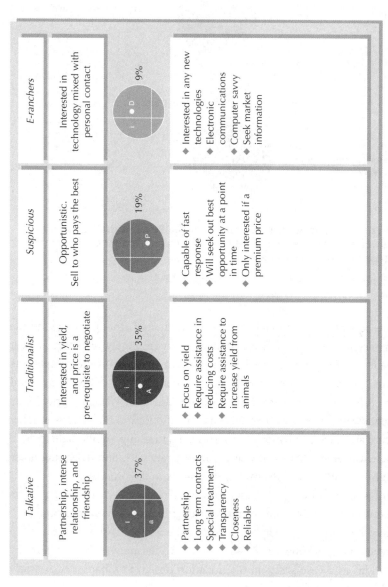

FIGURE 12.6 ◆ **Cattle supplier (ranchers) segmentation in Brazil**

Source: Adapted from information supplied by Axia Consulting, Brazil (2008)

By synchronizing orders through scores of contract manufacturers, sub-contractors, and suppliers in more than a dozen countries around the world, Adidas managed to get the top team's gear on retailers' shelves – duplicating those sales triumphs in every other country as their national teams advanced through the series. What's more, Adidas's flexible supply chains (I would call them Agile), delivered these sales without pre-investment in materials or finished product.[9]

The four generic supply-side supply chains

The four generic supply-side supply chains are depicted in Figure 12.7. We will now describe the characteristics of each in more detail.

Continuous replenishment supply chains – supply-side

The abbreviated details of this type of supply chain are depicted in Figure 12.8 overleaf. As in the case of the equivalent demand-side supply chains discussed in Chapters 7 to 10, we will mainly focus our discussion and comments on the capability levers that determine if the intended procurement strategies are to be fully implemented or not. The key, as before, is in getting the right subculture in place.

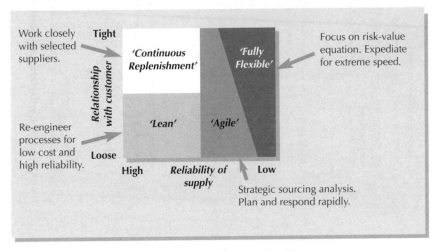

FIGURE 12.7 ◆ **Four generic supply chains – supply-side**

	'TRUSTED & RELIABLE'	CLOSE WORKING RELATIONSHIPS WITH SELECTED SUPPLIERS
MARKET SEGMENT		...where relationship matter most
		Collaboration zone
PROCUREMENT STRATEGY	VALUE PROPOSITION	**STRATEGIES** ◆ Share information ◆ Seek strategic partnerships ◆ Seek long-term stability ◆ Build mutual trust
INTERNAL CULTURAL CAPABILITY	**CULTURAL LEVERS** ◆ Orgnl design ◆ People positioning ◆ Processes ◆ IT/systems ◆ KPIs ◆ Incentives ◆ Job design ◆ Internal comms ◆ T&D ◆ Role modeling ◆ Recruitment	**'GROUP' SUBCULTURE** ◆ Relationship cluster ◆ Ensure bias in cluster is towards personnel with F in their MBTI profile ◆ Standard processes, e.g., supplier management ◆ SRM (SAS) ◆ Emphasis on loyalty and retention ◆ Encourage participative schemes ◆ Authority/autonomy negotiated by consensus ◆ Consultative; face-to-face ◆ Team building ◆ Managers with ISFT/MBTI profile (I code) are ideal ◆ Recruit team players
LEADERSHIP	LEADERSHIP STYLE	**COACH** ◆ Conscientious ◆ Lead by teaching and example ◆ Concerned for others ◆ Loyal, committed, politically astute ◆ Seeks agreement by consensus

FIGURE 12.8 ◆ *Continuous replenishment supply chains – supply-side*

Organization design. Procurement specialists will be part of the *continuous replenishment* cluster already shown in Chapter 7. We will show the two components, demand and supply-side, together in the same diagram in Chapter 13.

People positioning. As with all clusters, while not every member will have the same preferred operating style, it is important to engineer the selection of personnel so that the bias is appropriate, in this case a relationship bias, or F (feeling) in terms of the Myers-Briggs Type Indicator (MBTI) profiles and I (Integrator) in P-A-D-I language.

Processes. Stable processes are important where you want to faithfully replicate the same behavior each time, every time. And everyone should know what these are. In this case we expect that supplier management will be one of the key processes deployed.

IT/systems. The automatic choice here is the SAS Supplier Management System (SRM), with its different modules. The key is to choose who you want to be among your strategic suppliers, and then manage them on a sensitive, systematic basis.

Key Performance Indicators (KPIs). As we have said before, forget about measuring a long list of performance attributes, and select one or two that are the deal-breakers, those that 'move the needle' and are what we call 'biased' in the desired direction. In the case of procuring from loyal suppliers, we might choose to measure retention time as a de facto measure of loyalty, as well as monitor the share of the supplier's business that we represent.

Incentives. Once the KPIs are clear to members of this cluster, everyone will tend to work together to achieve them, encouraged by schemes that share the rewards fairly among the team.

Job design. For this cluster the name of the game is consensus. No one goes out on a limb and takes risks with strategic suppliers. Everything is fully discussed and agreed, with little individual autonomy allowed.

Internal communications. Everything is discussed face-to-face, and the meetings are frequent and sometimes long.

Training and development. No rash brainstorming required with this group – well-planned, team-building exercises are needed to develop trust between the individuals in the cluster.

Role modeling. If there is a particular profile of behavior to be admired and replicated by individuals in this particular cluster it is the ISFT (introvert-sensing-feeling-thinking) in the MBTI profile, or I in our P-A-D-I code.

Recruitment. If you want a certain behavior, a sure way of getting it is to recruit personnel with both the appropriate mindset **and** the technical competence. This is a refinement on what companies like Li & Fung have been doing, and represents a logical progression as they search for even higher levels of performance from their people.

Leadership style. The natural leaders that emerge from the multidisciplinary clusters will be very much a *Coach* in this environment, where day-to-day dealings are with loyal suppliers and loyal customers. It is reassuring when team members see the same values as they hold being exhibited by leaders inside their business and within their external stakeholders.

Lean supply chains – supply-side

Organization design. The cluster in this case is as described for customer segments in Chapter 8; it is designed around core processes to achieve high reliability at lowest possible cost.

People positioning. It is important to engineer the selection of personnel so that the bias is right, in this case a cost bias or S (sensing) in MBTI terms, or A (Administrator) in our P-A-D-I code.

Processes. This particular supply chain places a lot of emphasis on re-engineered processes, so Six Sigma techniques will be very applicable.

IT/systems. For best results it's essential to have an ERP system installed and functioning well. The alternative of a mix of legacy systems held together with middleware is a possible alternative, but is usually not as effective as having the one unified system.

Key Performance Indicators (KPIs). For this configuration, the emphasis moves away from relationships, to pure cost control and reliability, hence the measurement of unit cost, DIFOTEF; and a particular focus on forecast accuracy.

Incentives. For members of this cluster conformance is mandatory, and no member of the teams should try to do his or her own thing.

...focusing on streamlining processes for low cost and high reliability

MARKET SEGMENT	'PROCESS DRIVEN'	RE-ENGINEERING PROCESSES FOR LOW COST AND HIGH RELIABILITY
PROCUREMENT STRATEGY	VALUE PROPOSITION	**STRATEGIES** ◆ Strategic sourcing ◆ Product category rationalisation ◆ Re-design of product range
INTERNAL CULTURAL CAPABILITY	CULTURAL LEVERS ◆ Orgnl design ◆ People positioning ◆ Processes ◆ IT/systems ◆ KPIs ◆ Incentives ◆ Job design ◆ Internal comms ◆ T&D ◆ Role modeling ◆ Recruitment	**HIERARCHIAL SUBCULTURE** ◆ Organize clusters around core processes ◆ Ensure clusters have bias towards personnel with S in their MBTI profile ◆ Re-engineer all processes and standardize ◆ Replace legacy systems with ERP system ◆ DIFOTEF; forecast accuracy; unit cost ◆ Conformance to buying policies ◆ Centralized control – rules and regulations apply ◆ Regular; structured; on need-to-know basis only ◆ Emphasis on analysis and measurement ◆ Managers with ISTJ MBTI profile (A code) are ideal ◆ Recruit players with deep analytical skills
LEADERSHIP	LEADERSHIP STYLE	**TRADITIONALIST** ◆ Leads by procedure; precedent ◆ Implements only proven business practices ◆ Cost controller; efficiency focus ◆ Uses information to control ◆ Seeks stability ◆ Is risk averse

FIGURE 12.9 ◆ *Lean supply chains – supply-side*

Job design. In this supply chain, nothing is left to chance in the desire for consistency and reliability. The specific duties of every member of the cluster is spelled out in detail, and is known and understood by all other members.

Internal communications. Communications are very formal and structured, albeit quite detailed. This is a fact-based subculture, and because of the sheer volume of data floating around, personnel are often included on a need-to-know basis only.

Training and development. This cluster thrives on analysis and measurement of supplier performance, in an objective non-emotional way. Relationships with suppliers are not encouraged in any way. Business is business.

Role modeling. The ideal role model is the detailed, conscious cost-controller type, and this is reflected in an ISTJ (introvert-sensing-thinking-judging) MBTI profile or A (Administrator) in our P-A-D-I coding system.

Recruitment. Clearly, team members with highly tuned analytical capabilities are highly valued, although not every member of the cluster has to be equally hot on the numbers.

Leadership style. The natural leader to emerge in this cluster will be the hard-nosed, fact-based, cost-controller type who uses information cunningly and, above all, avoids any form of risk in transactions with suppliers or indeed customers.

(See Figure 12.9).

Agile supply chains – supply-side

Organization design. The cluster in this case is as described in Chapter 9, and is designed around satisfying demanding customers who come and go from our customer list. We therefore need to encourage suppliers to build capacity to help us satisfy sudden changes in demand.

People positioning. It is important to engineer the selection of personnel so that the bias is right, in this case a speed bias or N (intuition) in MBTI terms or P (Producer) in our P-A-D-I code.

...where quick response is paramount

| MARKET SEGMENT | | RAPID RESPONSE IN VOLATILE DEMAND SITUATIONS |

PROCUREMENT STRATEGY

'PLANNED CAPACITY'

VALUE PROPOSITION

STRATEGIES
- Encourage suppliers to build capacity
- Select several preferred suppliers with available capacity
- Ensure fast decision-making in every case
- Change product designs to speed supply
- Use postponement techniques

INTERNAL CULTURAL CAPABILITY

CULTURAL LEVERS
- Orgnl design
- People positioning
- Processes
- IT/systems
- KPIs
- Incentives
- Job design
- Internal comms
- T&D
- Role modeling
- Recruitment

RATIONAL SUBCULTURE
- Build on speed cluster
- Ensure bias in team is towards personnel with N in the MBTI profile
- Minimize number of processes; re-engineer
- Install software applications such as SCP; APS; NOM
- Absolute speed of response
- Achieve targets; cash and in-kind bonuses
- Authority/autonomy established by clear and published limits
- Formal; regular; action-oriented
- Problem-solving; resource allocation and management
- Managers with ENTJ MBTI profile (P code) are ideal
- Recruit personnel who are results-driven

LEADERSHIP

LEADERSHIP STYLE

COMPANY BARON
- Leads by objectives (MBO)
- Embraces change
- Goes for growth
- Focuses on what's important
- Analytical; fact-based negotiations

FIGURE 12.10 ◆ *Agile supply chains – supply-side*

Processes. Here the emphasis is on re-engineering processes to reduce their number and complexity.

IT/systems. For best results we should install software applications that help us to test various supply scenarios, and at what cost.

Key Performance Indicators (KPIs). For this configuration, the emphasis moves away from relationships and cost to pure speed of fulfillment.

Incentives. Members of this cluster must be able to meet customers' uncertain demands, irrespective of a scarcity of pre-information. Each member of the team works in an individual, albeit complementary, fashion to achieve set targets, and rewards are often in the form of bonuses.

Job design. Job descriptions are clear and boundaries are known and understood by all team members.

Internal communications. Communications are very formal, regular and action-oriented. No long meetings for this cluster, just quick advice and then get on with it.

Training and development. This cluster thrives on problem-solving exercises. The task is to make all team members fully familiar with best-practice resource allocation and trade-off techniques, because that is what they have to do most of the time.

Role modeling. The ideal role model is the detailed conscious *Company Baron*, who is driven to achieve agreed objectives, and will stop at nothing to do so. This style is reflected in an ENTJ (extrovert-intuition-thinking-judging) or ESTP (extrovert-sensing-thinking-perceiving) MBTI profile, which is P (Producer) or Pa (Producer-administrator) in our P-A-D-I logic.

Recruitment. Clearly, team members with finely tuned analytical and judgment skills are highly valued, although not every member of the cluster has to be equally driven.

Leadership style. The natural leader to emerge in this cluster will be the hard-nosed *Company Baron* who lives by the MBO creed: management by objectives. They are happy to lead from the front and take risks.

(See Figure 12.10).

Fully flexible supply chains – supply-side

Organization design. The cluster in this case is as described in Chapter 10, and is designed around 'hedge and deploy' principles. There is usually a single cluster to handle unplannable and unexpected situations, and all members of the cluster are selected for their ability to operate in unfamiliar situations. This cluster may be comprised of full-time or part-time volunteers.

People positioning. It is important to engineer the selection of personnel so that the bias is right, in this case a creativity bias or P (perceiver) in MBTI terms or D (Developer) in our P-A-D-I code.

Processes. Processes are almost non-existent as personnel react real-time on the ground to an evolving emergency.

IT/systems. While human intervention is at a high level in this type of supply chain, any and all IT/systems will be invoked if they can assist produce a solution fast.

Key Performance Indicators (KPIs). For this configuration, the emphasis moves away from relationships, cost and speed to finding creative solutions to the problem, very fast. Cost and to some extent relationships matter naught.

Incentives. For members of this cluster, risk-taking is highly rewarded because a solution must be found. Mistakes occur in this environment but are not penalized.

Job design. Job descriptions are non-existent as most team members must multi-task.

Internal communications. Communications are spontaneous and informal as the action is taking place. This is the time for doing first and asking forgiveness later.

Training and development. This cluster thrives on developing lateral thinking to meet unexpected problems.

Role modeling. The ideal role model is the detailed the ENFP (extrovert-intuition-feeling-perceiving) MBTI style, or D (Developer) in our P-A-D-I code.

...where nothing is impossible

MARKET SEGMENT	'OPPORTUNISTIC'	CREATE INNOVATIVE SOLUTIONS, VERY FAST
PROCUREMENT STRATEGY	VALUE PROPOSITION	**STRATEGIES** ◆ Have nominated personnel on stand-by of full-time duty ◆ Deploy assets across various geographies ◆ Have certain suppliers ear-marked for emergency situations ◆ Possibly place implants inside selected supplier organizations ◆ Encourage capacity build among selected suppliers
INTERNAL CULTURAL CAPABILITY	**CULTURAL LEVERS** ◆ Orgnl design ◆ People positioning ◆ Processes ◆ IT/systems ◆ KPIs ◆ Incentives ◆ Job design ◆ Internal comms ◆ T&D ◆ Role modeling ◆ Recruitment	**'ENTREPRENEURIAL' SUBCULTURE** ◆ A single problem-solving cluster ◆ Ensure bias in the cluster toward personnel with P in their MBTI profile ◆ Very few if any. Decisions made locally to suit situation ◆ Use whatever systems applications necessary ◆ Emphasis on finding creative solutions to problems, very fast ◆ Reward individual effort and risk-taking ◆ Autonomy through empowerment ◆ Spontaneous and informal ◆ Lateral thinking ◆ Managers with ENFP MBTI profile (D code) are ideal ◆ Recruit enterprising, resourceful personnel
LEADERSHIP	LEADERSHIP STYLE	**VISIONARY** ◆ Leads by inspiration, is authentic ◆ Informal ◆ Decisive ◆ Values innovation ◆ Values knowledge ◆ Expects subordinates to take accountability

FIGURE 12.11 ◆ *Fully flexible supply chains – supply-side*

Recruitment. This type of supply chain demands very enterprising and resourceful personnel, and a lot of testing is involved in finding this relatively rare quality.

Leadership style. The natural leader to emerge in this cluster will be the hard-nosed Visionary who is authentic and much respected by other team members.

(See Figure 2.11).

When customers become suppliers – reverse logistics

Reverse logistics is becoming more and more common as manufacturers and retailers accept that they have responsibilities to take back product, either because it is faulty, or at the end of its useful life for subsequent disposal.

A.T. Kearney has provided a useful definition of the send-it-back or take-it-back phenomenon that is becoming increasingly apparent across a range of customer markets. 'Reverse logistics encompasses all the activities associated with the return of goods, regardless of condition or reason for return, for the purpose of extracting value or ensuring proper disposal.'[10] Products can be returned because of customer preference ('I don't like it!'), to fulfill customer expectations about a company's environmental responsibilities, or to meet growing regulatory requirements around issues such as reducing waste to landfill. A wide range of options now exists for products to be returned and this in itself creates complexity (as well as opportunities) for supply chains, as depicted in Figure 12.12 overleaf. The problem of meeting reverse demand is only worsening as more customers embrace online purchasing as a method of acquiring products, and then, for whatever reason, want to return it to the place where they purchased it.

Perhaps *dynamic alignment* offers a way through this increasing complexity, just as it has helped with the forward-looking element of the supply chain on the demand-side. If we could limit the number of return options to a relatively few pathways, and focus resources on these few supply chains, the cost of the reverse activity would be significantly reduced. Let's have a look at four possible return pathways (supply chains) consistent with our experience on the demand- and supply-sides.

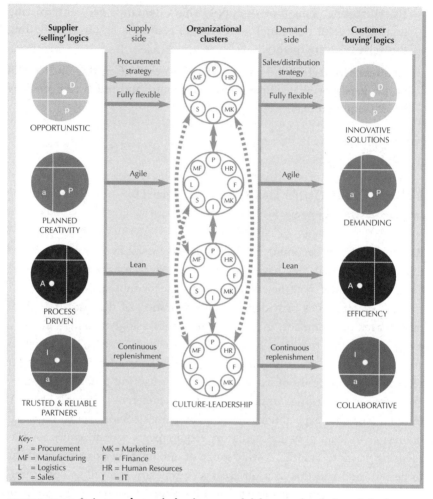

FIGURE 12.12 ◆ A new dynamic business model for supply chains of the future

1. The *continuous replenishment* return path – where relationships are the key driver[11]

Bessemer is an Australian company that has made and distributed premium quality aluminum cookware for more than 40 years. It offers customers a 40 per cent discount on a new product with a trade-in of any existing product. Many of Bessemer's customers are loyal devotees of their product and this very attractive incentive keeps them re-purchasing. However, as the items have a longer-than-normal life-cycle, the re-purchase period may be eight to ten years after the original sale.

In many respects, this is a very savvy approach. Returns constitute a third of the total aluminum used in production. At a cost per ton at the time of writing of more than US$2,000, and as recycled product requires considerably less processing effort, the economics are compelling. The offer also enhances the premium brand image by providing an additional benefit, and positions Bessemer as a responsible corporate citizen that is concerned about the full life-cycle of the product.

The return path is supported by the extensive national network used for forward movements, and the complexity is minimized because the returned item is introduced into the return path when it is exchanged for the new item. When each depot reaches an economic transfer quantity (usually a pallet), the items are dispatched, generally on the same vehicle delivering new product. The quantities returned, after many years of this operation, are also quite predictable.

This is a classic example of leveraging a loyal Ia (Integrator-administrator) customer base and developing a stable and cost-effective return operation around the predictability that that relationship brings. The *continuous replenishment* return path will often be built on dependencies. In this case, the manufacturing operation is highly dependent on the returns for inputs, and the marketing arm is dependent on the incentive to maintain and build an ongoing relationship with customers. Stable patterns also lend themselves to fine tuning based around analytics, and in this case the variability of supply is a key element in the analysis.

2. The *lean* return path – where cost is the key driver

Where items are expected to have no reclaimable value, or where there is regular and stable recycling of low-value inputs, the key driver is usually cost, and the emphasis is on routine patterns with minimal need for management intervention.

Ideally, the local waste recycling system for households should be designed around the reliability and rigor of a lean path so as to keep costs down. That will enable paper, glass, steel and aluminium to be removed on a weekly or fortnightly basis and directed through a predictable separation process, when the materials can be collected returned for re-use or new production. The company need not intervene in this process – or engage with the customers – at any stage.

3. The *agile* return path – where time is the key driver

Where there is an opportunity for resale, *time* usually needs to be the key driver in the returns process. Studies of Hewlett-Packard's Equipment Management and Remarketing (EMR) operation[12] found that laptops being refurbished for resale in secondary markets could take more than four months to go through the various phases of staging and processing before being made available for sale. Obviously the recovery value of computer equipment deteriorates rapidly with time, and time lost equates to value lost in these markets. One source of delay in this process was the use of the same manufacturer for refurbishment as for original equipment production. Inevitably new production was given a higher priority. A complicating factor in this market was also management's perception that they needed to limit sales of refurbished items to put a floor under the price of new laptops. However, on closer analysis during this study, it was found that the markets for each were distinctly different and there was little substance to this concern.

Time-sensitive returns should be treated as a value stream not a waste stream. The priority is to manage lead times, avoid bottlenecks and support the operation with a flexible organization structure geared around identifying and quickly capturing market opportunities as they emerge.

4. The *fully flexible* return path – where it's all about risk management

Whereas the *fully flexible* supply chain features rarely in the forward supply chain, in the reverse supply chain it is a feature of every major manufacturer's armory – but hopefully only in their contingency plans. A *fully flexible* path requires fast, dynamic and creative responses to unforeseen situations. For most companies this means recall programs, natural disasters or other, similarly high-risk situations.

The recall program is an important reverse logistics situation. It requires detailed contingency planning with specialized arrangements, and capacity commitments from logistics providers that can be turned on immediately they are needed. Despite all the planning, however, when the situation arises it will inevitably also require creative and fast decisions to respond to the particular situation. Reputational risk is so high in these situations that cost cannot be a consideration, just as holding or paying for spare capacity can often be justified as a risk minimization strategy.

The sustainability dimension and corporate social responsibility

Sustainability has swept on to the business scene in the past decade as consumer consciousness of the environment has grown. National governments have ignored this new movement at their peril, and some indeed have fallen because they did not take sustainability seriously. V.D.R. Guide[13] has calculated that the annual generation of waste in Western Europe is 550kg per person, exceeding the current target by 83 per cent, and is trending towards doubling by 2020. This problem is not going away soon! It has to be addressed.

Whether the solution is straight-out disposal, re-manufacturing, or refurbishment, all these options require cost-effective reverse logistics solutions. All will need to comply with the new battery of regulations increasingly emerging from concerned governments. It looks like supply chain design will become part of the corporation's legislative risk management and corporate governance.

It appears that the only sensible way forward is to design (or re-design) demand-side, supply-side and reverse logistics elements of an enterprise supply chain coincidentally because of the intense interdependency. This is the task for corporate managements and governments in the next decade. Solutions must be found as time begins to run out.[14]

Defining ideas

1 The supply-side is just the mirror image of the demand-side. Therefore, use the same segmentation techniques for your supplier base as used for the customer base.

2 Not surprisingly, we find four similar behavioral selling logics on the supply-side as we identified on the demand-side.

3 By aligning your procurement strategies with the previously identified dominant behavioral selling logics you will achieve a more efficient spend: witness what happened at JBS Swift in Brazil.

4 As we found on the demand-side, the key is to build the appropriate capability to underpin the execution of your procurement strategies via the four main types of supply-side supply chains.

5 **Challenge** to the reader: have you re-connected your supply-side to the demand-side of your enterprise supply chains?

CHAPTER 13

Hybrid supply chains

Surfacing the new realities

The preceding chapters in this book all culminate in this chapter, where we summarize the 16 possible combinations of supply chain configuration observed on the ground in enterprises worldwide.[1] We have termed these 'hybrids,' and they co-exist in various combinations depending on the marketplace being served. Indeed, the various combinations can also operate in parallel with each other, a situation that demands that multiple alignment techniques be applied at both ends of enterprise supply chains. If ever there was a final condemnation of the one-size-fits-all mentality so common in contemporary supply chain management, this is it.

If only the world was linear! Then we could more easily manage supply chains to match our customer segments. But there are inherent subtleties in different types of supply chains.

It is therefore important to understand that alignment with customers (and suppliers) does not always work on a linear one-to-one basis. Mixed supply chain combinations are sometimes the best solution, but have to be applied skillfully. We called these 'hybrid' supply chains in our discussion of organizational design in Chapter 6. As befits the cluster organization of the future, these supply chains can be any combination of the four demand-side and four supply-side supply chains depicted in

Figure 13.1. In Figure 13.2 we outline the 16 possible pathways of supply chains, but of course not all of these are feasible. We will look at the most common types of hybrid supply chains, and illustrate these with current examples.

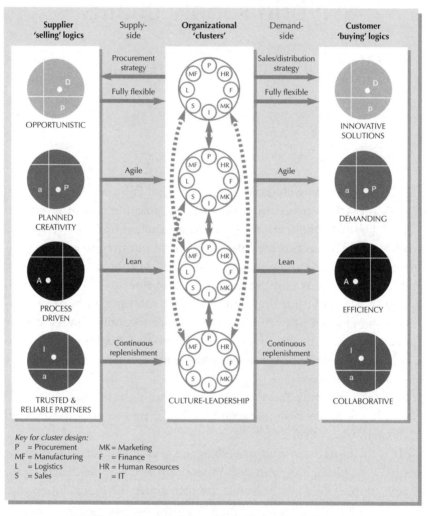

FIGURE 13.1 ◆ **Different combinations of hybrid supply chains**

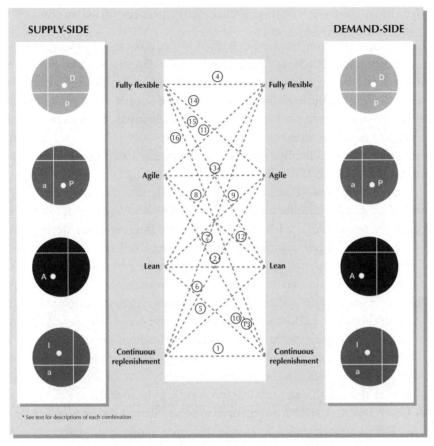

FIGURE 13.2 ◆ The 16 possible combinations of hybrid supply chains –
including the four main generic types

The 16 hybrid supply chains

The approach we will use in the following examples is to specify the
demand-side component first, followed by the **supply-side** component
in the overall enterprise supply chain. Note that the companies may have
more supply chain configurations than those quoted; this is not a comprehensive list of their active supply chain configurations.

1. Continuous replenishment – continuous replenishment

Li & Fung is the consummate enterprise when it comes to owning strong relationships at both ends of the supply chain. On the demand-side, the Hong-Kong based company set up individual multi-disciplinary clusters for each individual new account. On the supply-side, each cluster develops strong relationships down to the individual factory level. The emerging problem with this approach is that with 300 clusters now in operation, these individual 'tribes' are beginning to compete with each other for capacity in the individual supplier.

Lever Brothers (Thailand), one of Thailand's largest fast moving consumer goods manufacturers, has the *continuous replenishment* supply chain on both sides. With diverse products ranging from detergents to ice-cream to personal care products, Lever Brothers' hybrid supply chain addresses fluctuating production by working to a shared forecast on the demand-side. To support this dual arrangement there is a specific program to train staff in the competences required to operate each configuration. Lever Brothers is aiming to have these two supply chain configurations synchronized and integrated throughout the business.

BOC Gases, now part of the Linde Group, uses a similar arrangement when supplying bulk gas, onsite gas, and safety gear to their major customers in the health care, mining and metals industries. In the same way as Lever Brothers, BOC is synchronizing the demand-side and supply-side of their supply chains to ensure that their stable and reliable service is maintained for their many loyal customers. With collaboration a distinguishing feature of the *continuous replenishment* supply chain, it is double collaboration in this hybrid!

Unipart Group in the United Kingdom used this type of supply chain configuration in their strategic partnership with Jaguar Cars. With such a quality brand as Jaguar, Unipart knows that reliability, quality and collaboration are essential. As a major logistics services company, Unipart has developed their own philosophy to enshrine commitment to *lean* principles, called 'The Unipart Way,' which they seek to share with customers. Unipart says, 'We believe that no other logistics organization has developed 'lean thinking' to the extent that we have.'[2] We would argue, however, that 'The Unipart Way', being built around collaboration, is closer to the Continuous replenishment supply chain than the more cost-focused Lean operation.

2. Lean – lean

Lever Brothers (Thailand) has developed a manufacturing plant for their production of the well-known Sunsilk range of hair care products. The plant services two distinct supply chains. One of these is *lean-lean*, based on steady demand and therefore steady production. The other is in the next combination discussed.

Benetton also use this type of straight-through single type configuration for their pre-season dispatch of apparel to franchisees; they call it their 'sequential dual' supply chain.[3] Benetton use the dual configuration to supply garments ordered by franchisees before the beginning of the fashion season. It is very much 'push' focused. Features of this supply chain configuration are: make-to-forecast; sourcing teams focused on low-cost sourcing; and logistics teams focused on forecasting, inventory management and distribution.

Cochlear, the global company providing hearing solutions for the hearing-impaired, also use the *lean-lean* combination to meet that part of their global demand that is scheduled by hospitals and doctors. This high technology manufacturer, based in Australia, has, for this segment of customers, ample lead time to fulfill to a published schedule while doing so in a low-cost way.

BOC Gases use the *lean-lean* combination to meet the demand for gas cylinders and safety gear to their retail outlets.[4]

The **Ministry of Defence (MOD)** in the United Kingdom has some challenges with running parallel supply chains. It has to switch between maintenance mode in peacetime (*lean-lean*) to quick response in wartime (*agile-agile*). If they try to manage both supply chains with the same management system, it will be very difficult to optimize either – as a result, MOD carries huge inventories, and has incompatible performance management systems.

As *lean* initiatives are essentially designed to strip out waste from supply chains, including inventory and excess capacity, one outcome is to make the system less stable. Indeed, as with 'fly-by-wire' technology in aeronautics, the issue is stability. How close can you get to zero inventory and full utilization of resources without the system failing? In this case the failure is in meeting customers' expectations. On the other hand, if we try to increase stability by building in inventory, time and capacity buffers, agility will suffer. So the solution is to combine the two in some way rather than adopt one or other approach alone.

Ryanair, the Irish low-cost airline, has been able to minimize input costs and, therefore, the cost of fares on the demand-side. Consumers can buy tickets on the internet and pay for extras on-board if they choose. There is no loyalty club, no meeting customers and little or no advertising – as is befitting a *lean* operation!

The Dabbawallahs of Mumbai use this supply chain configuration every day as they deliver their home-cooked lunches to clients in the Mumbai CBD, at an impossibly low cost. This business successfully delivers 150,000 meals a day; doing so with such a high degree of accuracy.

Likewise **Haier**, the normally *agile* white goods manufacturer in China, has used a lean supply chain configuration to deliver white goods to parts of the United States market at the lowest possible cost.

CSR Gyprock the Australian building materials company uses this configuration when servicing the bulk plaster board needs of distributors and large commercial builders. The building materials manufacturer uses *lean-lean* principles for their bulk business, but needs different supply chain hybrids for other markets and products, as discussed below.

3. Agile – agile

Benetton also uses a straight-through *agile-agile* supply chain configuration in parallel to its lean configuration discussed above. This is designed to move apparel quickly to market within the season in a very short timeframe. They call this variation their 'integrated dual' supply chain.[5] Features of this configuration are make-to-order (pull) and a modular organization structure. Their key performance indicator is delivery time to customers.

BOC Gases use this combination when supplying gas cylinders and safety gear to small- and medium-sized enterprises, generally by direct delivery to reduce the lead time and maintain responsiveness.

Marks and Spencer, the British retailer, used this configuration in the 1990s, somewhat unsuccessfully.

4. *Fully flexible – fully flexible*

Most of the examples in this category will come from humanitarian disasters such as the 2004 Indian Ocean tsunami, and more recently the Haiti earthquake of January 2010. Increasingly the agencies involved in responding to these situations, however, are seeking to increase their preparedness by building both stocks and relationships with suppliers and third party logistics providers, thereby introducing elements of continuous replenishment and lean on the supply side, while maintaining the emphasis on being fully flexible and capable of any level of response on the demand side.

5. Lean – continuous replenishment

Gerdau Steel in Brazil has decentralized the production of long products using market-mills located in regional markets to allow efficient access to customers. On the supply-side, Gerdau fosters long-term relationships with its suppliers. Above all, the company tries to avoid any type of disruption by keeping dependence on any one supplier or customer to a maximum of 10 per cent of revenue.

Toyota and Honda are perfect examples of this combination. Both are automotive makers and both have formed remarkable partnerships with their Tier One supply base, resulting in lower cost components. They provide a clear case of collaboration on the supply-side leading to a lean result on the demand-side.

Tesco, the leading UK supermarket chain, also use this configuration among others. Their suppliers now perform many of the functions previously undertaken by Tesco, and the result is a lean supply chain at the demand-end, supported by a *continuous replenishment* configuration largely supported by suppliers. However, this is probably more an example of Tesco's power in the channel than true collaboration. Wal-Mart operates much the same way in their supply chain arrangements with suppliers.

Filtronic Comtek, which manufactures cellular base stations for the telecommunications industry, has embraced lean manufacturing principles on the demand-side. However the company concedes that strategic supplier relationships were essential to make it work and keep the company competitive.[6]

6. Agile – continuous replenishment

Marks and Spencer used the *agile-continuous* configuration in the 1990s when they relied on a collaborative relationship with their predominantly domestic UK supply base, and it worked well because replenishment times were relatively short. However, due to downward pressure on pricing, Marks and Spencer mistakenly changed their sourcing strategy to focus on the Far East, and that's when their problems multiplied. The retailer had underestimated the logistics difficulties associated with this new sourcing strategy, and paid the price.

Campbell Soups use this type of configuration, among others, to service their retail customers.

7. Fully flexible – continuous replenishment

The examples of this supply chain hybrid will often come from the 'event' business. From football games to music festivals the long lead times involved and the history of past events gives the organizers and caterers time and information to collaborate with suppliers. 'On the day', however, the operation must become fully flexible on the demand side, responding within very short time-frames to changes in conditions. As heat-wave conditions hit the Big Day Out concert in Sydney in January 2010 for example (registering 41°C) the demand for water from the 53,000 concert-goers increased by multiples placing intense pressure on the supply chain.

As noted earlier many NGOs and humanitarian agencies, who are responding to much less predictable events, see opportunities to move their supply chains at least partially towards this model.

8. Fully flexible – lean

Honda also demonstrated a lot of flexibility when they were able to build the Honda Accord in an old truck plant with minimal disruption during the changeover, as the demand for trucks fell and cars increased.[7]

9. Agile – Lean

This is one of the most common combinations in this increasingly volatile world.

BMW are a good example of this type of supply chain configuration. According to Rich Morris, 'flexibility . . . is the ability to shift production of different models among different plants, as demand shifts in different global markets'.[8]

Staroup in Brazil were forced to launch their 'survivor' project in January 2007, when their major customer for jeans, Levi's, announced they were shifting their sourcing to China. Up to that point Staroup had supplied all Levi's women's jeans sold in the US and was using an *agile-lean* configuration. After some experimentation, Staroup converted to an *agile-fully flexible* configuration to out-cycle their Chinese competitors and save a major part of their Levi business. See further comments below.

Cochlear is another company that uses the *agile-lean* combination for a large part of their business. During the past five years, Cochlear have been working to develop scale on the supply-side and agility on the demand-side. The motivation for this transformation was Cochlear's strong but somewhat unpredictable growth in international markets, which was influenced by an increasing product range, customer demand for more customization, and categories of institutional customers will minimal demand planning capability.

On the supply-side, Cochlear have secured their supply base for components and accessories by working closely with key suppliers and by acquiring their largest supplier, upon whom they were critically dependent. In manufacturing/assembly, lean principles were adopted along with the introduction of innovative new manufacturing technology. Postponement techniques, and locating inventory buffers along the chain, have led to increased responsiveness on the volatile demand-side. The result has been reduced production cycles and increased flexibility. The changes have also resulted in improved operational efficiency, increased customer service levels and more successful introductions of new products.

CSR Gyprock who you will recall from an earlier example also use this combination: servicing their 'Pick Centres' (for assembling assorted orders) with a *lean* configuration and these in turn service smaller residential customers who have dynamic requirements and demanding delivery needs with an *agile* response.

The **Hunter Valley Coal Chain** in Newcastle, Australia, managed by Port Waratah Coal Services (PWCS), has aimed to be *lean* from the mine pit/loading point to port (on the supply-side) and *agile* from the port stockpile to on-board the ore carrier which is waiting for dispatch to end users (on the demand-side). Focus on the differing requirements of their end-users, however, is suggesting new combinations. The reliable demands for much of the coal used in power stations in several key markets such as Japan could lend itself to an information-driven continuous replenishment supply chain on the demand side, while the unpredictable requirements of that part of the market dominated by traders and parts of the spot market will always ensure an agile supply chain is also required.

Daewoo Shipyards[9] in Korea is another outstanding example of the successful application of a hybrid supply chain configuration.

Daewoo Shipyards completes a new super-tanker or container ship every 36 hours, or more than 200 a year. They are valued at US$75 million to US$100 million each. How can that be possible?

Several ships are constructed line abreast, and up to 20 sections or blocks for each ship are built off-line, simultaneously. This is the lean part of the supply chain. These blocks, weighing several thousand tons each, are completed with all the fittings inside – piping, electricals, hydraulics – everything. They are transported from other areas of the site at the last minute and welded together, painted and launched, as fast as possible as the next ship is waiting to be assembled.

This is postponement in action on a massive scale. So it is not just a phenomenon that happens with apparel and electronics. This is heavy industry with a capital 'H'. All of this is also achieved with a well-paid labor force – Korea is no longer a low-cost labor country. So, here again, we see an innovative combination of *lean* and *agile* supply chains at work.

Viterra (previously ABB Grain) does something similar to Daewoo when shipping grain to their worldwide customer base.

With New Zealand's geographic isolation and its dependence on imported grain for the animal feed and flour industries, efficient supply chain management requires suppliers like ourselves to understand millers' annual requirements and sometimes unexpected demands.

Our solution is to locate strategic storage at sites adjacent to the mills. This provides the millers with certainty of supply, and also flexibility in purchasing to meet demand either on a spot or forward basis. The advantage of this is to optimize supply chain efficiencies both in the country of origin, sea freight and on-shore New Zealand storage sites.[10]

The development of the **Land Rover** Freelander, otherwise known as the CB40 Project,[11] is another demonstration of combining *lean* and *agile* supply chains.

> Two of the Freelander project's many unique features are: the design of a large part of the new vehicle using standard components and processes (*lean*); and the combined in-built 'design redundancy' of other components to shorten the time required at assembly, to reduce the waiting time for customers (*agile*).
>
> To achieve this, Land Rover's supply base was limited to 146, and fully integrated into the project at the concept phase. Suppliers were also encouraged to participate in component design and subsequent logistics processes and physical operations. In truth, this was one of the first projects in any industry to invoke a higher-order level of collaboration between multiple parties in the extensive supply chains involved, right through to the dealer network.[12] It set the scene for others to follow.

Fantastic Furniture, Australia's fastest-growing furniture chain, has their own Fantastic Lounge Factory which produced 113,000 sofas in 2004/05, about one every three minutes! It was clearly using postponement techniques and an *agile-lean* supply chain combination, albeit on a somewhat smaller scale than Daewoo Shipyards, but just as effective. As always, you look behind the scenes and you find an entrepreneur and quality leadership at the top; it never fails. Who said Australia can't match the lower labor-cost countries for productivity, work practices and sheer passion?

Zara is world famous for their ability to work within a 15-day cycle to replenish their store network with newly designed fashion apparel. This is very much a case of *agile* on the demand-side and *lean* on the supply-side. Their main competitor, the Swedish firm H&M, is not far behind, with a 20-day replenishment cycle.

Zara is designed in a vertically integrated way. They manufacture 50 per cent of their products and outsource the residual 50 per cent. They integrate backward for design, fabric procurement and coloring processes, and forward integrate for market research and running their own retail chain.

Haier, which also featured earlier, set up manufacturing facilities in California as this was their major export market. In effect, they traded off some of the benefits of low cost production in China for responsiveness to the demands of customers in the domestic US market.

10. *Continuous replenishment – lean*

Shouldice Hospital[13] in Canada has refined and smartly executed their approach to a particular customer segment with a single health problem, thanks to their hybrid configuration.

> Shouldice Hospital has a unique service – it treats only people with inguinal hernias. These patients are in and out of the hospital in three days and back to work in about ten days, compared to the usual hospital stay of seven to ten days, followed by up to six weeks for full recovery. The streamlined approach of this hospital and the focus on one type of operation has resulted in expertise in the preparation of the patient, surgery procedure, recovery program and rehabilitation – as well as an international reputation attracting 'customers' from all over the globe.
>
> Over 95 per cent of hernia patients are male, and Shouldice Hospital has developed its systems to address the needs of this customer category. This is achieved by maximizing the information and control the patient has in the procedure and minimizing time lost from work; which further contributes to the speed of recovery. The shortened time for recovery has decreased the negative impact on both the patient's family and their business.
>
> Patients are admitted in the afternoon and allocated to a group that they are responsible to and for during their stay in the hospital. The group eats their meals together in the equivalent to a hotel dining room (in both quality of food and style). Hospital rooms in Shouldice do not have their own bathroom – instead patients have to get up and walk to the bathroom. At every step the patients are encouraged to return to routine activity. On the first afternoon the groups are taken through a complete explanation of the medical procedure.

The next day operations are performed without a general anaesthetic; instead they are given a combination of a local anaesthetic and sedatives (they are semi-conscious). After the procedure is completed the patient is helped to walk back to their bed – in contrast to conventional approaches to hernia recovery, where patients are restricted to complete bed-rest for almost a week after the operation. The same day patients are up and walking (very slowly) in the manicured gardens of the hospital. They are required to walk to meals and exercise with their group.

Two days later they are discharged from the hospital after following a program of increased gentle exercise and instruction on how to continue the healing process. Annually, Shouldice Hospital has sold-out reunions for their patients in a five-star hotel. The venue is packed with more than 1,500 patients who come to rejoin 'their' group to catch up and celebrate.

The **Virginia Mason Hospital** fully embraced lean principles on the back end in order to provide a reliable but patient friendly service at the demand-end of its supply chains.

BOC Gases uses a customer friendly front-end supply chain when servicing selected long term contract customers in the health care, mining, and metal industries.

CSR Gyprock used this type of configuration when servicing retail trade centres located around the country to support the relationship and network needs of the small builder/tradesmen.

Louis Vuitton, a unit of Louis Vuitton Moet Hennessy (LVMH), the world's largest luxury goods company, overhauled its manufacturing processes in 2005/06 in an effort to reduce costs.[14] We assume the sell prices did not change though!

Other luxury-goods brands are following suit, eg., Versace, Giorgio Armani, Burberry, Cartier and Prada.[15]

Interestingly, Louis Vuitton are now considering a joint-venture in India in a further overhaul of its supply chain.[16]

11. *Fully flexible – agile*

This is the **Formula One pit stop** or **Dell** replacing 1,000 PCs lost in Hurricane Katrina, in super quick time.

12. Lean – agile

This combination has been seen in some parts of the red meat industry, where availability of supply can be highly unpredictable, influenced by a range of factors including weather. Businesses with ongoing contracts with retailers and export customers must do whatever is necessary to source and negotiate supply terms to fulfill their ongoing commitments, and to keep volume moving through their plant to absorb overheads.

Procter & Gamble also use this approach when supplying volume products to Wal-Mart.

13. Continuous replenishment – agile

Marks and Spencer in the UK used this combination until they moved away from their domestic suppliers in favor of low-cost source markets in the Far East in the late 1990s.

Once again, red meat and other businesses built around the natural unpredictability of agriculture are a key source of examples for this hybrid. Where customers have regular and planned requirements and the relationship has been built over time to share this information, the business (such as **Stockyard Beef** in Australia) find themselves needing to 'convert' the unpredictability of upstream supply into the steady flow required to maintain the loyalty of their collaborative customers.

14. Agile – fully flexible

This is the supply chain configuration ultimately adopted by **Staroup** in Brazil to out-cycle their Chinese competitors and retain a large proportion of the Levi women's jeans business in the US market.

15. Lean – fully flexible

This is the type of configuration needed, and occasionally evident, where Ministries of Health and Not-For-Profit (NFP) organizations attempt to keep a steady flow of life-critical drugs (such as insulin) moving to affected populations in Third World countries within very tight budgetary constraints. While the base level operation in these situations needs to be designed around low cost and reliability, there also needs to be a highly flexible 'back-up' supply chain that is available in emergencies, avoiding the need to hold high stocks and spare capacity in the primary channel.

16. Continuous replenishment – fully flexible

Another unusual combination – Egged Bus Company in Israel, which has to try and run a user-friendly service amidst the constant threat of suicide bombers blowing up their buses.

Defining ideas

1 There is clear evidence of the occurrence of all 16 types of supply chain 'hybrid' combinations in the Gattorna taxonomy.

2 In the sort of volatile world that we now live in, and expect to continue, it is not surprising that the most prevalent combination appears to be *Agile-Lean*.

3 Enterprises should also be aware that they must identify and select which three or four combinations they want to participate in, and put all their resources behind these. In this case it would be very useful to know the proportions of the business going down each of the main supply chain combinations.

4 **Challenge** for the reader: from the list of 16 listed above, what hybrids can you identify running through your own enterprise?

CHAPTER 14

New business models for new supply chains

The miracle of 'embedded alignment'

T o this point we have been striving to demonstrate how an enterprise can re-align with its customers, suppliers and third parties. This type of transformation takes time, tenacity and, above all, leadership.

But for some enterprises, time is not on their side. Something more radical is required to achieve the desired alignment in a much shorter time-frame. In some cases, even survival is at stake. This is where we need to shift gears and go in search of new business models that can be applied to the whole enterprise and its constituent supply chains.

The idea is to go beyond conventional outsourcing, and instead look for ways to establish a consortium that has the required capabilities to complete the task, and do it fast, without the usual internal resistance. Everything must come together – innovation; cultural fit; advanced organization designs; and above all, a leadership style that's prepared to try something new and reap the rewards of a quantum improvement in operational and financial performance. There have been successes in this regard, but not enough. This situation will change as the operating environment gets progressively tougher and new-style leadership takes on the odds in search of the increased rewards sought by all stakeholders.

A 'business model' is simply the way an enterprise organizes itself to make money. It's the core logic of how your business creates value in a sustainable way. *New* business models are just that – new and often innovative ways of organizing the enterprise to make money on a sustainable basis. Can you think of a genuinely **new** business model? According to Johnson and his colleagues,[1] 'there's really no point in instituting a new business model unless it's not only new to the company but in some way new or game-changing to the industry or market. To do otherwise would be a waste of time and money.' Today they come in both formal and informal arrangements. Perhaps the best known are the models nurtured in industry clusters first identified by Michael Porter in 1990.[2] Examples include information technology in Silicon Valley and biotechnology at nine locations across the United States. Other examples include banking in Switzerland and movie production in Hollywood and of course India's own Bollywood. These clusters act as 'incubators' for new ideas and set the direction for industry. Rubbing shoulders with each other helps to share knowledge, excite passions and encourage more than a bit of intense competition, as well as intensifying the development of associated industries. This simply doesn't happen in other environments, at least not in such an intense, industry-focused way. Industry clusters in Europe have generated world-class industries, from ceramics in Italy, fashion in Paris, Milan and London and more recently New York and Tokyo, to the original watch/clock industry, and cut flowers in the Netherlands, as our case example below describes. Perhaps a contemporary example of this clustering arrangement can be found in the form of 'Logistics City States' such as Singapore and Dubai.[3]

Have you seen the seeds of new ideas appearing in your industry? Fortunately, new business models are emerging in a multitude of different formats in different industries around the world. In particular, new business solutions in publishing,[4] tobacco[5] and aviation fuel[6] exist today. The airline industry has its alliances, brokers and call centres; SMART cars, an alliance between Daimler-Chrysler and SWATCH, is focused on achieving an environmentally friendly design; Arshiya International in India is building a completely new third-party logistics provider (3PL)/ fourth-party logistics provider (4PL) business model; eco-tourism is emerging as a significant industry segment; and many other examples are at different stages of development.

All of these new-breed business models are based on **the principle that it is better to bring together the required combinations of** *capabilities*, **fast, in a new integrated organization** rather than trying to develop them organically over time. The resulting hybrid businesses bring to life the idea of 'embedded alignment'. The desired alignment with customers is created and embedded almost instantaneously in the new enterprise. There's an almost immediate end to the hard work of trying to change your internal culture to achieve alignment; the required alignment is embedded from the very start. Sound easy? We will get to the hard part later.

The cut flower market in the Netherlands is an example of a highly per-ishable luxury product being transformed into a global product through an innovative business model. The market origins are from the late 1800s when vegetable growers started auctions to sell their own produce instead of selling through wholesalers. The wholesalers tended to foster intense competition between the growers – driving down prices. This developed into the flower auctions known today, that are owned by the growers in a cooperative that helps set market prices and provides an exchange of information on future market trends. Basically an anteced-ent of the 'open auctions' that were all the buzz when first 'discovered' in the 1990s.

This innovative solution to unbalanced power in the supply chain (where the wholesalers dominated) fostered a cluster of industries with strong links to the cut flower market. Not all of these industries are directly involved in the 'Dutch auctions' yet have formed a service or supplier to the industry. For example, the Netherlands, with its limited land mass, has cut flowers as one of its exports – which initially seems counter-intuitive. However, due to the early development and adoption of glasshouses in this country the cut flower market was facilitated by a state-of-the-art glass production industry. Glasshouses provided the means for intensive cultivation of land, resulting in both high yields and more standardized product. Even new technology developed in The Netherlands is now being used at the Melbourne Cricket Ground to promote the growth of grass in the shadow of the giant stands.

Other well-developed industries closely associated with cut flowers in the Netherlands are the strong agricultural businesses (dairy, agron-omy), horticulture products (fertilizers and pesticides), horticultural education and training, along with the innovative logistics developed since the mid-1990s that allows the transportation of perishable prod-ucts around the globe. The cluster comprises a range of products and

---

services – from horticultural advice and innovative packaging for the global transport of flowers, to state-of-the-art logistics systems, fertilizers and pesticides and glass products for green houses.

You might ask: 'Why do we need new organizational formats in the first place? My business is travelling along very well, thank you.' One very good reason, particularly if you are a small to medium-sized business, is **scale**. Scale is critical simply because it gives businesses greater operating efficiencies and competitiveness. That means, you may be faced with new competitors, perhaps not just yet . . . but watch them enter your market soon! Let's face it, in many smaller economies the size of entire industries is less than a single organization in other parts of the world, particularly in the northern hemisphere. If you are in a smaller economy and you want to compete, you need to find new ways to achieve scale – even if only artificially. In this context, a report by Booz Allen Hamilton proposed the concept of 'virtual scale', which allows smaller companies to 'compete with industry giants by pooling resources with carefully chosen partners'.[7] This is not an unreasonable concept, but it relies heavily on the companies' ability to form strong and lasting alliances. The new scaled-up organization will only survive if there is an 'equity' structure to hold it together when the going gets tough, as it surely will, as we shall see.

There is also the *diminishing returns* effect of just doing more of the same, as depicted in the first two levels of Figure 14.1. Re-inventing the organization, even using sophisticated alignment principles described in earlier chapters, has its limitations, mostly to do with the time to fully execute plans. Therefore, we have to seek out more radical forms of organization formats.

Why are radical formats necessary? Surely, they are risky? Paradoxically, I don't think they are – indeed they are essential. For too long enterprises have segmented their customer base using institutional, geographical and other internal parameters. This immediately 'disconnects' the non-customer-facing operations from the most important people in the business: *customers*. No wonder they fail to get a clear view of what customers want! Unfortunately, the idea of weaving multiple supply chains into the fabric of a business is still a foreign concept. In addition, the underlying mechanisms that cause cultural resistance to new initiatives are still largely a mystery

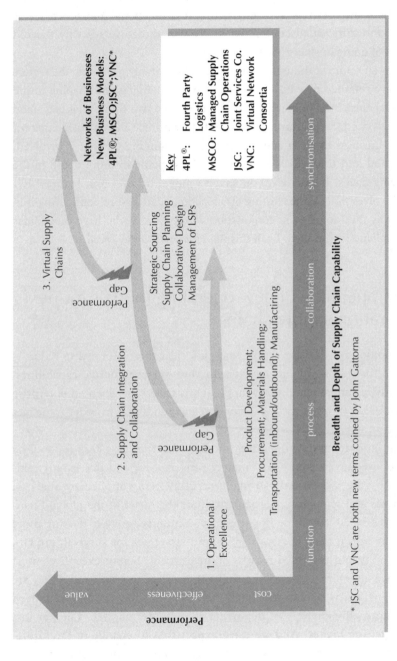

FIGURE 14.1 ◆ Performance/capability continuum

Source: Adapted from Figure I.1 in Gattorna (2003), p. xi

to executives brought up in a predominantly functional world, where specializations are preferred and rewarded. Cross-functional interaction seems almost too difficult to contemplate. We can therefore see why the old models of doing business have prevailed!

I am an optimist though. Businesses will inevitably overcome the factors that have retarded new business models from emerging and shaping future supply chains. But you need to watch out for the two things that can stand in the way: a lack of **management will** to embrace the changes inherent in new business models; and a lack of understanding of what is involved, both good and the bad. We will pursue this theme in more depth in the following pages. Ultimately, you have to move to Level 3 in Figure 14.1. This involves pulling the existing organization apart and re-configuring it in some way, but doing so in conjunction with partners who have capabilities to complement your own. I call this the *Humpty Dumpty effect.*

The imperative of new operating models for next generation supply chains

You should take decisive action when it's clear that you need to radically re-align the needs of your market with your current internal capabilities. Similarly, a fundamentally new approach is called for when an enterprise cannot break through the *capability wall* surrounding it in order to deliver its own strategies.

But embracing new operating models is not an easy task for today's C-level executives. Many are innately conservative, and this is only reinforced by the increasingly stringent scrutiny being applied by analysts, investors, and regulators, particularly since the onset of the global financial crisis in 2008-9. The investment community today is looking more critically at top management's plans and strategies for survival, growth, profitability and projected returns on investment. Senior executives must convince investors they have the ability to 'execute to plan'; and if they are proposing a new operating model, they have to show that it will indeed be a more efficient way of deploying shareholder capital. The bar just keeps getting higher! And we can't expect that to change in the future. If anything, the scrutiny is set to increase. The recession in the wake of the financial crisis made sure of that. With supply chains accounting for up to 80 per cent of the enterprise's capital investment and 60 per cent of working capital,[8] they are already coming under almost daily scrutiny by financial analysts around the world. It is therefore imperative that management finds new supply chain operating models that are more capital efficient[9] and less demanding in terms of up-front investment requirements. One of the most exciting recent developments has been the wider adoption of the Cash Flow Return on Investment (CFROI)[10] metric developed by Boston Consulting to measure the health and relative wealth of an enterprise. CSFB Holt's ValueSearch database of cash flow and valuations of tens of thousands of companies across the globe has detected a significant correlation between future share price performance (expressed as market capitalization) and CFROI as described by Joel Litman and Mark Frigo in their paper.[11] On this basis it seems that this financial metric (depicted in Figure 14.2) is superior to other more traditional accounting ratios. CFROI gets under the covers and exposes what is really going on inside a company's operations and finances.

Indeed, if we look at the leading companies of the past decade, their market performance is matched by their CFROI. Nokia – one of the most positive change stories of the last 25 years – has had a spectacular growth in its CFROI. While transforming itself from a timber company into one of the world's leading high-tech companies, Nokia has ensured that ample funds are available to sustain high investment levels in competitive-building assets. This in turn has helped the company out-perform the market in terms of share price. And it is right in the middle of another major transformation as it seeks to out-compete Apple. Li & Fung is another enterprise that has successfully transformed itself from a small trading company[12] to a global high-performance, full-line supply chain service provider. In fact HSBC reported in the *Wall Street Journal* that Li & Fung's current profit measure, EBIT/Revenue (3.4 per cent in 2004), understates the company's real performance, which when measured by EBIT/Gross Profit is 36.9 per cent in the same year.[13] At the other extreme is Enron, whose demise was probably predictable given 18 consecutive years during which its CFROI failed to beat the cost of capital. This could be attributed in part to the way Enron's leadership responded to the quarterly reporting pressures for on-going performance improvement. Compare this with the more European style of Nokia's leadership,

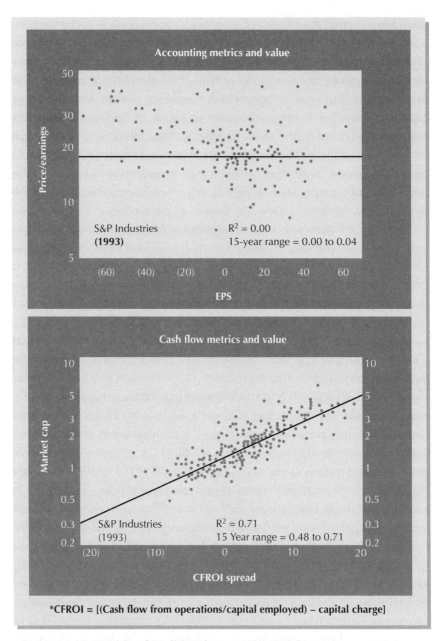

FIGURE 14.2 ◆ **CFROI and traditional accounting metrics**

Source: CSFB Holt

where the emphasis has been on satisfying all key stakeholders by building a sustainable business.

The CFROI metric gives us a mechanism to help predict the future performance of publicly listed companies. It's no surprise that the best performing companies on world share markets exhibit relatively high CFROIs over a five-year period – and have superior alignment with their respective marketplaces. Take a look at BMW, Gillette and Wal-Mart – all examples of this phenomenon.[14] They also have cost-effective supply chain operations, supported by strong asset investment programs. But other equally well-known companies, many of them global brands, are struggling to achieve acceptable levels of performance, and probably do not have the luxury of time to take the long view about performance improvement. It is this latter group that must look for new business models that will improve their performance, fast, just to survive.

However, because CFROI is a complicated equation, some analysts prefer to use Return on Invested Capital (ROIC), Economic Profit (EP) and Total Return to Shareholders (TRS). The combination of these three metrics provides very powerful insights into the operating performance of a business – and its ability to return value to its shareholders – as depicted in Figure 14.3.

ROIC is calculated as NOPAT (or EBITA*1-tax)/Invested Capital, and in simple terms this is a measure of how well a business performs in terms of generating operating profit from the capital it has invested in the business. When we subtract the costs associated with investing this capital – otherwise known as the Weighted Average Cost of Capital (WACC) – we come to an economic profit figure, representing the true value that a business has generated from its operations. Economic Profit is currently regarded as the most important metric when analyzing the value creation ability of a business. Furthermore, there have been several studies into the correlation of EP and TRS over the years: showing a strong R^2, i.e., providing evidence that to improve shareholder returns, managers should focus on optimizing their Economic Profit. However, it is important to note that EP only calculates the historical cash-flow generation of a business, and so is not appropriate for calculating current share price, or indeed, future share prices.[15]

Why am I giving you all this financial detail? If you believe as I do that supply chains are the business, a notion first introduced in Chapter 1, then

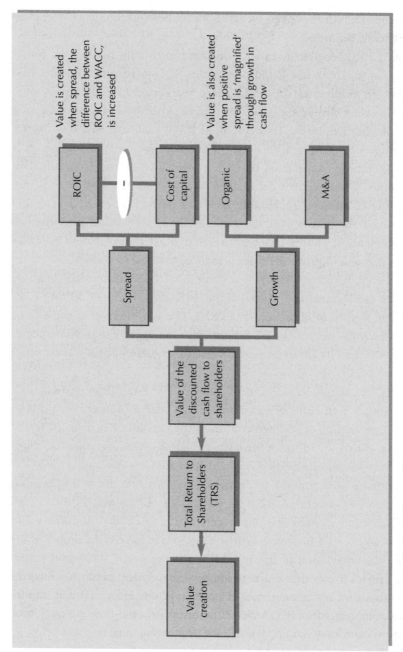

FIGURE 14.3 ◆ **Value creation road map**

Source: Accenture, copyright 2005

it's logical to look at overall business performance to see how well your enterprise supply chains are performing. The two are inextricably linked.

It has all been painfully slow!

New business models in supply chains were first seriously considered circa 1996 when Accenture[16] invented and trade-marked the fourth-party logistics concept, better known simply as 4PL®. Accenture originally defined the 4PL® model 'as a supply chain integrator that assembles and manages the resources, capabilities, and technology of its own organization, with those of complementary service providers, to deliver a comprehensive supply chain solution'.[17] The motivation for this organizational innovation grew out of the very real frustration that shippers around the world were experiencing with their 3PLs, sometimes referred to as Logistics Service Providers (LSPs). This category of third-party provider first emerged in the mid-1970s as an outgrowth of single-mode transportation and warehouse service companies. Unfortunately, few of these companies have been able to successfully make the transition to the satisfaction of their shipper customers, as evidenced by the 1994 survey carried out in Britain among 250 companies across several industries.[18] Only a third of the sample felt that their expectations were being met on a consistent basis; the other two-thirds were unhappy. Hardly a resounding endorsement!

Can you remember the thinking that drove the emergence of 3PLs? About 20 years earlier, some businesses – predominantly Fast-Moving Consumer Goods (FMCG) companies – took the first tentative steps towards outsourcing elements of their distribution function. Often it was for the wrong reasons, such as to excise industrial relations issues. However, a genuine rationale existed for outsourcing at the time, and it is worth recalling this:

> **Strategic**: it was thought that senior management would be freed up to focus on core competences. However, it was found that substantial senior management time was still required after the move to outsourcing, to coordinate and review 3PL performance.

> **Financial**: a reduction in total costs and associated working capital requirements was thought to be a natural outcome of outsourcing, but

in those early days the experience was that a continuous reduction in operating costs was minimal after the initial 'honeymoon period' of six to 12 months.

Operational: a simpler industrial relations climate was expected, but in fact the industrial action was simply transferred to the new 3PL organization, and this factor continued to affect the client's business for a few decades.

One of the biggest factors to undermine the success of outsourcing – and perhaps the most unexpected – was the on-going internal resistance experienced. People inside the outsourcer organization strongly opposed the proposed outsourcing arrangement and this inevitably made life difficult for both parties. In other words, the biggest competitors that the early 3PLs faced were in fact internal (functional) competitors, and this situation continues today.

But perhaps the biggest issue for the fledgling 3PL organizations between 1970 and 2000 was their inability to develop the 'creative solutions' so much sought after by their shipper clients. Clearly these new logistics service organizations lacked the essential *innovation gene* needed for success. This failing was due to their lack of scale in talent and strategic thinking, which in turn was a throwback to their operational roots. Over the succeeding three decades, much has changed in the global, regional and local 3PL marketplace; fewer, larger, more sophisticated organizations now fill this space and there has been a discernible closing of the original *capability gap* between shippers' expectations and their perceptions of 3PL capabilities to meet these expectations.[19]

The 4PL® business model, which brings together a select combination of principal parties with a number of minor equity parties with special capabilities, was born as a direct result of the doubt that accompanied the early development of 3PLs. But it too has suffered, albeit in a different way; the original design concept and operational philosophy behind the 1996 version, depicted in Figure 14.4, has largely been lost or become confused over the past decade.[20] Indeed, several factors combined to force compromises: relatively long lead-times in the negotiation phase; the pure scale of the proposed new business model; and the apparent rigidity of the 4PL® design. Many current versions of 4PL®s look nothing like the originally intended design.

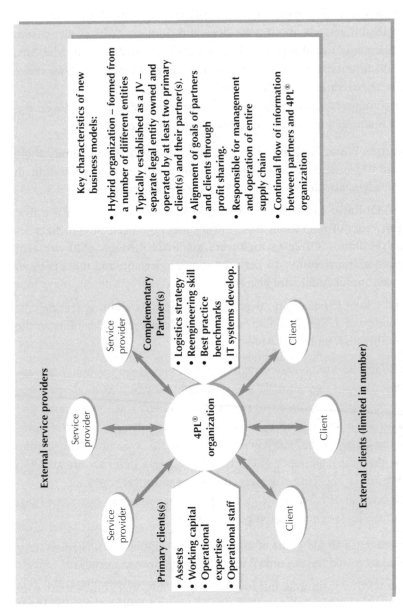

Key characteristics of new business models:

- **Hybrid organization – formed from a number of different entities**
- **Typically established as a JV – separate legal entity owned and operated by at least two primary client(s) and their partner(s).**
- **Alignment of goals of partners and clients through profit sharing.**
- **Responsible for management and operation of entire supply chain**
- **Continual flow of information between partners and 4PL® organization**

External service providers

Service provider

Service provider

Service provider

Primary clients(s)

- **Assests**
- **Working capital**
- **Operational expertise**
- **Operational staff**

Complementary Partner(s)

- **Logistics strategy**
- **Reengineering skill**
- **Best practice benchmarks**
- **IT systems develop.**

4PL® organization

Client

Client

Client

External clients (limited in number)

FIGURE 14.4 ◆ Classic 4PL® new business model

Source: Adapted from Figure 27.4 in Gattorna (1998), p. 43

Nevertheless, some 20 genuine 4PL®s have been designed and built across multiple industries around the world, and Figure 14.5 shows a sample of these. The early 4PL® prototypes (1994 to 2002) taught us many valuable lessons about what does and does not work in the design and implementation of new supply chain business models. These lessons, which are discussed in more detail below, should be heeded as we move to the next generation of business model.

Early adopters of the original 4PL® business models have enjoyed significant financial and operational improvements; for example:

Thames Water Utilities (UK): 10 per cent reduction in supply chain costs; 40 per cent reduction in inventory; 70 per cent reduction in backorders; and achievement of 97 per cent service levels.

New Holland Logistics (Italy): US$67 million savings in the first seven years of operation; this venture has now been bought back by New Holland. These savings were achieved through a 20 per cent reduction in inventory; 15 per cent saving in freight; and more than 90 per cent order fulfillment accuracy.

Ford Clasa (Spain): an on-going annual supply chain operating cost reduction of US$6.7 million, together with increased flexibility in the assembly mix; and reduced in-plant stock.

These examples are consistent with my own experience in building business cases for a range of 4PL®s. In virtually all cases, annual operating costs were reduced by up to 40 per cent, net of any shut-down costs, and that is on top of one-off savings in capital investments. And just as importantly, the degree of difficulty in implementing this type of transformation was less than the experience of changing an existing or legacy organization from the inside out. Unfortunately, this is not intuitively obvious.

The original 4PL® design was specifically structured to overcome most if not all the issues encountered by early 3PLs:

1 **Strategic:** a single point of contact for all supply chain requirements designed to reduce the time demands on senior management.

2 **Financial:** continuous improvement and on-going re-negotiation of Service Level Agreements (SLAs) as a central feature of the new 4PL® organization.

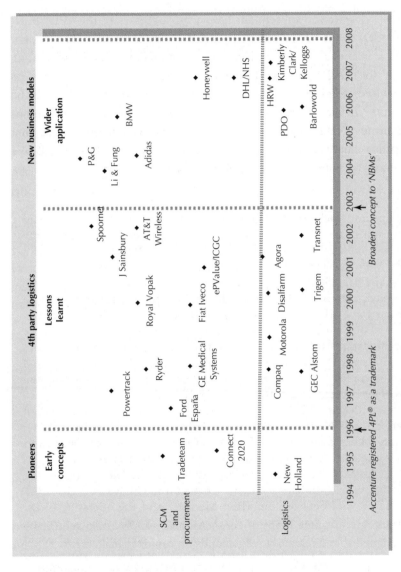

FIGURE 14.5 ◆ Historical evolution of 4PL® style new business models

Source: Accenture

3 **Operational**: the simple act of establishing an entirely new entity meant that staff and management could be carefully selected, thereby reducing possible union and internal cultural resistance.

However, despite the subsequent hard-won successes of the 4PL® business model, it has been difficult to maintain the integrity of the design. In fact, it is not unusual these days to hear that companies are requesting 'tenders' for a 4PL® provider, just as you would do in the days when 3PLs were invited to respond to a Request For Quotation (RFQ) for specific contracts.[21] In the process, some of the essential elements that differentiate 3PL and 4PL® business models have been lost. One thing is for certain: you cannot simply issue a tender in the conventional sense for a 4PL®! The Petroleum Development of Oman (PDO) is a case in point.

Petroleum Development of Oman (PDO) is owned jointly by the Omani government and Royal Dutch Shell, with the former having the majority interest and management control. In 2003–04, PDO decided to set up a 4PL® to move its onshore oil rigs and undertake associated cargo transport and handling.

From the outset, PDO made the decision to go out to a worldwide tender for a '4PL® Manager,' which was to be given the task of raising and operating the consortium of contractors needed to carry out the specific tasks involved. They subsequently awarded a five-year contract to Tibbett & Britten, a UK-based 3PL with no prior experience in oil field operations. This company had the lowest tender, and was accepted by PDO because they wanted to prove that the cost of their logistics operations could be significantly reduced. Things just went downhill from there. Tibbett & Britten was subsequently taken over by Exel Plc, another UK-based 3PL which, after reviewing the contract, decided to persevere even though they too had no previous oil field experience.

Against advice to the contrary, PDO insisted on setting up the 4PL® with back-to-back contracts – between themselves and the 4PL® Manager, and between the 4PL® Manager and the operating 3PLs. Ostensibly this was because PDO, as a government-owned entity, was within the purview of the Government Tender Board and could not enter into equity-based arrangements with private enterprises. They clearly had not heard of Public Private Partnerships (PPP). Poor leadership at the 4PL® Manager and continued tension between PDO Logistics and the other party meant that performance was

---

unacceptable. In addition, the internal PDO customer, Well Engineering, was also unhappy with both performance and cost.

The obsession with cost reduction was demonstrated to be invalid when it was pointed out that by adding additional assets (and cost), rigs could be moved faster and therefore have less down-time between holes, thereby producing more revenue for PDO and reducing the total number of rigs needed in the field. In this instance, agility led to lower total cost although rates were still a focus in the cargo haulage area.

When Deutsche Post DHL took over Exel Plc in December 2005, they also inherited the PDO 4PL contract in Oman, and again there was a change in leadership personnel at the 4PL® Manager. Unfortunately, these personnel came to their new positions with predominantly 3PL operational experience. Nothing had changed despite two rotations in ownership! Indeed, this has been one of my key observations in this whole saga: the inability of 3PLs to step up to the 4PL® role and manage differently. They keep reverting to what they know – which is the 3PL *modus operandi*. And this has badly affected the relationship with the three specialist rig-moving 3PLs, all Omani owned, who do the actual work day-to-day and generally do it well in what is a harsh operating environment.

The performance of the overall consortium has improved significantly in the past 12 months, with something of the order of 12 drill string-months saved through treating this as an *agile* rather than a *lean* supply chain.

But the underlying problems remain, and it is hard to see how this type of performance can be sustained into the future under the current management regime. The key problem is that the contractual arrangements between the owner, PDO, and the 4PL® Manager, Bahwan DHL, is still driven by a cost-saving mentality, and the KPIs reflect this. Similarly, for the 4PL® Manager to reach its own operational and financial objectives it feels complelled to engage in an adversarial relationship with the 3PL subcontractors, squeezing them for lower rates at every turn, without themselves adding the required value in the form of innovative techniques for the benefit of all parties. This first contract was due to end in January 2010 and has subsequently been extended for two years while a second generation 4PL® contract is prepared for tender.

Hopefully, valuable lessons have been learned and the next generation contract will not suffer from the same difficulties. The key is to only seek expressions of interest from suitably qualified companies with significant experience in this type of oilfield operations. It's just too difficult to learn on the job!

Perhaps the only independent research[22] published on the comparative value created by a true 4PL® business model revealed that the EV/EBITDA[23] earned by a genuine 4PL® was a factor of three to five times greater than the more conventional single mode or 3PL models. So why do 3PLs aspiring to the 4PL® manager role inevitably revert to type? It's the culture factor I suspect. See Figure 14.6 for more detail on the relative profit performances of the different levels of logistics provider.

Some single-mode companies developed variations of the 4PL® business model to operate in parallel with their core business. For example, Spoornet, the freight division of South African Railways, has been working on several collaborative industry-level models for several years. These models involve developing customized e-marketplaces for suppliers and buyers in several major industries, and attaching a 4PL® style *virtual management company* to coordinate the fulfillment task that is physically carried out by other 3PLs and single-mode transportation companies. The success of this venture is still being assessed, but this configuration could well be the forerunner of future *supply chain industry solution* models (see Figure 14.7). Another example is found in New Zealand with the commodity company M-co, which operates internationally in markets for gas and electricity commodities and telecommunications.[24]

The key lesson that has emerged from the early experience with 4PL® business models in their various forms over the past 15 years is that it still takes a tremendous leap of faith by management to embrace an organization design that is so radically different from conventional experience. But then that is what leadership is about. However, C-level executives simply do not feel comfortable engaging in such new styles of organization design that are relatively untested under different types of operating conditions; especially given the increased market scrutiny these days. People are playing it safe. Typically, the easy way out is to embrace the 'norm' and undertake large-scale transformations of **existing** organization structures. What if the same mindset had been adopted in the area of product development? Answer: little or no progress, and probably extinction by now. That's why it is so hard to reconcile the slow progress made by many global companies such as Philips, Samsung and Sony in their supply chain business models, compared to the rapid rate of innovation on the product side of their business. Perhaps we should shift some product development executives into logistics and supply chain functions and see what they can achieve in a short time!

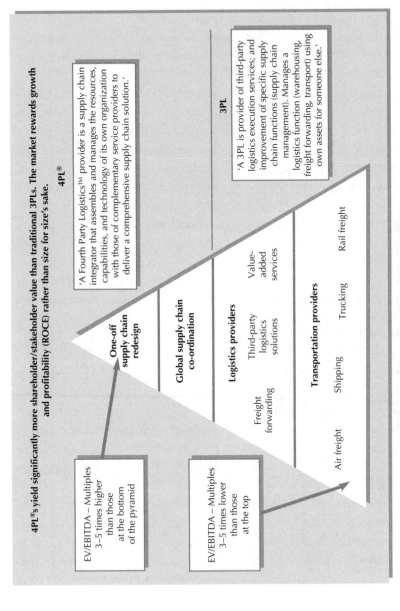

4PL®s yield significantly more shareholder/stakeholder value than traditional 3PLs. The market rewards growth and profitability (ROCE) rather than size for size's sake.

4PL®

'A Fourth Party Logistics™ provider is a supply chain integrator that assembles and manages the resources, capabilities, and technology of its own organization with those of complementary service providers to deliver a comprehensive supply chain solution.'

3PL

'A 3PL is provider of third-party logistics execution services; and improvement of specific supply chain functions (supply chain management). Manages a logistics function (warehousing, freight forwarding, transport) using own assets for someone else.'

EV/EBITDA – Multiples 3–5 times higher than those at the bottom of the pyramid

EV/EBITDA – Multiples 3–5 times lower than those at the top

One-off supply chain redesign

Global supply chain co-ordination

Logistics providers

Third-party logistics solutions

Value-added services

Transportation providers

Air freight

Freight forwarding

Shipping

Trucking

Rail freight

FIGURE 14.6 ◆ **Relative profitability of logistics service provider (LSP) models**

Source: Adapted from 4PL Report, Dr Jochen Vogel, Lehman Bros, 2001

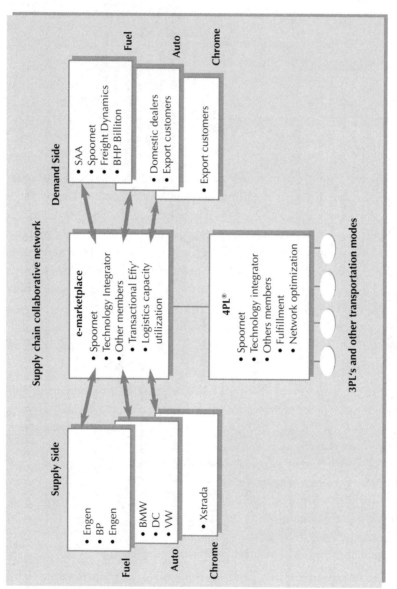

FIGURE 14.7 ◆ A railway attempting to transform itself

Source: Accenture; SA Railways

The difficulties in executing 4PL® designs has led me to search for new and more flexible structures during the past seven years. Interestingly, during the same period, significant progress has been made in adapting 4PL® concepts and principles to the service sector. A good example is the British health care logistics provider NHS Logistics, which is described in a case study in my earlier book *Living Supply Chains*.[25]

Outsourcing in the twenty-first century – getting it right

'Outsourcing' is not a term that I use with any relish these days, because it has too many different meanings, and in any event has largely been devalued by association with high-profile failures in the past two decades. The experience of Marks and Spencer in 1998, when it turned its back on local UK suppliers and opted to outsource all its apparel requirements to distant markets in the Far East, is a good example of what can happen when the blind pursuit of cost savings leads to quite the opposite outcome. We will consider 'outsourcing' further in Chapter 15.

At this stage I prefer to describe the nine principles that should be followed in developing and operating the next generation of supply chain business models:

1 Ensure the new service company is co-owned and co-managed; this holds the disparate members of the consortium together and motivates them to achieve shared goals. It does what a contractual arrangement can't. This is a criterion that has been largely overlooked in the many new business models that were tried during and after the e-commerce era, when we saw numerous one-sided marketplace models emerge only to fail.[26] My own preference is to go all the way and develop industry supply chain solutions that involve the *equity* participation of key stakeholders in a particular industry. The arguments against such an open approach will be discussed later in this chapter.

2 Facilitate rapid realization of benefits (cost savings, profitability and revenue generation); investors and analysts will no longer tolerate back-loaded benefits. Those days are gone forever.

3 De-risk the implementation of new systems technology and other operational processes; this will help gain the confidence of the investment community.

4 Take advantage of any state-of-the-art assets that are readily available from other specialist players; there is simply not enough time to grow assets, competences and capabilities organically in major competitive markets.

5 Reduce up-front implementation costs through financial engineering practices and careful choice of consortium partners. This lowers investment requirements and enhances asset efficiency.

6 Infuse a subculture of innovation and continuous improvement through some conscious corporate genetic engineering. This is essential for success of the venture and quite feasible if you understand the internal behavioral forces in play.

7 Embed pre-determined KPIs and corresponding incentives (for all parties) in the new organizational design. Every party involved must make a fair return if the consortium is to succeed and stay together. See Figure 14.8 for typical commercial arrangements.

8 Recognize all the risks involved in this new style of business model, and confront them head-on.

9 Use the OODA loop to 'out-cycle' your competitors' supply chains, in speed of decision-making as well as action.

The result is a completely new type of execution model that will deliver scale at speed and, paradoxically, at lower risk than traditional change initiatives. Why? As has been argued throughout this book, it's the *people factor* that will ultimately decide the success or failure of a major transformation, and everything else fades into insignificance. I think this approach of bringing together the *best-of-the-best* resources and capabilities in a consortium-style structure will also overcome the negative aspects of performance observed in numerous mergers and acquisitions (M&A) over the past decade – and they too were in search of scale, but overlooked a few key issues such as cultural compatibility! An Accenture White Paper[27] documents some of the value-destruction which has occurred during the pursuit of scale via M&A activities, and concludes that: 'the scale-driven perspective is not without merit; it is simply incomplete'.[28] I agree with

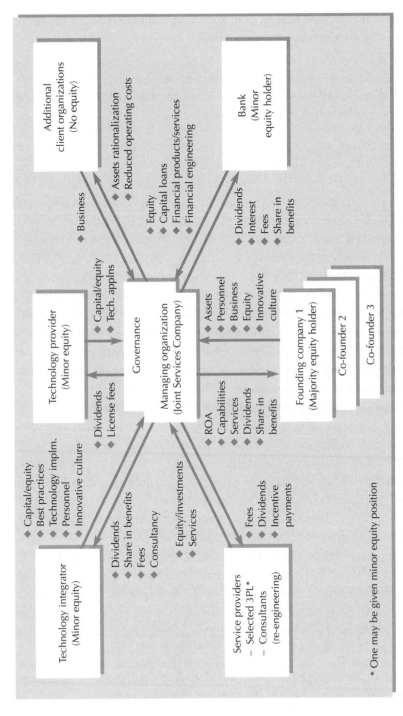

FIGURE 14.8 ◆ **How each member of a joint services company (JSC) earns a ROI**

Source: Adapted from Figure 9.8 in Gattorna (2006), p.220.

this point of view, and suggest that we have found the missing piece of the puzzle – the joint services company (JSC).

The next generation of business models

What does the next generation of supply chains look like? The Level 3 *virtual supply chains*, depicted in the performance/capability continuum (Figure 14.1), paints a future involving new business models configured in different ways. We have updated versions of the original 4PL® and newer business models such as Managed Supply Chain Operations (MSCO), JSCs, and Virtual Network Consortia (VNC), otherwise known as 'Networked Supply Chains'. The speed with which these models are adopted is largely in the hands of the shipper principals who own the business being transacted. They must take the lead and drive selection of the various equity and capability partners required to make such entities a success for all the parties involved. It takes an entrepreneurial (or deal-making) culture in the set-up stage to do this, but the potential rewards are enormous. For example, I was involved in one business case in the oil industry where the principal partners saved 36 per cent off their baseline operating costs, mainly through rationalizing terminals and transportation capacity. The partners were previously competitors. Such is the quantum of benefits possible from these new models – the potential cannot be ignored for long, irrespective of previous concerns and biases.

The good news is that there is emerging evidence that global and regional LSPs have significantly closed the *capability gap* that was both real and perceived among their shipper principals/customers over the past five years.[29] For example, Deutsche Post Worldwide Network (DPWN), with its acquisition of Exel Logistics, now has a complete array of logistics and supply chain capabilities available under the one brand, DHL. However, a lot of this early promise has been destroyed in the aftermath of the global financial crisis. It is therefore an opportune time for a new generation of business models to emerge on to the scene, ones that are far more flexible than previous versions. These would typically have the following five characteristics in addition to the nine already articulated:

1 Built-in 'sunset clauses' that provide consortium members with more flexibility to enter and exit the joint venture as required.

2   The major shareholding principals would have the **option of either rolling-over or folding the entity after a fixed period** (say seven to ten years), and buying the capabilities back on the basis of a pre-agreed formula.

3   More attention should be given to including **both sides of an industry** (buyers and sellers) in the proposed JSC; this is an essential ingredient for success in the future. One-sided arrangements simply won't fly in the future – they never have.

4   **Banks and other financial institutions would be encouraged to join the JSC as minority equity partners.** For them there is also the added sweetener of capturing all the other financial services required by consortium members.

5   More attention should be paid to the **requirements of government regulatory bodies** such as the Competition Commission (UK); the Australian Competition and Consumer Commission (Australia); the Commerce Commission (NZ); and the International Trade Administration (US). These statutory bodies should ideally be included in discussions at an early (design) stage. This will assist the approval process because these authorities will see, at close quarters, the cost-based rationale for these new organization structures. It is unlikely that straight out mergers and acquisitions will receive the same sympathetic treatment because they inevitably reduce consumer choice.

The best chance of introducing these new generation models will be in Europe and the Asia-Pacific region as competitive pressures build, but this is truly a global issue. Pressure for change will ultimately determine the rate and location of adoption.

The only difference between the proposed business model of the JSC and the more advanced virtual network consortia is that the latter version will make it even easier for equity holders to enter and exit the virtual management company on a 'plug-and-play' basis. These differences are summarized in Figure 14.9.

Doctoral research is currently underway on this category of 'networked' models to determine if operational effectiveness can be further increased through a more informal configuration than even that proposed by the virtual network consortia.[30]

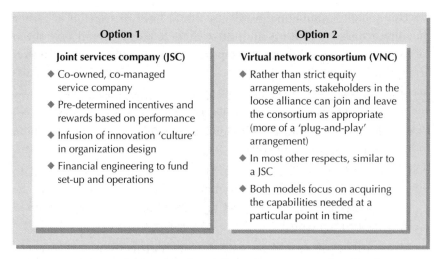

Option 1	Option 2
Joint services company (JSC)	**Virtual network consortium (VNC)**
◆ Co-owned, co-managed service company	◆ Rather than strict equity arrangements, stakeholders in the loose alliance can join and leave the consortium as appropriate (more of a 'plug-and-play' arrangement)
◆ Pre-determined incentives and rewards based on performance	
◆ Infusion of innovation 'culture' in organization design	◆ In most other respects, similar to a JSC
◆ Financial engineering to fund set-up and operations	◆ Both models focus on acquiring the capabilities needed at a particular point in time

FIGURE 14.9 ◆ Execution models that deliver change at speed and scale

Source: Adapted from Figure 9.9 in Gattorna (2006), p.223.

What's so different about the joint services company model?

I have shied away from using the term 'outsourcing' for most of this chapter because it normally conjures up failed contractual arrangements, where one party has given an external party business to carry out on its behalf, usually under tightly worded legal-style conditions. Too often the 'performance' measures become self-fulfilling prophecies of failure! Within two or three years the business is again back in-house and the 3PL is discarded. We have witnessed this scenario many times during the past few decades, as neither the principal (owner of the business being transacted) nor the 3PL provider has been able to find the right balance between capability, price, innovation and service.

The JSC model is a far different proposition. The structure of the organization, its incentive/reward systems and funding arrangements are all designed to bring together parties that have the necessary array of capabilities for a particular task. These ingredients are critical for success. The one-to-one contracts used with 3PLs have failed in all but the most common operational situations. As customers become more demanding, particularly in the fast-moving consumer goods, automotive and electronic high-technology industries, suppliers must look for solutions outside their own resources and those of their immediate 3PL contractors. These solutions will require the unique combination of a particular array of capabilities for a specific task that are only available from across multiple organizations. Selecting and bringing such parties together, and keeping them motivated and rewarded for a significant period (say seven to ten years), is the challenge facing many global multinational companies today. While there are three main options (and variations around each), the one most likely to achieve a quantum improvement in performance is the JSC business model, as shown in Figure 14.10.

Based on the parameters in Figure 14.9, it seems almost foolhardy to either: a) embark on major change programs and take all the up-front risk while waiting for the promised benefits to accrue (traditional consulting) or b) lose control of particular business functions in pursuit of short-term cost reductions (traditional outsourcing), when a third option exists. This is the development of a co-owned, co-managed delivery model where capability is built and executed very fast in order to provide shareholders with almost immediate results. This is what global financial centres want to see, and this is how to give it to them. The paradox is that this approach is technically easier and less risky to engineer in change management terms. It will deliver much improved results, faster, and is better than taking what appears to be the safer, slower, internal change-management pathway to improved performance. In the end, it is the internal cultural *forces of darkness* that will undo the best laid transformational plans, and have done many times in the past. But there are risks in the suggested approach as well, which we will now consider more closely.

Risks associated with forming a JSC

Clearly, forming any new business model carries its share of risks. But for 4PLs®, most if not all of these risks were flushed out during the prototype era of 1994 to 2003. The way to reduce the risks is to study them in detail and consider the remedies.

The structure, motivation and funding options that define strategic transformation programs place clear daylight between the value of this approach compared to either traditional contract-style outsourcing or 1990s-style consulting services

Feature	Client-hosted solution	Outsourcing solution	Strategic transformation and joint services company
◆ Ownership and risk	◆ Borne 100 per cent in-house	◆ Contracted out	◆ Jointly owned
◆ People	◆ Bought-in resources	◆ Transferred	◆ Enhanced career path
◆ Objective	◆ Process improvement	◆ Cost reduction	◆ Share price growth
◆ Motivation	◆ Policy and compliance	◆ Cost reduction	◆ Mutual shared goals
◆ Incentives	◆ Milestones	◆ Cost-based service rewards	◆ Fusion of all partners' share prices
◆ Funding	◆ 100 per cent in-house	◆ Outsourcing provider	◆ Own, or other third parties
◆ Focus	◆ Template roll-out	◆ Cost reduction	◆ Capability at speed
◆ Control	◆ Program management	◆ By contract only	◆ Improved and flexible
◆ Future option	◆ Sustain non-core activity	◆ Return difficult	◆ ROI easier to get
◆ Strategy	◆ Better IT	◆ Cost reduction	◆ Market leadership

Why should a company embark on such a pivotal change program and either (a) take all the risk and the upfront costs while waiting for the benefits (traditional consulting) or (b) lose control of business functions in pursuit of short-term cost reductions (traditional outsourcing) when there is a co-owned execution model able to build capability to drive shareholder value with immediate results?

FIGURE 14.10 ◆ **Comparing the three outsourcing options**

Source: Adapted from Figure 9.10 in Gattorna (2006), p.225

1. Founding partners

The first and perhaps most difficult task is to find at least two founding partners of like minds for the JSC; cultural 'fit' is essential for success. The principal partners can be drawn from the same industry or a related industry. The key is to find two enterprises, preferably at the big end of their industry, that have products with the same or similar *handling* characteristics and/or going to the same or similar delivery destinations. If two such parties cannot be found, or if they can be found but are not willing to pool their businesses to significantly increase scale, then it's simply not possible to launch this class of business model. In other words, don't try it!

But you could try looking in the large process industries, where companies have downsized for several years and cannot find any new avenues for reducing costs. They offer a good potential source for partner enterprises. Another source could be fragmented industries where only a few majors exist, beyond which there is a long tail of small- to medium-sized enterprises; examples would be the pharmaceutical and alcoholic beverage industries. In each case, a JSC configuration will bring major benefits to both major and minor (complementary) parties that join the original venture.

By the way, the idea often gets stifled at this point by senior executives who use the 'we are not prepared to give up our competitive advantage in logistics' argument, or 'we really believe this is the way to go but we don't want to be the first.' Interestingly, every time I hear these comments opposing the formation of a JSC, it invariably comes from executives in enterprises whose logistics and supply chain performance is nothing near 'competitive' in the first place; they are quite simply in denial.

2. Ownership structure

Once the two (or three, maximum) principal partners have been identified and agree to spin-off a new management company to manage their joint logistics operations, it is time to agree the all-important equity structure. The principal partners will usually take the majority of the equity between them. The next task is to decide on what specialist capabilities are needed to service the combined business, and from where these are likely to be sourced. It is all about capabilities, and these should be sourced from best practice enterprises which then become complementary or minor equity partners in the new venture. **Equity** is essential for all active members of the consortium, because it provides the basic motivation to stay together and help each other in a non-contractual environment. The other part of this motivation is provided by setting appropriate performance milestones and corresponding incentives/rewards, which all parties share according to their equity position. These elements of the organization design will make a big difference if and when the going gets tough. No such fall-back is in place for the so-called 4PL® manager that is formed through the tender process. Yet, several enterprises have tried to go this route.[31]

One interesting variant of the 4PL® equity-based formula described above is HRW Logistics & Industrial Services BV in the Netherlands. This is a consortium of three 3PLs: Wagenborg BV, Den Hartogh BV and Reym BV. All three companies are independently owned subcontractors in their own right, and have a largely complementary range of services which are offered to companies in the oil and gas business. HRW's major client is Shell EPE, which in the Netherlands is called Nederlandse Aardolie Maatschappij B.V.

HRW's scope of activities includes such categories as: cargo/ transport; lifting and hoisting; fluids transport; industrial cleaning; maintenance service; de-icing; tank supply; and supply chain.[32] Each company has a third of the equity in HRW. The board of HRW, which is constituted of executives from the three subcontractors, appoints the CEO, and the CEO in turn has an organization that undertakes added value planning; IT facilities; HSE-compliance; aggregated viewpoint; and shared administrative activities. This is a version of my 'Control Tower' concept, and it works very well.

Apart from difficulties during formation in 2007, when one of the original shareholders clearly did not make a good cultural 'fit', the existing structure is working well, uninhibited by contractual disputes highlighted in the earlier PDO example. This is why equity participation is so crucial to success.

---

3. Perceived independence

A board and executive team should be installed to run the new entity so that the newly formed JSC is perceived to be independent from its major shareholders. Independence could become a vital issue if you later decide to publicly list the new company and launch it as a supply chain provider in its own right. Such a scenario would have been thought impossible some years ago, but it's likely to be played out in several countries as pressure on margins builds to intolerable levels.

4. Secondement of best talent

You should look to seconde or permanently transfer the best talent from the founding enterprises to the new (virtual) management company. This is an essential ingredient for success. Transferring staff can help you to sidestep the usual internal resistance to change and put in place only those personnel who passionately want to be involved in the new venture, a type of genetic engineering! It is important to minimize the cultural differences between staff in the JSC, and indeed to shape a new culture quickly. The design of the organization structure will be an important factor in success, and should be approached using the principles already outlined in Chapter 6.

5. Organization life-cycle

The principal shareholders should reach initial agreement on the life of the organization, with a minimum of seven, but preferably ten, years in the first phase. To lessen the concern in the formation stage it is recommended that a 'pre-nuptial' clause be agreed between all parties to the effect that at the end of the initially agreed life of the entity, the principals have the option to buy-back their respective business and capabilities according to a pre-agreed formula. On the other hand, if the principals agree, the arrangement can be extended for another term, at which time a similar review and decision is contemplated. This clause provides the flexibility that did not exist in early versions of the original 4PL® business model and its absence may have contributed to the slow acceptance of that model.

6. Scope of operations

At a very early stage in the development of the JSC, you should define and agree on the exact scope of operations among all partners, and the partners' specific roles within that scope. The principle is that no party should be part of the JSC unless they bring one or more of the unique assets or capabilities required to execute the business of the venture. No passive investors are welcome.

7. Financial engineering

One of the most vital roles is the financial engineering of the new venture. The financials have to make the JSC immediately viable, and it is here that major financial service institutions have an opportunity to lead. Sadly, too many of our modern financial institutions are not prepared to do so, and are missing out on huge opportunities to capture future revenue streams; but they must take some risk at the outset to reap later rewards. I strongly believe there is **less** risk for banks and other financial institutions in getting involved in this type of business model. As a principal partner, they would invariably have a seat at the board table, and would be able to influence the management of the new entity, rather than simply stand aside as an external observer and/or mortgage broker. This insider role just became even more important in the wake of the global financial crisis.

Some limited activity is already starting to happen in this area of financial engineering, with GE Commercial Finance (GECF) and Barclays Bank taking the lead. GECF has combined with DHL to roll out a new inventory ownership product called Trade Distribution Services. This product is directly designed to address concerns of manufacturers with their cash-to-cash cycles and the consequent impact on working capital. Under the proposed arrangement, GE Commercial Finance takes ownership of the finished goods inventory from the seller's point of shipment until the buyer's just-in-time point of purchase. GE owns the inventory and DHL manages it while in transit between seller and buyer. There are benefits in this arrangement for all the parties involved, so we are likely to see more of the same as other enterprises recognize the benefits potentially available, at relatively low risk. Unfortunately, Sarbanes-Oxley in the US has undermined the successful development of this model, which is a great pity because that was not the intention of the legislation.[33] Meanwhile Barclays have formed a dedicated group under the name Barclays Logistics, and they are pursuing the development of new financing products and limited involvement in joint ventures. They are treating this development as very much 'experimental' in the early stages.

8. Ability to meet performance milestones

Clearly, if targeted savings/benefits are not achieved on time the whole venture is at risk, as the equity players will not realize the forecasted ROI. But if the partners can meet the conditions described above it is unlikely that they will fail to achieve their targeted savings. At the outset, JSC managers should lay out the proposed milestones for the life of the venture; transparency in the initial stages is important for the cohesiveness of the new organization structure. This approach was followed by the former Andersen Consulting (now Accenture) and a North Sea oil exploration consortium in 1994, and proved to be a winning initiative.

But how will we achieve the *embedded alignment* referred to at the start of this chapter? The new 'service company' will ideally own little or no infrastructure, other than technology, and will in effect coordinate and manage an array of hand-picked 3PLs to achieve the desired outcome.

One of these outcomes will be to fulfill all the Service Level Agreements (SLAs) entered into with the owner-principals and other external organizations. This will by definition require the JSC to deliver different levels of service to achieve the multiple supply chain alignment already discussed in Chapter 2. However, it is more than likely that the new entity will be capable of delivering the required responses, in parallel, and cost-effectively; because it will be specifically designed to do this from the outset. This is in effect *embedded alignment*.

Going beyond the business that the founding partners bring to the JSC, there is a risk that future expansion will be limited if other companies in the industry, especially direct competitors, are unwilling to add their business to the growing pool. They may not have a choice if the model is designed well from the start and grows rapidly to a dominant position, but if the cost economies of the JSC are not clearly evident, other companies may choose not to join the burgeoning industry supply chain solution. This is now less of a risk than a decade ago, but it becomes real if the JSC is launched without at least two major industry players.[34]

9. Availability of best 3PLs

Another early risk in forming a JSC is that the best 3PLs in the logistics industry, and relatively few exist across the globe, may not be immediately available because of long-term contractual commitments that cannot easily be set aside in the short term. It may be necessary to negotiate exits from existing contracts in crucial cases.

10. Excessive disruption

There is always the risk of excessive disruption to the existing business during the establishment phase of the JSC. The best strategy is to plan for this and then execute as fast as possible. Given that an entirely new organization is being set up, the risk of 'cultural resistance' will be minimal, and if the new staff members are selected carefully, most will welcome the rapid pace of change. Going slow in implementing change these days is a recipe for failure, because a slow pace allows competitors and internal forces alike to mount more strident defenses. In any case it's unlikely that the disruption will be any worse than that encountered in an internal transformation project. At least in the case of the JSC, most if not all the action takes place 'off-line', thereby minimizing disruption to the mainstream business.

11. Culture

The cultural challenge for JSCs is to encourage *entrepreneurial behavior* and embed a subculture of *innovation* early in the life of the new organization, while encouraging a focus on *continuous improvement*. The current crop of 3PLs generally lack these cultural capabilities and will probably never have the resources and mindset to fully develop and sustain them. And yet these are the very attributes that client organizations desire most, because they know that it will reduce costs on a progressive and sustainable basis over time. The 'rate game' cannot be sustained indefinitely; something has to give.

12. The risk of doing nothing

The biggest risk of all is of course doing nothing, or just as bad, continuing to embrace traditional change management practices because they appear to be safe and risk free. Indeed, nothing could be further from the truth, as we have already demonstrated in Chapter 4. I have never forgotten the concept of 'tensegrity' first introduced to me by Colin Benjamin, many years ago; the idea that building protection around a company, and indeed an industry is quite the wrong thing to do, because eventually that protection is removed, for some reason, and the unprepared on the inside just collapse in a heap. The more appropriate way to prepare for change is to inject yourself with change, regularly, and desensitize yourself to its harsh realities. Transforming organizations is a risky business at the best of times, and attempting to carry out major change coincidentally with operating the company is akin to *do-it-yourself brain surgery* – it is seldom successful. Therefore, other less conventional ways must be sought to achieve the quantum improvements in operational and financial performance that await the brave.

Going forward: new complexities and new solutions

Increasingly in the future we can expect to see enterprises of all types experimenting with different combinations and permutations of business models in search of performance improvement. Although the risks associated with introducing new organization formats were once considered unacceptably high, the situation now is quite the reverse; the risk of **not** embracing new business models is even higher, and from what we now know about the difficulties of transforming organizations from the inside out, it is easy to see why this is so.

However, as always, everything comes back to the quality of executive leadership, and their individual and joint resolve to innovate to succeed in the difficult times that surely lie ahead.

One significant development in the last few years is that of a jointly managed agency whose prime function is to share information, called an 'Infomediary'. I have a different name for it, 'Lead Box', but we will come to that.

Prashant Yadav of the MIT-Zaragoza International Logistics Program and colleagues from other groups[35] have been researching the problem of inadequate forecasts and lack of demand visibility for essential medication in developing countries. This is causing higher levels of risk for pharmaceutical companies and other channel members, as well as disincentives to invest and a general lack of alignment between the parties in the corresponding supply chains. They have conceived the idea of a

'Global Health 'Infomediary,' which collects information from funding agencies, procurement agents, national buyers and other parties who have a wealth of information, but don't currently share it. The revolutionary aspect of the Infomediary is that it generates **aggregated** – and country-level forecasts by product type. This is a massive development. Being able to view data at an aggregated level is crucial in this and other industries where demand and supply conditions are volatile. My colleague Deborah Ellis is currently conducting doctoral studies into this very issue, focusing on the supply of insulin to developing countries for the treatment of Type 1 diabetes.[36]

Something similar has been in operation at Cash Services Australia (CSA) for several years. This is an enterprise jointly owned by Australia's four major trading banks, ANZ, Commonwealth, Westpac and NAB. It effectively gathers the 'in-demand' information for the cash requirements of each bank, aggregates the data, and then manages the optimal pick-up and delivery of cash throughout the Australian economy every day, using several armored car companies as subcontractors (see Figure 14.11). All this is done within operating guidelines set by the Reserve Bank of Australia. Again, this is another case of demand aggregation being used to fulfill individual requirements in an optimal way.

CSA was formed in 2001, when the Reserve Bank of Australia transferred to the trading banks its traditional role of managing the physical distribution of notes and coins.

Significantly, CSA is authorized by the Australian Competition and Consumer Commission (ACCC) to use aggregated customer information to optimize the distribution and processing of cash, and to achieve economies of scale for the benefit of the industry as a whole. This might sound like bank talk, but in fact it's pure 4PL® speak!

CSA was required to give an undertaking to the ACCC that each customer can only see i) their own data and ii) aggregated industry data for at least three customers. The undertaking also spells out the control on data and software that protects each bank's competitive information from the other customers of CSA. Regular audits are part of these controls.

So, despite the regulation, it is still possible to build an industry-level solution for the benefit of all participants. Why have we not seen more of this style of design? Refer to Figure 14.11 for a before and after view.

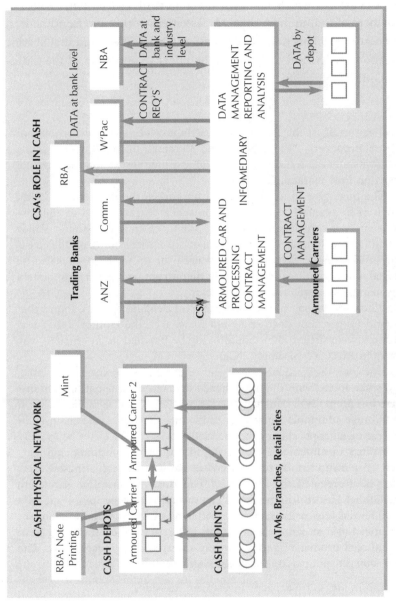

FIGURE 14.11 ◆ The new business model at Cash Services Australia (CSA)

Source: Carpenter Ellis

The final example illustrates the same principle but involves a very different industry-coal. My consulting firm was advising Port Waratah Coal Services (PWCS), which manages the export of 100 million tonnes of mainly thermal coal to more than 75 customers worldwide, from the Port of Newcastle, 150 kms north of Sydney, Australia. We found that sharing information was critical to ensuring the effective operation of the industry's unique supply chain.

Coal exporting at the Port of Newcastle involves a complex equation: 17 coal producers, 27 load points and 39 mines; three rail track owners; two owners of rail rolling stock; a single port authority; and the terminal operator, Port Waratah Coal Services.

The huge growth in the demand for coal in the five years to 2008, much of it volatile because of the presence of traders, led to capacity problems along the length of the coal supply chain in the Hunter Valley region, and was manifested in queues of ore carriers sitting off the coastline of Newcastle. Some of them waited for up to three weeks to be loaded, costing millions of dollars in demurrage, and generating quite a few newspaper headlines in the process!

When we deconstructed four years' of demand data we found that around 60 per cent of the demand for coal in the Hunter Valley was extremely consistent. This could easily be handled in an efficient way using, in effect, a *lean* supply chain.

However, the residual 40 per cent of demand was extremely volatile, and when mixed with the other steady demand component, all patterns were lost from view. This volatile component could be serviced, but it would take additional capacity at different points along the chain. This was the *agile* supply chain alive and well!

PWCS's problem was that it could not get an on-going aggregate view of demand similar to the view we had gained in the one-off exercise. We developed the idea of a 'Lead Box' organization, similar to the Global Health Infomediary. The notion is to keep important data confidential, hence the name. The idea was to set up an independent organization that gathered data from different sources, including individual coal producers and their customers, and aggregated this. The data would then be usable at three levels, to:

1. inform long-term capacity investment decisions;
2. inform the allocation of coal supply chain capacity to individual producers; and

3. lead to short-term optimization of the supply chain operations, involving stockpiles; train scheduling; maintenance schedules; berthing sequences, etc.

The overall scheme is depicted diagrammatically in Figure 14.12. It has not yet been implemented because of the vested interests of stakeholders in the Hunter Valley coal chain, but it's inevitable that this type of structure will be needed if the demand for coal continues. In a similar way to the banking industry, it is likely that the competition regulator, the ACCC, will agree to this shared arrangement for the good of the industry, which is facing stiff competition from South Africa, Indonesia and Brazil.

From our experience at PWCS and other places where it is necessary to share infrastructure, it becomes very obvious that some type of 'Infomediary' is going to be an essential element of future designs where there are multiple users of the available infrastructure; parties are just going to have to learn to share information, albeit in a confidential environment. Our view of what this will look like is depicted in Figure 14.13 on page 373.

Finally, a sneak preview of the future, and it comes from India.[37] Driven by the visionary thinking of Ajay Mittal, Chairman of Arshiya International, we are seeing the development of a completely new business model in India, from scratch. The concept, which is now a partial reality, is to build Free Trade Warehousing Zones (FTWZs) in five major Indian cities, connected by a rail network traversed by trains owned by Arshiya International to transport containers, 90 per rake, between the FTWZs which are configured like a diamond across India. Hanging off each FTWZ is a Virtual Distribution Network, involving hundreds of 3PLs controlled by Arshiya's own information systems, to make the 'last mile' deliveries.

Throw in the fact that India's complex tax system has been simplified specifically to accommodate this new model, and you have a revolutionary new way to service both domestic and export/import customers. Figure 14.14 (on page 374) is a schematic of the new model. The future is in capable hands in India, and elsewhere if this style of thinking spreads across geographies as I am sure it will. We have to learn to expect innovations emanating from unexpected places.

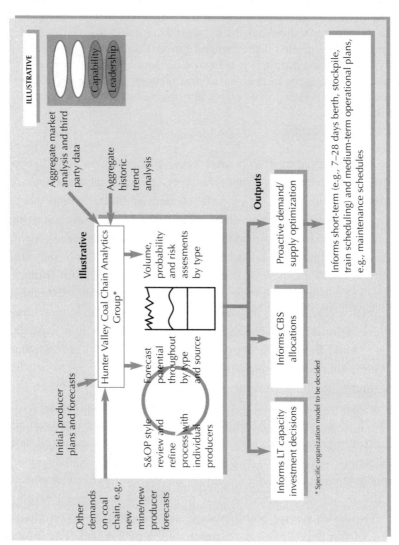

FIGURE 14.12 ◆ A new business model to manage demand and capacity planning at Port Waratah Coal Services

Source: Unpublished PWCS presentations by Gattorna Alignment Pty Ltd, March 2008

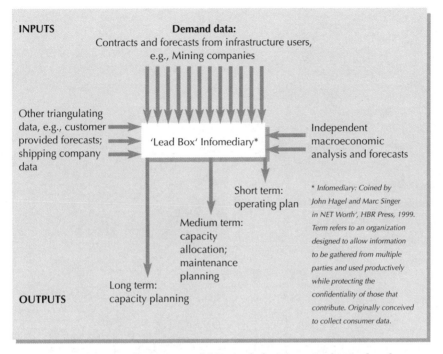

INPUTS

Demand data:
Contracts and forecasts from infrastructure users,
e.g., Mining companies

Other triangulating
data, e.g., customer
provided forecasts;
shipping company
data

'Lead Box' Infomediary*

Independent
macroeconomic
analysis and forecasts

Short term:
operating plan

Medium term:
capacity
allocation;
maintenance
planning

Long term:
OUTPUTS   capacity planning

* Infomediary: Coined by
John Hagel and Marc Singer
in NET Worth', HBR Press, 1999.
Term refers to an organization
designed to allow information
to be gathered from multiple
parties and used productively
while protecting the
confidentiality of those that
contribute. Originally conceived
to collect consumer data.

FIGURE 14.13 ◆ **A new business model is needed to manage demand and capacity planning in multi-user supply chains . . . the 'Lead Box' concept**

Defining ideas

1   Incredible opportunities exist for those prepared to step up to the plate and go well beyond simple operational excellence. We must wake up to the fact that it is 'supply chain versus supply chain' from now on, rather than company versus company as in the past. Within a decade it will be networks versus networks!

2   Go all-out for cultural compatibility and alignment of objectives with your key partners/stakeholders and other consortium members, from the very start.

3   For any new business model to be successful, it has to be equity-based. This is one of the most important insights I've gained from my work over the past decade or so. This type of arrangement helps to keep the consortium together and focused when the going gets tough, as it surely will.

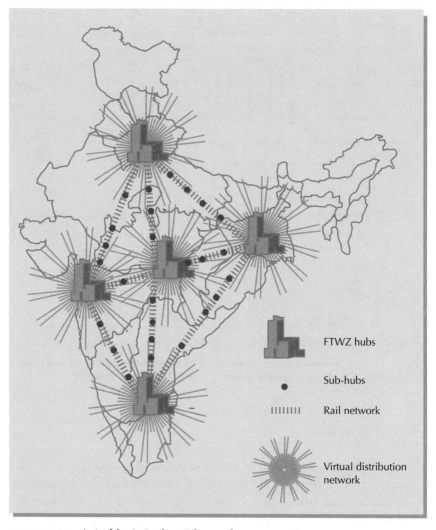

FIGURE 14.14 ◆ Arshiya's Project Diamond

Source: Adapted from Figure 27.5 in Gattorna (2006), p.381

4 New models already exist and are being trialed by leading companies. Go and have a look at these and see what can be learned.

5 The 'Infomediary' or 'Lead Box' is an exciting development, and has the potential to take a huge quantum of costs out of supply chain networks; it just requires the courage to either lead or be a member of such a consortium.

6 **Challenge** to the reader: it is inevitable that many struggling enterprises will have to embrace a new business model if they are to survive? Is your business in that category? And are you ready to lead such an initiative?

CHAPTER 15

Delivering dynamic supply chains

An agenda for the next decade

So far in this book we have focused on analyzing the status quo and sought frameworks that will help us to re-align the enterprise to its various markets. Now we must look to the future, not in a predictive way, but rather, attempt to identify and assess in a practical way the critical issues that are already out there and, believe me, are coming towards us over the next decade. I call these the 'Exocets' that could affect your business and its supply chains. Each issue will be briefly analyzed and its priority re-assessed so that you can consider the level of resources and effort that should be assigned to each. To be forewarned is to be forearmed!

This is not the end; rather, it is the beginning of the new era of *dynamic supply chains*. We now know much more about the sometimes mysterious mechanisms that shape and drive today's complex supply chain networks. We know that viewing supply chains as a linear set of inanimate structures and systems both misunderstands the modern supply chain and underestimates its potential for being a source of competitive advantage. The real driver in the supply chain today is **people**: we are dealing with living systems propelled by the personality and behavior of people both inside and outside the enterprise. Our *dynamic alignment* model showed us how to treat the supply chain as a set of dynamic mechanisms. This is no more linear than the complex, changing world in which we operate! For the first time, this model gives us a clearer view of our customer segments and helps us to align the culture and leadership styles of the business to the dominant buying behavior of each customer group. The *dynamic alignment* framework then helps us to work through the different types of supply chains likely to impact our business: and how to understand, manage and synchronize these to our advantage.

What do you think are the top strategic issues facing your enterprise supply chains? I believe that understanding the dynamism of the supply chain will help us face the major challenges expected to appear over the horizon during the next decade, 2010 to 2020. There are certainly many – from the need to be socially responsible and sustainable, to managing fluctuating oil prices, through to gaining and retaining top talent in our supply chains and managing partnerships with new outsourcing formats. Each new issue is likely to have a different impact on your business depending on your preparedness – whether you analyze and prioritize the issues as they emerge, or whether you fail to consider the future and simply react to crisis after crisis, engulfing your business in uncertainty. In this penultimate chapter we will explore how *dynamic alignment* in our supply chains can help to weather the storm and make life more beneficial for customers, employees and shareholders alike.

Here come the Exocets

As we begin to understand more about the world in which supply chains operate, it is a case of the more we find out, the more we realize we don't know. We have come a fair way in the past 50 years, but there is a lot more we need to learn in the next decade. There is always some warning of future events, however subtle, and Kenneth McGee of Gartner, Inc. quotes examples such as Three Mile Island and the Space Shuttle *Challenger*, to demonstrate this point.[1]

After scanning the horizon, I have come up with 13 issues, or Exocets, that I think will affect the way enterprise supply chains perform during the next decade. To help us prioritize this list, I will use an issues analysis technique that I developed in the 1980s.[2] It is simple to use, but very effective. Indeed, I still find executives using this technique 15 years after I first introduced them to it. First, however, let me define an 'issue'. An 'issue'

*is anything that is either impacting now or will impact at some
time in the future on the performance of the organizational unit
under review; in this case, the enterprise and its supply chains.*

An issue defined in this way can come from anywhere in the organization's
operating environment, which is why I refer to them as Exocets. But unlike
a real Exocet, they may have either a positive or negative influence on their
target. My approach involves listing and briefly describing each issue in
no particular order, then assessing the priority of each to the business and
plotting each issue on the impact/urgency matrix shown in Figure 15.1.
The guidelines for this approach are described in each box of the 3 × 3
matrix. This is, in effect, a prioritization technique designed to help you to
assess the issues and then guide you in your decisions about how and when
to allocate resources in order to alleviate or enhance their impact.

How do issues emerge in your business? Do they suddenly occur in a
crash, as in a crisis? Or do they linger on the horizon for some time before
unleashing their full force? You will see in Figure 15.1 that issues normally enter the matrix at the top left-hand box, where they very often go
unnoticed. Over the succeeding years they can drift around in the matrix,
and may not be noticed until they reach crisis proportions and appear in
the bottom right-hand box. Then it's time for 'crisis management'. Many
executives spend their lives doing nothing more than reacting to the issues

		Impact		
		Low	Significant	Major
Urgency	Low	New entry	Periodic review	Monitor continuously
	Significant	Periodic review	Closely monitor	Planned/ delayed response
	Major	Monitor	Planned/ quick response	Crisis – respond immediately

FIGURE 15.1 ◆ **Critical strategic issues impact/urgency matrix framework**

that become crises. The idea of the impact/urgency matrix is to push back the boundaries, study the issues as they occur, so that you can get out of crisis mode. Interestingly, issues are like radio waves – they are in the air that surrounds us, but we can only do something about them early if we tune in to the right wavelength. So, once we have clearly identified an issue and understood the likely implications of its presence, we can either continue to monitor its progress through time, or take immediate or more measured action. If the matrix is re-visited on a regular (say quarterly or six-monthly) basis, the movement of issues can be monitored and action taken in a proactive way. The aim of course is to avoid further crises.

I remember working with John Rickard, Group Chief Executive of Hooper Baillie Industries, an Australian mini conglomerate, during the mid-1980s. His problem was that the board was acquiring diverse companies, often without involving him; e.g., tanneries, vineyards and office interiors. John was always in a 'crisis'. One day about a year after we had been systematically plotting and managing the issues that arose across his various businesses, he remarked to me, 'I feel there's something wrong – I don't seem to have any crises these days', or words to this effect! What had happened was that the issues management technique had helped him get ahead of the crisis and anticipate events so that he had more time to do what he was paid for as Chief Executive: lead the conglomerate, provide direction and work more systematically on shaping his portfolio of businesses to achieve the desired performance.

Global critical strategic issues facing supply chains of the future

Below is the original list of the 13 strategic issues that I published in *Living Supply Chains* (2006) as most likely to have an impact on the performance of enterprise supply chains over 2006 to 2016. I now want to update Issues 1 to 13 and re-prioritize them in the light of business developments of the past four years; and add four new issues, 14 to 17, that have emerged since 2006. The issues are listed in no particular order.

1 **Sustainability** in supply chains in the light of pressures for ecological, social and corporate responsibility. This issue to be split into two parts:

   1a. **Sustainability;** and

   1b. **Corporate social responsibility (CSR).**

2 The **impact of oil prices** on cost-to-serve.

3 The future practice of **outsourcing,** in all its different forms.

4 The wider adoption of supply chain 'principles' by **service organizations.**

5 **Vulnerability** of contemporary supply chains to sudden **disruptions;** risk management regimes.

6 The rise of **genuine collaboration** in enterprise supply chains.

7 Tapping the **talent** inside and outside enterprises.

8 Learning to design and manage **multiple organization formats.**

9 Coping with the national, regional and global **spread of supply chain networks.**

10 Adoption of the **whole-of-enterprise mindset** in managing supply chain operations.

11 **Collaborating with the enemy.**

12 **Innovation (all forms), product design and product life-cycles.**

13 Learning to manage **inherent complexity** in supply chains.

14 The impact of **pricing regimes** on supply chain performance.

15 **Financial links** in enterprise supply chains.

16 The role of **knowledge management** in developing intelligent supply chains.

17 Developing a **subculture of continuous improvement** in enterprise supply chains.

Is that a priority? Assessing where to put the effort

Your enterprise could be operating in quite a unique environment and therefore have different strategic issues to those listed above. But I have judged these issues using my experience across a broad range of sectors and assigned each a specific level of priority, as shown in Figure 15.2. I have shown the original position assessed in 2006, and also provided their updated position as at the end of 2009. The positions of the four new issues are provided for the first time.

I will discuss each of the top-priority issues and comment briefly on how the application of *dynamic alignment* principles may assist in resolving each. I will start with the issues in the 'crisis management' box first, i.e., 5, 1a, 2 and 17; then issues 1b, 2, 7, 12 and 15; and finally 3, 4, 6, 8, 13 and 14. The rest will not be analyzed in detail but will instead be monitored. This is the suggested order of priority for your business, until your resources run out.

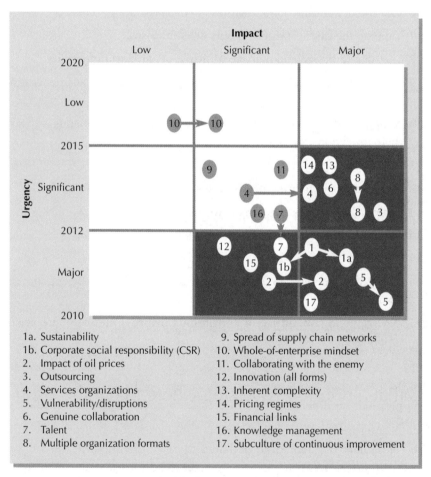

FIGURE 15.2 ◆ Assessment of critical strategic issues facing enterprise supply chains

Issue 5. Vulnerability of contemporary supply chains to sudden disruptions; risk management

Sudden failures in supply chains can be due to multiple causes, including the following:[3]

- Disruptions: natural disasters, terrorism, and war.
- Delays: due to inflexibility of supply.
- Systems: failure of technology infrastructure.
- Forecasts: inaccurate forecasts; lack of forecasting.
- Capacity: capacity inflexibility; and the list goes on.

One such failure occurred in March 2000 when lightening hit a power pole in Albuquerque, New Mexico. The strike caused a massive surge in the surrounding electrical grid, which in turn started a fire at a local plant owned by Royal Philips Electronics NV, damaging millions of microchips. Nokia, a major customer of the plant, almost immediately began switching its chip orders to other Philips plants, as well as to other Japanese and American suppliers. Thanks to its multiple-supplier strategy and responsiveness, Nokia's production suffered little during the crisis. In contrast, L.M. Ericsson, another mobile-phone customer of the Philips plant, employed a single-sourcing policy. As a result, when the Philips plant shut down after the fire, Ericsson had no other source of microchips, which disrupted its production for months. Ultimately, Ericsson lost $400 million in sales.[4]

This was a spectacular example where two different approaches to risk led to very different outcomes; but many more risks abound in the way supply chains are designed and operated. For instance, if *lean* principles are taken too far, and stocks of components and finished goods in the pipeline are reduced to very low levels to cut costs, it will become susceptible to even the smallest disruption in supply or fluctuation in demand. In these situations, it is prudent to hold reserves of inventory along the supply chain in different stages of completion. This in-built redundancy costs money, but has to be offset against the cost of lost sales and lost customers through non-supply.

Given the rise of terrorism, which has injected even more uncertainty into the operation of global supply chains, the solution is to put much more thought into developing risk mitigation strategies, **before** something happens. Hau Lee and Michael Wolfe suggest six strategies:[5]

1   Comprehensive tracking and monitoring – to detect a security breach at the earliest possible stage.

2   Total supply chain visibility – so that you can respond in a meaningful way once the extent and location of a security breach or other disruption is known.

3   Flexible sourcing strategies – we saw how important this is in the case of the fire at the Philips microchip plant.

4   Balanced inventory management – the importance of reviewing 'safety stocks' has been brought back into focus, after years of cutting and trimming inventories to reduce costs.

5   Product and process re-design – this has taken on new significance, and led directly to the development of postponement techniques. Indeed, one of the strategies used by Nokia to mitigate the problems caused by the fire at the Philips plant was to re-design its microchips so that they could be sourced from alternative suppliers.

6   Demand-based management – which means influencing demand with pricing and other offers to upgrade to the next level of product. Dell does this very well.

The fully *flexible* supply chain configuration, described in Chapter 10, would surely help to secure supply chains in most eventualities and protect them against the impact of sudden shocks. In particular, the cluster organization design and corresponding Entrepreneurial subculture are essential ingredients for success in such unforgiving circumstances. Indeed, Professor Yossi Sheffi of MIT highlights the role of culture in his book *The Resilient Enterprise*.[6] He too believes that resilience and flexibility in an organization derive largely from having the appropriate culture in place.

In the context of the *dynamic alignment* model, a fast-reacting Entrepreneurial subculture will often be the key to aligning your firm successfully, irrespective of the processes and technology. Nokia demonstrated this when the fire occurred at its microchip supplier; Dell epitomizes the fast-moving culture of a high-tech company, as does DHL in its express business. All the necessary traits for developing a resilient organization, underpinned by an Entrepreneurial subculture, have been discussed in

Chapter 10. Yossi Sheffi has also defined similar elements for achieving the necessary dynamic culture for a *fully flexible* supply chain; these are:[7]

◆ continuous communications among informed employees;

◆ distributed power;

◆ passion for work; and

◆ conditioning for disruption.

Changing and shaping the culture so that it can cope with sudden disruptive events in supply chains is the key starting point in preparing for unexpected events. Anything can happen – it's just a matter of where and when. So we shall see much more emphasis on developing both variants of *fully flexible* supply chains in the future.

Update: If anything, this issue of potential disruptions to the supply chain has become more critical over the last four years, as indicated in Figure 15.2 by the movement of Issue 5 towards the bottom right-hand corner of the matrix, in the 'crisis – respond immediately' zone. There is now clear evidence of the impact of disruptions in research carried out by Kevin Hendriks and Vinod Singhal.[8] They found that average shareholder returns dropped by 33.08 per cent in a three-year period, from one year before a disruption was announced to two years after the announcement.[9] That's a staggering figure! They quote two examples of recent disruptions that have had a major effect on the companies involved: Mattel's product recall of lead-tainted toys[10] and Boeing's Dreamliner delays.[11] Airbus had similar problems with its Airbus 380. In fact EADS, the Airbus parent company, reported that 'its net income dwindled to €99 million in 2006, from €1.68 billion a year earlier. This was due largely to €2.5 billion in charges directly related to a two-year delay in the A380 deliveries.'[12] Another high-profile disruption occurred in Japan at Rikon Corp., a supplier to all eight of Japan's automakers. It caused the suspension of production, which resulted in widespread customer disruption. Perhaps the most high-profile disruption of the last decade occurred in Texas City in 2005 when the BP Refinery exploded, killing 15 people and injuring 500. This event was so serious that it has been the subject of drawn-out legal proceedings and an official inquiry[13] and was one of the contributory factors in the resignation of Lord Browne, BP's CEO.[14]

More recently, we have witnessed the sudden and dramatic disruption to world commerce (and supply chains) caused by the eruption of Eyjafallajokull, the Icelandic volcano.

With the frequency and level of disruptions seemingly on the increase, the only solution is to 'design redundancy into supply chains wherever possible', according to Jim Thomas of CEM Axiom Manufacturing Services.[15] Thankfully, because of the increasing awareness of disruptions and their negative impact over an extended period on the affected enterprise, a lot more attention is now being given to risk mitigation and building resilience into enterprise supply chains.[16] This process is likely to continue for the foreseeable future. A company that does this well is Wal-Mart, as evidenced by the way it responded to the Hurricane Katrina disaster.[17]

Issue 1. Sustainability in supply chains

In the 2006 edition of my book I joined 'sustainability' and 'corporate social responsibility' together. However, although the two topics are inextricably intertwined, they deserve to be treated separately, and in any event, more seems to have happened on the 'sustainability' front than in the CSR area over the past four years.

Issue 1a. Sustainability

Sustainability is a big issue, looming large in the minds of all types of enterprises, public and private. Rising community pressure over human rights and globalization brought sustainability to prominence in the 1990s. Business was forced to 'take a closer look at sustainable development, particularly its social dimension,' writes Charles Holliday in his book *Walking the Talk*:

> *Companies such as Shell, Nike, and BP were unprepared for consumers' ability to get their concerns into the boardrooms. In a globalised and transparent world, managing a company's reputation becomes a central element in managing a corporation.*[18]

Sustainability is therefore a relatively new concept, albeit a complex one. When supply chains, also underdeveloped as a concept, are added to the mix, complexity increases. 'Nevertheless, this is where business, value creation and sustainability meet reality, in difficult-to-manage and increasingly globalized and commoditized supply chains,' a report on sustainability in the supply chain points out. 'Sustainability in the supply chain is fundamentally about identifying problematic social, environmental and H&S [Health & Safety] issues throughout the supply chain, assessing their impacts and risks, and then trying to improve them.'[19]

Investors and fund managers are not only increasingly scrutinizing companies for their supply chain performance, as discussed in Chapter 14, but they are also looking at the enterprise's performance on sustainability issues, including the environment, human rights, occupational health and safety, ethics and social responsibility. Australian funds manager AMP Capital Investors is one such firm. Senior research analyst Dr Ian Woods reviews company performance against sustainability criteria in order to decide whether or not to recommend investment in such firms. The reason for doing so is clear, says Woods: 'sustainable companies in the end will outperform other enterprises.'[20] AMP and other firms have mounted a *Sustainable Future Funds Research* effort to understand if there are any risks associated in investing in these companies, beyond the normal financial analyses. A recent article in *Fortune* magazine seems to reinforce this trend to look beyond the bottom line and demand corporate social responsibility from the Fortune Global 100 and others.[21] This subject is getting hot!

Update: You only have to have followed the events up to and during the Copenhagen Climate Change Conference in December 2009 to know that this topic, particularly as it affects climate change and the environment, and national economies, to know just how hot this topic is. For this reason I have moved it to the right and down in the crisis management box of 'pressing urgency' and 'major impact'. Solutions, or at least a consensus on the way forward, must be found in the next few years by both developed and developing nations if the Earth's environment is not to be damaged irreparably. The question to be answered by all stakeholders is: is 'sustainability' a problem or an opportunity? An Australian perspective on this critical question is provided in a short report prepared following key meetings in Melbourne and Sydney with industry leaders.[22]

Companies at the forefront of sustainable practices along the length of their supply chains are Hewlett-Packard and Wal-Mart, simply because they have focused resources on this area over the past few years. One of

Asia's leading 3PLs, Linfox Logistics, has also achieved a reduction in average annual energy consumption of around 5 per cent a year with its Linfox Energy Efficiency program.

The Australian Research Institute in Education for Sustainability (ARIES) at Macquarie University conducted extensive research into how enterprises could move towards more sustainable business practices, and developed the following six insights.[23]

1 Adopt a clear, shared vision for the future;

2 Build teams, not just champions;

3 Use critical thinking and reflection;

4 Go beyond stakeholder engagement;

5 Adopt a systemic approach; and

6 Move beyond expecting a linear path to change.

These six insights/principles are equally applicable to enterprises everywhere.

Ultimately, the adoption of sustainanle practices by business enterprises will largely depend on the weight of consumer demand, and this is gradually building. Indeed, it is possible that we are seeing the formation of two subsegments inside the more conventional 'Collaborative' segment, ie., Ia, where the values point to maintaining a 'relationship' with the environment, and Id, where the values point to introducing innovations that support the idea of protecting the environment. Supply chain designers inside enterprises will need to take these emerging developments in mind as they think about their supply chain configurations in the future.

Issue 1b. Corporate social responsibility

Putting in place sustainability policies, and often public reporting of the results, is paying off for enterprises such as BP, BT, Intel, Procter & Gamble and Tesco; they have all been acknowledged and admired for their stand on corporate social responsibility.[24] Interestingly, they all have strongly performing supply chains integral to their businesses. While not suggesting there is a causal link here, the same sound thinking that drove them to pursue sustainable growth policies is also likely to be the same as their approach to their supply chains.

This demonstrates an ability to think and behave in the face of complexity. The pharmaceutical company Novo Nordisk's approach to sustainable supply chain management is firmly rooted in the twin principles of company values and risk management. The company has developed its own self-evaluation program which it administers to suppliers, and if necessary it requires its suppliers to submit to social and environmental audits. As always, it's the best companies that come to the fore. At Nokia, CSR involves acknowledging that the business has an impact on society at large and the environment, so it behaves accordingly. Another company that sees things a little differently from many others is IKEA. Goran Carstedt, former Volvo and IKEA Senior Executive, thinks the leadership challenge 'is to stop treating companies like machines that need to be driven', and as his friend Arie de Geus wrote over a decade ago in *The Living Company*, 'accept that a company is a community with all the complexity of a living organism.'[25] His attitude to sustainability is summed up as follows: 'it's so sad when people think the purpose of business is shareholder value alone. That's like saying the purpose of life is oxygen. Of course it's needed, but it's the customers, co-workers, and the organization's place in society that create that value, and that's why they have to come first.'[26]

There is a cost to sustainability, a real cost in terms of the financial and human resources required, with no immediate prospects of payback. But it's becoming a requirement of doing business, just as occupational health and safety (OH&S) is now part of every business. The companies that don't move forward with sustainability initiatives will in the end be forced to do so by government policy. If they wait until they are coerced, the danger is they will be well behind their competitors. Leading companies are acting to ensure they are ahead of the regulatory game. Witness environmental policies that are now commonplace – clean air requirements to reduce air pollution, environmental impact assessments for new developments and reporting on greenhouse gas emissions. Interestingly, Wal-Mart was widely criticized for its operating practices and attitude to labor in 2005, but has since developed a new set of priorities that signals a substantial shift (for the better) in its stance on both environmental and social issues.[27] No firm is too big to ignore the growing demands for more sustainable practices.

Several companies are starting to extend sustainability principles across their supply chains. Nestlé Philippines Inc. (NPI) launched a Greening of the Supply Chain (GSC) initiative involving 42 of its upstream channel partners.[28] The GSC initiative involves educating business partners on environmental management. The initiative has improved performance and relationships between NPI and its suppliers. Adidas-Salomon, the footwear and apparel company, which outsources most of its production to more than 500 factories around the world, demands that all its suppliers adopt self-governance on the sustainability issue. Adidas-Salomon has implemented a system of scoring and monitoring suppliers' performance on social and environmental matters.[29] Major competitor Nike, the global footwear and sports clothing company, was the first in the industry to disclose its supplier base in its new corporate social responsibility report. Nike believes 'the potential benefits to industry and factory workers outweigh the possible competitive risks.'[30]

The issue is not going away and indeed will loom larger in the next decade, particularly for those companies falling behind in this area. Application of *dynamic alignment* principles will help to pinpoint and understand the areas of potential misalignment between the stakeholders in particular industry supply chains and more broadly – remember, *dynamic alignment*, first and foremost, applies to the whole enterprise, not just to the supply chains they are part of. However, it can be used to guide the formulation of strategies to close identified gaps where sustainability is the focus, and the benefits that flow from this action to stakeholders will vary.

Update: From what I can observe, CSR as a business philosophy has not developed as fast as might have been expected over the past four years. For this reason I have moved it from 'major' to 'significant' impact, but increased the urgency slightly.

For some companies it has taken a crisis to get their CSR practices sorted out; look at Mattel,[31] which initially dragged its feet when the first accusations emerged about the toys they manufactured in China being contaminated with lead paint. After a slow start they are now one of the leaders in CSR.

Two companies that have caught my eye in the past few years are both Brazilian – Marcopolo S.A. and Natura. Marcopolo, which manufactures bus bodies and their components, holds about a 43 per cent share of the Brazil local market, and 6 to 7 per cent of the global market. Marcopolo's shares are listed on BOVESPA (the Sao Paulo Stock Exchange). The company has made a very successful transformation from a family-owned and managed business to a company with widely dispersed ownership and a high level of corporate governance, as evidenced by several awards for its social responsibility.[32]

Natura is the leading company in the Brazilian cosmetics sector. It is 'committed to the quality of its relationship with stakeholders, [and has] established a sustainable business model, focused on constant innovation and improvement of its products.'[33]

Another cosmetics company, L'Oréal, led by CPO Barbara Lavernos, 'is sold on the value of investing time and money in long-term supplier relationships and corporate social responsibility.'[34]

Meanwhile, the British retail giant Tesco, which buys much of its manufactured merchandise in poor countries, is under continual pressure to adhere to high labor standards. This is an ethical issue that concerns consumers, and is likely to become stronger over time. Indeed as 'fast fashion' becomes a reality, store chains such as Top Shop, Miss Selfridge and Gap are struggling with this conflict between business competitiveness and the need to provide fair pay and conditions to the people working in the factories where their merchandise is made. Chocolate is another product where the same issue exists and is still unresolved despite pleas to the contrary.

Then there's the situation at Pacific Brands in Australia where the CEO, Sue Morphett, retrenched 1,850 workers and sent their jobs offshore. Is that ethical? And is the shareholder the only stakeholder that should be considered? If you listen to Arie de Geus, the answer is definitely no. So despite many stories of improvements in CSR during the past five years, I am left with the distinct impression that there is still a long way to go in this area of business.

Issue 2. Impact of oil prices on cost-to-serve

No one quite knows where the oil price will go over the next decade, but high oil prices will clearly have a negative impact on the global economy, and therefore on the supply chains that link national and regional economies. If, for instance, rising oil prices cause a shift in customer buying behaviors throughout supply chain networks, it may mean each party in the network has to change their emphasis. High oil prices in the US\$75 to US\$100 per barrel range will significantly affect both the energy input costs for manufacturing and the fuel costs for all types of transport. To stay aligned with any shifts in customer preferences, enterprises will need to watch markets very carefully, and adjust inputs to production, production processes, and transportation arrangements. If you do this, you will postpone any rise in cost-to-serve for as long as possible.

Update: When I prepared the last critical issues assessment in January 2006, the oil price was hovering between US$60 to $70 per barrel. No one could foresee that it would hit over US$140 per barrel in July 2008. By January 2010, with the world's major economies still in recession, oil is already back to US$80 per barrel. One thing we can be fairly sure of is that energy in the future will be expensive when compared to previous decades, whether it is carbon-based or renewable. The days of cheap energy are gone forever. For this reason I have moved this issue squarely into the crisis management box; right now, so little is being done that we're going backwards not forwards. That trend will have to be reversed within five to ten years.

Issue 17. Developing a subculture of continuous improvement in enterprise supply chains

This is a new issue I have added to the critical issues matrix for the first time. The reason for its inclusion, and its prominent high-priority position, is that we simply won't be able to extricate ourselves from the complexities we are dealing with in enterprise supply chains – unless we have more firms switched on to a continuous improvement subculture. Indeed, this issue goes hand in hand with Issue 12 on all types of innovation. Innovation, and the corresponding Entrepreneurial subculture, is the only thing that will save us now. It's time to pour the necessary resources into addressing this issue, which needs the will of the board and CEO to fix. No one else has the command of resources that will be required, or the leadership clout to produce the required change in mindset to match the Entrepreneurial subculture. Now is the time to embrace 'disruptive technologies'[35] in an effort to catch up for ground lost over the past several decades.

Issue 12. Innovation, product design and product life-cycles

The variability of supply and demand are the two big killers of smooth supply chain operations. However, you can reduce some of the variability in supply through smart design that allows for ease of manufacture and assembly (postponement). You will need to have quality assessment routines in place, particularly in the early stages of a new product launch. Innovation will also be vital, not just in the product development stage but throughout the supply chain itself. Today many enterprises favor innovation in product and product design rather than innovation in manufacturing and supply chain areas. On the demand-side of the supply chain, you can avoid variability by strategically stocking product at various locations along the supply chain, essentially building capacity ahead of demand. This also means ensuring contract manufacturers build manufacturing capacity and trained people capacity, ahead of demand. This may run counter to some *lean* principles, but if a specific product requires unrelenting agility, then building in redundant capacity is the only answer. The cost has to be weighed against the potential for lost revenue by keeping to more conventional cost-based methods in managing the supply chain. Finally, in some product-supply chain combinations, complexity rises exponentially quicker than the growth in product sales, and in this situation significant innovation is usually required at process, technology and people levels. To achieve *dynamic alignment,* continuous improvement (Issue 17) and innovation (Issue 12) must be pursued in all four generic types of supply chain, although here again the subcultures that underpin innovation are not naturally present in *continuous replenishment* and *lean* supply chains, and therefore the task is all that much harder.

Update: This issue stays where I originally placed it – in the 'planned/ quick response' box for 'pressing urgency' and 'significant impact' issues. There is no shortage of new ideas – the problem is to convert ideas into action on the ground. It takes courage, leadership, tenacity, and resources. Ideas matter, but conversion into practice matters even more.

Issue 15. Financial links in enterprise supply chains

This too is a new issue to watch for on the horizon. I have inserted it here because of the major credit crunch caused by the global financial crisis, which went very close to crippling global business – and therefore supply chains. This issue has several dimensions:

1 Making real the clear connection between supply chain execution and financial performance;[36]

2 Using new financial ratios such as CFROI and TRS to assess real performance of enterprise supply chains;[37]

3 The emergence of tax considerations in the so-called tax-aligned supply chains.[38] Arshiya International, the new Indian 3PL/4PL®, has designed its entire strategy around the advantages of using free-trade zones for its warehousing and rail transport network;

4 Innovative ways to link finance and the physical flow of product and information in supply chains. As already mentioned in Chapter 14, DHL has attempted to develop this area in conjunction with GE Finance but growth has been hampered by the Sarbanes- Oxley legislation, or at least the way business interpreted it.

The issue of financial links in supply chains may seem to be vexed as we recover from the GFC, but, surprisingly, the issue has untapped potential to deliver future value. The smart players will be members of enterprise supply chains who engineer new financial structures and prevent the tightening of credit from stymieing their plans. Watch this space! I have positioned it in the 'planned/quick response' box because it represents a genuine area of value extraction for enterprises over the next decade. The sooner they get started the better.

Issue 7. Tapping the talent inside and outside enterprises

Growing or acquiring talent is likely to be one of the biggest issues for the most successful (and unsuccessful) businesses over the next decade. For some, especially the large global consultancies, they see this issue as already at crisis point, and in some cases is holding back the growth of certain firms. Perhaps an even bigger crisis for enterprises, and supply chain management alike, is how to develop leadership talent to execute the types of strategies suggested in this book. Unfortunately, many executives believe that leadership development is a job for the human resources department. This is the worst possible misconception.[39]

Update: I originally had this issue in the 'monitor' section in my previous edition, but in the last four years it has emerged as a much more pressing issue, hence the revised position in the 'planned/quick response' box. Attracting talented people is one of those areas where we should be applying supply chain principles to the problem. If we want talent 'on demand', we have to approach the issue this way.[40] In this situation, the talented personnel are the stock that we must work to retain, even through downturns, if we want our business is to grow.

Companies that clearly do a good job with acquiring and retaining talent are IBM, GE, EDS, Dow Chemicals, Capital One, Citibank, Corning, Johnson & Johnson, Procter & Gamble and Pepsico; they all have different but effective approaches.

The other factor that has emerged following the financial crisis and subsequent global recession is that boards in major companies around the world are already looking for new leaders to replace the existing incumbents. Why? They are betting on the need for a very different leadership style over the next decade from that we have witnessed for the past decade, one that can handle increased volatility. And they are right.

Issue 3. Future practice of outsourcing, in all its forms

It is becoming clear that outsourcing is not a simple task, for either the outsourcer or outsourcee. As was outlined in Chapter 14, enterprises outsource for one main reason: to access required capabilities and to do so at a minimum cost. Unfortunately, most companies that have either outsourced the manufacture of key products and components, or outsourced logistics functions, have often not had a happy experience.

Management consultancy firm Booz Allen Hamilton reported in 2001 that high-tech companies such as Cisco, Sony, Palm, Hewlett-Packard, Apple and Philips had found that outsourcing did not met their expectations and had in fact caused them some complications in their operational and financial performance.[41] The report highlighted one of the major flaws in outsourcing: the inevitable and fundamental conflict in objectives between the Original Equipment Manufacturers (OEMs) and Contract Equipment Manufacturers (CEMs) who actually make the product. In short, OEMs such as Cisco need 'flexibility' to meet sudden changes in demand; and CEMs such as Solectron and Jabil Circuit need 'predictability' rather than flexibility for their production schedules. Never the two shall meet! This remains a big issue today, which is making supply chains rougher rather than smoother to manage.

A study by Deloitte Consulting highlights that some of the world's largest organizations have started to recognize 'the real cost and inherent risks in outsourcing'.[42] The report argues that 'organizations looking for differentiated growth solutions should avoid outsourcing when based solely on cost saving'. Further, 'companies should outsource only commodity functions to guard against a loss of knowledge and should plan for short-term outsourcing to prevent vendor dependency'.[43] Zara does just this; in fact, it keeps the difficult work inside and only outsources the simple tasks.

Do any of the problems and issues highlighted by Deloitte sound familiar to you? I believe the new business model proposed in Chapter 14 will deliver a more successful approach to outsourcing for the next generation of the economy and associated labor markets. The model brings together companies that want work done along their supply chains, with other parties that have the particular *capabilities* to best carry out that work. The organizational format can be a partnership or, better still, an equity-based consortium. The parties in a consortium should be able to make good returns, but most importantly of all, the principals (OEMs or retail distributors) which own the business should retain control of their business, and be rewarded for creating scale of operations and knowledge. The *dynamic alignment* model provides useful guidance in these circumstances because it helps to ensure that 'rapid alignment' is achieved in the new joint venture, highlighting how to make the objectives, culture and leadership of all the parties compatible.

When I worked in the Australian office of Accenture, our consulting assignments certainly revealed some of the best and the worst of outsourcing arrangements operating at the time. Accenture has listed its top five considerations in achieving better outsourcing[44] and it is useful to discuss these here as they reinforce the features of the joint services company (JSC) model introduced in Chapter 14. Get these features of the outsourcing arrangement right and the benefits will flow.

1. Have a partnering approach to outsourcing

Your selection of the right partner is crucial, and is now regarded as one of the new competences that enterprises must be good at. Once the selection is complete, you have to commit to each other in virtually a 'professional marriage,' and managing the relationship becomes the key to success. It's important that partners be both competency and culturally compatible. Key attributes to look for in a partner are:

- *demonstrated leadership*, capability and a track record for delivery in outsourced activity;
- *flexibility* in approach, and willingness to shape a contract that works for both parties;
- willingness to take on a business risk-reward contract structure – business is of a strategic nature to the supplier as well as the buyer; and
- willingness to be transparent in working towards mutual trust as well as risk and reward.

So, *flexibility, team approach, trust, shared objectives* and *compatible culture* are all vital ingredients of success in outsourcing deals. For these to occur, all parties in a consortium need to share similar relationship values and business outcomes. The cultures need to mesh so that everyone is in agreement about what end results to focus on. The *dynamic alignment* model will be a useful tool to achieve this.

2. Use outsourcing to drive strategic change

A significant success factor is to use outsourcing to achieve enterprise-wide strategic impact on the buyer's organization, rather than outsourcing to accomplish lower operational costs or higher process efficiencies. The outsourcing relationship should be used to achieve business objectives that cannot be accomplished by the buyer organization without leveraging the strong points of the service provider's organization.

3. Use risk-reward structures to motivate performance

Incentive-based pricing structures pay significant dividends. As usual it is a case of 'the greater the risk, the greater the reward'. The reward is not paid to the service provider unless they achieve the specified desired result of the buyer organization. Incentive-based pricing or risk-reward structures are always evident in successful outsourcing arrangements. These structures provide an effective way to motivate providers to achieve challenging goals that will greatly impact the buyer organization's ability to compete.

Examples of risk-reward structures include the following:

◆ Gain share on savings achieved in operating costs.

◆ A reward for improved performance.

◆ A combination of the above.

◆ A reward for achieving a unique objective, such as target cost-to-serve, or percentage movement in share price.

4. Adopt a beneficial deal structure

You should be prepared to spend time up-front on developing joint objectives. Structure the deal using business principles that are beneficial to both parties. Due diligence is also a critical step and should be used to establish the governance structure, joint business objectives, and commercial payment structure. You should also clearly articulate the desired business outcomes and key success factors and measures.

Partnership 'operating principles' should be built into the program. Agree working principles that ensure a 'win–win' relationship. Share information openly to secure a robust business case. And spend time understanding each other's company philosophy.

5. Avoid outsourcing problems

Poor due diligence or assessment can have a negative impact on the outsourcing arrangement. Some of the problems include:

◆ Buyer not properly prepared at various stages of the process, e.g., value of assets may not be known; lack of resources through transition and implementation phases.
Recommendation: you need to work with the partner to capture baseline data, and assign dedicated resources to work on the deal to clearly identify business objectives, desired outcomes and potential risks.

◆ Buyer has unrealistic expectations, e.g., buyers often do not understand their roles and responsibilities during and post-transition. **Recommendation**: agree business principles and roles and responsibilities early during discussions with outsourcing partner.

◆ Buyer makes poor judgments, e.g., ineffective service level specifications; lack of linkage of contract to business outcomes. **Recommendation**: agree business outcomes and link service level agreements to outcomes.

Update: I am leaving this issue where it was positioned in my earlier book, because I don't think anything significant has happened in this area, in either impact or urgency. In terms of life-cycle, it seems that the outsourcing experience is still in the early stages. There has been some tendency for a 'myopic pursuit of low-cost country sourcing',[45] but this cost-mitigation strategy is coming to an end as today's low-cost countries become tomorrow's emerging markets. That changes a lot of things.

Issue 8. Learning to design and manage multiple organization formats

Where to then, for your organization design? Clearly, a simple, straightforward format of days past will not provide the appropriate mix of supply chains needed to respond effectively to the desires of today's customers. Your supply chain performance will depend on your ability to design and manage three or four organizational formats within your current structure. This sounds like a complex task, and it is. But if we accept that the marketplace for most product categories is fragmenting, then we must also accept that this shift will have to be reflected in the way organization structures are configured. This book has stressed that customers exhibit several dominant buying behaviors; now you will need at least four types of organizational clusters to cover these primary behaviors, as depicted in Figure 15.3 overleaf.

No doubt maintaining the coexistence of four sometimes opposing organization formats inside a single enterprise is something you have studiously avoided in the past. But it's become obvious that the old singular formats cannot possibly respond to the emerging range of different buying behaviors that today's customers exhibit. Leading management thinker Peter Drucker has in effect been saying something similar for more than 36 years. In 1974 he wrote that:

an organization should be multi axial, that is, structured around work and task, and results and performance, and relationships, and decisions. It would function as if it were a biological organism, like the human body with its skeleton and muscles, a number of nervous systems, and with circulatory, digestive, immuno-logical, and respiratory systems, all autonomous yet interdependent. But in social structures we are still limited to designs that express only one primary dimension. So, in designing organizations, we have to choose among different structures, each stressing a different dimension and each, therefore, with distinct costs, specific and fairly stringent requirements, and real limitations. There is no risk-free organization structure. And a design that is the best solution for one task may be only one of a number of equally poor alternatives for another task, and just plain wrong for yet a third kind of work.[46]

How prophetic his words were!

How do you view organizational structures? I see them acting as the 'straitjackets' in which we put people to work; work structures have an inordinately powerful impact on the performance of the enterprise as a whole, and supply chains in particular. Hierarchies have thrived for too long and have largely outlived their usefulness. The functional mindset that dominates so many enterprises needs to be broken down and dispersed into customized clusters, as described in Chapter 6 if maximum value is to be extracted for all stakeholders.

Apart from the cluster organizational model I am proposing, other variants have been tried in an attempt to align the enterprise with its rapidly fragmenting market. The McKinsey 'atom' structure,[47] which disaggregated organizations into smaller decision-making units to force greater accountability at lower levels of the organization, has been briefly reviewed in Chapter 6. Donald Sull reports that Haier, China's largest home appliance manufacturer, has adopted what he calls a *flexible hierarchy* structure.[48] This is 'an organizational form in which top executives set top–down priorities for the organization, but allow middle managers and employees great latitude in negotiating their specific objectives and autonomy in executing them.'[49] This sounds very much like a version of

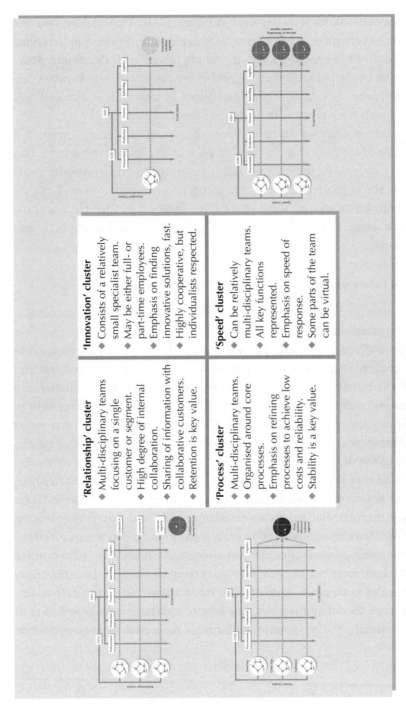

'Relationship' cluster
- Multi-disciplinary teams focusing on a single customer or segment.
- High degree of internal collaboration.
- Sharing of information with collaborative customers.
- Retention is key value.

'Innovation' cluster
- Consists of a relatively small specialist team.
- May be either full- or part-time employees.
- Emphasis on finding innovative solutions, fast.
- Highly cooperative, but individualists respected.

'Process' cluster
- Multi-disciplinary teams.
- Organised around core processes.
- Emphasis on refining processes to achieve low costs and reliability.
- Stability is a key value.

'Speed' cluster
- Can be relatively multi-disciplinary teams.
- All key functions represented.
- Emphasis on speed of response.
- Some parts of the team can be virtual.

FIGURE 15.3 ◆ **Multiple organization formats within an enterprise**

the organizational clusters depicted in Figure 15.3. Whatever the case, the point is to recognize the importance of organization design in achieving alignment of the enterprise and its supply chains with the marketplace, and focus enough of your thinking and resources to radically improve current practices. As you've probably gathered by now, this is a crucial area where much work remains to be done in the next decade.

Update: I need say no more about organizational design, except that the sense of urgency to get a suitable fix is increasing, year-by-year. This is why I have re-positioned the issue down in the crisis response zone, because the urgency and impact are taking on crisis proportions. Let's see what enterprises take up some of the ideas outlined in Chapter 6 over the next few years. It won't be an easy transition, but it will surely be a winning move!

Issue 6. The rise of genuine collaboration in supply chains

I have probably said enough about this issue in Chapter 7, but it concerns me that seller enterprises continue to throw resources at buyer enterprises in supply chains, when there is clearly no chance of ever achieving equitable collaboration. You can talk about trust and governance all you like, but if the buyer enterprise doesn't have deeply embedded collaborative values, you can forget about collaboration. The task for management in the future is to read the situation earlier in the cycle of the buyer–seller relationship, and make a call whether or not you are in the *zone of collaboration*. In the meantime, let's cut the rhetoric!

Update: In the intervening four years between editions there has been a lot of noise surrounding 'collaboration', but I'm not sure the message has got through that we are only talking about 'requisite' collaboration after all. Requisite collaboration involves responding in a requisite way: not too much or too little, but just enough. As there hasn't been much progress or learning on this front, I prefer to keep the collaboration issue in the same place: in the 'major impact' box. Sooner or later enterprises have to clarify their view on how to handle collaboration in their supply chains – today and into the future. I have given my prescription in Chapter 7.

Issue 13. Learning to manage inherent complexity in supply chains

I doubt if you or any other senior manager today will dispute my contention that 'complexity' is increasing. Complexity comes in many forms, but to mention a few, there is the proliferation of SKUs; shorter product life-cycles; demands by customers for ever quicker service; external factors such as increasing oil prices; an imbalance of channel power in many industries; sourcing from distant global locations; and the list goes on. Where can we go for some respite from this multi-headed, accelerating band-wagon which is practically unavoidable in today's world order? Our problem is that complexity will define today's and tomorrow's world. As they say, you can run but you can't hide!

Let's turn to scientific theory for some guidance on how to cope with this issue of complexity. *Ashby's Law of Requisite Variety*[50] is one of the laws common to all systems. To paraphrase, it says that as systems become more complex through increased variety, then the corresponding complexity-resolution devices have to become correspondingly sophisticated. In effect, to manage complexity in supply chains – and supply chains are *living systems* – we have to absorb 'variety', otherwise the whole system is likely to become unstable, and at worst, collapse, in some cases catastrophically. To overcome potential instability, systems have to be designed with in-built redundancy to allow them to suffer and absorb unexpected shocks of the type we have been discussing in this and earlier chapters. If we try to eradicate all redundancy, such as in the pursuit of ever lower costs in supply chains, supply chains are likely to become brittle and fail. We have to embed redundancy into certain types of supply chain configurations, in particular *agile* and *fully flexible* supply chains, if they are to be flexible and resilient enough for extreme market conditions. In light of this, perhaps we have brought a lot of complexity upon ourselves by trying to squeeze too much out of our current supply chain designs. They are simply not equipped to cope with rapidly changing demand patterns. This realization only reinforces the need to recognize and implement the concept of *multiple supply chain alignment*. And this is a dynamic situation – because different supply chain configurations will need to operate either in parallel to or in some linear combination. The future world will look like this whether we like it or not.

Update: This issue is being addressed by companies with varied degrees of success. I have kept it in its original position, in the 'planned/delayed response' box, but I could have easily let it slip down towards the crisis response zone. It will become progressively more critical that complexity is addressed, otherwise performance improvement in enterprise supply chains will be impaired. My philosophy on this issue is very clear: tackle complexity at source, i.e., the marketplace, and work back from there. If you try to tackle it at some later point, say inside the business, you will find yourself always in reactive mode; this is very inefficient and wearing on everyone involved.

Issue 14. The impact of pricing regimes on supply chain performance

I have added this as a new issue because it has such a big influence on the performance of enterprise supply chains. I have positioned it in the top left corner of the 'planned/delayed response' box because its influence is only just becoming apparent, and will take some time to understand and harness to good effect.

The important point for this issue is that the pricing regimes associated with the four generic supply chain types will all be different. Why? Just as customers have different values that dominate and drive their buying behavior, pricing will also be an influence. Pricing is one of the attributes in the hierarchies that have an impact on customer behavior.

The task for us is to take conventional knowledge on pricing mechanics, converge it with our new understanding of customer preferences, and use this to shape differential value propositions and constituent operational strategies. Chung Chee Kong has perhaps gone the furthest of any researchers in making the connection between behavioral segmentation and pricing.[51]

Issue 4. Adoption of supply chain 'principles' by service organizations

Service enterprises vary in only one respect from product enterprises: their product is intangible. They still have networks of nodes, all of which are some form of processing point, or dispensing point for their services. And those nodes where all the activity takes place are usually tied into an information network. Banks, indeed all kinds of financial service institutions, are enterprises that have multiple supply chains or pathways running through them. And yet very few of these institutions have systematically adopted supply chain principles to shape their various responses to the marketplace. They are years behind FMCG and hi-tech companies in this respect, and the gap continues to widen. A great opportunity awaits discovery.

Update: I have relocated the position of this issue into the 'planned/delayed response' box because it is an issue that is looming larger for financial service institutions, particularly following the global financial crisis. Given the pressure coming from regulatory authorities and consumers alike, this issue can no longer be ignored. It would be safe to say that there are billions of dollars in value locked up in financial and other service institutions that will only be extracted when supply chain principles are systematically employed.

Monitor the rest

Issues 9, 10, 11 and 16 all fall into the monitoring category. However, like all issues, it's possible that some of these too will move into the high-priority (shaded) area of Figure 15.2 and require resources and direct action in the years ahead. In the meantime, a parting word on each.

Issue 9. Coping with the national, regional and global spread of supply chain networks

The globalization of supply chain operations is well established for the leading players in several industries, from electronics high-technology and fashion to automotive and third-party logistics. But for many other companies the wave is just breaking over them. What to do? My advice is to look and learn from the supply chain experiences of enterprises that have gone before you, irrespective of your industry.

Update: I have left this issue in its original central position on the grid, in the 'closely monitor' zone, although it's possible the current push to introduce climate change initiatives to reduce their carbon footprint will cause a rethink of regional and global supply chains . That would see the issue shift into a higher-priority box. We shall see.

Issue 10. Adoption of the whole-of-enterprise mindset in managing supply chain operations

This might seem a long way off, but I hope that one of the outcomes of this book is that more enterprises will realize the value in taking a whole-of-enterprise approach to their business. One day, I hope we can sound the death knell for the narrow myopic view of the supply chain that has characterized the development and management of logistics and supply chains over the past two decades. Perhaps no more telling is the realization that supply chain management today is a strategic business issue requiring top management attention. As US supply chain 'guru' Clifford Lynch said in a keynote speech delivered in Athens, 'in a globalized business environment, with goods without country, the only true Supply Chain Manager in a corporation is the CEO, because nobody else has full control of the cradle-to-grave process'.[52]

Update: This issue still seems like it is on a far-off horizon, although the best-of-the-best companies like Nokia, Dell and Apple are moving in that direction. So I have kept it at the same level of urgency, while moving it's likely impact from 'Low' to 'Significant' on the grid.

Issue 11. Collaborating with the enemy

Collaborating with competitors is difficult for two reasons. First, most executives cannot cope with the ambiguity of collaborating with a competitor in the supply chain, and at the same time competing in the marketplace. Well, get used to it, as the ambiguity is set to increase to new, higher levels in the next decade. In some parts of the world, collaborating with competitors is the **only** way to achieve the scale to compete on a level footing with major international players that have more natural scale at their disposal.

And second, how do you draw the line between collaboration and collusion? That's tricky, especially when your reputation is at stake over any 'unfair' or restrictive trading practices. In the future you will see that companies have to manage the strict requirements of certain government regulatory bodies that have been expressly set up to stop the domination of a few industry players over the majority of smaller players. We mentioned this issue in Chapter 14, but it's a long way from being resolved.

Perhaps some education of the regulatory agencies about the modern supply chain is in order! Or at the very least, getting them involved in the supply chain design discussions at an early stage.

Update: There has not been much progress on this issue over the last four years, but as pressure mounts to find new ways to compete, collaboration will surely be revisited.

Issue 16. The role of knowledge management in developing intelligent supply chains

This issue was originally an integral part of Issue 7, tapping into the talent of your organization, but the growing importance of knowledge has led me to make it an issue in its own right. Going hand-in-hand with talent is the requirement to help key talent in the enterprise with personal knowledge management. These managers will need help to keep track of and manage the information they encounter in their daily working likes.[53] In fact, today's organizational designs are particularly difficult for knowledge workers or professionals because of the difficulties of moving information across functional boundaries.[54] John Mangan and Martin Christopher have provided a comprehensive review of the knowledge areas, competences and skills that tomorrow's supply chain managers will need to have, as a minimum.[55] It reads like a general manager's job description. Surprised? I don't think so.

Update: The reality is that knowledge is a strategic resource in supply chains, and we must find ways to make the most of it.[56] The first, most important element of corporate knowledge is to 'know your customers'. For this you will need the assistance of a Customer Relationship Management (CRM) system – that is where you start the journey towards the 'intelligent supply chain'. Kate Andrews has devised categories for the different types of knowledge required for the four generic supply chains.[57] Her framework provides an excellent guide to ensuring your company's intellectual resources 'fit' your firm's customer segments just as much as the subculture and leadership. Knowing your customer – intelligently – is the way of the future. There's a gold mine to be found and tapped!

Defining ideas

1   Your world will be full of 'Exocets' (or issues) coming at you over the horizon, both from inside the firm and the external operating environment. The trick is to see them coming early, and prepare.

2   Select the issues that are likely to have the biggest impact both positive and negative) on your business, and allocate resources to them as a matter of priority.

3   After a while, if you follow this prescription the incidence of crises in your enterprise supply chain will significantly diminish, and you will have some thinking time for continuous improvement initiatives and the introduction of performance-enhancing innovations.

4   **Challenge** to the reader: have you identified the critical issues that are impacting (or likely to impact) your business over the next few years? If so, and have you prepared contingency plans to handle them?

CHAPTER 16

Meeting of minds

Joining the dots to create *dynamic* institutions

R ather than end at the beginning, it seems appropriate that we should end with evolution. In their book *Presence*, Peter Senge and his colleagues say that 'nowhere is it more important to understand the relation between parts and wholes than in the evolution of global institutions and the larger systems they collectively create'.[1] They point to the observation made by Arie de Geus that 'the twentieth century witnessed the emergence of a new species on Earth – large organizations, notably global corporations'.[2] De Geus continues: 'This is a historic development. Prior to the last hundred years, there were few examples of globe-spanning institutions. But today, global institutions are proliferating seemingly without bound, along with global infrastructures for finance, distribution, supply, and communication they create'.[3] Clearly, these global institutions require the delivery capability, speed, agility, and performance made possible by a global network of supply chains.

Even if you are not a global business, no organization on Earth can isolate itself from this phenomenon. Trying to segment your business according to single customers and targeting each and every one of them is simply not feasible. Now more than ever we need to understand how people behave and interact as *groups* within these extended supply chains. The *dynamic alignment* model we have outlined in this book seeks to give you the tools to identify, design and execute the most common supply chain configurations – and the corresponding dominant buying behaviors that they serve. As the title *Presence* suggests, supply chains are omnipresent and pervade our lives; they may be unseen, seemingly operating in subliminal ways, but they underpin the conduct of all enterprise and the way we as customers and consumers demand and receive goods and services. As humans, our behavior is shaping and driving these modern extended supply chains; not the other way around. If events go as predicted, the **presence** of *dynamic supply chains*, and all that they encompass, will loom large in all our lives in the years and decades to come.

So let's draw all the threads together. In this book we have traversed some of the old ways of thinking about supply chains and found them wanting at best, flawed at worst. We can see now that contemporary supply chains are pervasive. And they are so much more than warehouses, transport and technology. Supply chains are by their very nature living and dynamic organisms, ever evolving in response to their particular operating environment.

Understanding supply chains in this way means we can configure and re-configure them, just like any cellular structure in nature. Paradoxically, it is going to make the task of managing the enterprise much simpler and more rewarding in the future. With your supply chains forming part of a much broader business ecosystem, you can survive and thrive by designing and operating supply chains configurations that have an embedded *dynamism* that facilitates on-going *dynamic alignment* between the enterprise and all its stakeholders.

How to do this? The *dynamic alignment* model and the supply chains described throughout this book show you how to group processes, assets and people into modular structures or 'clusters' that can be quickly re-configured and re-aligned to changing customer buying behaviors. As in nature, the secret is to have simple building blocks that are endlessly re-configurable to create sophisticated 'life forms'. This means your enterprise will need to develop or acquire multiple *capabilities* that can be compartmentalized, combined and unwound at speed, something akin to 'cellular manufacturing'.

But unlike cellular manufacturing, *alignment* is likely to occur in a much less controlled environment, so maintaining all the elements in synch is much more difficult over sustained periods. But if *dynamic alignment* principles are followed, it is still possible. We know – we have done it! And so have others. Businesses such as Apple (US), General Accident (now CGU Insurance), Li & Fung (Hong Kong), DHL Taiwan, Fonterra (New Zealand), Elgeka (Greece), Dell (US), Nokia (Finland), Procter &

Gamble (US), Wal-Mart (US) and a growing band of enlightened enterprises are leading the way.

Remember, success is all about understanding customers' 'buying behaviors', developing matching *value propositions* and underpinning these with an organization design that flexes according to customers' needs. And any and all of this will only happen if the leadership of your enterprise is in harmony with the target market. Are you in harmony?

After understanding customers, leadership is the most important ingredient for success. With the right leadership, the best strategies for identifying and targeting customers in separate supply chains will surely follow – breathing even more life into your *dynamic supply chains*.

With that said, we leave you with a challenge which was made to me by a leading executive in the fast moving consumer products industry when we met in Boston in November 2009 to discuss *dynamic alignment* concepts and practices.

He felt that it was imperative to make a choice if a company is to remain competitive, and he encouraged me to provoke the readers of this book into making such a *choice*: a choice between adopting many of the ideas in this book; or simply staying with the *status quo*, and risk missing out attracting the best customers, the best suppliers, the best talent and everything else that goes along with winning in today's ultra-competitive world. I have offered you, the reader, a genuinely new *frame-of-reference* to work with; it is now up to you to run with it and become part of a global groundswell which is building towards improved alignment in enterprise supply chains around the world.

In effect, the challenge I am making to the readers of this book is to consciously go out there and 'disrupt' your enterprise with this new model and way of thinking about supply chains. Be like Honda, Virgin, and other like them that have created extreme value through disruptive thinking. Don't be like Sun Microsystems and, more recently, Toyota who have suffered because they failed to disrupt their previous success formulae as markets shifted. As Adam Hartung says, 'Teachers may tell you to sit still, but if you want your business to succeed, you had better start disrupting'.[4]

Over to you now! Above all else, don't be one of those enterprises that becomes hopelessly lost in the maze depicted in the picture overleaf, and eventually becomes extinct. The difference between success and failure is very small, sometimes infinitesimal, but you have now been given a road map through that maze – **use it or lose it!**

FIGURE 16.1 ◆ Maze of complexity

Appendices

Appendix 2A.1

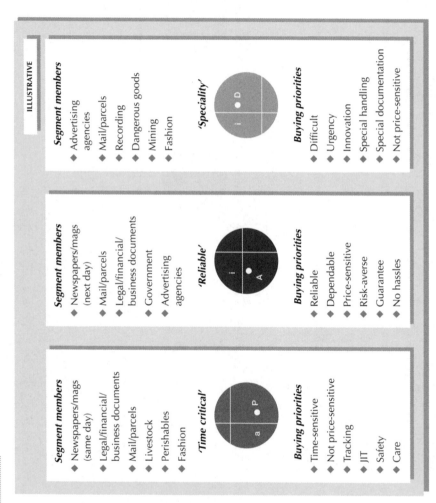

Time critical

Segment members

- Newspapers/mags (same day)
- Legal/financial/ business documents
- Mail/parcels
- Livestock
- Perishables
- Fashion

Buying priorities

- Time-sensitive
- Not price-sensitive
- Tracking
- JIT
- Safety
- Care

Reliable

Segment members

- Newspapers/mags (next day)
- Mail/parcels
- Legal/financial/ business documents
- Government
- Advertising agencies

Buying priorities

- Reliable
- Dependable
- Price-sensitive
- Risk-averse
- Guarantee
- No hassles

Speciality

Segment members

- Advertising agencies
- Mail/parcels
- Recording
- Dangerous goods
- Mining
- Fashion

Buying priorities

- Difficult
- Urgency
- Innovation
- Special handling
- Special documentation
- Not price-sensitive

Product/service category – express small packages

ILLUSTRATIVE

Segment members

- Kodak
- Hewlett-Packard
- LL Bean
- Chrysler
- Bechtel
- Polygram

'Collaborative'

Buying priorities

- Partnership relationships
- Reliability > price
- Budgets
- Quality and safety
- Stability

Segment members

- Hoechst
- Westinghouse
- 3M
- Nissan Nth America

'Fair Deal'

Buying priorities

- Reliability – 'on-time'
- Quality and service guarantee
- Customer focus
- Fair negotiations
- Cost effectiveness

Segment members

- AMP
- J&J Medical
- Bank of America
- New Hampton Inc.
- Paul Fredrick Shirt
- Mobile Telesystems Communications Equipment

'Efficiency'

Buying priorities

- Reliability > speed
- Cost is the final evaluation criterion
- Access to information
- Timely and accurate information

Segment members

- General Motors
- AT&T
- IQ software
- Motorola Inc.
- Lillian Vernon

'Premium'

Buying priorities

- Speed > reliability
- Product availability
- Flexibility
- Communication
- Competitive pricing

Product/service category – express logistics

Appendix 2A.3

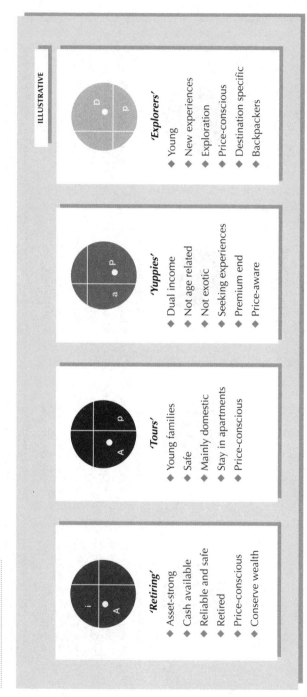

ILLUSTRATIVE

'Retiring'
◆ Asset-strong
◆ Cash available
◆ Reliable and safe
◆ Retired
◆ Price-conscious
◆ Conserve wealth

'Tours'
◆ Young families
◆ Safe
◆ Mainly domestic
◆ Stay in apartments
◆ Price-conscious

'Yuppies'
◆ Dual income
◆ Not age related
◆ Not exotic
◆ Seeking experiences
◆ Premium end
◆ Price-aware

'Explorers'
◆ Young
◆ New experiences
◆ Exploration
◆ Price-conscious
◆ Destination specific
◆ Backpackers

Product/service category – leisure travel

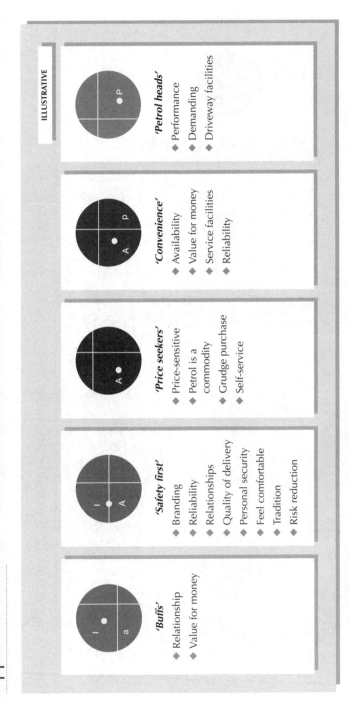

ILLUSTRATIVE

'Bufis'
◆ Relationship
◆ Value for money

'Safety first'
◆ Branding
◆ Reliability
◆ Relationships
◆ Quality of delivery
◆ Personal security
◆ Feel comfortable
◆ Tradition
◆ Risk reduction

'Price seekers'
◆ Price-sensitive
◆ Petrol is a commodity
◆ Grudge purchase
◆ Self-service

'Convenience'
◆ Availability
◆ Value for money
◆ Service facilities
◆ Reliability

'Petrol heads'
◆ Performance
◆ Demanding
◆ Driveway facilities

Product/service category – gasoline

Appendix 2B.1

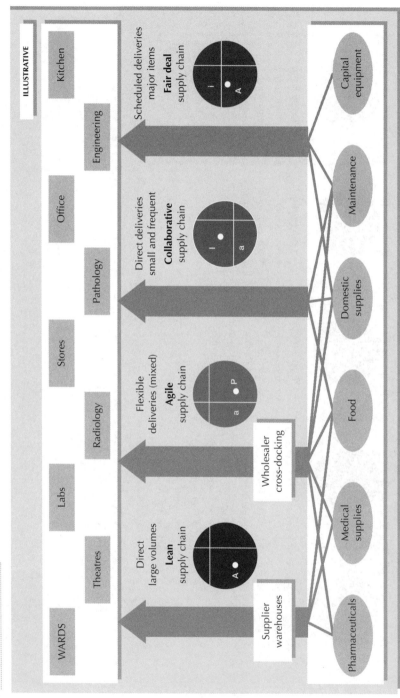

Multiple supply chains in the healthcare industry

Appendix 2B.2

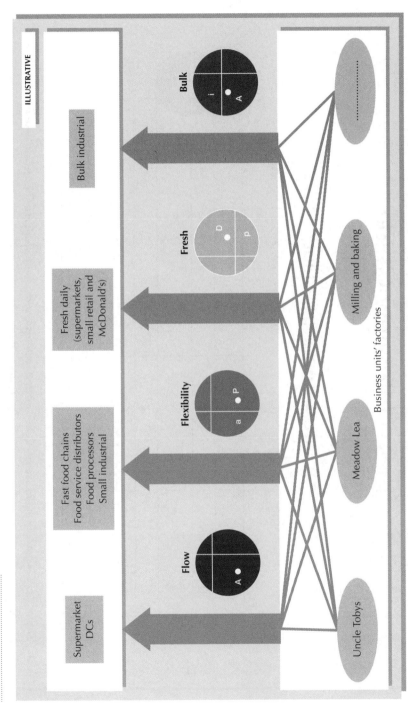

Multiple supply chains in processed food manufacturer Goodman Fielder Limited

Appendix 2C

Segmenting customers along behavioral lines – Interview Guide

CUSTOMER INTERVIEW GUIDE

Customer: .... (In this case, ABC Logistics)

CUSTOMER:	
Interviewee:	
Contact Details Phone:	Email:
Position:	
Appointment Time and Date:	
Interviewed by:	
Background on Company	

Thank you for agreeing to this interview. We are trying to understand more about ABC Logistics' customers and about the aspects of service that different customers value.

First, some background questions:

1. **What services does ABC Logistics provide to your business? What markets are they in?**
   (do not ask this if it is known from research)

   ....

   ....

   ....

   ....

2. How long has ABC Logistics been a provider to your company?
   Do you know why they were originally selected?

   ....

   ....

   ....

   ....

3. Is ABC Logistics a small or large proportion of your total spend on 3PLs?

....

....

....

....

4. Could you describe your strategy in the market that ABC Logistics serves? What role does ABC Logistics play in this strategy?

....

....

....

....

5. What are your fundamental expectations of any business that provides these services?

6. Which is most important? Why?

7. How well does ABC Logistics **perform** against these expectations?

....

....

....

....

8. I would like to ask you some questions now that will help us to understand more fully the relative importance of various aspects of the service you need from a logistics service provider.

For each aspect, I will read you 4 statements. Could you please consider the relative importance of each, and then allocate 100 points between each statement to reflect that importance.

Section A:

	Statements	Score	Logic
a.	That we have a **supportive and involved relationship** with the Logistics Provider		I
b.	That they **respond quickly** to our changing needs		P
c.	That they control costs and keep the **rates down.**		A
d.	That they bring us **new ideas** and approaches		D
		100	

Note any comments made:

....

....

....

Section B:

	Statements	Score	Logic
a.	The Logistics provider is **reliable and consistent** in their performance		A
b.	They keep **up to date** with innovations in their industry		D
c.	They are aware of changes to our service expectations and needs, and **respond**		P
d.	They **understand** and **support** our brand		I

100

Note any comments made:

....

....

....

Section C:

	Statements	Score	Logic
a.	They can come up with **solutions** to get us out of trouble when needed		D
b.	They are known to be highly **trustworthy and reputable**		I
c.	Their management is **readily available** when we need them		P
d.	They have solid **administration and controls** in the business		A

100

Note any comments made:

....

....

....

Section D:

	Statements	Score	Logic
a.	They are adaptable and can work in unpredictable situations		D
b.	They have the **lowest rates** in the industry		A
c.	They are **loyal** and act as a partner		I
d.	They can **make things happen** quickly when necessary		P

100

Note any comments made:

....

....

....

9. Any other comments or feedback?

THANK YOU FOR YOUR TIME

Logic Assessment

QUALITATIVE:

KEY POINTS FROM EXPECTATIONS AND OPEN ENDED QUESTIONS (INCLUDE LOGISTICS FOR EACH):

ILLUSTRATIVE

FORCED CHOICE RESULTS:
Record score in each quadrant

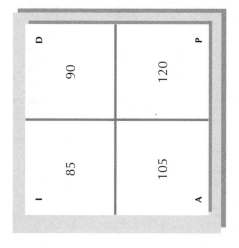

D	
90	85
120	105
P	**A**
	I

OVERALL ASSESSMENT OF 'BUYING' LOGICS:

Appendix 3A.1

Strategy issues associated with the 'pragmatic' segment ('AP' logics)

ILLUSTRATIVE

Value proposition

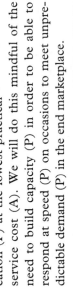

Our aim is to consistently (A) deliver products and services to your customers and your specification (P) at the lowest practical service cost (A). We will do this mindful of the need to build capacity (P) in order to be able to respond at speed (P) on occasions to meet unpredictable demand (P) in the end marketplace.

Value proposition issues

1. Execute to principal specification
2. Keep the principles aware of all the details
3. Risk averse
4. Very close control and monitoring of expenses
5. Forecasting
6. Returns

Capability issues

A. People positioning
B. Re-evaluation of processes
C. IT systems
D. Incentives
E. Role modeling
F. Problem-solving
G. Resource allocation and management

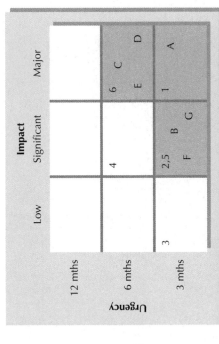

Strategy issues associated with the 'solutions' segment – 'Pd/Id' Logics

ILLUSTRATIVE

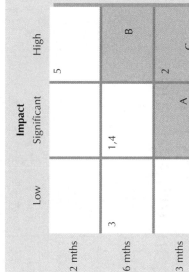

Value proposition

We are committed to finding creative ways (D) to service your market needs, at speed (P). For some of your customers this will mean working with you on a shared basis (I) to find creative solutions (D) and for others we will lead all the way (P).

Value proposition issues

1. Early identification of new opportunities in the market
2. Emphasizing rebuilding trust, especially with the 'Id' principles
3. Adapt to principal's new product ideas
4. Have a steady stream of new products introduction
5. Sharing market intelligence with the principals

Capability issues

A. Market intelligence gathering
B. New products screening methodology
C. Risk management

Appendix 3B

Planning template for converting issues into solutions and actions

ISSUE: Can be negative or positive *Must relate to a vision, which could be value proposition*		ASSUMPTIONS: (As required)		
OBJECTIVE(S) Must be tangible. It must be able to say when complete – timeframes ('by June 2011') – and specific measures ('by 10 per cent')				
STRATEGIES (WHAT)	ACTION STEPS (HOW)	Action responsibility	Start	Complete (WHEN)

Appendix 4A.1

Culture mapping methodology

Organizational Culture Mapping

Organizational culture has been described as the *'psychological life of an organization.'* It is the unwritten values and assumptions that most people in the organization understand and work within – their shared meaning of the situation. More anecdotally it has been described 'as the way we do things around here'.

Culture mapping is a method of understanding and depicting organizational culture. There are various approaches to mapping culture, but what is ultimately important is the usefulness of the results. There is little value in mapping culture where there is no context for what it reveals. The context in the business setting is the strategy that the business wishes to pursue, which in turn is driven by the market or markets in which it operates.

The culture mapping approaches used to support the *dynamic alignment* model produces results which can be easily considered in relation to the other three levels of the alignment framework, i.e. the market, strategy and leadership. In fact, the method of depicting culture uses the same metric system (the PADI logics) that are used throughout alignment.

The organization's culture (and the culture of subgroups) is assessed on nine dimensions, which include autonomy, communication and change tolerance. The nine dimensions measured have been identified in many research studies as key elements of culture (although due to the subjective and perceptual nature of culture there could be an almost infinite number of other dimensions present).

Culture Mapping for Alignment involves a survey of employees that explores their attitudes and beliefs about their workplace. Questions relate to both the *current* situation and the *preferred* situation. The distance between *current* and *preferred* is of interest because it can indicate the level of cultural tension within the group examined, but *preferred* is not considered to be the same as *ideal* culture. *Ideal* culture can only be determined by understanding the marketplace or stakeholders to which the organization must ultimately deliver value. For this reason culture mapping is usually conducted in parallel with some form of market or stakeholder segmentation.

The format of the result of Culture Mapping for Alignment and examples of the information that can be gleaned from the different data and culture dimension cuts are shown below.

Source: Prepared for John Gattorna by Deborah Ellis, Carpenter Ellis, 2009

Appendix 4A.2

Example of a culture map

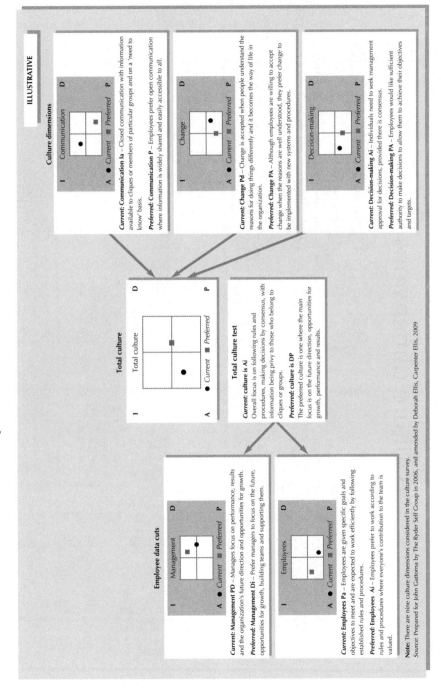

ILLUSTRATIVE

Culture dimensions

Communication

Current: **Communication Ia** – Closed communication with information available to cliques or members of particular groups and on a 'need to know' basis.

Preferred: **Communication P** – Employees prefer open communication where information is widely shared and easily accessible to all.

Change

Current: **Change Pd** – Change is accepted when people understand the reasons for doing things differently and it becomes the way of life in the organization.

Preferred: **Change PA** – Although employees are willing to accept change when the reasons are well understood, they prefer change to be implemented with new systems and procedures.

Decision-making

Current: **Decision-making Ai** – Individuals need to seek management approval for decisions, provided there is consensus.

Preferred: **Decision-making PA** – Employees would like sufficient authority to make decisions to allow them to achieve their objectives and targets.

Total culture

Total culture test

Current: **culture is Ai**
Overall focus is on following rules and procedures, making decisions by consensus, with information being privy to those who belong to cliques or groups.

Preferred: **culture is DP**
The preferred culture is one where the main focus is on the future direction, opportunities for growth, performance and results.

Employee data cuts

Management

Current: **Management PD** – Managers focus on performance, results and the organization's future direction and opportunities for growth.

Preferred: **Management Di** – Prefer managers to focus on the future, opportunities for growth, building teams and supporting them.

Employees

Current: **Employees Pa** – Employees are given specific goals and objectives to meet and are expected to work efficiently by following established rules and procedures.

Preferred: **Employees Ai** – Employees prefer to work according to rules and procedures where everyone's contribution to the team is valued.

Note: There are nine culture dimensions considered in the culture survey.

Source: Prepared for John Gattorna by The Ryder Self Group in 2006, and amended by Deborah Ellis, Carpenter Ellis, 2009

Appendix 4B

Culture dimensions (1)

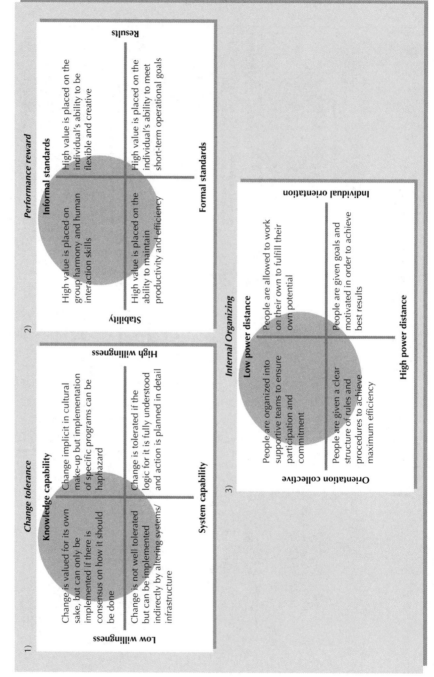

Culture dimensions (2)

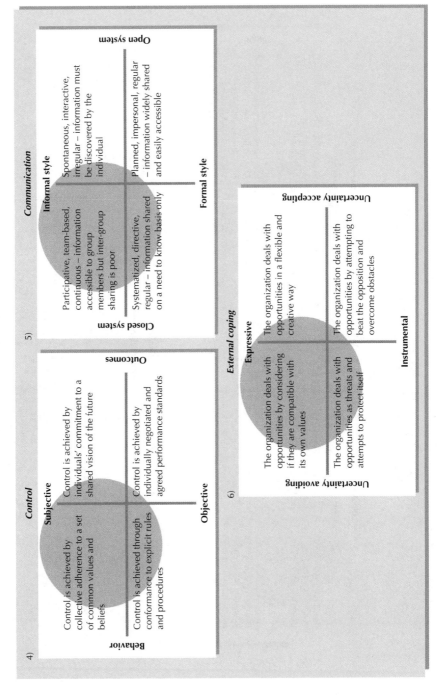

Control

4)

Subjective

Control is achieved by individuals' commitment to a shared vision of the future

Control is achieved by individually negotiated and agreed performance standards

Control is achieved by collective adherence to a set of common values and beliefs

Control is achieved through conformance to explicit rules and procedures

Objective

Behavior

Outcomes

Communication

5)

Informal style

Spontaneous, interactive, irregular – information must be discovered by the individual

Planned, impersonal, regular – information widely shared and easily accessible

Participative, team-based, continuous – information accessible to group members but inter-group sharing is poor

Systematized, directive, regular – information shared on a need to know basis only

Formal style

Open system

Closed system

External coping

6)

Expressive

The organization deals with opportunities in a flexible and creative way

The organization deals with opportunities by attempting to beat the opposition and overcome obstacles

The organization deals with opportunities by considering if they are compatible with its own values

The organization deals with opportunities as threats and attempts to protect itself

Instrumental

Uncertainty accepting

Uncertainty avoiding

Source: Developed from Hofstede data 2006

Culture dimensions (3)

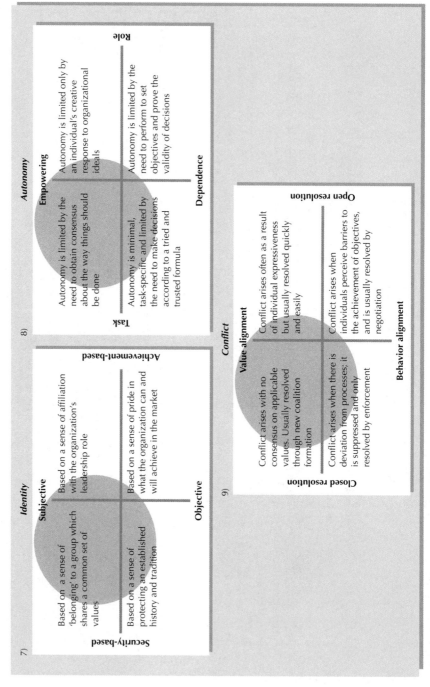

7)

Identity

Subjective

Based on a sense of 'belonging' to a group which shares a common set of values

Based on a sense of affiliation with the organization's leadership role

Based on a sense of protecting an established history and tradition

Based on a sense of pride in what the organization can and will achieve in the market

Security-based

Achievement-based

Objective

8)

Autonomy

Empowering

Autonomy is limited by the need to obtain consensus about the way things should be done

Autonomy is limited only by an individual's creative response to organizational ideals

Autonomy is minimal, task-specific and limited by the need to make decisions according to a tried and trusted formula

Autonomy is limited by the need to perform to set objectives and prove the validity of decisions

Task

Role

Dependence

9)

Conflict

Value alignment

Conflict arises with no consensus on applicable values. Usually resolved through new coalition formation

Conflict arises often as a result of individual expressiveness but usually resolved quickly and easily

Conflict arises when there is deviation from processes; it is suppressed and only resolved by enforcement

Conflict arises when individuals perceive barriers to the achievement of objectives, and is usually resolved by negotiation

Closed resolution

Open resolution

Behavior alignment

Source: Developed from Hofstede data 2006

Appendix 4C

'Quick' culture mapping diagnostic

Source: Prepared for John Gattorna by The Ryder Self Group, 2006

Each question has four statements. **Read each question first** and then rank the four statements, allocating a 4, 3, 2 or 1 to each statement to indicate how often that situation occurs at work, where:

4 = Most often and 1 = Least often

Use 4, 3, 2 or 1 only once when ranking the four statements in each question. Rank all statements.

Management

Current

1. a. Our managers are focused on setting performance targets to be achieved and results

   b. Our managers are focused on analysis, planning and budgets

   c. Our managers are focused on the company's future direction and opportunities for growth

   d. Our managers are focused on building teams and a supportive environment

Employees

Current

2. a. Each of us is given specific goals and objectives to meet

   b. We have clear rules, guidelines and procedures to follow

   c. As individuals, we are expected to work on our own to fulfill our potential

   d. We value everyone's contribution to the team

Communication

Current ☐ ☐ ☐ ☐

3. a. Information is openly shared and easily accessible

   b. We get information on a 'need to know only' basis

   c. We stumble across the information we need

   d. Those who are part of a clique or group are privy to information

Change

Current ☐ ☐ ☐ ☐

4. a. Change works best when everyone understands the reasons for doing things differently

   b. Change works when new systems, rules and procedures are put in place to do things differently

   c. Change is the way of life in our organization

   d. Change is acceptable when we all agree how it should take place

Decision-making

Current ☐ ☐ ☐ ☐

5. a. We can make decisions that allow us to achieve our objectives and targets

   b. We can only make decisions with management approval

   c. We are free to make any decisions we like

   d. We can make decisions as long as everyone agrees

Thank you for taking the time to complete this questionnaire.
Please score your result overleaf

Culture mapping – self-scoring

Instructions

1. Transpose your rankings to each question in the culture mapping questionnaire into the following scoring sheet:

	Q1 Management	Q2 Employees	Q3 Communication	Q4 Change	Q5 Decision-making	TOTAL
P – Producer	1a	2a	3a	4a	5a	
A – Administrator	1b	2b	3b	4b	5b	
D – Developer	1c	2c	3c	4c	5c	
I – Integrator	1d	2d	3d	4d	5d	

2. Add your responses across the table, writing a total score for each row in the total column.

3. Write the total scores into the calculation below to get your Z diagonal and X diagonal plotting scores.

P total _____ *less* **I** total _____ = **Z** plot _____

A total _____ *less* **D** total _____ = **X** plot _____

4. Make a mark on the Z diagonal to represent the Z plot score. If it is a + value, this mark will be somewhere in the P quadrant. If it is a – value, this mark will be somewhere in the I quadrant.

Culture mapping – self-scoring

Instructions cont'd

5. Make a mark on the X diagonal to represent the X plot score. If it is a + value, this mark will be somewhere in the A quadrant. If it is a – value, this mark will be somewhere in the D quadrant.

6. Extrapolate your Z plot at right angles to the Z–Z diagonal, and your X plot at right angles to the X–X diagonal until they intersect. This intersection point is the 'centre-of-gravity' of the culture for the unit being mapped

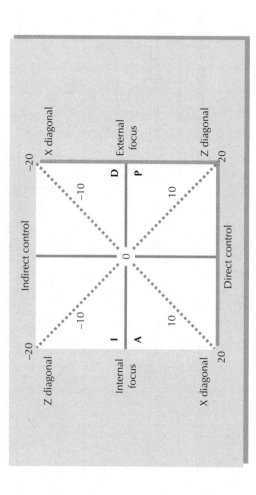

Source: Prepared for John Gattorna by the Ryder Self Group, 2006

Appendix 4D

Change pathways: 'Evolutionary' change (1)

Option 1: Consolidate current position

- Improve cultural coherence
- Remove negative climate influences
- Measure business unit productivity; reward efficiency
- Emphasize past achievements
- Define 'how we do things' statement

Option 2: Move towards Group culture

- Multi-level/functional team-building
- Introduce bottom-up planning
- Reduce power distance; TMT role modeling
- Joint, peer job design
- Personal interaction skills training

Option 3: Move towards Rational culture

- Individual results – based on job design
- Measure performance against objectives
- Reward achievement; speed of response
- Research and wide communication of prevailing market conditions
- Delegate, decentralize decision-making
- Install task force issue resolution process

Source: Adapted from Appendix 3D in Gattorna (2006), p.293

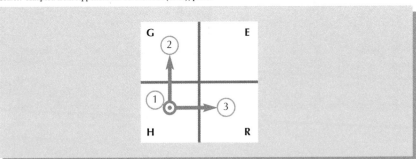

Change pathways: 'Evolutionary' change (2)

Option 1: Consolidate current position

◆ Improve cultural coherence

◆ Remove negative climate influences

◆ Measure by objectives, reward performance

◆ Emphasise current achievements

◆ Define 'what we are fighting for' statement

Option 2: Move towards Hierarchical culture

◆ Direct objectives towards efficiency, productivity, on a collective basis

◆ Centralize 'important' decision-making

◆ Define jobs by method

◆ Develop policy manuals; reward adherence

◆ Control information flows

Option 3: Move towards Entrepreneurial culture

◆ Assign open-ended problems; reward creativity of solutions

◆ Emphasise the long-term 'strategic' view of performance

◆ Reward experimentation/ideas

◆ TMT role model – tolerance of risk and error

◆ Remove all systemic barriers to change

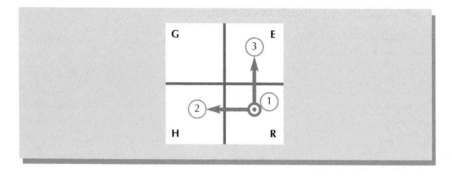

◆ Evaluate knowledge capability and spend (lavishly) on individual development

Source: Adapted from Appendix 3D in Gattorna (2006), p.294

Change pathways: 'Revolutionary' change (1)

Consolidate current position

◆ Nurture any signs of the right momentum

◆ Identify systemic resistance/barriers

◆ Build change power-base

◆ Raise status of R&D function

Phase I: Re-direct system focus

◆ From rules to 'guidelines'

◆ Set market-related objectives for each job

◆ De-centralize structure

◆ Research and communicate pressure for change

◆ Train all personnel in marketing based skills – internal customer service?

◆ Streamline administrative/reporting procedures

◆ Measure market impact; reward individuals

◆ TMT role modeling – high energy

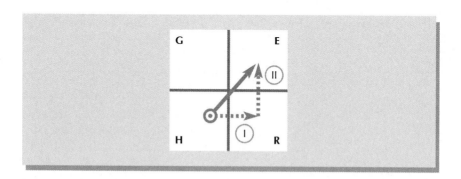

Phase II: Loosen control mechanisms

◆ Recruit individuals with D–P capability

◆ Introduce 'what if' scenario building into planning process

◆ Reduce power-distance; flatten structure

◆ Make individuals accountable

◆ Encourage/reward 'good ideas'

◆ Formulate appropriate human resource management (HRM) strategy

Source: Adapted from Appendix 3D in Gattorna (2006), p.295

Change pathways: 'Revolutionary' change (2)

Consolidate current position

♦ Nurture any signs of the right momentum

♦ Identify sources of philosophical resistance

♦ Select and convert change affiliates

♦ Raise status of operations and marketing functions

Phase I: Make values explicit

♦ Define values, and develop policy manuals based on these values

♦ Formalize communication/meeting practices

♦ Define lines of authority, decision-making

♦ Measure and reward productivity, efficiency

♦ Close control loopholes, especially job descriptions

♦ Training in systems, methods and time management

Phase II: Redirect control mechanisms

♦ Recruit individuals with A–P capability

♦ Introduce appropriate systems and processes

♦ Market awareness communication campaign

♦ Restructure towards product/market matrix

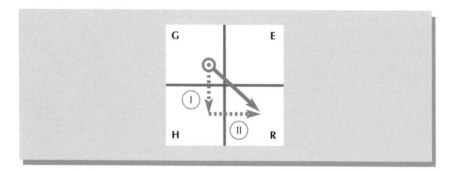

◆ Introduce individual accountabilities for performance Bottom-up planning process

◆ Formulate performance-oriented HRM strategy

Source: Adapted from Appendix 3D in Gattorna (2006), pp.293–96

Appendix 5A

Formulating a vision statement

The task of formulating a vision statement is quite daunting. Certainly, it is rarely achieved by taking executives away on a weekend retreat to debate the future of the organization. Our experience over years of empirical work with top management teams is that a template is required when embarking on this undertaking. This, combined with a facilitated real-time environment, is the only way to achieve a meaningful, yet practical, vision statement. We have developed a vision template through working with hundreds of management teams over two decades; it has four components as indicated below, all of which are essential.

1. Contextual

The first component of our vision template is the context within which the particular organizational unit is operating. Leaders need to consider the role or unique contribution that the unit makes to the larger organization. The idea is to test whether or not the organization has an ongoing role in which a vision is indeed appropriate. In many cases organizations struggle to pass this first hurdle and consequently doubt is cast on long-term viability from the outset. Typically, the internal contributions of supply chains will be in terms of cash generation; working capital reduction; ownership of the pipeline through which products move to market; and custodianship of the inventory.

2. Business definition

In the second component, the organization needs to describe clearly what the business of the organization is now and is likely to be in the future. Too many vision statements fail at this point because they describe the business in terms of what the organization does from day to day – and that may change. However, there is only one way to describe the business or boundary of the organization, and that is in terms of the needs the organization has set out to satisfy, for either internal stakeholders or external customers. If organizations follow this method, their definition of the business will remain constant over time. Contrary to popular opinion, the fundamental needs of customers do not change over time; only the way organizations go about satisfying those needs. That usually has something to do with the ever-changing technology landscape. However, technology and geography, combined with customers' needs, also may be used as part of the 'boundary' definition. So, the vision statement can be thought of as a 'boundary' or 'positioning' statement. This view is consistent with strategic alignment that we use to anchor all our supply chain work. It is also consistent with our view that organizations have supply chains plural rather than one supply chain as envisaged by previous writers on the topic. To understand this concept, think in terms of several conveyor belts running inside an organization, all at different speeds and with different operating characteristics. The same product can travel down any conveyor or pathway.

3. Distinctive competence

Distinctive competence is the third component of our vision statement template and is perhaps the most difficult to understand and operationalize. Internal to the organization, distinctive competence attempts to identify the essential skills, capabilities and resources that underpin current and future success. It involves identifying those things that the organization does particularly well compared to competitors in the same business domain. Generally, a true distinctive competence is not easy to copy or emulate in the short to medium term.

Clearly, you must look for potential distinctive competencies among an organization's strengths. In our experience, most organizations lack this 'silver thread' or 'essence' running through the business, and this is one of the reasons why they are seemingly always struggling to achieve differential advantage in the marketplace; distinctive competencies underpin differential advantages.

If the conclusion is that no such unique competence exists, then try to define what competence you want to build and start the long process of growing it organically within the business. If in the rare case a genuine distinctive competence is uncovered, then the required action is to nurture and develop it further. Unfortunately, there have been many cases over the last few decades where distinctive competencies have been ignored and lost through neglect, very often as an outcome of mergers and acquisitions. In these examples, the business cases on which the mergers/acquisitions were approved will not be delivered.

A defensible distinctive competence, according to Quinn, Doorley and Parquette (1990) in the *Harvard Business Review*[i], usually derives from outstanding depth in human skills, logistics capabilities, knowledge bases, brand loyalty and other intangibles that competitors cannot easily replicate, and which lead to demonstrable value for the customer. In any event, distinctive competences can either be grown organically over time or bought as part of an acquisition, albeit with due care in the latter case. The most difficult distinctive competencies to compete against are those that are qualitative rather than quantitative, for example, a company's culture or tacit knowledge. In both examples, the competence is deeply embedded in the organization and almost impossible to unbundle and extract.

Finally, unlike physical assets, Prahalad and Hamel (1990)[ii] observed that a distinctive competence can be used simultaneously in several applications, does not wear out, and can be combined in various ways to create new opportunities. Indeed, a distinctive competence can be used to screen or filter any new opportunities being considered and, in this way, it helps the organization maintain focus.

4. Future indicators

This final component in the vision statement template is designed to give the overall statement a dynamic character as it is the only component of the four that is likely to change materially from year to year. Future indicators are designed to provide a sense of future direction and the initiatives likely to be pursued in the medium term. In effect, future indicators are a catalog of the organization's major strategies and are important enough to be included in the vision statement. Over time, the organization will modify these directional statements gradually as it weaves a path through its operating environment.

This then completes the template. As indicated, the 'personality' of the organization is best captured in the flavor of its vision statement, and the flavor should ideally reflect the dominant logic of the operating environment. At least four flavors of vision statement are possible, and the one chosen will be embedded eventually in the predominant culture of the organization.

i Quinn, J.B., Doorley, T.L., Paquette, P.C. (1990) 'Beyond products: service-based strategy', *Harvard Business Review*, 68 (March–April), 58–66.
ii Prahalad, C.K. and Hamel, G. (1990), 'The core competence of the corporation', *Harvard Business Review*, 68 (May–June), 79–91.

Appendix 5B

Examples of supply chain vision statements

The supply chain groups of several large organizations in Australia and New Zealand have developed vision statements for their supply chains. The statements illustrate the depth of thinking involved in formulating a vision. While they might look relatively long at first, remember that once the hard graft of formulating a statement is achieved and the vision has been internalized by those involved, the statement can be shortened. Through this process, people will think of the full weight and content of the longer statement when they see the slogan. The names of the companies involved in the examples below are real.[i]

Myer Grace Department Stores (MGDS) supply chain vision

The logistics function within MGDS is the custodian of the supply chain (or pipeline) that links customers with suppliers. Supply Chain is charged with the professional management of those considerable resources that participate in the complex task of moving merchandise through the pipeline, i.e., facilities, systems, personnel and capital. The actual merchandise in the pipeline remains the 'property' of the merchandise function, but we are the facilitators. In effect, supply chain is an internal contractor, which has the potential to influence significantly the Department Stores Group overall profit by optimizing the service-cost equation.

The Supply Chain function has several 'stakeholders', and in meeting their respective needs we effectively define our business. For example:

Suppliers: look to Supply Chain to fulfill elements of the strategic partnership arrangements entered into with the merchandise function for the purpose of achieving mutual profitability.

Merchandise function: is an internal client that requires Supply Chain to shorten the strategic lead times that merchandise inventory is in the pipeline to Stores. Management of this lead time has tremendous leverage on the group's overall profitability. We collaborate with merchandise personnel at the interface with suppliers, and manage the merchandise on their behalf from that point on.

Stores function: is another internal client which requires Supply Chain to deliver merchandise to every store according to previously agreed service levels, and in some cases to arrange final delivery to, and installation in, customers' premises. We also liaise with stores on a range of matters that affect the management of merchandise, such as packaging, price-marking, allocations, storage, facilities design and handling practices at the back door.

We liaise with marketing in regard to promotional campaigns, packaging, and other special conditions that influence the flow of merchandise. Finally, it is our ultimate aim to contribute to customer satisfaction by collaborating with all internal functions, as well as suppliers. Our scope of operations is Australia and New Zealand. Supply Chain owns the methodologies and procedures that facilitate the cost-effective flow of merchandise from suppliers to stores and on to customers. These methodologies include leading edge physical and information systems, supported by a logistics orientation among all our personnel. Because we are responsible for the operation of such a comprehensive network of facilities, we can make things happen.

For the future, the supply chain function intends to develop and implement a blueprint for quantum change that will take Alpha to the forefront of supply chain practice in department stores, worldwide. To achieve this we must institute and manage major changes in the way we currently do things. Our task is to ensure that no competitor out performs MGDS in a supply chain sense; that stock in the 'pipeline' is managed expeditiously, and that the entire supply chain (including the supplier component) comes under our influence – all of which adds up to a competitive advantage for MGDS at the point of sale. We are determined to realize most, if not all, the potential savings available through improved supply chain practices.

For this reason measurement systems and corresponding standards will be established along the supply chain. Technology will be applied as appropriate in the form of hardware and software. In regard to the latter optimization models and other decision support systems will be a priority, as will EDI links with suppliers. We are mindful that supply chain man-ages major elements of the company's assets and as such we will seek to ensure acceptable rates of return on these investments. As an additional incentive, we propose to operate the function as a profit center, servicing its various stakeholders to pre-arranged service levels for a predetermined cost to them.

DHL Airways Express Logistics vision

DHL Airways Express Logistics exists to enhance and complement DHL Airways' current business, and to tap new emerging opportunities in the international express distribution market. DHL Airways is com-mitted to expanding its service offering to selected customers and we have an important role in this expansion program. In the process, DHL Airways Express Logistics will increase in sophistication – which will have a positive spin-off on the core business, increase competitiveness, build customer loyalty, and contribute to corporation profits. However, it is important that our management remains fully cognizant of the impact that the logistics operation may have on existing network facilities and other key resources servicing the core business.

Our business is to facilitate the cost-effective, time definite movement of product through customers' supply chains, worldwide. In this, we effec-tively reduce the risk and complexity for our customers, thus allowing them to focus on their respective business(es). For our part, it is essential that we gain an in-depth understanding of customers' business and adopt a consultative selling approach, supported by advanced decision support technology, when formulating appropriate response(s). Such an approach will be able to change the 'rules' in the marketplace and dilute the current preoccupation with transport rates.

We have a truly global company at our disposal, providing an inter-national network of express shipping, pick-up and delivery capabilities, interconnected with a reservoir of local knowledge about individual country-markets worldwide. We also have an adaptive culture, capable of flexible responses to customers' needs and a desire to access further com-petencies relevant to our business (e.g., relationship management of other suppliers of specialist services in the supply chain).

For the future, it is important that we position DHL Airways in that part of the overall third party logistics services spectrum which best protects and leverages our evolving core competencies. This will involve careful market segmentation and ultimately, selection of customers with genuine international requirements – which we feel we can meet within specified resource limitations – and whose products have handling and market characteristics, which align with our capabilities. Development of our logistics services portfolio will be evolutionary, consistent with our experience curve. It is important that we avoid the 'over-customization trap', and instead develop a portfolio of standard service products which are capable of being combined in unique ways to satisfy the individual needs of our customers.

In that it is likely that we will necessarily have to enter into and play the lead role in developing strategic relationships with key suppliers, we should continue to develop our sourcing and relationship management skills.

i Myer Grace Department Stores have since split into two separate entities: Myer Stores and Grace Bros. Stores.

Appendix 7A.1

Supply chain relationship *enablers* – at three levels

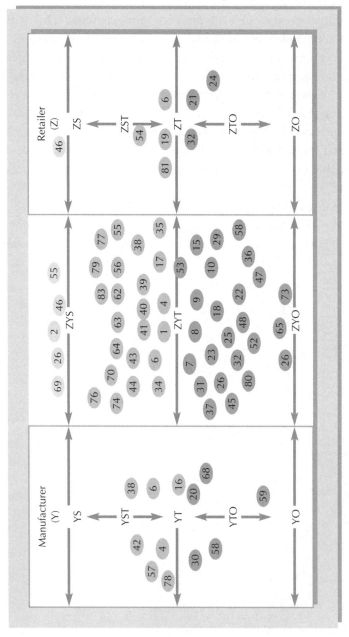

Source: Barratt, Mark A. (2002). See endnote 5 in Chapter 7 for full bibliographical details.

Key for relationship enablers

STRATEGIC
2 Board to board dialogue
26 Multiple level relationships
46 Senior management commitment
55 Communicable strategy
69 Ongoing board level dialogue

TACTICAL
1 Advanced problem notification
4 Capability to share information
6 Collaborative/information-based culture
16 Information critical mass
17 Information quality
19 Interdependency recognition
34 Mutual understanding
35 Mutual agreed processes
38 Openness
39 Opportunism versus collaboration
40 People relationship skills
41 Proactive approach
42 Problems not symptoms
43 Relationship commitment
44 Relationship manager

54 Benefit demonstration
55 Communicable strategy
56 Context dependent relationship
57 Creative thinking
62 Full process review
63 Individual chemistry
64 Integrated relationships
70 People relationship facilitators
74 Supply chain manager
76 System enabled processes
77 Understanding buying behavior
78 Understanding demand aggregation
79 Understanding information requirements
81 Understanding role of suppliers
83 Vendor managed inventory

OPERATIONAL
7 Common objectives and goals
8 Common philosophies
9 Communication
10 Communication mechanisms
15 Identifying communication channels
18 Integrated suppy chain plan

20 Internal communication
21 Internal understanding
22 Joint replenishment decisions
23 Jointly defined processes
24 Long-term commitment
25 Mean what is said
26 Multiple level relationships
30 Mutual honesty
31 Mutual recognition
32 Mutual respect
36 Ongoing partner recognition
37 Ongoing trust development
45 Seeking industry best practice
47 Share future plans
48 Shared KPIs
52 Understanding partner's issues
58 Customer implants
59 Customer team clusters
65 Integrated supply chain operations
68 Maintain current information
73 Solving operational issues
80 Understanding role of people

Source: Barratt, Mark A. (2002)

Appendix 7A.2

Supply chain relationship *inhibitors* – at three levels

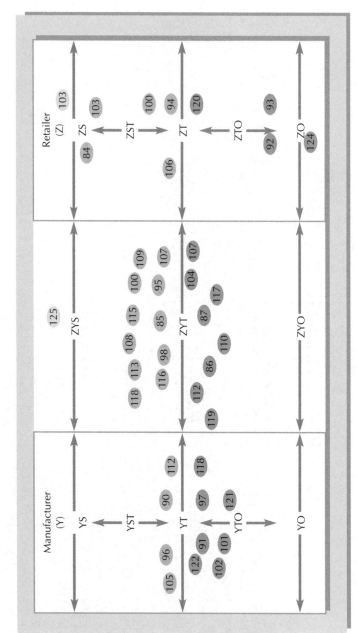

Source: Barratt, Mark A. (2002)

Key for relationship *inhibitors*

STRATEGIC

103 Mechanistic relationship behavior
125 Poor strategic relationships

TACTICAL

84 Adopting a 'customer' mentality
85 Commercial pressures
90 Forecast driven DC
94 Increasing competitive environment
95 Information exchange accuracy
96 Information overload
98 Joint initiative resources
100 Lacking senior management commitment and support
105 Not sharing future production plans
106 Panic buying behavior
107 Perceived supplier performance
109 Poor personal relationships
112 Role of EPOS
113 Short-term focus
116 Timeliness of information exchange
118 Collaboration slippage

OPERATIONAL

86 Cost-focused
87 Cultural differences
91 Forecast-driven production
92 Functional-based teams
93 Functional silo mentality
97 Information starved
101 Managing change
102 Managing promotions
104 Misunderstanding decision implications
107 Perceived supplier performance
110 Product lead-times
112 Role of EPOS
117 Underestimating the scale of change required
118 Collaboration slippage
119 Differing trading strategies
120 Functional management style
121 Information location
122 Organizational size
124 Poor in-house logistics

Source: Barratt, Mark A. (2002)

· 463 ·

Strategic partnering technique – overview

'*No matter how much the world changes, buyers, sellers and third parties will always need each other.*' (Anon)

Perhaps the single most strategic issue facing companies today is the overhaul and consequent re-design of their supply chains, i.e., the commercial and physical arrangements made with other parties in order to provide consumers or corporate users with access to products and services. This pressure for change has been brought about through rapid developments in most marketplaces.

Unfortunately, in most industrial situations the conflict between the various parties in distribution channels and supply chains continues, generally with a 'zero-sum' result. Often conflict arises because buyers and suppliers have different expectations of each other's role in the value-adding process of selling and distribution. Conflict can also arise when one member in a supply chain introduces innovations which ensure the benefits remain with the innovator, while corresponding costs flow to the parties in other parts of the chain.

However, perhaps the major source of conflict between supply chain parties is the lack of understanding each has of the other's business and respective market positioning. Usually, one party is more sophisticated than the other, and consequently a 'mis-communication gap' can easily arise between the two. Strategic Partnering can help close this gap, and get the two parties relating to each other in a much more positive fashion. Our experience is that in such situations, resources are better allocated and a 'win–win' condition arises wherein **both** parties achieve additional profitability – to their mutual satisfaction.

The important thing here is that two parties in a given supply chain commit to a **unique** rather than **exclusive** relationship, and that this relationship is systematized rather than simply relying on more fragile personal contacts.

Customer/supplier loyalty – the key to success

Enlightened enterprises throughout the world are recognizing the value of developing sustained cooperation with other supply chain members. Enduring cooperative relationships are the key to successful marketing in the new millennium as indicated below in a modified version of Raphael's ladder of loyalty. Too often we work tirelessly to move a customer (or supplier in the reverse case) up through the various phases of customer loyalty, as depicted, only to lose them at the Advocate stage. Often getting them back on the bottom rung of the ladder is much more costly in time and money than careful 'maintenance' of the relationship would have been in the first instance. But by then it's too late.

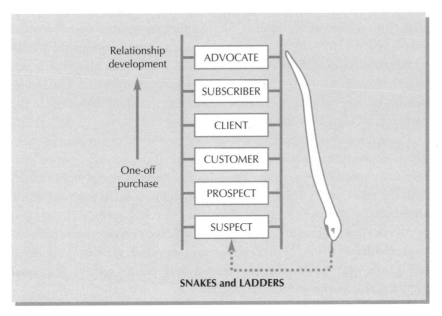

Raphael's ladder of loyalty

Upgrading the relationship

Our experience indicates that many of the problems that arise between buyers and suppliers occur because managers take a low level and generally unplanned approach to the relationship, i.e., solving operational problems as they arise. However, the secret is to set the correct context early – at the highest possible managerial level – and then cascade the understanding which arises from this meeting of minds downwards through the two collaborating organizations via a series of horizontal communications between the two. The workshop-driven methodology we have developed to achieve this is described next.

Appendix 7B.2

Strategic partnering technique – steps

Process methodology

Step 1 Vision formulation

This step produces vision (or philosophical) 'what we stand for' statements from both parties. The process significantly reinforces the awareness of the necessity to understand each other's business position and aspirations. It also prepares the way for an understanding of any conflict points wherein the companies may not fundamentally share the same objectives, *yet both exist to serve the same end user or consumer.*

Step 2 Environmental scan

This step seeks to flush out and understand the various elements of the economic, government, consumer and organizational environment which do, or would, influence the proposed 'partnership.'

Step 3 Issues formulation

This step solicits and documents critical issues from both individual companies and jointly held perspectives. These issues are seen to be significant in as much as they can have a major impact on performance in a predetermined time frame.

Step 4 Issues identification and definition

This step 'tests' each issue with pressure questions in an attempt to understand the rationale for its selection. The objective is to clearly sort out symptoms and causes.

Step 5   Issues prioritization

This step determine and graphically documents the position of the issues on an impact/urgency matrix to ensure that the resources available are allocated correctly. It also provides the key to the ongoing monitoring of issues which require attention when further resources become available.

Step 6   Issues break-out

This step translates the issues (those selected as critical, given the resources) into

- Assumptions
- Objectives
- Strategies
- Action plans
- Time frames
- Budgets
- Monitor points
- Responsibilities

and ensures that both partners in the 'partnership' understand and agree on what is to be done, by whom, and by when, to achieve the jointly agreed results.

Appendix 7B.3

Strategic partnering technique – methodology

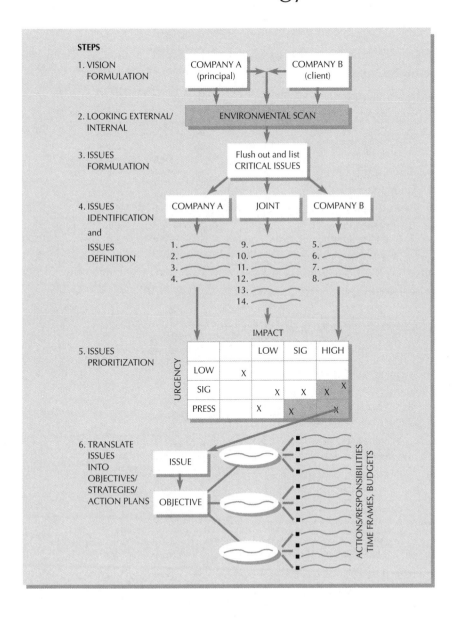

STEPS

1. VISION
   FORMULATION

2. LOOKING EXTERNAL/
   INTERNAL

3. ISSUES
   FORMULATION

4. ISSUES
   IDENTIFICATION
   and
   ISSUES
   DEFINITION

5. ISSUES
   PRIORITIZATION

6. TRANSLATE
   ISSUES
   INTO
   OBJECTIVES/
   STRATEGIES/
   ACTION PLANS

Appendix 8A

Phases in developing a network optimization model

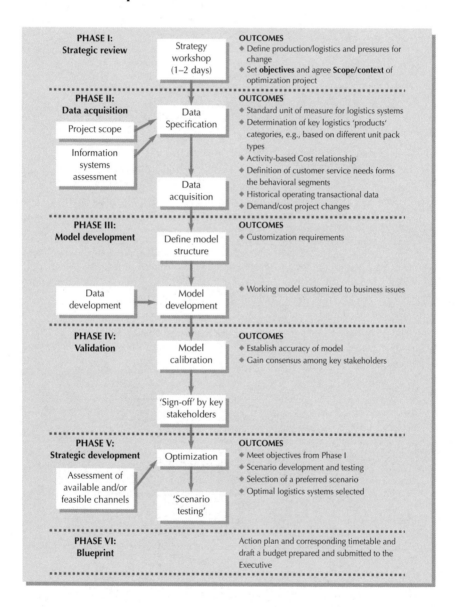

Notes

Chapter 1

1 Gattorna, John (2009), 'Fix your supply chains and you fix the company (and the Economy)', *Supply Chain Asia*, May/June, pp. 24–25.

2 'Thriving in a recession: value chain strategies at work', from the AMR Research *Value Chain Strategies Team*, 16 April 2008.

3 James, David (2006), *Leading Edge*, a column in *Business Review Weekly* Magazine, 16–22 November, p. 57.

4 Simon, Bernard and Reed, John (2009), 'GM announces rebirth with vow to start listening to its customers', *Financial Times*, Saturday 11 July/Sunday 12 July/Asia edition, p. 1.

5 Ibid.

6 Surowiecki, James (1998), 'Dark days at Sunbeam', *The Motley Fool*, posted Friday April 17 at 12:30am ET, www.slate.com/id/2650.

7 I am indebted to Emeritus Professor Malcolm McDonald who coined this term.

8 CFROI = [(Cash flow from operations / capital – capital charge], generally expressed as a percentage. CFROI percentage spread correlates positively with share price and market capitalization.

9 The business units that comprised Goodman Fielder at the time were: Ingredients, Meadow Lea Foods, Milling & Baking, Steggles and Uncle Tobys.

10 Kirby, Julia (2003) "Supply chain challenges: building relationships", a conversation with Scott Beth, David N. Burt, William Copacino, Chris Gopal, Hau L. Lee, Robert Porter Lynch and Sandra Morris', *Harvard Business Review*, July, pp. 64–73.

11 This is the author's own assessment based on more than 100 consulting assignments.

12 Jackson, Tony (1998) 'Melding of minds to master the intangibles – management sharing knowledge', *Financial Times*, 15 June, 15 Online edition, sourced from http://global.factiva.com.simsra.cl.net.ocs.mq.edu.au/ha/default.aspx.

13 Friedman, Thomas, L. (2005) *The World is Flat: A Brief History of the Twenty-first Century*, Farrar, Strauss & Giroux, NY.

14 Friedman, Tom (2009), Interview with Leigh Sales on *ABC Lateline*, 26 March 2009. Refer www.abc.net.au/lateline/content/2008/s2527420.htm

15 Neuschel, Robert P. (1967) 'Physical distribution – forgotten frontier', *Harvard Business Review*, March–April, Vol. 45, No. 2, pp. 125–134.

16 Stolle, John F. (1967) 'How to manage physical distribution', *Harvard Business Review*, July–August, Vol. 45, No. 4, pp. 93–100.

17 *See Signature Concepts* at www.johngattorna.com.

18 Porter, Michael E. (1979) 'How competitive forces shape strategy', *Harvard Business Review*, March–April, Vol. 57, No. 2, pp. 137–145.

19 Advertisement for one-day national management conference in Dublin and Manchester, in *business life*, the in-house magazine published by British Airways, September 2004.

20 'Siberian Siren', *Sunday Times*, Singapore, 11 July 2004, p. 31.

21 Chessell, James (2005) 'Lion boss eschews champagne tastes', *Sydney Morning Herald*, Monday 23 May, p. 34.

22 Bryan, Lowell L. and Joyce, Claudia (2005) 'The 21st-century organization', *McKinsey Quarterly*, No. 3, pp. 25–33.

23 Akumatsu, K. (1962) 'A historical pattern of economic growth in developing countries', *Japanese Economic History 1600–1962*, Vol. 1, pp. 1–23. Akumatsu applied the wild geese analogy to economic theory, specifically the adoption of new technology by Asian nations.

24 Photograph from Getty Images: The Australian 4,000 metre men's pursuit cycling team competing at the Beijing Olympics.

25 Coase, R.H. (1937) 'The nature of the firm', an essay in *4 Economica NS*, pp. 386–405, quoted in Williamson, O.E. and Winter, S.G. (eds) (1991) *The Nature of the Firm*, Oxford University Press, New York, NY, pp. 19–31.

26 Shiller, Robert J.(2009), in an interview with Leigh Sales on *ABC Lateline*, 4 February, 2009.

27 Labovitz, G. and Rosansky, V. (1997) *The Power of Alignment: How great companies stay centred and accomplish extraordinary things*, John Wiley & Sons, New York, NY.

28 Chorn, N.H. (1987) 'The relationship between business-level strategy and organizational culture', unpublished PhD thesis, Witwatersrand University, Johannesburg.

29 Gattorna Strategy Consultants Pty Ltd, Sydney, Australia, 1985–95.

30 See Adler, G., Fordham, M. and Read, H. (eds) (1971) *The Collected Works of CG Jung Volume 6: Psychological Types* (translated by R.F.C. Hull), Bollingen Series 20, Princeton University Press, Ewing, NJ.

31 Adizes, Ichak (1979) *How to Solve the Mismanagement Crisis*, 1st printing, Dow-Jones-Irwin; 5th Printing (1985), Adizes Institute, Santa Monica, CA.

32 Gerard W. Faust, President, Faust Management Corporation, Poway, CA (previously President of the Adizes Institute).

33 Gosfield, Josh and Lopez, Nola (1996) 'Levi's changes everything', *Fast Company*, No. 3, June/July.

34 Huckboy, Jamie (2005) 'Queen B', in *Harper's Bazaar*, September, pp. 118–120.

35 Fly-by-wire technology is an electronically managed flight system, which uses computers to make the aircraft easier to handle, while further enhancing performance and safety. More details can be found at www.airbus.com. See also Gattorna, J. (ed.) (1998) *Strategic Supply Chain Alignment: Best practice in supply chain management*, Gower Publishing, Aldershot, pp. 633–634.

36 An observation frequently made to the author during his research and consulting.

37 Russell, Jeffrey (2009), 'Rapid and sustained cost management: a tool for unprecedented times', *Supply Chain Asia*, March/April, p. 17.

Chapter 2

1 These additional building blocks include 'fit' of personnel in the organizational structure, internal communications, performance measurement regimes and incentives, planning systems, training and development initiatives, recruitment and role modeling.

2 Holweg, Mattias and Pil, Frits K. (2001) 'Successful build-to-order strategies start with the customer', *MIT Sloan Management Review*, Vol. 43, No. 1, Fall, pp. 74–83.

3 Standard Industrial Classification (SIC) is the US government system for classifying industries to enable the analysis of data by different industry types.

4 Davenport, Thomas H., Harris, Jeanne G. and Kohli, Ajay K. (2001), 'How do they know their customers so well?', *MIT Sloan Management Review*, Vol. 42, No. 2, Winter, p. 63.

5 Ibid.

6 Ings-Chambers, Edwina (2004) 'In the mood', *Financial Times*, 30–31 October, p. W14.

7 Nunes, Phil F. and Cespedes, Frank V. (2003) 'The customer has escaped', *Harvard Business Review*, No. 81, Issue 11, November, pp. 96–105.

8 Ibid., p. 105.

9 Fisher, Marshall L. (1997) 'What is the right supply chain for your product?', *Harvard Business Review*, Vol. 75, No. 2, March–April, pp. 105–116.

10 Ibid., p. 106.

11 Ibid., p. 109.

12 Lee, Hau L. (2002) 'Aligning supply chain strategies with product uncertainties', *California Management Review*, Vol. 44, No. 3, Spring, pp. 105–119.

13 Ibid., p. 119.

14 Johnson, Alan (2004) 'Decision time for consumer manufacturers', *Manufacturing Monthly*, May, p. 26.

15 Booz Allen Hamilton (2003) Smart Customization: Profitable Growth Through Tailored Business Streams, White Paper, 7 pp.

16 Ibid., p. 1

17 Byrnes, Jonathan (2005) 'You only have one supply chain?', *Working Knowledge*, Harvard Business School, 1 August. Sourced from http://www.hbswk.hbs.edu.

18 Ibid.

19 Ibid.

20 Ibid.

21 A.T. Kearney (2004) *How Many Supply Chains Do You Need?*, 13 pp., A.T. Kearney, Chicago, IL.

22 Godsell, Janet (2005) 'Demand chain strategy: the missing link', *Management Focus*, Cranfield School of Management, No. 22, Spring, pp. 4–7.

23 Ibid., p. 7.

24 Melnyk, Steven A., Davis, Edward W., Spekman, Robert E., and Sandor, Joseph, in a short article adapted from 'Outcome-Driven Supply Chains', which appeared in the Winter 2010 Issue of MIT *Sloan Management Review*.

25 Anderson, David (2005), 'Quick-change supply chain', *ASCET*, Vol. 7, 13 September, 6 pp. Sourced from http://www.ascet.com/documents.asp?d_ID=3432.

26 Ibid., p. 1.

27 Nunes, Phil F. and Cespedes, Frank V. (2003) 'The customer has escaped', *Harvard Business Review*, Vol. 81, No. 11, November, pp. 96–105.

28 Ibid., p. 100.

29 Hall, Louise, and Robotham, Julie (2009), 'Hospital to divide and conquer waiting lists', *Sydney Morning Herald*, Wednesday 29 July, 2009, p. 5.

30 Monahan, Sean and Nardone, Robert (2007), 'How Unilever aligned its supply chain', *Supply Chain Management Review*, November 2007, p. 48.

31 As defined by Hofstede, who was one of first to extensively research the influence of national cultures on work-related values. One of his early articles: Hofstede, Geert (1983) 'National cultures in four dimensions', *International Studies of Management and Organization*, Vol. 13, No. 1/2, Spring/Summer, pp. 49–74.

32 Adapted from original work first published by Gattorna Strategy Consultants Pty Ltd, (1991) 'Pathways to Customers: reducing complexity in the logistics pipeline', *Strategy Spotlight*, Vol. 1, No. 2, October, pp. 21–30.

33 *Zara* (2003) 'Case study', written by Ferdows, K., Machuca, J.A.D. and Lewis, M. Available from The European Case Clearing House, Cranfield University, England and USA, 15 pp.

34 Lee, H.L (2004) 'The Triple-A supply chain', *Harvard Business Review*, Vol. 83, No. 1, October, pp. 102–112.

35 Ibid., p. 112.

36 McAdam, R. and Brown, L. (2001) 'Strategic alignment and the supply chain for the steel stockholder sector: an exploratory case study analysis', *Supply Chain Management: An International Journal*, Vol. 6, No. 2, pp. 83–94.

37 August, B. (2002) 'Aligning the supply chain to anticipate developing market trends', unpublished conference paper, delivered at the Kenan Institute, Asia, March.

38 Evans, Simon (2005) 'New Foster's unit flexes muscle', *Australian Financial Review*, 30 May, p. 16.

39 Ibid.

40 Gettler, Leon (2005) 'Foster's has a big ambition, a very big ambition', *The Age*, 28 September, p. 14.

41 After Kim, W. Chan and Mauborgne, R. (2005) *Blue Ocean Strategy: How to create uncontested market space and make the competition irrelevant*, Harvard Business School Press, Boston, MA.

42 See forthcoming paper in *Interfaces*, by Coltman, Tim, Gattorna, John and Whiting, Stuart, 'Realigning service operations strategy at DHL Express', due 2010; 40, 3, 175–183. http://interfaces.journal.informs.org/current.dtl.

43 For example, in a market with just a few major customers, each customer in effect can be equivalent to a market. In these situations more sophisticated techniques are required to identify the different buying behaviors present inside each major customer.

44 Prof. Andy Fearne of Kent University (UK) is doing a lot of ground-breaking work in this area.

45 SLIM, designed at MIT by Professor Jeremy Shapiro and associates.

46 Wagner, Stephen N., Bolton, Jamie M. and Nuthall, Linda (2003) 'Supply chain network optimization modeling', Chapter 2.1 in Gattorna, John L. (ed.), *Handbook of Supply Chain Management*, Gower Publishing, Aldershot, pp. 89–104; and Jimenez, Sue, Brown, Tim and Jordan, Joe (1998) 'Network-modeling tools: enhancing supply-chain decision-making', Ch. 19 in Gattorna, John (ed.), *Strategic Supply Chain Alignment*, Gower Publishing, Aldershot, pp. 302–324.

Chapter 3

1 Christopher, Martin, Peck, Helen and Towill, Denis, 'A taxonomy for selecting global supply chain strategies', *International Journal of Logistics Management*, Vol. 17, No. 2, 2006, p. 277.

2 Refer to article by the author: 'The key to successful innovation in enterprise supply chains', *Supply Chain Asia*, November/December 2009, pp. 18–19.

3 See Ch. 16 in Gattorna (2009), *Dynamic Supply Chain Alignment*, Gower Publishing, 'DHL Taiwan: Aligning the express business with customers', by Stuart Whiting, pp. 221–238.

4 Linfox Logistics, operating in Australia, New Zealand and across 11 Asian countries have adopted this approach, reducing their client base from 312 to 101 in the past two years and at the same time doubling revenue and profit.

5 The company is Elgeka S.A, one of Greece's largest FMCG distributors of branded goods.

6 Spivey, Duane, (2009), 'The OODA loop and learning', *Chief Learning Officer*, Vol. 8, pp. 30–33.

7 Baker, B., (2006), 'Timely decisions', in *PM Network*, p. 20.

Chapter 4

1 Anders, George (2003) 'The Carly Chronicles,' *Fast Company*, February, p. 70.

2 Coutts, Louis (2004) 'Culture clubs,' *Business Review Weekly*, July 22–28, p. 57.

3 Schien, Edgar H. (1992) *Organizational Culture and Leadership*, 2nd ed, Jossey-Bass., San Francisco, CA, p. 12.

4 Characteristics of the 'dark side' were prepared for John Gattorna by The Ryder Self Group, and derived from their organizational culture mapping work over the past 20 years. Since 2004, the 'dark side' has been clearly differentiated for each of the four generic subcultures.

5 Cameron, Kim S. and Quinn, Robert E. (2000) published details of their Organizational Culture Assessment Instrument (OCAI) in *Diagnosing and Changing Culture*, Pearson Education, Upper Saddle River, N.J. Their framework is very similar to our own P-A-D-I based framework applied to mapping culture, which was developed a decade earlier.

6 Hofstede, Geert (1980) *Culture's Consequences: International Differences in Work-Related Values* (Cross Cultural Research and Methodology), Sage Publications, Newbury Park, CA.

7 Firoz, Nadeem M., Maghrabi, Ahmad S. and Kim, Ki Hee (2002) 'Think globally manage culturally,' *International Journal of Commerce and Management*, Vol. 12, Nos. 3 and 4, pp. 32–50.

8 Hofstede, Geert & Associates (1998) *Masculinity and Femininity: The Taboo Dimension of National Cultures*, Sage Publications, Newbury Park, CA.

9 Fonterra behavioral segmentation analysis carried out in 2000–01.

10 First mentioned in a *Fortune* article by an executive of Texas Instruments in the 1980s.

11 'Reinventing Motorola', *Business Week*, 9 August 2004, p. 98.

12 'Culture change inspires revival', Leo D'Angelo Fisher interviews Peter Widdows, in *Business Review Weekly*, February 8-14, 2007, pp. 52–53.

13 Neilson, Gary L. and Pasternack, Bruce A. (2005) 'The cat that came back,' *strategy+business*, No. 40, Fall, pp. 32–45.

14 Timmons, Heather (2007), 'Culture blamed for BP blast', *Australian Financial Review* (January 17), p. 9. Reprinted from the *New York Times*.

15 Petronius, AD 66, Roman Centurion.

16 General Accident has since merged worldwide with Commercial Union to form one global company, CGU Insurance Group.

17 Stevens, Greg (2003) 'Changing a culture to become more innovative – faster than ever before', *inKNOWvations*, February, 4 pp.

18 Ibid., p. 2.

19 Ibid.

20 Evans, Simon (2005) 'New CEO wants Amcor out of the silo', *Australian Financial Review*, Thursday 25 August, p. 19.

21 Refer to Blackmores brochure, 'People, Product, and Passion', p. 2. www.blackmores. com.au

22 I am indebted to Andrea Ehlers for making me aware of this trend. Andrea is Director of a Sydney-based commercial interior design firm specializing in 'brand and the built environment'.

23 This is quoted verbatim from a conversation the author had with Andrea Ehlers, one of the Watermark Architecture consultants who took part in the AMP project that helped turn the company around.

24 Beer, Michael and Eisenstat, Russell A. (2000) 'The silent killers of strategy implementation and learning', *Sloan Management Review*, MIT, Summer, Vol 41, No. 4, p. 29.

25 Ibid., pp. 31–32.

Chapter 5

1 Kotter, John P. (1990) 'What leaders really do', *Harvard Business Review*, May–June, pp. 103–111.

2 Ibid., pp. 105 and 107.

3 Ibid., p. 103.

4 Deborah Ancona, Thomas W. Malone, Wanda J. Orlikowski, and Peter Senge, 'In praise of the incomplete leader', *Harvard Business Review*, February, 2007, pp. 92.

5 Ibid.

6 Hanley, Mike, (2005) 'Really, truly – forget charisma. The latest leadership gift is authenticity. And if it doesn't come naturally, you can learn to be real', *Australian Financial Review BOSS*, May, pp. 52–5. Article based on a forthcoming book by Goffee, Rob and Jones, Gareth, *Why Should Anyone Be Led by You*, Harvard Business School Press, Boston, MA., 2009.

7 Ibid., p. 52.

8 Sir Clive Woodward's speech at the Chartered Institute of Transport and Logistics (CILT) Annual Conference, Birmingham, 26 June, 2007.

9 Refer www.eyethinksport.com for more information.

10 Grenny, Joseph, 'Leadership international influence', *Business Week*, Special Report, June 5, 2009, p. 1.

11 Ibid., p. 2.

12 Clarke, John (2005) *Working with Monsters: how to identify and protect yourself from the workplace psychopath*, Random House Australia, Sydney.

13 Ibid., pp. 56–57.

14 Cromie, Ali (2005) 'The Big Profit' Interview with Chip Goodyear, CEO BHP Billiton, on *Business Sunday*, Nine Network, Australia, 28 August.

15 Ashlee Vance, 'A tough second act for the executive that revitalized HP', *International Herald Tribune*, Business Asia with Reuters, Monday 27 April, 2009, p. 14.

16 Mentioned in a review by Brian Bremner, 'The gaijin who saved Nissan', *Business Week*, 31 January 2005, p. 12. Bremner was reviewing the book by Carlos Ghosn and Philippe Ries, *SHIFT: Inside Nissan's Historic Revival*, Currency/Doubleday, 2005.

17 Hilb, Martin (2005) 'New corporate governance: from good guidelines to great practice', *New Corporate Governance*, Vol. 13, No. 5, September, pp. 569–581.

18 Refer to article by Miranda Devine, 'A bureaucratic child of our times', in *The Sydney Morning Herald*, April 24–25, 2010, p. 7.

19 Geoff Colvin, 'Leader machines', in *Fortune*, 1 October, 2007, p. 60.

20 Ibid., p. 65

21 Ibid., p. 66.

22 Ibid., pp. 66–67.

23 Ibid., p. 67.

24 Ibid.

25 Ibid.

26 Schieffer, Alexander (2003) 'The Essence of Leadership and the Power of Networks: an Interview with Margaret Wheatley', *Reflections*, Vol. 4., No. 4, pp. 69.

27 Ibid.

28 The Myers-Briggs Type Indicator or MBTI® is the original and best known instrument in its category. It is the registered trademark of Consulting Psychologists Press, California.

29 Another possible instrument is the Predictive Index (PI), but the disadvantage of this is that it then has to be translated into the P-A-D-I code to be of any use in making comparisons.

30 Burrows, Peter (2005) 'The new broom starts to sweep at HP', *Australian Financial Review*, 25–26 June, p. 30.

31 Burrows, Peter (2001) 'The radical: Carly Fiorina's bold management experiment at HP', *BusinessWeek*, February 8; online edition www.businessweek.com.

32 Ibid.

33 Salter, Chuck (2004) 'And now the hard part; JetBlue is cool. Can David Neeleman make it great?', *Fast Company*, May, pp. 66–75.

34 Fung, Victor, Fung, William K. and Wind, Yoram (Jerry) (2008) *Competing in a Flat World; Building Enterprises for a Borderless World*, Wharton School Publishing, Upper Saddle River, NJ.

35 Lee, Hau L. (2004) 'The Triple-A Supply Chain', *Harvard Business Review*, October, pp. 102–112.

36 Ibid, p. 112.

37 See Gattorna, John L. and Tang, M. (2003) 'Formulating a supply chain vision', Ch. 1.2 in Gattorna, John L. (ed.) *Handbook of Supply Chain Management*, 5th edn, Gower Publishing, Aldershot, pp. 11–35.

38 Van Lee, Reggie, Fabish, Lisa and McGaw, Nancy (2005) 'The value of corporate values', *strategy+business*, No. 39, pp. 1–14.

39 'In praise of Peter Drucker', *The Guardian*, 17 November 2005, p. 34.

Chapter 6

1 Remember what the Japanese General said after the successful attack on Pearl Harbor which brought the US into World War II: 'The seeds of tomorrow's failures are sown in today's success', or words to that effect.

2 Gattorna, John (2006) *Living Supply Chains*, Ch.2., pp. 30–66.

3 This is the same as Figure 2.4 in Ch. 2.

4 Kim, Soo Wook (2007) 'Organizational structures and the performance of supply chain management', *International Journal of Production Economics*, Vol. 106, pp. 323–345.

5 Gulati, Ranjay (2007), 'Silo Busting; how to execute on the promise of customer focus', *Harvard Business Review*, May, pp. 98–108.

6 Ibid., p. 102.
7 Morgan, Gareth (2006) *Images of Organization*, Sage Publications, London
8 The author was working in a consulting capacity for Fletcher Challenge at the time and made these observations
9 Bryan, Lowell L., and Joyce, Claudia (2005) 'The 21st Century Organization', *The McKinsey Quarterly*, Number 3, New York, p. 26.
10 Barber, Felix, and Morieux, Yves (2005) 'More than Talent', in *Perspectives*, The Boston Consulting Group, p. 6.
11 Robertson, Peter W. (2005) 'Adaptive supply chains: from command-and-control to control – commands', in *MHD supply chain solutions*, May/June, p. 63.
12 Ibid.
13 Day, George (1999) 'Aligning Organizational Structure to the Market', *Business Strategy Review*, Vol. 10, Issue 3, Autumn, p. 35.
14 Semler, Ricardo (1993) *Maverick*, Warner Books, London; and Semler, Ricardo (2003), *The Seven-Day Weekend*, Random House, London.
15 A commendation by Charles Handy, commenting on Ricardo Semler's first book, *Maverick*.
16 People and Coaches, Irizar Group, Issue 36, October 2006; http://www.irizar.com/eng/o/filosofia.htm
    See also the Irizar story by Luxio Ugarte (2004) *Sinfonia o Jazz, Koldo Saratzaga y el modelo Irizar*, Granica, S.A. Barcelona.
17 Cottrill, Ken (2005), 'It takes a village to run a supply chain', *Supply Chain Strategy*, Harvard Business Review Publishing.
18 See http://www.aeraenergy.com/ website for more information.
19 Guidewire, A. (2007) 'Sprinting to success, a case study developed by IMD', Lausanne, Switzerland, 12 pp.
20 Refer to Douglas, M.A. and Strutton, D. (2009) 'Going 'purple': can military jointness principles provide a key to more successful integration at the marketing-manufacturing interface?', *Business Horizons*, Vol. 52, No. 3, pp. 251–263, 19 May.
21 Jenkins, Mark (2006) 'How to win and keep on winning: performance lessons from Formula One Motorsport', unpublished paper, Cranfield School of Management, 4 pp. See also Jenkins, Mark (2009) *Performance at the Limit: Business Lessons from Formula 1 Motor Racing*, 2005.
22 Carter, Phillip L., Carter, Joseph R., Monczka, Robert M., Blascovich, John D., Slaight, Thomas, H. and Markham, William J. (2007) 'Succeeding in a dynamic world: supply management in the decade ahead', A joint research initiative of CAPS Research Institute for Supply Management and A.T. Kearney, p. 131.
23 Ibid., p. 95.
24 Fletcher Challenge Energy (1996) 'The integrated energy company', internal document, 17 December, p. 14.
25 Mintzberg, Henry (1981) 'Organization design: fashion or fit?', *Harvard Business Review*, January/February, pp. 103–116.
26 Ibid. p. 115
27 Ibid.
28 Fung, Victor K., Fung, William K. and Wind, Yoram (2008) *Competing in a Flat World*, Wharton School Publishing, Upper Saddle River, NJ.
29 A comment made during a teleconference between the author and Victor Fung on 1 April 2009.
30 Fung *et al.* (2008), p. 86.
31 What they did is recorded in a seven-minute CD called: 'The FIFA World Cup 2006 – the ultimate supply chain event', produced by Adidas and Deloitte, 2007.

32 Press release by Adidas on 7 March, 2007 from their headquarters at Herzogenaurach, Germany.

33 First-quarter 2009 pretax profit at Adidas fell 97% to $12 million, for all intents and purposes the break-even level. The earnings were way below expectations and prompted a 9 per cent drop in Adidas shares. http://www.businessweek.com/globalbiz/blog/europeinsight/archives/2009/05/adidas_profit_w.html

34 I would like to acknowledge the quality research work of Wendy Sadler-Moyes in her supply chain management report, 'Organizational structures – examples and variants', an unpublished paper prepared for her MBA at the Macquarie Graduate School of Management, Sydney, 2009.

35 Larsen, H.H (2002), 'Oticon: unorthodox project-based management in a "spaghetti organization"', *Human Resource Planning* (USA), Vol. 25, No. 4, pp. 30–37.

36 Ibid.

37 Sadler-Moyes, Wendy (2009), p. 5.

38 Weintraub, M. (2006) 'Transforming the procurement organization for a new era', Oracle White Paper, p. 2

Chapter 7

1 Clark, Theodore H. (1994) 'Campbell Soup Company: a leader in continuous replenishment innovations', Case Study 9-195-124, Harvard Business School, 14 October, 21 pp.

2 I am indebted to Bill Gill, Managing Director, Joe White Maltsters, for this example of a *continuous replenishment* supply chain.

3 Anthony Burgmans, CEO, Unilever, speaking at the 6th ECR (Efficient Consumer Response) Conference, Edinburgh, 2001.

4 Mitchell, Sue (2002) 'Super market forces', interview with Roger Corbett in *AFR BOSS* magazine, *Australian Financial Review*, 2 January, pp. 43–44.

5 Barratt, Mark A. (2002) 'Exploring relationships and information exchange in grocery supply chains: a case study of enablers and inhibitors', unpublished PhD thesis, Cranfield University.

6 See Appendix 7A.1 for a list of the 83 cultural *enablers*.

7 See Appendix 7A.2 for a list of the 34 cultural *inhibitors*.

8 In Ch. 6 of Living Supply Chains (Gattorna, 2006), I focused on what I called a 'process' design; see Figure 6.1, p. 140. The added subtlety introduced in this book is that the process teams are actually multidisciplinary ' clusters'.

9 Kaplan, Robert S. and Norton, David P. (1992) 'The balanced scorecard: Measures that drive performance', *Harvard Business Review*, Vol. 70, No. 1, January/February, pp. 71–79.

10 Kaplan, Robert S. and Norton, David P. (2005) 'Managing alignment as a process', *Balanced Scorecard Report*, Harvard Business School Publishing, July–August, 6 pp.

11 Humphries, Andrew S. and Wilding, Richard D. (2004) 'Long term collaborative business relationships: the impact of trust and C3 behavior', *Journal of Marketing Management*, Vol. 20, pp. 1107–1022. See also Ch. 3 in Gattorna (2009), 'Building relationships that create value', pp. 67–80.

12 See Lambert, Douglas M. and Knemeyer, Michael A. (2004) 'We're in this together', *Harvard Business Review*, December, pp. 114–122.

13 Gratton, Lynda (2007) 'Building bridges for success', in Understanding the Culture of Collaboration, a special supplement in *The Financial Times*, 29 June, p. 2.

Chapter 8

1 Vitasek, Kate, Manrodt, Karl B. and Abbott, Jeff (2005) 'What makes a lean supply chain?', *Supply Chain Management Review*, October, pp. 39–45.
2 Womack, James P., Jones, Daniel T. and Roos, Daniel (1990) *The Machine that Changed the World: Based on the MIT 5-million dollar Study on the Future of the Automobile*, Rawsons Associates, New York, NY.
3 Black, Cherie (2008) 'To build a better hospital, Virginia Mason takes lessons from Toyota plants', *Seattle Post-Intelligencer*, 15 March.
4 Ibid.
5 Hill, T. (2004) 'Designing service delivery systems', Ch. 5, *Operations Management*, 2nd edn, Palgrave Macmillan, p. 117.
6 Chandrasekhar, Ramasastry and Menor, Larry (2004) *Dabbawallahs of Mumbai (A)*, Case 9B04D011, Richard Ivey School of Business, 22 pp.
7 Comment made by Don Meij, CEO/Managing Director of Domino's Pizza Australia and New Zealand (16 May 2005) at MGSM Networker meeting, Sydney, Australia; www.mgsmnetworker.net.
8 SCOR (supply chain operations reference) model was developed by the Supply Chain Council, a not-for-profit organization that commenced in 1996–97. SCOR is a process model designed to improve efficiency and productivity through the use of best practices, standardized terminology, a cross-functional framework along with common metrics. For more information go to www.scor.com.
9 EDLP was a concept developed by Wal-Mart and Procter & Gamble at the end of the 1990s. It has not become a universal practice, although many retail organizations have tried to mimic this arrangement.
10 I am indebted to my colleague Deborah Ellis, Principal of Carpenter Ellis, for this example, August 2005.
11 Cowley, Mark (2005) 'BlueScope Steel – a case study in adapting to a global manufacturing market', a paper presented at the Smart Conference, Sydney, 2 June.
12 'Jeffrey Liker: The Thought Leader Interview', an interview with Jeffrey Rothfeder, *strategy +business*, Issue 51, Summer 2008, p. 107.
13 Ibid., p. 108.

Chapter 9

1 The 'bullwhip' effect is where poor information sharing, long lead times and inaccurate forecasts cause ever increasing fluctuations as demand signals move from consumers upstream towards the supply end.
2 Glatzel, Christoph, Helmcke, Stefan and Wine, Joshua (2009) 'Building a flexible supply chain for uncertain times', *The McKinsey Quarterly*, Premium Edition, March, p. 3.
3 See IBM Australia's advertising campaign, which started in March 2003, to communicate its vision of 'e-business on demand' to a wider business community. http://www.bandt.com.au/news/87/0c014b87.asp
4 This is where customer account profitability regimes come in.
5 Fonterra placed embargoes on certain production from certain of its processing factories so that production allocated against forecasts for 'collaborative' customers would not be interfered with.
6 Henry, Jim (2009) 'BMW says flexible, not lean, is the next big thing in autos', BNET Auto Blog, 24 November, p. 1.

7 Ibid., p. 2.
8 Spivy, Duane (2009) 'The OODA loop and learning', *Chief Learning Officer*, Vol. 8, Issue 1, pp. 30–33.
9 Baker, B. (2005) 'Timely decisions', *PM Network*, p. 20.
10 I am indebted to Professor Donald Sull, London Business School, for this example, Chantilly, 7 October 2005.
11 Sull, Donald H. with Yong Wang (2005) *Made in China*, Harvard Business School Press, Boston, MA.
12 The companies Sull was clearly referring to would come from the following list: Haier (Appliances, TVs); Lenovo (Computers); TCL (TVs, Mobile phones); Wahaha (Beverages); Gome (Electronics); Geely (Cars); Bird (Mobile phones); Tsingtao (beer); Li-Ning (Clothing, shoes); and Yonghe King (Fast food).This list we sourced from Roberts, Dexter, 'China's Power Brands', *BusinessWeek*, 8 November 2004, pp. 52, 53.
13 Fine, Charles, H. (2005) 'Are you modular or integral? Be sure your supply chain knows', *strategy+business*, No. 39, Summer, pp. 499–506.
14 Ibid., p. 502.
15 Ibid., p. 503.
16 Ibid.
17 Gupta, Vivek and Radlika, A. Neela (2005) 'Li & Fung: the global value chain configurator', Case ref. 305-052-1, ICFAI Center of Management Research, Hyderabad, 28 pp.
18 See Chapter 11 in Gattorna (2009) for more detailed treatment of S&OP, pp. 159–176.
19 Ritter, Ronald C. and Sternfels, Robert A. (2004) 'When offshore manufacturing doesn't make sense', *McKinsey Quarterly*, online journal of McKinsey & Company, No. 4; www.mckinseyquarterly.com.
20 CEO Sue Morphet took the decision to lay off 1850 workers at Pacific Brands' Melbourne plant and move production of the Bonds product line off-shore, for strictly cost reasons. Pacific Brands is Australia's largest branded apparel supplier.
21 Op. cit, Ritter *et al.* (2004).
22 Ibid.
23 Ibid.
24 'Haier's aim: "Develop our brand overseas"', *Business Week* online, 31 March 2004, p. 2; http://search.businessweek.com.
25 Cienski, Jan (2005) 'Asia forces rethink for Polish clothing makers', *Financial Times*, Wednesday 26 October, p. 4.
26 Salter, Chuck (2001) 'This is one fast factory', *Fast Company*, No. 49, August, pp. 32–34.
27 Reeves, Phil (2008) 'How rapid manufacturing could transform supply chains', *Supply Chain Quarterly*, Quarter 4/2008, p. 32.
28 Ibid., p. 33.
29 Bleeke, Joel, A., 'Peak strategies', in *McKinsey Quarterly*, Spring, 1989.

Chapter 10

1 The concept of two variants in a *fully flexible* supply chain and their respective characteristics and names were developed by Kate Hughes, PhD scholar, Macquarie Graduate School of Management (MGSM), Sydney, Australia.
2 For more information about these disasters refer to Michael Whiting's Chapter 7, pp. 117–119 in Gattorna, John (2009) *Dynamic Supply Chain Alignment*, Gower Publishing, Farnham.

3 For more information on these various phases, refer Hughes, Kate, 'The Evolution of Fully Flexible Supply Chains', Chapter 5 in Gattorna, John (2009) *Dynamic Supply Chain Alignment*, Gower Publishing, Farnham, pp. 85–95.

4 In doctoral studies by Deborah Ellis at MGSM, Macquarie University, Sydney, 2009.

5 For more information contact Maeve Magner, Supply Chain Director, Clinton Foundation: www.clintonfoundation.org

6 Steinberg, Jessica (2003) 'Driving in the valley of the shadow of death', *Fast Company*, No. 74, September, p. 88.

7 Borger, Julian (2008) 'Lives lost through lack of leadership in UN response to humanitarian crises, Britain warns', Diplomatic Editor, *The Guardian*, 7 October, p. 4.

8 Murray, Sarah (2005) 'How to deliver on the promises: supply chain logistics', *Financial Times – Business Life*, 7 January, p. 9.

9 See Hughes, Kate (2009) 'The Evolution of Fully Flexible Supply Chains', in Gattorna, John (2009) *Dynamic Supply Chain Alignment*, Gower Publishing, pp. 85–95.

10 Ibid. p. 88.

11 Ibid. p. 91. I have altered Kate Hughes's original order of phases.

12 Ibid. p. 90.

13 Ibid. pp. 93–94.

14 http://www.londonprepared.gov.uk/downloads/lookingbackmovingforward.pdf

15 For more information about the diversity of tasks the UN is engaged in, refer to the case 'Logistics moving the seeds of a brighter future', by Ramina Samii and Luk N. Van Wassenhove, INSEAD, Fontainebleau, 2003, p. 23.

16 Dr Chris Morgan was a Lecturer at Cranfield Center for Logistics and Supply Chain Management, Cranfield University, prior to his untimely death in 2008.

Chapter 11

1 Adapted from 'The Triple-A supply chain revisited', *Supply Chain Asia* November/December 2008, pp. 38–41, and a more recent version published as Chapter 8 in Gattorna, John (2009) *Dynamic Supply Chain Alignment*, Gower Publishing, Farnham.

2 Hau L. Lee (2004) 'The Triple-A supply chain', *Harvard Business Review* October, pp. 102–112.

3 Ibid., p. 112.

4 Ibid., p. 105.

5 Details of this emerging concept were first published in: Gattorna, John and Walters, D.W. (1996) *Managing the Supply Chain: A Strategic Perspective*, Macmillan Press, London; and Gattorna, John (1998) *Strategic Supply Chain Alignment*, Gower Publishing, Aldershot.

6 Lee, 'The Triple-A supply chain', *op. cit.*, p. 105.

7 Ibid., p. 106.

8 Primarily Kate Hughes who is studying for her doctorate at Macquarie Graduate School of Management, Sydney, Australia.

9 'AAA Supply Chains in a Turbulent World', a webcast on SCM World, 3 December, 2009. Refer to link: https://scmworld.webex.com/scmworld/lsr.php?AT=pb&SP=EC&rID=6977742&rKey=F16FFBD1D155C369

10 Ibid.

11 Lee, 'The Triple-A supply chain', *op. cit.*, p. 106.

12 I coined the term *dynamic a alignment* (previously 'strategic alignment'), in 2005 and published early details of how it works in Gattorna (2006) *Living Supply Chains, op. cit.*

13 Lee, 'The Triple-A supply chain', *op. cit.*, 108.

14 Ibid.

15 See Chapter 16 for more details. DHL Taiwan was providing a largely fast express service to all customers. However, we discovered in fieldwork that this type of singular focus was over-servicing some customers and disaffecting others who simply wanted a reliable relationship-driven service at lower cost.

16 Lee, 'AAA supply chains in a turbulent world', *op. cit.*

17 See Chapters 7–11 for details of each of the 13 levers in each type of supply chain.

Chapter 12

1 Christopher, M., Jia, Fu, Khan, Omera, Mena, Carlos, Palmer, Andrew and Sandberg, Erik (2007) 'Global Sourcing and Logistics', Research Report, Cranfield School of Management, May, p. 3.

2 Ibid.

3 Kearney, A.T. (2004) 'When your suppliers talk . . . listen', *Executive Agenda*, Third Quarter, pp. 29, 30.

4 Bueler, Diane (2006) 'Supplier Segmentation – the Tool for Differentiation and Results', a paper presented at the 91st Annual International Supply Management Conference, Minneapolis Convention Center, Minneapolis, MN, 7–10 May.

5 Dyer, Jeffrey H., Dong, Sung Cho, and Chu, Wujin (1998) 'Strategic Supplier Segmentation: the next "best practice" in supply chain management', *California Management Review*, Berkley: Winter, Vol. 40, Issue 2, pp. 57–77.

6 Ibid., p. 58.

7 Ibid., p. 59.

8 Ibid.

9 Puryear, Rudy, Singh, Bhanu and Phillips, Stephen (2007), 'How to be everywhere at once', *Supply Chain Management Review*, May/June 2007, p. 10.

10 Kearney. A.T (2004), 'Shifting your supply chain into reverse', *Executive Agenda*, Third Quarter, p. 18.

11 I am indebted to my colleague Deborah Ellis for fleshing out this idea of return pathways.

12 Guide,V. Daniel R., Muyldermans, Luc and Van Wassenhove, Luk N. (2005) 'Hewlett-Packard Company Unlocks the Value Potential from Time-Sensitive Returns', *Interfaces*, July–August, 35, pp. 281–293.

13 Guide, V. Daniel R., Harrison, T.P. (2003) 'The challenge of closed-loop supply chains,' *Interfaces*, Vol. 33, No. 6, Nov–Dec, pp. 3–6.

14 This is the theme that runs all through Thomas L. Friedman's book *Hot, Flat and Crowded*, Allen Lane, New York, 2008.

Chapter 13

1 I am indebted to my colleague, Deborah Ellis, of Carpenter Ellis, for many of the examples mentioned in the text.

2 Case studies illustrating The Unipart Way can be found at: http://unipart.oxi.net/Home/tabid/36/language/en-US/Default.aspx

3 Perepu, Indu (2008) 'Benetton's 'Dual Supply Chain' System', ICFAI Center for Management Research, Case Study ref. no. 608-003-1, p. 12.

4 See note by MBA student Vinay Thomas, a former employee of BOC (T2, 2009, MGSM).

5 Op. cit., ICFAI case study (2008).

6 Sullivan, Paul (2004) 'Paradigm Shift', *Supply Chain Review*, 16 July, pp. 22–25.

7 Ibid. p. 1.

8 Comment by Rich Morris, VP BMW Manufacturing Co., in Henry, Jim (2009) 'BMW says Flexible, Not Lean, is the next best thing in Autos', BNET Auto Blog, 24 November, p. 1.

9 'Ship Ahoy', 60 Minutes television program, Nine Network Australia, 21 August 2005; reporter Richard Carlton.

10 I am indebted to Terry O'Connor, General Manager Corporate Services Director, ABB Grain, for this enlightening example, 7 December 2005.

11 Plant, Robert, Feeny, David and Mughal, Hamid (2000) 'Land Rover vehicles: the CB40, a project in nimbleness and flexibility', Case 600-001-1, Templeton College Publication, European Case Clearing House, Templeton College, Oxford, 19 pps.

12 I am indebted to Mike Bernon of the Cranfield Centre for Logistics and Supply Chain Management for his insights on this project.

13 Howell, R. and Heskett, J. (2004) 'Shouldice Hospital Limited', Case Study 9-805-002, Harvard Business School, 14 pp. See website www.Shouldice.com.

14 Passariello, Christina (2006) 'Louis Vuitton tries modern methods on factory lines', *Wall Street Journal*, Monday 9 October. Refer to website http://www.post-gazette.com/pg/06282/728653-28.stm.

15 Ibid.

16 Kurian, Boby and Singh, Amarpreet (2007) 'Louis Vuitton plans Asia plant in Pondy', *Times News Network*, Tuesday 9 January. Refer to website http://forums.thefashionspot.com/f57/louis-vuitton-paris-made-india-52636.html.

Chapter 14

1 Johnson, Mark W., Christensen, Clayton M. and Kagermann, Henning (2008) 'Reinventing your business model', *Harvard Business Review*, December, p. 57.

2 Porter, Michael E. (1990) *The Competitive Advantage of Nations*, Free Press, New York, NY.

3 For more information about Dubai World Central Logistics City, see Ch. 25 in Gattorna (2009), pp. 347–360.

4 A form of 4PL® is taking shape among some leading members of the Australian publishing industry. Refer to Report Ad Rem, *The Australian Book Industry; challenges and opportunities*, prepared by Accenture and Industry Sciences Resources, 2001, 32 pps.

5 A 3PL-driven collaborative model exists in Australia to service the retail and wholesale tobacco markets.

6 Sydney Mascot International Airport has a system for aviation fuel where provider companies share the cost of infrastructure on a time-share basis. This means natural competitors are still competing, while collaborating to reduce costs in a specific area of their supply chains.

7 Hardman, Doug, Messinger, David and Bergson, Sara (2005) 'Virtual scale: alliances for leverage', *strategy+business*, 14 July, Booz Allen Hamilton, p. 1; published online at http://www.strategy-business.com/resiliencereport/resilience/rr00021?pg=0.

8 Based on my own assessment over the past two decades of consulting.

9 Where the returns generated are consistently greater than the cost-of-capital.

10 Expressed as an equation, CFROI = [(Cash flow from Operations/Capital Employed) – Capital Charge].

11 Litman, Joel and Frigo, Mark L. (2004) 'When strategy and valuation meet; five lessons from return driven strategy', *Strategic Finance*, August, pp. 31–39.

12 Magretta, Joan (1998) 'Fast, global and entrepreneurial: supply chain management, Hong Kong style. An interview with Victor Fung', *Harvard Business Review*, Vol. 76, No. 5, September/October, pp. 102–114.

13 Kissel, Mary (2005) 'Li & Fung may be more valuable than its profit measure shows', 'Heard in Asia' column, *Wall Street Journal*, Tuesday 25 October, p. 19.

14 Litman, Joel and Frigo, Mark L. (2004) 'When strategy and valuation meet: five lessons from return driven strategy', *Strategic Finance*, August, pp. 31–39.

15 I am indebted to Will Lock of Accenture (UK) for his help in clarifying the various financial ratios mentioned in the text for assessing the performance of business enterprises.

16 Then called Andersen Consulting.

17 See Gattorna, John (1998) 'Fourth-party logistics: en-route to breakthrough performance in the supply chain' in Ch. 27 in Gattorna, John (ed.) *Strategic Supply Chain Alignment: best practice in supply chain management*, Gower Publishing, Aldershot, pp. 425–445.

18 1994 Andersen Consulting Survey of 250 UK companies. The industries surveyed were: consumer, retail, oil, gas and chemical, industrial and utilities.

19 Alpha Research Consortium (2004) *Characteristics, Strategies and Trends for 3PL/4PL in Australia*, Logistics Association of Australia, March, p. 86.

20 For more detailed information on the 4PL® model, see Ch. 27 in Gattorna, John (ed.) (1998) *Strategic Supply Chain Alignment*, Gower Publishing, Aldershot.

21 Petroleum Development of Oman (PDO) issued such an RFQ in 2003.

22 Vogel, Jochen (2001) 4PL® Report, March, Lehman Bros, London.

23 EV/EBITDA, i.e., Economic Value/Earnings before Interest and Tax Depreciation and Amortization.

24 M-co developed after the deregulation of New Zealand's power industry. Company information can be found at www.nz.m-co.com

25 See short case description in Gattorna, John (2006), pp. 214–218.

26 For example: Corprocure in Australia; Transora in the United States.

27 Breene, Tim and Nunes, Paul F. (2004) 'High-performance business – is bigger always better?', *Outlook*, Accenture, No. 3, pp. 19–25.

28 Ibid., p. 25.

29 Alpha Research Consortium (2004) 'Characteristics, Strategies and Trends for 3PL/4PL® in Australia', Logistics Association of Australia, 30 March.

30 Ogulin, Robert (2005) 'Coordination in networked supply chains', PhD thesis work-in-progress, Macquarie Graduate School of Management, Sydney.

31 The Petroleum Development of Oman (PDO) has attempted to form a 4PL® by tender for the task of moving exploration equipment; the winning company has encountered early difficulties, which are now being addressed.

32 Extracted from HRW's Vision statement, 2009.

33 For more information, see Barratt, Mark, Savidge, Matthew, and Barratt, Ruth (2006) 'Sarbanes-Oxley: Is it good for your supply chain', *Supply Chain Management Review*, November, pp. 34–40.

34 This was the experience with the Thames Water – Accenture Connect 2020 venture, which although successful, was unable to attract other utilities to join and bring with them additional volume that would have driven the experience curve down at an even faster rate than was achieved with just the one major principle.

35 Levine, Ruth, Pickett, Jessica, Sekhri, Neelam and Yadav, Prashant (2008) 'Demand forecasting for essential medical technologies', *American Journal of Law & Medicine*, 34: 269–297.See Section B, 'Create a Global Health Infomediary', pp. 294–295.

36 Ellis, Deborah, PhD candidate at Macquarie Graduate School of Management, 2009 – Research topic: 'Evaluating the supply chains supporting insulin-dependent diabetes patients in developing countries'.

37 Refer to interview of Ajay Mittal by Turloch Mooney in *Supply Chain Asia*, January/ February, 2009, pp. 27–29 and Ch. 27 in *Dynamic Supply Chain Alignment*, 'China and India: Future Giants of Supply Chain Developments in the Twenty-first Century', by Paul W. Bradley, Gower Publishing, pp. 371–395.

Chapter 15

1 McGee, Kenneth, G. (2004) *Heads Up: How to anticipate business surprises and seize opportunities first*, Harvard Business School Press, Boston, MA.

2 Gattorna, John L. (1991) 'Exocets and Equilibrium', *Strategy Spotlight*, the in-house journal of Gattorna Strategy Consultants Pty. Ltd., Vol. 1, No. 1, February, pp. 8–12.

3 Adapted from Chopra, Sunil and Sodhi, ManMohan S. (2004) 'Managing risk to avoid supply-chain breakdown', *MIT Sloan Management Review*, Fall, p. 54.

4 Ibid., p. 53.

5 Lee, Hau L. and Wolfe, Michael (2003) 'Supply chain security without tears', *Supply Chain Management Review*, January/February, pp. 12–20.

6 Sheffi, Yossi (2005) *The Resilient Enterprise: overcoming vulnerability for competitive advantage*, MIT Press, Cambridge, MA.

7 Ibid., p. 255.

8 Hendriks, Kevin B. and Singhal, Vinod, R., (2009) 'Managing disruptions in contemporary supply chains', Ch. 22 in John Gattorna (ed.) *Dynamic Supply Chain Alignment*, Gower Publishing, Farnham, pp. 311–321. See also Singhal, Vinod and Hendricks, Kevin (2007) 'Disruptive influences', in *CPO Agenda*, Summer, pp. 58–63.

9 Hendriks, Kevin B. and Singhal, Vinod, R., (2009) 'Managing Disruptions in Contemporary Supply Chains', p. 313.

10 Ibid p.319.

11 Ibid. p.320.

12 Clark, Nicola, (2007) 'Worst year at Airbus hurts EADS', *International Herald Tribune*, 10–11 March, p. 17.

13 See Hopkins, Andrew (2009) *Failure to Learn: the BP Texas City refinery disaster*, CCH Australia, for the full story.

14 John Browne has referred in detail to this event in his memoirs, *Beyond Business* (2010) Weidenfeld & Nicolson, London.

15 Jim Thomas, quoted in *Manufacturing Business Technology* Report, Reed Business Information, 9 September 2007, p. 2.

16 Michelman, Paul (2007) 'Building a Resilient Supply Chain', Conversation Starter, Harvard Business Online, 14 August. http://blogs.harvardbusiness.org/cs/2007/08/building_a_resilient_supply_ch.html
This article originally appeared in the October issue of *Supply Chain Strategy*.

17 Hendriks, Kevin B. and Singhal, Vinod, R. (2009) 'Managing Disruptions in Contemporary Supply Chains', p. 318.

18 Holliday, Charles, O. Jr., Schmidheiny, Stephan and Watts, Philip (2002) *Walking the Talk: the Business Case for Sustainable Development*, Case Study 38, Berrett-Koehler Publishers, San Francisco, CA, p. 22.

19 'No writing on the wall? Sustainable Development as a Business Principle in the Supply Chain', a discussion paper by The Nordic Partnership, 2003, p. 2. See http://www.nordicpartnership.org.

20 Conversation with Dr Ian Woods at a University of Wollongong Supply Chain Forum, Sydney, 29 June 2005. AMP Capital Investors writes research papers on issues affecting the Socially Responsible Investments (SRI) industry. See www.ampcapital.com.au.

21 Demos, Telis (2005) 'Managing beyond the bottom line', *Fortune*, 3 October, pp. 70–75.

22 *Sustainability – Problem or Opportunity?* A report by Russell Reynolds Associates and Circ Consulting, Melbourne and Sydney, 2008, 8 pps.

23 *Shifting towards sustainability; six insights into successful organizational change for sustainability* (2006) Australian Research Institute in Education for Sustainability (ARIES), Macquarie University, Commonwealth of Australia, 54 pps.

24 Fittipaldi, Santiago (2004) 'When doing the right thing provides a pay-off', *Global Finance*, January, pp. 18–22.

25 Hall, James (2005) 'Designer Companies', *AFR BOSS* magazine, *Australian Financial Review*, January, p. 40.

26 Ibid., p. 41.

27 Birchall, Jonathan (2005) 'Wal-Mart sets out stall for a green future', *Financial Times*, Wednesday 26 October, p. 17.

28 Holliday, Charles, O. Jr., Schmidheiny, Stephan and Watts, Philip (2002) *Walking the Talk: The Business Case for Sustainable Development*, Berrett-Koehler Publishers, San Francisco, CA., pp. 170–171.

29 Ibid. pp. 118–120.

30 'The Nike factory challenge', Ethical Corporation, News Release, 16 May 2005, p. 1.

31 Gapper, John (2007) 'No reason to put Mattel on the rack', *Financial Times*, 17 September, p. 13.

32 For more detail see 'Marcopolo', in *Case Studies of Good Corporate Governance Practices*, Global Corporate Governance Forum, International Finance Corporation, World bank Group, 2006, pp. 50–57.

33 'Natura', in *Case Studies of Good Corporate Governance Practices*, (2006) p. 58.

34 John, Geraint (2008) 'Because it's worth it', an interview with Barbara Lavernos, CPO Agenda, Spring, p. 39.

35 New ways of doing things that disrupt or overturn the traditional business methods and practices. For example, steam engine in the age of sail, and the internet in the age of post office mail. Refer to website: http://www.businessdictionary.com/definition/disruptive-technology.html

36 Presutti, William D. Jr., and Mawhinney, John R. (2007) 'The supply chain-finance link', *Supply Chain Management Review*, September, pp. 32–38.

37 In calendar 2009, the *Logistics Magazine* TOP 25 Enterprise Supply Chains in Australian Listed Companies were assessed using CFROI as the main selection criterion.

38 See also Campbell, Brett and Rodi, Alyson, 'Tax-aligned supply chains', Ch. 24 in John Gattorna (ed.) *Dynamic Supply Chain Alignment*, pp. 337–346. See also Irving, Dan, Kilponen Gary, Markarian, Raffi, and Klitgaard, Mark (2005) 'A tax-aligned approach to SCM', *Supply Chain Management Review*, April, pp. 57–61.

39 Cohn, Jeffrey M., Khurana, Rakesh and Reeves, Laura (2005) 'Growing talent as if your business depended on it', *Harvard Business Review*, October, pp. 62–70.

40 Cappelli, Peter (2008) 'Talent on Demand: applying supply chain management to people', *Knowledge@Wharton*, 20 February, pp. 1–5.

41 Booz Allen Hamilton (2001) 'Out of Sorts with Outsourcing', New York, 25 July.

42 Deloitte Consulting (2005) *Calling a Change in the Outsourcing Market*, April, p. 2.

43 Ibid., p. 3.

44 Internal paper prepared by Ming Tang, Partner, *Asia-Pacific Supply Chain Practice*, Accenture, 2003.
45 Ellis, Simon (2008) 'The case for 'profitable proximity', *'Supply Chain Quarterly*, Council of Supply Chain Management Professionals, Quarter 3, p. 56.
46 Drucker, Peter F. (1974) 'New templates for today's organizations', *Harvard Business Review*, January–February, pp. 45–51.
47 This was a new organizational format that McKinsey & Company tried out with various clients in the early 1990s, but it has not been widely adopted.
48 Sull, Donald N. (2005) *Made in China: What Western Managers Can Learn from Trailblazing Chinese Entrepreneurs*, Harvard Business School Press, Boston, MA, p. 107.
49 Ibid.
50 Ashby, W.R. (1956) *An Introduction to Cybernetics*, Chapman & Hall, London; and by the same author: (1954) *Design for a Brain*, 2nd edn, John Wiley, New York, NY.
51 Chung, Chee Kong, 'Supply chain configurations and the impact of different pricing strategies', Ch. 13 in John Gattorna (ed.) *Dynamic Supply Chain Alignment*, pp. 189–205.
52 'Outsourcing in the new supply chain environment', Media Release, Supply Chain Management Forum, Athens Hilton, Athens, 25–26 November 2005. See www. scmforum.org
53 Miller, Ron (2005) 'The evolution of knowledge management', November, *EContent*, pp. 38–41.
54 Lowell, Bryan L. and Joyce, Claudia (2005) 'The 21st-century organization', *McKinsey Quarterly*, No. 3, pp. 24–33.
55 Mangan, J. and Christopher, M. (2005) 'Management Development and the supply chain manager of the future', *International Journal of Logistics Management*, Vol. 16, No. 2, pp. 178–191.
56 Hult, G.Tomas M., Ketchen, David J. Jr., Cavusgil, S.Tamer and Calantone, Roger J. (2006) 'Knowledge as a strategic resource in supply chains', *Journal of Operations Management*, 24, pp. 458–475.
57 Andrews, Kate (2009) 'The importance of intellectual capital and knowledge in the design and operation of enterprise supply chains', Ch. 26 in John Gattorna (ed.) *Dynamic Supply Chain Alignment*, pp. 361–370.

Chapter 16

1 Senge, Peter, Scharmer, C. Otto, Jaworski, Joseph and Flowers, Betty Sue (2005) *Presence: Exploring Profound Change in People, Organizations, and Society*, Nicholas Brealey Publishing, London, p. 7.
2 See De Geus, Arie (1997) *The Living Company*, Nicholas Brealey Publishing, quoted in Senge, P. *et al.*, *Presence*, p. 7.
3 Ibid.
4 Adam Hartung, 'To succeed you must seriously disrupt. That's what separates winners from losers'. http://www.forbes.com/2010/03/01/disrupt-change-innovation-leadership-managing-hartung.html?partner=email.

Select bibliography

Aker, David A., *Spanning Silos; the new CMO Imperative*, Harvard Business School Press, Boston, MA, 2008.

Adizes, Ichak, *How to Solve the Mismanagement Crisis*, 1st printing, Dow-Jones-Irwin, 1979; 5th printing, Adizes Institute, Santa Monica, CA, 1985.

Adler, G., Fordham, M. and Read, H. (eds), *The Collected Works of C.G. Jung Vol. 6: Psychological Types* (translated by R.F.C. Hull), Bollingen Series 20, Princeton University Press, Ewing, NJ, 1971.

Ashby, W.R., *An Introduction to Cybernetics*, Chapman & Hall, Boston, MA, 1956.

Ashby, W.R., *Design for a Brain*, 2nd edn, John Wiley, New York, NY, 1954.

Avery, Gayle C., *Leadership for Sustainable Futures: achieving success in a competitive world*, Edward Elgar, Cheltenham, UK, 2005.

Avery, Gayle C., *Understanding Leadership: Paradigms and Cases*, Sage Publications, London, 2004.

Bacon, Terry R. and Pugh, David G., *The Behavioral Advantage: What the Smartest, Most Successful Companies Do Differently to Win in the B2B Arena*, AMACON, New York, NY, 2004.

Barker, Joel A. and Erickson, Scott W., *Five Regions of the Future: Preparing Your Business for Tomorrow's Technology Revolution*, Penguin, New York, NY, 2005.

Beck, John C. and Wade, Mitchell, *Got Game: How The Gamer Generation is Reshaping Business Forever*, Harvard Business School Press, Boston, MA, 2004.

Benfari, Robert with Knox, Jean, *Understanding Your Management Style: Beyond the Myers-Briggs Type Indicators*, D.C. Heath, Lexington, MA, 1991.

Berger, Andrew J. and Gattorna, John L., *Supply Chain Cybermastery: Building High Performance Supply Chains of the Future*, Gower Publishing, Aldershot, 2003.

Bossidy, Larry and Charan, Ram, *Execution: The Discipline of Getting Things Done*, Crown Business, New York, NY, 2002.

Bourne, Lynda, *Stakeholder Relationship Management: a Maturity Model for Organisational Implementation*, Gower Publishing, Farnham, 2009.

Brooks, Frederick P. Jr, *The Mythical Man-Month: Essays on Software Engineering*, Addison-Wesley Longman, Boston, MA, 1995.

Browne, John, *Beyond Business*, Weidenfeld & Nicolson, London, 2010.

Bryan, Lowell L., and Joyce, Claudia (2005) 'The 21st-Century Organization', *The McKinsey Quarterly*, No. 3, pp. 25–33.

Christopher, Martin, *Logistics and Supply Chain Management: Creating Value-Adding Networks*, 3rd edn, FT Prentice Hall, London, 2005.

Christopher, Martin and Peck, Helen, *Marketing Logistics*, 2nd edn, Elsevier Butterworth-Heinemann, Oxford, 2004.

Clarke, John, *Working with Monsters: How to Identify and Protect Yourself from the Workplace Psychopath*, Random House, Sydney, 2005.

Cohen, Shoshannah and Roussel, Joseph, *Strategic Supply Chain Management: The Five Disciplines for Top Performance*, McGraw-Hill, New York, NY, 2005.

Cokins, Gary, *Performance Management: Finding the Missing Pieces (to Close the Intelligence Gap)*, John Wiley, New York, NY, 2004.

Conner, Daryl R., *Managing at the Speed of Change: How Resilient Managers Succeed and Prosper Where Others Fail*, Villard, New York, NY, 1992.

Conner, Daryl R., *Leading at the Edge of Chaos: How to Create the Nimble Organization*, John Wiley, New York, NY, 1998.

Cranfield School of Management, *Supply Chain Vulnerability*, Report on behalf of DTLR, DTI and Home Office, 2002.

Davenport, Thomas H. and Prusak, Laurence with Wilson, H. James, *What's The Big Idea? Creating and Capitalizing on the Best Management Thinking*, Harvard Business School Press, Boston, MA, 2003.

De Geus, Arie, *The Living Company: Habits for Survival in a Turbulent Business Environment*, Harvard Business School Press, Boston, MA, 1997.

Friedman, Thomas L., *The World is Flat: A Brief History of the Globalized World in the 21st Century*, Penguin Books, London, 2005.

Friedman, Thomas L., *Hot, Flat, and Crowded: why the world needs a green revolution-and how we can renew our global future*, Allen Lane, New York, NY, 2008.

Fritz, Robert, *Corporate Tides: The Inescapable Laws of Organizational Structure*, Berrett-Koehler Publishers, San Francisco, CA, 1996.

Fung, Victor K., Fung, William K. and Wind, Yoram, *Competing in a Flat World: Building Enterprises for a Borderless World*, Wharton School Publishing, Upper Saddle River, NJ, 2008.

Gabel, Jo Ellen and Pilnick, Saul, *The Shadow Organization in Logistics: The Real World of Culture Change and Supply Chain Efficiency*, Council of Logistics Management, Oak Brook, IL, 2002.

Gattorna, J.L. and Walters, D.W., *Managing the Supply Chain: a Strategic Perspective*, Macmillan Business, London, 1996.

Gattorna, John (ed.), *Strategic Supply Chain Alignment: Best Practice in Supply Chain Management*, Gower Publishing, Aldershot, 1998.

Gattorna, John L., *Handbook of Supply Chain Management*, 5th edn, Gower Publishing, Aldershot, 2003.

Gattorna, John, *Living Supply Chains: How to mobilize the enterprise around delivering what your customers want*, FT Prentice Hall, Harlow, 2006.

Gattorna, John, *Dynamic Supply Chain Alignment: a New Business Model for Peak Performance in Enterprise Supply Chains Across All Geographies*, Gower Publishing, Farnham, 2009.

Gibbs, Richard and Humphries, Andrew, *Strategic Alliances & Marketing Partnerships: gaining competitive advantage through collaboration and partnering*, Kogan Page, London, 2009.

Goldratt, Eliyahu M., *Theory of Constraints: and How it Should be Implemented*, North River Press, Great Barrington, MA, 1990.

Goold, Michael and Campbell, Andrew, *Designing Effective Organizations: How to Create Structured Networks*, Jossey-Bass, San Francisco, CA, 2002.

Handy, Charles, *The Elephant and The Flea: Reflections of a Reluctant Capitalist*, Harvard Business School Press, Boston, MA, 2001.

Herzlinger, Regina, E., *Market-Driven Health Care: Who Wins, Who Loses in the Transformation of America's Largest Service Industry*, Perseus Books, Cambridge, MA, 1997.

Hofstede, Geert, *Cultures Consequences: International Differences in Work-Related Values (Cross Cultural Research and Methodology)*, Sage Publications, Newbury Park, CA, 1980.

Hofstede, Geert, *Cultures Consequences: Comparing Values, Behaviors, Institutions, and Organizations Across Nations*, 2nd edn, Sage Publications, Newbury Park, CA, 2001.

Hofstede, Geert and Hofstede, Gert Jan, *Cultures and Organizations: Software of the Mind*, 2nd edn, McGraw-Hill, New York, NY, 2005.

Hofstede, Geert & Associates, *Masculinity and Feminity: The Taboo Dimensions of National Cultures*, Sage Publications, Newbury Park, CA, 1998.

Holliday, Charles O. Jr, Schmidheiny, Stephan and Watts, Philip, *Walking the Talk: The Business Case for Sustainable Development*, Berrett-Koehler Publishers, San Francisco, CA, 2002.

Horne, Alistair, *The Age of Napoleon*, Modern Library, New York, NY, 2004.

Honold, Linda and Silverman, Robert J., *Organizational DNA: Diagnosing Your Organization for Increased Effectiveness*, Davies-Black Publishing, Palo Alto, CA., 2002.

Hopkins, Andrew, *Failure to Learn: the BP Texas City Refinery disaster*, CCH, Australia, 2009.

Ibarra, Hermina, *Working Identity: Unconventional Strategies for Reinventing Your Career*, Harvard Business School Press, Boston, MA, 2003.

Itami, Hiroyuki with Roehl, Thomas W., *Mobilizing Invisible Assets*, Harvard University Press, Cambridge, MA, 1987.

Jung, C.G., *Memories, Dreams, Reflections*, Fontana Paperbacks, London, 1983.

Kaplan, R.S. and Norton, D.P., *The Balanced Scorecard*, Harvard Business School Press, Boston, MA, 1996.

Kaplan, Robert S. and Norton, David P., *Alignment: using the balanced Scorecard to create corporate Synergies*, Harvard Business School Press, Boston MA, 2006.

Kim, W. Chan and Mauborgne, Renee, *Blue Ocean Strategy: How to Create Uncontested Market Space and Make the Competition Irrelevant*, Harvard Business School Press, Boston, MA, 2005.

Labovitz, George and Rosansky, Victor, *The Power of Alignment: How Great Companies Stay Centered and Accomplish Extraordinary Things*, John Wiley, New York, NY, 1997.

Lencioni, Patrick, *The Five Temptations of a CEO: a Leadership Fable*, Jossey-Bass, San Francisco, CA, 1998.

Lewis, Michael, *The Big Short: Inside the Doomsday Machine*, Allen Lane, London, 2010.

Lewis, Richard D., *Finland, Cultural Lone Wolf*, Intercultural Press, Boston, 2005.

Littauer, Florence, *Personality PLUS*, Revell, Grand Rapids, MI, 2007 (fourth printing).

Lynn, Barry C., *End of the Line: the rise and coming fall of the global corporation*, Doubleday, New York, 2005.

Low, Jonathan and Kalafut, Pam Cohen, *Invisible Advantage: How Intangibles Are Driving Business Performance*, Perseus Publishing, Cambridge, MA, 2002.

Management Today Series, *The Power of Culture: Driving Today's Organisation*, Australian Institute of Management, McGraw-Hill, Sydney, 2004.

Mant, Alistair, *Intelligent Leadership*, Allen & Unwin, Sydney, 1997.

Marsh, Nick, McAllum, Mike and Purcell, Dominique, *Strategic Foresight: The Power of Standing in the Future*, Crown Content, Melbourne, 2002.

MacFarlane, Hugh, *The Leaky Funnel: Earn More Customers by Aligning Sales and Marketing to the Way Businesses Buy*, Bookman Media, Melbourne, 2003.

McGee, Kenneth, G., *Heads Up: How to Anticipate Business Surprises and Seize Opportunities First*, Harvard Business School Press, Boston, MA, 2004.

Messner, Reinhold, *Moving Mountains: Lessons on Life and Leadership*, Executive Excellence Publishing, Provo, UT, 2001.

Morrell, Margot and Capparell, Stephanie, *Shackleton's Way: Leadership Lessons From The Great Antarctic Explorer*, Nicholas Brealey, London, 2001.

Nadler, David A. and Tushman, Michael L., *Competing by Design: The Power of Organizational Architecture*, Oxford University Press, New York, NY, 1997.

Neilson, Gary L. and Pasternack, Bruce, A., *Results: Keep What's Good, Fix What's Wrong, and Unlock Great Performance*, Crown Business, New York, NY, 2005.

Ouspensky, P.D., *The Psychology of Man's Possible Evolution*, Vintage Books, New York, NY, 1974.

Pandya, Mukul and Shell, Robbie, *Lasting Leadership: What you Can Learn from the Top 25 Business People of Our Times*, Wharton Publishing and Pearson Education, Upper Saddle River, NJ, 2005.

Penrose, Edith, *The Theory of the Growth of the Firm*, 3rd edn, Oxford University Press, Oxford, 1995.

Pitelis, Christos (ed.), *The Growth of the Firm: The Legacy of Edith Penrose*, Oxford University Press, Oxford, 2002.

Porter, Michael E., *The Competitive Advantage of Nations*, The Free Press, New York, NY, 1990.

Roberts, John, *The Modern Firm: Organizational Design for Performance and Growth*, Oxford University Press, New York, NY, 2004.

Robbins, Stephen P. and Judge, Timothy A., *Organizational Behavior*, 13th edn., Pearson: Prentice Hall, Upper Saddle River, NJ, 2009.

Rudzki, Robert A., Smock, Douglas A., Katzorke, Michael and Stewart, Shelley, Jr, *Straight to the Bottom Line: An Executive Roadmap to World Class Supply Management*, J. Ross Publishing, Fort Lauderdale, FL, 2006.

Rummler, Geary A. and Brache, Alan P., *Improving Performance: How to Manage the White Space on the Organization Chart*, 2nd edn, Jossey-Bass Publishers, San Francisco, CA, 1995.

Samuels, Martin, *Command or Control: Command, Training and Tactics in the British and German Armies, 1888–1918*, Frank Cass, London, 1995.

Semler, Ricardo, *The Seven-day Weekend: a Better Way to Work in the 21st Century*, Arrow Books/Random House, London, 2003.

Senge, Peter, Scharmer, C. Otto, Jaworski, Joseph and Flowers, Betty Sue, *Presence: Exploring Profound Change in People, Organizations, and Society*, Nicholas Brealey, London, 2005.

Sheffi, Yossi, *The Resilient Enterprise: Overcoming Vulnerability for Competitive Advantage*, MIT Press, Cambridge, MA, 2005.

Sull, Donald N., *Revival of the Fittest: Why Good Companies Go Bad and How Great Managers Remake Them*, Harvard Business School Press, Boston, MA, 2003.

Sull, Donald N., *Made in China: What Western Managers Can Learn From Trailblazing Chinese Entrepreneurs*, Havard Business School Press, Boston, MA, 2005.

Sveiby, Karl Erik, *The New Organizational Wealth: Managing and Measuring Knowledge-Based Assets*, Berrett-Koehler Publishers, San Francisco, CA, 1997.

Towill, Denis and Christopher, Martin, *International Journal of Logistics: Research Applications*, Vol. 5, No. 3, 2002, pp. 233–309; www.tandf.co.uk/journals.

Ugarte, Luxio, *Sinfonia o jazz? Koldo Saratxaga y el Modelo Irizar*, Granica, Barcelona, 2004.

Viguerie, Patrick, Smit, Sven, and Baghai, Mehrdad, *The Granularity of Growth; making choices that drive enduring company performance*, Marshall Cavendish Business, and Cyan Communications, London, 2007.

Williamson, Oliver E. and Winter, Sidney G. (eds), *The Nature of The Firm: Origins, Evolution, and Development*, Oxford University Press, New York, NY, 1993.

Womack, James P., Jones, Daniel T. and Roos, Daniel, *The Machine that Changed the World: Based on the MIT 5-million Dollar Study on the Future of the Automobile*, Rawsons Associates, New York, NY, 1990.

Index

A word about the author

Dr John Gattorna

John Gattorna has spent a lifetime working in and around supply chains, in many different capacities – line executive, researcher, consultant/ adviser and teacher. He is passionate about the subject matter – some might say obsessive.

In the late 1980s, John became disenchanted with the lack of conceptual depth in the 'logistics' field; and as it turned out this did not improve much as logistics thinking morphed into 'supply chains' in the 1990s. So he started to search for a new model/framework that would better inform the design and operation of enterprise supply chains seeking to satisfy customers and consumers. And he found it; *dynamic* alignment.

For the last two decades John has been working with companies around the world to take his new model from the conceptual stage to a finer level of granularity. It has been a complex task because it has involved learning about, and combining, several disciplines – consumer/ customer behavior; internal cultural capability of the enterprise; leadership styles; and of course the operational aspects of corporate logistics networks and supply chains. The unique thing about John's perspective is that he presents a multi-disciplinary approach to the design and management of supply chains, and this requires an eclectic mindset.

He has written several books along the way as his thinking evolved, but his two most recent titles have been seminal: *Living Supply Chains* (FT Prentice Hall, Harlow, 2006), and *Dynamic Supply Chain Alignment*, Gower Publishing, Farnham, 2009). We hope his work will inspire you to innovate in your enterprise at this critical time in our history because that is the path to survival and sustained success in an increasingly volatile world.

John welcomes your comments, and can be contacted on his personal email address: john@johngattorna.com.

It is also worthwhile to keep up with his many short articles published in magazines around the world, and his numerous speaking engagements. You can do this by visiting his personal website: www.johngattorna.com.